TEXT, PLAY, AND STORY
The Construction and Reconstruction of Self and Society

Edited by
Edward M. Bruner
University of Illinois, Urbana-Champaign

1983 Proceedings of
The American Ethnological Society
Stuart Plattner, Proceedings Editor

WAVELAND
PRESS, INC.
Prospect Heights, Illinois

For information about this book, write or call:

Waveland Press, Inc.
P.O. Box 400
Prospect Heights, Illinois 60070
(708) 634-0081

Contents

Acknowledgments. On behalf of the American Ethnological Society I would like to thank the Wenner-Gren Foundation for Anthropological Research for their generous support so that foreign scholars could attend the 1983 AES meetings in Baton Rouge. I would also like to thank Stuart Plattner, AES Society/Proceedings Editor, who saw this volume through the production process, and Theresa L. Sears, our copyeditor, whose editorial skills and eye for detail greatly enhanced this proceedings volume.

Edward M. Bruner
Editor and Symposium Organizer

Foreword

The American Ethnological Society was organized in 1842 in New York City with the aim of supporting "inquiries generally connected with the human race."[1] The first *Transactions* volume was published in 1845. The present volume is the *Proceedings* of the 1983 annual meeting of the American Ethnological Society and continues a long if sometimes interrupted tradition.

The spider symbol on the cover is a design element in Hopi Indian pottery, taken from a set of silver medallions made by Mr. Emory Sekaquaptewa of Hopi Crafts, Arizona. The medallions were given to the students winning the American Ethnological Society's annual Elsie Clews Parson prize paper competition from 1970 until 1980, when the price of silver made the prize prohibitively expensive. The sole remaining medallion is retained by the Society as its presidential emblem. This medallion was worn by Edward M. Bruner in 1982.

Following American Ethnological Society tradition, outgoing president Bruner organized the keynote symposium during the next annual meeting. This volume is the proceedings of that symposium on "Text, Play, and Story: The Construction and Reconstruction of Self and Society," held on 11–14 February 1983, in Baton Rouge, Louisiana. The American Ethnological Society met in conjunction with the Southern Anthropological Association and the Association for the Anthropological Study of Play, during Mardi Gras. Symposium participants were encouraged to visit New Orleans following the academic meeting for participant observation. Readers will note the appearance of a playful theme throughout the volume and should be aware that Professor Bruner planned it so. The American

Ethnological Society takes pleasure in acknowledging its gratitude to the Wenner-Gren Foundation for Anthropological Research for help in bringing distinguished foreign visitors to participate in this meeting.

Notes

1. "From Ethnologists to Anthropologists: A Brief History of the American Ethnological Society," by Robert Bieder and Thomas Tax, in *American Anthropology: The Early Years* (1974 Proceedings of the American Ethnological Society), John Murra, ed. pp. 11–12. 1976, St. Paul: West.

Stuart Plattner
Proceedings Editor
American Ethnological Society
University of Missouri, St. Louis

Introduction:
The Opening Up of Anthropology

Edward M. Bruner
University of Illinois, Urbana-Champaign

As a text is influenced by its context, so are anthropology meetings affected by their settings, in this case a Louisiana Mardi Gras. The papers in this volume were presented at the American Ethnological Society meetings held in Baton Rouge in mid-February 1983. Following the meetings, many of us attended Mardi Gras in New Orleans. I was pleased to see a group of serious academics wearing sets of colored beads and outlandish T-shirts, cheering at the Rex and Zulu parades, fighting for trinkets thrown from the floats, jostling with the crowds and struggling to make sense of the multiplicity of ever-changing images and sounds of a festivity that overwhelms an entire city. I had been pleased earlier to see these same academics struggling in their papers to move beyond the confines of the now-familiar paradigms of structuralism and symbolic anthropology that have engulfed our discipline in the past. Both the carnival and these papers were moved by the same spirit of openness and freedom.

After the papers had been presented and the festivities had ended, alone in my study with editor's pencil in hand, I confronted the problem of how to organize the papers in the volume. The contributors were selected because of the quality of their previous research and because of their common interest in text, play, and story, but the topics of the papers turned out to be a melange: Apache stories, an Israeli archaeological site, a mental health center in the Midwest, life histories of religious leaders, children's narratives, Burmese sentences, Menippean satire, Ilongot rage, a folklore parade in Spain, Brazilian Carnaval, Newfoundland mumming, monkey performances in Japan, and the Olympic Movement in Puerto Rico. Clearly, anthropologists these days have no respect for the traditional definition of our discipline.

On closer inspection, however, a division can be made between those papers oriented toward narrative and those oriented toward performance. This distinction is based on subject matter emphasis and is what I use here as an organizational convenience. Part I, on "Narrative," contains papers by Basso, Bruner and Gorfain, Schwartzman, Peacock, and Sutton-Smith, all of whom write about stories and the narrative process. Part III, on "Performance and Inversion," contains papers by Fernandez, DaMatta, Handelman, Ohnuki-Tierney, and MacAloon, all of whom write about such performative genres as parades, carnival, ritual, and games. The three papers in the middle, by Becker, Boon, and Rosaldo, make up part II, "Shaping the Text," and relate more to the subtitle of the symposium, to "the construction and reconstruction of self and society." Sir Edmund Leach was asked to present his reflections on the papers at the conclusion of the Baton Rouge conference and his thoughts appear as the Conclusion.

In these introductory comments, I choose not to present a summary of each paper in sequence. The papers are clearly written and speak for themselves; each is by an established scholar and each is a unique contribution. Rather, I prefer to stress the common themes and convergences in theory and method that crosscut the diversity of subject matter. Building on the papers as well as the conference discussion, I articulate here the general sense of the symposium, at least as I understand it.

The feeling was widespread at Baton Rouge that the conference was exciting and evocative and that anthropology is clearly changing, but no ready rubrics surfaced to characterize the changes. Those characterizations offered at Baton Rouge appear too formulaic—for example, from structuralism to deconstruction, or from rules to interpretation. Certainly, the changes evidenced at Baton Rouge are part of a larger, ongoing discourse, one occurring not only in anthropology but in the other social sciences and the humanities as well. The objective, however, is to highlight our anthropological contribution to that larger discourse. In the anthropological enterprise, as Geertz (1973a) has reminded us, we develop theory as we work through bodies of data, and the papers in this volume are all data-based. Anthropologists do not usually write pure theory. Instead, they use theory to achieve an interpretive understanding of some aspect of social life, which is one of the great strengths of the discipline. But the common directions must then be teased out of the data base within which they are embedded. This is what I attempt here.

To begin at the beginning, the main title of the symposium, "Text, Play, and Story," was not intended to be as theoretically significant as the subtitle, "The Construction and Reconstruction of Self and Society." What is implied by this subtitle is that self and society are not taken as given, as fully formed, fixed, and timeless, as either integrated selves or functionally consistent structures. Rather, self and society are always in production, in process; and one of our tasks as anthropologists is to specify how, in concrete instances and in different cultural settings, this shaping and reshaping takes place. All the contributors to this volume accept this general proposition, although some state the theme more explicitly than others. John MacAloon, for example, in his paper on the Olympics in Puerto Rico, shows how games shape politics. For him, Olympic sports are not simply epiphenomena that symbolically express, functionally reinforce, or reflexively comment on preexisting social-political formations; rather, they contribute to the determination of such formations. Sports help to affect the outcome of the political process. Play and games, storytelling, verbal arts, parades, carnivals, rituals, and performance are also means by which the reshaping occurs.

In her paper on a mental health center, Helen Schwartzman rejects the empiricist view of organizations as stable, concrete, objective, and essentially unproblematic entities. She begins with the stories told by participants about the organization and about themselves, and she suggests that the narrative framework is the best model to study organizations as a social construction. The stories told within the mental health center generate organizational activity, not just comment on it, and they sometimes transform the work experience, shape and sustain the participants' image of the organization, and help in the construction of organizational reality.

Keith Basso's paper is multifaceted. Among other things, he tells the story of a young Apache girl who returns from an off-reservation school to attend an Apache puberty ceremony. Inappropriately, she comes to the ceremony with her hair rolled up in oversized pink curlers, a shocking offense to the sacredness and integrity of the occasion. Nothing is said during the ritual itself, but weeks later the girl's grandmother relates an oral narrative associated with a particular geographical site about an Apache who tried to behave like a white man and about the misfortunes that subsequently occurred because he did not follow the Apache way. We are given an analogy between a story and an event.

All Apache oral narratives are connected with one or another feature of the geographical landscape, such as a natural spring, arroyo, or tree. The Apache refer to the use of narrative as "shooting with stories," as if the teller shoots an arrow that can correct someone's misconduct. The narrative becomes a powerful corrective that works on the person's mind, so much so that many years later, whenever the person passes by the particular geographical place associated with the narrative, he or she is reminded of the previous transgression. It is a repeatedly painful experience, one that produces feelings of shame and guilt and a periodic reexamination of one's life course.

Basso shows us, then, how Apache oral narratives are used in situations where transgressions have occurred to modify a person's future behavior—to reshape a self—and simultaneously to reconstitute Apache tradition. In the process, the geographical landscape is transformed into a moral one as natural ecological features become symbolic of cultural standards and become meaningful in a deeply personal sense. The Apache countryside is imbued with moral injunctions in the enduring association of place, story, and person. In a sense, the land tells its own story, recalling previous events and incidents of Apache misconduct, invoking moral correctives, and reshaping self and society. In Basso's terms, sites become mnemonic pegs, the land becomes a keeper of tradition, an arroyo becomes a grandmother.

A point that emerged during our discussion is that the Apache countryside does not have the "same" meaning for everyone. A particular natural spring and its associated oral narrative may be widely known, part of shared cultural knowledge, but the same narrative may have been told by many persons on separate occasions with relevance to disparate transgressions. On the same day, it is entirely possible that two or three individuals might pass by the same natural spring and that each person would recall a different incident and a different telling by a different grandmother. Thus, knowledge of oral narratives is shared but the meaning of any one is personal. Individuals read the Apache landscape in terms of their own life experiences.

Similar points are made by Edward M. Bruner and Phyllis Gorfain regarding the relationship between story and place. Masada, a tourist and pilgrimage site in Israel, was resurrected to serve the explicitly political purpose of shaping an emerging national state. The story of Masada is about a group of zealots who chose mass suicide rather than surrender to their Roman conquerors. It is a story that valorizes heroism, resistance, and freedom, qualities necessary for a new nation whose status is disputed by hostile neighbors. But controversy has arisen in present-day Israeli society over the use and interpretation of the story. Political controversies are debated in terms of the Masada story, in part because the story itself is filled with ambiguity and paradox and presents a series of semiotic and epistemological dilemmas. As the original event occurred over 2000 years ago, the gap between the original and subsequent tellings is particularly transparent, leading to problems of authority and interpretation and revealing the constructed nature of the narrative process.

To attach such a paradoxical and controversial story to the most solid of sites, to a massive and immovable mountain, is a device to fix meaning, to stabilize the fragile interpretive process. To generalize beyond the Apache and Israeli data, possibly sacred sites, holy places, national shrines, pilgrimage localities, monuments, graves, and tombs all serve to lend some measure of stability and credibility to what are essentially ephemeral and ever-changing narrative constructions by individuals and groups.

Stories and their sites have a complex relationship. Once a feature of the landscape is named, it is thereafter marked as a special place and distinguished from the unlabeled earth and rock and vegetation that surround it. Without at least a name, there would be no culturally significant site, just raw natural environment. Labels, as cultural artifacts, transform nature into marked, delimited places. But to attach a story to a site does so much more, as Basso and Bruner and Gorfain suggest. Names may construct the landscape but stories make the site resonate with history and experience. Stories introduce a temporal dimension, making sites the markers of the experiences of groups and historical periods, not just markers of space. In spite of the inevitable changes that occur with each retelling of the story, the now culturally constituted landscape, in its solid materiality and sequentiality, authenticates the story. The permanence of the site becomes an anchor for an elusive story.

It is generally acknowledged that if the narrative focus is to be useful for anthropologists, stories cannot be viewed simply as abstract plot structures isolated from their cultural context. We know that stories must be seen as rooted in society and as experienced and performed by individuals in cultural settings. Basso, Bruner and Gorfain, and Schwartzman advance our understanding by showing how these general ideas are refined and carried out in actual studies. They stress given tellings of particular stories by persons located within real social groups. We see how stories are used and enacted in specific historical situations by the Apache, the Israelis, and by the staff of a mental health center. Most significantly, we learn that the meanings of a story are the constructions placed on it in a particular telling by socially positioned persons at given historical moments. We have moved quite far in these papers from the notion of an abstract story that reflects societal values, or from the notion that meaning is inherent in the text.

Certainly, there are abstract stories such as an Apache narrative or the Masada story. I do not deny the existence of a basic story; however, every time such a story is told or referred to, even here and now in this very sentence, it is placed in a particular context and given meaning by a reader. Tellings and readings always involve active selves engaged in an interpretive process, selves that are historically positioned in a given time, place, and social situation. But while the meaning of a story is dependent on these very contextual variables, the telling of the story also can create its own context. The story itself, even if referred to indirectly, may evoke its own mental images, associations, and feeling tone for a particular teller or reader, and thus at least contribute to the construction of the context. The question was raised in Baton Rouge, Are there not some boundaries or limitations on the possible interpretations of any story? There may well be, but given only the basic story, one never knows in advance of a particular telling the constructions that may be placed on it; these are emergent from the here-and-now of the moment. Once the story is told, however, that telling, by the way it is introduced, by its rhetoric, by the style with which it is told, and by other variables of the telling, does limit and restrict the interpretive options.

Basso clearly demonstrates how individual Apaches actually experience oral narratives. Tourist-pilgrims know the basic story of Masada, but on the site, as they climb the mountain, the temporal extension of the narrative is duplicated in the spatial extension of movement through the site. The experience of the story is transformative and induces reflexivity in that a standardized cultural account, a basic story, is taken over and related to one's own life situation, leading individuals to reflect on themselves and on uses of the story. Cultural narratives become personal narratives. Further, the individuals who experience the story do so at a particular point in a life career, at a given age and phase in the life cycle, so that tellings always involve an intersection of culture and autobiography. The constructions of self are simultaneously cultural constructions in that they reconstitute the Apache way, the Israeli sense of nationhood, or the participants' image of their mental health center, to use the examples considered thus far.

In discussing performance and narrative, it is not my intent to merge the two or to ignore the differences between them. They correspond to Schwartzman's meetings and stories, to Leach's ritual and myth (see his concluding remarks), to incidents and accounts, or in the most general sense to any event and its representation. I do not agree that ritual and myth are simply transformations of one another insofar as one exhibits the "same" basic structure as the other. The differences between a performance and a story are an important object of investigation, as is the tension between them. My own perspective is more phenomenological. For me, no representation can fully exhaust the images, feelings, and meanings emergent from an event. As I have written elsewhere, "Every ethnographer is painfully aware of the discrepancy between the richness of the lived field experience and the paucity of the language used to characterize it" (Bruner in press). Of course, there can be no lived experience without language, but neither can language fully encompass lived experience.

What is essential, however, is not to confuse an event with an account, which is one of the key points of James Peacock's paper. He presents the life histories of religious leaders in three cultures and shows that variation in the pattern of their life stories corresponds to differences in the Islamic, Christian, and Buddhist religious orientations of the three tellers.

Peacock urges us to take life history as narrative, as a story told to someone in a given context. The act of reading, hearing, and interpreting the life history, according to Peacock, becomes part of the history of that life history as the text is placed in ever more ramifying contexts. He advocates that we analyze the pattern and narrative structure of a life story rather than cannibalize it by using fragments as juicy tidbits to liven up a descriptive ethnography, or selecting isolated incidents to illustrate a theoretical point. Nor should we ignore the pattern in the story and the way that our informants organize their own life experiences by going beneath or behind the text for a deep psychodynamic interpretation. For Peacock, a life history is a story, told or elicited, and the narrative structure should be kept intact and analyzed as such. Life histories are accounts, representations of lives, not lives as actually lived.

There may be a correspondence between a life as lived, a life as experienced, and a life as told, but the anthropologist should never assume the correspondence nor fail to make the distinction (Turner 1982, in press). A life as lived is what actually happens. A life as experienced consists of the images, feelings, sentiments, desires, thoughts, and meanings known to the person whose life it is. One can never know directly what another individual is experiencing, although we all interpret clues and make inferences about the experiences of others. A life as told, a life history, is a narrative, influenced by the cultural conventions of telling, by the audience, and by the social context. One can envision a case in which a life as lived, experienced, and told may tend to correspond. Given the American ideal of success, achievement, and acquiring position and wealth as one moves through the life cycle, I suppose it is possible that one could live, experience, and tell about one's life in such terms, but this would imply a remarkable concordance between the ideal and the real, without any out-of-phase incidents. The individual would have to be a letter-perfect copy of his culture, with no discrepancy between outer behavior, inner state, and how he chooses to characterize those behaviors and states in the stories told about them. Such a correspondence would deny the problematic that animates the papers by Roberto DaMatta, Don Handelman, and Emiko Ohnuki-Tierney. The usual American success story is told to fit the conventional narrative pattern and is not necessarily a reflection of inner states or outer behavior. Narrative patterns are acquired cultural conventions, a conclusion supported by Brian Sutton-Smith's material, as well as by Peacock.

At this point, the empiricist may raise an objection: In all this talk about stories and constructions, have we lost sight of the real world, of history and culture as it exists "out there"? Is anthropology being submerged in literary criticism? Is ethnography reduced to stories? Or, as Gellner writes[1] in support of Evans-Pritchard, "He had far too much sense of political and external reality to be drawn to their cloud-cuckoo-lands where you invent your world by your concepts." In this proceedings volume, are we taking our readers into a "cloud-cuckoo-land" where we invent the world by our stories? Such issues did arise in our discussion in Baton Rouge.

Polemics aside, every historian must distinguish between the realm of past events and the stories he tells about them (White 1973). Every ethnographer must understand the distinction between the sociocultural realities he observes in the field and his genuine efforts to represent such realities in an ethnographic account. Anyone producing a life history has the obligation to consult written records, to confirm his material with other members of the culture, to participate in his consultant's life during his stay in the field, and to use whatever methods may be available to validate the reliability of his data. Nevertheless, a life history is still a story, a representation of a life, not a life as lived or experienced.

Another way to put what Peacock, Basso, A. L. Becker, and others in this volume are advocating is to respect what I call the "integrity of the text" rather than to dissolve that text into our ever-changing theoretical frames. I realize that this is what many of us have always taught in our introductory anthropology courses, but it takes on added meaning and a new significance when some of our best anthropologists state how they have misrepresented and misinterpreted the indigenous text and how they eventually came to understand what their consultants had claimed for themselves. When Becker began to study the Burmese language 20 years ago, he made a written transcription of his consultant's statements according to the linguistic conventions of the era, conventions he learned in graduate school. His consultant examined what the young linguist-anthropologist had written in his notebook and said that Becker was violating Burmese writing and language. Becker had the authority of Leonard Bloomfield, structural linguistics, and Western science behind him, so it was not really an even match; except that now, 20 years later, Becker has come to recognize the sense in which his consultant was correct. His paper in this volume is about how he indeed violated Burmese language and cosmology and how, through successive approximations over the years, he has come to represent it more accurately, that is, closer to the Burmese model rather than to some illusion of scientific objectivity. Basso's paper, too, can be read as a record of his 20-year effort to understand the claims that the Apaches make about themselves.

The encounter between ethnographer and native consultant is presented by Becker and Basso as a kind of story, using the metaphor of the initiate (as James Fernandez pointed out in the conference discussion). Both Becker and Basso have come to respect the integrity of the indigenous text.

We must begin with that text, with Burmese sentences and Apache narratives—or with rituals, parades, and carnivals—recognizing all the while that such sentences and narratives and performances are the representations that the Burmese and the Apaches make to themselves. We cannot assume a priori that we know what a sentence or a narrative means to a people unless we examine it in their cultural context. As anthropologists, our first responsibility is to respect people's accounts of their experiences as they choose to present them. We may not necessarily accept their claims or representations, but we had better understand them.

When we begin with the peoples' representations, the relationship between their representations and our own is always problematic. We could say that their representations—their sentences, stories, parades, and performances—are their interpretations of their own experiences, a first-order interpretation. Geertz's (1973b) cockfights and Turner's (1974) social dramas are of the first order, and our analyses are second-order representations, our interpretations of their interpretations. Just as our informants have active selves that engage in an interpretive process, ethnographers, too, are interpretive beings. In Renato Rosaldo's terms, both informants and ethnographers are historically situated, positioned subjects. Rosaldo is against descriptions of stories or rituals as anonymous and mechanical, unrelated to the attempts of active persons to make sense of the real-life situations in which they find themselves. Thus, I advocate a context-centered anthropology based on the interpretations made by active agents, both native consultants and anthropologists. We not only want to connect cultural descriptions with personal ones, social processes with active selves, but we also want to relate our consultants' first-order interpretations to our own second-order ethnographic accounts and theories.

The contributors to this volume have been quite innovative in this respect. In our Western tradition we usually make a sharp separation between subject and object, between the privileged anthropologist and the native peoples as the object of study. To use Michael Herzfeld's terms from our discussion, we are the "theoretical beings" and they are "the field." But in the papers collected here, that distinction is blurred.

Schwartzman, for example, first became interested in the organization she studied because of the stories she had heard about it. She began systematic investigations only to find that the data came to her in the form of more stories, which is the way her consultants chose to present information about themselves, and she then wrote an anthropological account of the stories. In the process, an organization described by informants as "crazy" becomes, in the literature, "organized anarchy"; but the two are very similar indeed. In his paper Basso tells two stories, one about his personal interaction with Nick Thompson, his key Apache consultant, and the other about his ethnographic interpretation of Apache oral narratives. The two stories are interspersed at regular intervals throughout the paper. We might ask, Is the first story of the relationship between Basso and Thompson simply a series of amusing anecdotes, rather like after-hours conference conversation in which people sit around and swap field experiences, whereas the other story is solid ethnography? I think not. I suggest that both stories are related in complex ways and that both are equally serious anthropology. Taken together, we not only hear talk about the Apache landscape but also about the Apaches talking about talk about their landscape. Sutton-Smith tells a story about his raconteur father and his rebellious older brother, who would parody the father's stories, and suggests that this may be related to his lifelong belief in the dialectic between the relevance of storying and its destruction, between order and disorder. He also writes that developmental psychology may have swallowed the Western hero tale, suggesting that a particular narrative form—a story—comes to be taken as a model for a scientific discipline, a point also made by Schafer (1980) for psychoanalysis. In the course of coming to terms with his own grief, Rosaldo reexamines Ilongot views about grief; in his paper the two perspectives are played off against one another. What the Ilongot said about their grief helped Rosaldo to understand his own, particularly that the Western definition of grief did not admit rage, a rage which a grieving Rosaldo felt but could not at first articulate. In a sense, it is impossible to tell where Rosaldo's story leaves off and the Ilongot story begins, one of the virtues of his contribution. Thus, some of these papers comment on themselves: Sutton-Smith on storying and Rosaldo on anthropologists.

Not only do these papers blur the comfortable distinction between the theorizing subject and the object of study, they also question the familiar separation between synchrony and diachrony. From the conceptual position developed here—that self and society are generated as they are expressed—it follows that every expression is also a change, if for no other reason than no event is an exact duplicate of any previous event. Radcliffe-Brown made much of the distinction between statics and dynamics, between sociology and history. He was also concerned with process, separating processes of replacement from processes of transformation—which is precisely the distinction we do not accept here. Rather, we agree with Sahlins (1981:67) that "what begins as reproduction ends as transformation." Culture changes as it is enacted, in practice. As every present act incorporates the past and anticipates the future, temporality is built into our descriptive accounts, a position long incorporated into the work of Victor Turner (1974, 1982). In brief, we no longer accept a sociology that deals only with the static present as opposed to a history concerned with a dynamic past.

In her study of monkey performances, Ohnuki-Tierney finds that a purely synchronic study leads to erroneous conclusions, even in interpreting the meaning of a present event. In prefeudal Japan, the monkey and its outcaste trainer have religious significance and are mediators; in feudal Japan, monkey and trainer become entertainers and are marginals. For the trainers, the monkey performance transforms nature to culture, but for the nonoutcaste Japanese there is an inversion, from culture to nature. Ohnuki-Tierney concludes that it is essential for an understanding of monkey performances in Japan to combine sociology and history as the limitations of synchronic structuralism become more apparent.

Becker's paper is an elegant statement of change as reshaping, based on a contextual theory of meaning and on his view of all language use as translation. He rejects the view of grammar as a system of rules that map a logical deep structure onto a surface structure. That theory is exclusively formal and the computer is the natural metaphor for language processing. Becker's own view of grammar is based on a different perspective of language, one involving time and memory. He sees grammar as context shaping; persons learning to reshape prior texts in new contexts. The constraints of the first view of grammar are structural and logical; the constraints of the second are pragmatic and rhetorical. Insofar as the focus is on reshapings in new contexts, language, too, is viewed as always in production.

Some recent critics of structuralism have rejected language as an analogy for society. But much depends on whose theory of language is being rejected or accepted, Chomsky's or Bakhtin's. Rather than abandon the linguistic analogy, the contributors to this volume choose a different view of language. It is striking that, independently, four of the papers in the volume quote or refer to Bakhtin. In his perspective, language is not restricted to grammatical rules, fixed meanings, or monologic readings. For Bakhtin (1981), language is alive; it is an uninterrupted process of historical becoming. There is no such thing as a language, in his view, but rather many overlapping intersecting contradictory languages. Bakhtin stresses plural voices and multiple languages in dialogic interplay.

A recurrent theme in Bakhtin, Wittgenstein, and the papers here is that it is impossible to interpret a text based on an examination of that text alone. Interpretation, either by anthropologists or actors, depends on an understanding of the unstated or metacommunicative messages conveyed by the text but not necessarily embodied within that text. The unstated messages would be unrecognized or misinterpreted without detailed ethnographic knowledge of the cultural context and the actual situation in which the text appears. An accurate mechanical reproduction of the text, by film or tape, for example, may provide clues about meaning but would be

no substitute for knowledge of the mental associations and stocks of understandings of the participants in the event. Interpretation depends on knowledge of context and background. Bruner and Gorfain show that some tellings of the Masada story are in response to previous criticisms or alternative
stories. There may be no direct references to these challenging tellings in the
authoritative Masada text, but that text nevertheless takes account of the
challenges and is shaped by them. Whatever the text may be—a sentence, a
story, a parade, a carnival—we must go outside the text to understand it. As
MacAloon tells us, what is happening in the Olympic Games makes no sense
without knowledge of the Puerto Rican political scene. And Fernandez's
subtle analysis of reflexive irony is entirely dependent on understanding recent Spanish history. The most ironic anthropological predicament of all
would be if a people took their own behavior as ironic commentary but the
ethnologist missed it because he held too close to a literal reading of the
text. DaMatta's examination of Brazilian Carnaval can only be understood
in terms of the misery and cultural conventions of everyday Brazilian society.

    To go outside the text is not to go to a hidden, deeper level below the
surface manifestations. In rejecting the multilayered view of society as consisting of a depth and a surface; in stressing context and the interpretive
process rather than rules; in questioning the subject-object and the syn-
chrony-diachrony distinctions; in emphasizing the dialogic rather than the
monologic, the pragmatic rather than the formal, the fluidity rather than
the fixity of meaning—this volume could be taken as a critique of structuralism. But our aim is to go beyond yet another critique to stress positive
contributions. These papers point to where we should be going, not to
where we have been. Not only are there many kinds of structuralisms, but
structuralism today is not the same as it was two decades ago.

    The question arose in our discussion, If not structuralism, then how
do we characterize the kind of anthropology being done by the contributors
to this volume? Others might identify most participants as symbolic anthropologists, but it is noteworthy that the term "symbolic anthropology" is
rarely mentioned in the papers, nor did it emerge in our discussion. There
was no emphasis on "symbols" as such. How about poststructuralism,
deconstruction, hermeneutics, or phenomenology? It would be premature
to apply any of these current labels to our enterprise because we differ
among ourselves and because the intellectual positions implied by any of
these labels is not consistent. Also, we are skeptical about forcing ourselves
into one or another tight category (itself a manifestation of our position).
Many of us have learned much from reading Derrida, Foucault, Barthes,
Ricoeur, Bakhtin, and Wittgenstein. But the point is that our prior text,
which as conservative culture bearers we are not yet ready to relinquish, is

simply a data-based social or cultural anthropology with a marked interpretive bent.

What I believe characterizes the papers included in this volume, for want of a more elegant phrase, is an "opening up" of anthropology, one that takes account of the spontaneity, improvisation, and innovation inherent in social practice, that sees culture as being in production, that is skeptical of fixed meanings and resolved endings and recognizes the inconsistency and ambiguity of social life. James Boon's paper is central in this respect. He contrasts one world as linear, sequential, causal, unified, rule-governed, and formal with another as nonlinear, open, and radically plural (see also Boon 1982). Building on Becker's (1979) characterization of the Javanese wayang, Boon extends the notion to encompass many more areas of social life as being wayang-like, including carnivals and anthropology conferences, where everything happens at once rather than in an orderly sequence; where images are as significant as words; and where what one hears are plural voices rather than monologic speech. The Boon-Becker wayang world is indeed strikingly like my own experience of the New Orleans Mardi Gras and the Baton Rouge AES conference.

That wayang world is surprisingly, or perhaps not so surprisingly, like the Sutton-Smith account of the stories told by very young children before they have learned the routinized narrative conventions. Western developmental psychology evaluates the stories of young children as somehow inferior to, or at least representative of, an earlier stage of development, for those stories lack clear endings or resolved plot structures. Sutton-Smith correctly questions that evaluation—how can we judge one as better than the other? There is indeed a similarity between young children's stories, wayang, carnival, anthropology conferences, contemporary French philosophy, and modern novels. If not the Id (Spiro 1979), then we may be approaching primary processing.

One way in which these papers open up anthropology is that they avoid monolithic interpretations. The metaphor of opening up appeals to me: I picture a huge "soft" rock filled with cracks, faults, and fissures. In the past, we have tended to gloss over the irregularities; but present-day anthropology stops to reexamine the cracks, probe the faults, and penetrate the fissures. We move into the open spaces of soft rocks, of metaphorical Masadas, and of society, using our concepts to explore new complexities of meaning. Rocks and social worlds are not monolithic.

Bruner and Gorfain describe the paradoxical Masada not as one story but as multiple stories in dialogic relationships. Ohnuki-Tierney analyzes the multiple structures of monkey performances as they evolved historically, taking readings from the perspective of the performers as well as from the nonoutcaste Japanese. Whereas some structuralists might

analyze the monkey performance and its variants in one synchronic moment, Ohnuki-Tierney deals with the historical process of performance as
enactments and meanings that change over time.

It is not only the analyses that have opened up in the sense of providing multiple perspectives but the very subject matter selected for study is
not fixed or bounded. A key to Ohnuki-Tierney's paper is that the status of
the outcaste Japanese is paradoxical; the outcastes today are equal in
modern Japanese society, but then again they are not equal. As MacAloon
makes clear, the national status of Puerto Rico is under discussion—some
favor independence, some a modified commonwealth, and others advocate
statehood and even closer ties to the United States. Puerto Rico may be a
separate entity as far as the Olympic Games are concerned, but politically
its status is neither here nor there. Israel is in a somewhat similar predicament; there is no doubt that it is a national state except that its national
status is not acknowledged by its neighbors, which is why symbols of statehood assume such extraordinary importance. The organizational status and
central mission of the mental health center described by Schwartzman is apparently not clear to anyone—which is what gives rise to an endless round
of committee meetings and stories. The center is a viable organization, but
then again it is not. These papers focus on what is ambiguous, paradoxical,
unclear, or unresolved in society itself and in its expressive forms.

Fernandez's paper is especially instructive for these matters. Ironic
commentary is rhetorical weaponry that arises because of the perceived incongruity between official pronouncements and the actual state of affairs in
Asturian political life. Fernandez shows that in the Asturian case, in a nation that produced Cervantes, the incongruity emerges because new pronouncements about political life are made but the structural apparatus of the
former world is still in place. Incongruity, however, could also arise in the
reverse situation, where the world changes but people keep saying the same
things. In any case, there can be no irony without incongruity, without the
realization that people are saying or are told one thing but find that they are
living another. Irony arises in the open space between what is said and what
is experienced. Such discrepancies may, in other circumstances, simply be
tolerated, or they may lead to nativistic movements or revolution. But here
the response is irony, both a playful counterstatement and a covert attack
that undermines authoritarian repression.

In his paper on Newfoundland mumming, Handelman focuses on
the space between the physical outside and the inside, on the disjunction
between exterior person and inner self, between stranger and community
member. Mumming was a drama of deception and truth, a performance
about concealment and revelation that served to erase the disjunctions, at
least temporarily. DaMatta reads Brazilian Carnaval as a complex poem, a

utopia of pleasure, sexuality, laughter, and abundance but read against the backdrop of everyday life where people are defined by their relationship to house and job, by familial repression and discrimination against women, by inequality. Carnaval takes what is ordinarily private, individual, and within the home and temporarily makes it open and public, in the street, in a magic, democratic, explosive, feminine world where eyes can meet and what people do is what they feel. Carnaval is a wayang or a children's story, operating in the space between obligation and desire.

These papers open up anthropology and focus on the ambiguous spaces in social life, probably as a response to current theoretical trends in the discipline. Although I have doubts about my ability to see beyond the epistemes of our historical moment, I believe we are moving toward a more accurate representation of the world as it is. At least I hope so. There is a freer spirit on the loose in our discipline now, one that is more fun and more open, like a children's story or a mardi gras. We can be more honest with ourselves and acknowledge the force of our own emotions. We are at liberty to merge with our subject matter and open up not only to anthropology but to ourselves. If the papers in this volume are representative, then we can all look forward to a more creative period.

Notes

1. This was brought to my attention by James Boon; I do not have the exact reference.

References Cited

Bakhtin, M. M.
   1981   The Dialogic Imagination. Michael Holquist, ed. Austin: University of
      Texas Press.
Becker, A. L.
   1979   Text-building, Epistemology, and Aesthetics in Javanese Shadow Theatre.
      In The Imagination of Reality. A. L. Becker and A. Yengoyan, eds. pp.
      211–243. Norwood, NJ: Ablex.
Boon, James A.
   1982   Other Tribes, Other Scribes. London: Cambridge University Press.
Bruner, Edward M.
   in press   Ethnography as Narrative. *In* The Anthropology of Experience. Victor
      Turner and Edward M. Bruner, eds. Urbana: University of Illinois Press.
Geertz, Clifford
   1973a   The Interpretation of Cultures. New York: Basic Books.

1973b   Deep Play: Notes on the Balinese Cockfight. *In* The Interpretation of Cultures. pp. 412–453. New York: Basic Books.

Sahlins, Marshall
1981   Historical Metaphors and Mythical Realities. Ann Arbor: University of Michigan Press.

Schafer, Roy
1980   Narration in the Psychoanalytic Dialogue. Critical Inquiry 7:29–53.

Spiro, Melford E.
1979   Whatever Happened to the Id? American Anthropologist 81:5–13.

Turner, Victor
1974   Dramas, Fields, and Metaphors. Ithaca: Cornell University Press.
1982   From Ritual to Theatre. New York: Performing Arts Journal Publications.
in press   Dewey, Dilthey and Drama: An Essay. *In* The Anthropology of Experience. Victor Turner and Edward M. Bruner, eds. Urbana: University of Illinois Press.

White, Hayden
1973   Metahistory. Baltimore: Johns Hopkins University Press.

I
Narrative

1

"Stalking with Stories": Names, Places, and Moral Narratives among the Western Apache

Keith H. Basso
Yale University

Shortly before his death in 1960, Clyde Kluckhohn made the following observation in a course he gave at Harvard University on the history of anthropological thought: "The most interesting claims people make are those they make about themselves. Cultural anthropologists should keep this in mind, especially when they are doing fieldwork." Although Kluckhohn's comment seemed tenuously connected to the topic of his lecture (he was speaking that day on the use of statistical methods in culture and personality studies), few of his students were distracted or annoyed. We had discovered early on that some of his most provocative thoughts were likely to come in the form of brief asides delivered casually and without apology at unexpected moments. We also learned that these ostensibly offhand remarks frequently contained advice on a topic that we were eager to know more about: ethnography and ethnographic research. Rarely, however, did Kluckhohn see fit to elaborate on his advice, and so it was only later, after some of us had become ethnographers ourselves, that we could begin to assess it properly.

I think that in this particular instance Kluckhohn was right. Attending carefully to claims that people make about themselves, and then trying to grasp with some exactness what they have claimed and why, can be a perplexing and time-consuming business. But when the work goes well—when puzzling claims are seen to make principled sense and when, as a consequence of this, one is able to move closer to an understanding of who the people involved imagine themselves to be—it can be richly informative and highly worthwhile. Indeed, as Kluckhohn implied in his textbook *Mirror for Man* (1949), it is just this sort of work that makes ethnography the singu-

larly valuable activity—and, he might have added, the singularly arresting
and gratifying one—it very often is.

     This essay focuses on a small set of spoken texts in which members
of a contemporary American Indian society express claims about themselves, their language, and the lands on which they live. Specifically, I am
concerned here with a set of statements that were made by men and women
from the Western Apache community at Cibecue, a dispersed settlement of
1100 people that has been inhabited by Apaches for centuries and is located
near the center of the Fort Apache Indian Reservation in east-central

Figure 1. Map showing location of the community of Cibecue on the Fort
Apache Indian Reservation, Arizona.

Arizona (see Figure 1). The statements that interest me, which could be supplemented by a large number of others, are the following.

1. The land is always stalking people. The land makes people live right. The land looks after us. The land looks after people. [Mrs. Annie Peaches, age 77, 1977]
2. Our children are losing the land. It doesn't go to work on them anymore. They don't know the stories about what happened at these places. That's why some get into trouble. [Mr. Ronnie Lupe, age 42; Chairman, White Mountain Apache Tribe, 1978]
3. We used to survive only off the land. Now it's no longer that way. Now we live only with money, so we need jobs. But the land still looks after us. We know the names of the places where everything happened. So we stay away from badness. [Mr. Nick Thompson, age 64, 1980]
4. I think of that mountain called "white rocks lie above in a compact cluster" as if it were my maternal grandmother. I recall stories of how it once was at that mountain. The stories told to me were like arrows. Elsewhere, hearing that mountain's name, I see it. Its name is like a picture. Stories go to work on you like arrows. Stories make you live right. Stories make you replace yourself. [Mr. Benson Lewis, age 64, 1979]
5. One time I went to L.A., training for mechanic. It was no good, sure no good. I start drinking, hang around bars all the time. I start getting into trouble with my wife, fight sometimes with her. It was *bad*. I forget about this country here around Cibecue. I forget all the names and stories. I don't hear them in my mind anymore. I forget how to live right, forget how to be strong. [Mr. Wilson Lavender, age 52, 1975]

If the texts of these statements resist quick and easy interpretation, it is not because the people who made them are confused or cloudy thinkers. Neither is it because, as one unfortunate commentator would have us believe, the Western Apache are "mystically inclined and correspondingly inarticulate." The problem we face is a semiotic one, a barrier to constructing appropriate sense and significance. It arises from the obvious circumstance that all views articulated by Apache people are informed by their experience in a culturally constituted world of objects and events with which most of us are unfamiliar. What sort of world is it? Or, to draw the question into somewhat sharper focus, what is the cultural context in which Apache statements such as those presented above find acceptance as valid claims about reality?

More specifically, what is required to interpret Annie Peaches's claim that the land occupied by the Western Apache is "always stalking people" and that because of this they know how to "live right"? And how should we understand Chairman Lupe's assertion that Apache children sometimes misbehave because the land "doesn't go to work on them anymore"? Why does Nick Thompson claim that his knowledge of place-names and historical events enables him to "stay away from badness"? And why does Benson Lewis liken place-names to pictures, stories to arrows, and a mountain near the community at Cibecue to his maternal grandmother? What should we make of Wilson Lavender's recollection of an unhappy time in California when forgetting place-names and stories caused him to forget "how to be strong"? Are these claims structured in metaphorical terms, or, given Western Apache assumptions about the physical universe and the place of people within it, are they somehow to be interpreted literally? In any case, what is the reasoning that lies behind the claims, the informal logic of which they are simultaneously products and expressions? Above all, what makes the claims make sense?

I address these and other questions through an investigation of how Western Apaches talk about the natural landscape and the importance they attach to named locations within it. Accordingly, my discussion focuses on elements of language and patterns of speech, my purpose being to discover from these elements and patterns something of how Apache people construe their land and render it intelligible. Whenever Apaches describe the land—or, as happens more frequently, whenever they tell stories about incidents that have occurred at particular points upon it—they take steps to constitute it in relation to themselves. Which is simply to say that in acts of speech, mundane and otherwise, Apaches negotiate images and understandings of the land which are accepted as credible accounts of what it actually is, why it is significant, and how it impinges on the daily lives of men and women. In short, portions of a world view are constructed and made available—bits and pieces of what Erving Goffman (1974) has called a "primary framework" for social activity—and a Western Apache version of the landscape is deepened, amplified, and tacitly affirmed. With words, a massive physical presence is fashioned into a meaningful human universe.

This universe of meanings comprises the cultural context in which the Western Apache texts presented earlier acquire their validity and appropriateness. Consequently, if we are to understand the claims set forth in these statements, portions of that context must be explored and made explicit. We must proceed, in other words, by relating our texts to other aspects of Western Apache thought—in effect, to other texts and other claims—and we must continue doing this, more and more comprehensively, until, finally, it is possible to confront the texts directly and expose the major premises on which they rest. As we shall see, most of these premises are grounded in an unformalized native model of Western Apache storytelling which holds that oral narratives have the power to establish enduring bonds between individuals and features of the natural landscape, and that as a direct consequence of such bonds, persons who have acted improperly will be moved to reflect critically on their misconduct and resolve to improve it. A native model of how stories work to shape Apaches' conceptions of the landscape, it is also a model of how stories work to shape Apaches' conceptions of themselves. Ultimately, it is a model of how two symbolic resources—language and the land—are manipulated by Apaches to promote compliance with standards for acceptable social behavior and the moral values that support them.

Should it appear, then, that these Western Apache texts lack substance or complexity, we shall see that in fact both qualities are present in ample measure. Should the aim of interpreting such modestly worded documents seem unduly narrow, or my strategy for trying to accomplish it too tightly bound up with an examination of linguistic and ethnographic particulars, it shall become evident soon enough that wider and more general issues in anthropology are very much involved. Of these, I suggest, none is more pressing or conspicuous than the reluctance of cultural ecologists to deal openly and in close detail with the symbolic attributes of human environments and the effects of environmental constructions on patterns of social action.

But I am getting ahead of myself. The problem is how to get started, and for advice on that matter I turn here, as I actually did in Cibecue seven years ago, to a gifted and unusual man. Teacher and consultant, serious thinker and salacious joker alike, he has so strongly influenced the content and organization of this essay that he has become, with his permission, a part of it himself—and so, too, of the interpretation it presents.

"Learn the Names"

Nick Thompson is, by his own admission, an old man. It is possible, he told me once, that he was born in 1918. Beneath snow-white hair cut short, his face is round and compact, his features small and sharply molded. His large, black, and very bright eyes move quickly, and when he smiles he acquires an expression that is at once mischievous and intimidating. I have known him for more than 20 years, and he has instructed me often on matters pertaining to Western Apache language and culture. A man who delights in play, he has also teased me unmercifully, concocted humorous stories about me that are thoroughly apocryphal, and embarrassed me before large numbers of incredulous Apaches by inquiring publicly into the most intimate details of my private life. Described by many people in Cibecue as a true "Slim Coyote" *(ma' ts'ósé),* Nick Thompson is outspoken, incorrigible, and unabashed.[1] He is also generous, thoughtful, and highly intelligent. I value his friendship immensely.

As I bring my Jeep to a halt on the road beside the old man's camp, I hear Nick complaining loudly to his wife about the changing character of life in Cibecue and its regrettable effects on younger members of the community. I have heard these complaints before and I know they are deeply felt. But still, on this sunny morning in June 1977, it is hard to suppress a smile, for the image Nick presents, a striking example of what can be achieved with sartorial *bricolage,* is hardly what one would expect of a staunch tribal conservative. Crippled since childhood and partially paralyzed by a recent stroke, the old man is seated in the shade of a cottonwood tree a few yards from the modest wooden cabin where he lives with his wife and two small grandchildren. He is smoking a mentholated Salem cigarette and is studying with undisguised approval the shoes on his feet—a new pair of bright blue Nike running shoes trimmed in incandescent orange. He is also wearing a pair of faded green trousers, a battered brown cowboy hat, and a white T-shirt with "Disneyland" printed in large red letters across the front. Within easy reach of his chair, resting on the base of an upended washtub, is a copy of the *National Enquirer,* a mug of hot coffee, and an open box of chocolate-covered doughnuts. If Nick Thompson is an opponent of social change, it is certainly not evident from his appearance. But appearances can be deceiving, and Nick, who is an accomplished singer and a medicine man of substantial reputation, would be the first to point this out.

The old man greets me with his eyes. Nothing is said for a minute or two, but then we begin to talk, exchanging bits of local news until enough time has passed for me to politely announce the purpose of my visit. I explain that I am puzzled by certain statements that Apaches have made about the country surrounding Cibecue and that I am anxious to know how to interpret them. To my surprise, Nick does not ask what I have been told or by whom. He responds instead by swinging out his arm in a wide arc. "Learn the names," he says. "Learn the names of all these places." Unprepared for such a firm and unequivocal suggestion (it sounds to me like nothing less than an order), I retreat into silence. "Start with the names," the old man continues. "I will teach you like before. Come back tomorrow morning." Nodding in agreement, I thank Nick for his willingness to help and tell him what I will be able to pay him. He says the wage is fair.

A few moments later, as I stand to take my leave, Nick's face breaks suddenly into a broad smile and his eyes begin to dance. I know that look very well and brace myself for the farewell joke that almost always accompanies it. The old man wastes no time. He says I look lonely. He urges me to have prolonged and abundant sex with very old women. He says it prevents nosebleeds. He says that someday I can write a book about it. Flustered and at a loss for words, I smile weakly and shake my head. Delighted with this reaction, Nick laughs heartily and reaches for his coffee and a chocolate-covered doughnut. Our encounter has come to an end.

I return to the old man's camp the following day and start to learn Western Apache place-names. My lessons, which are interrupted by mapping trips with more mobile Apache consultants, continue for the next ten weeks. In late August, shortly before I must leave Cibecue, Nick asks to see the maps. He is not impressed. "White men need paper maps," he observes. "We have maps in our minds."

Western Apache Place-names

The study of American Indian place-name systems has fallen on hard times. Once a viable component of anthropology in the United States, it has virtually ceased to exist, the inconspicuous victim of changing intellectual fashions and large amounts of ethnographic neglect. There are good reasons for advocating a revival. As early as 1900, Franz Boas, who was deeply impressed by the minutely detailed environmental knowledge of the Baffin Land and Hudson Bay Eskimo, suggested that one of the most profitable ways to explore the "mental life" of Indian peoples was to investigate their geographical nomenclatures (Boas 1901–07). In 1912, Edward Sapir made the same point in more general terms, saying that Indian vocabularies provided valuable insight into native conceptions of the natural world and all that was held to be significant within it. Later, in 1934, Boas published a short monograph entitled *Geographical Names of the Kwakiutl Indians*. This essay is essentially a study of Kwakiutl word morphology, but it demonstrates beautifully Boas's earlier ideas concerning the Eskimo: namely, that the study of place-name systems may reveal a great deal about the cognitive categories with which environmental phenomena are organized and understood. This tradition of research, which also included J. P. Harrington's (1916) massive treatise on Tewa place-names, began to falter in the years preceding World War II. A few brief articles appeared in the 1950s, and Floyd Lounsbury contributed an important paper on Iroquois place-names in 1960. Since then, however, little work has been done. Indeed, with the notable exception of Frederica de Laguna's (1972) long-delayed monograph on the Tlingit, I know of not a single study written by a linguist or anthropologist in the last 20 years that deals extensively or in depth with the place-name system of a North American tribe.[2]

One can only imagine how Boas or Sapir or Harrington might have reacted to Nick Thompson's interest in Western Apache place-names. They would have been intrigued, I think, but probably not surprised. For each of them had come to understand, as I am just beginning to at Cibecue, that American Indian place-names are intricate little creations and that studying their internal structure, together with the functions they serve in spoken conversation, can lead the ethnographer to any number of useful discoveries. All that is required is sound instruction from able native consultants, a fondness for mapping extensive areas of territory, and a modest capacity for wonder and delight at the large tasks that small words can be made to perform. And one more thing: a willingness to reject the widely accepted notion that place-names are nothing more than handy vehicles of reference. Place-names do refer, and quite indispensably at that; but in communities such as Cibecue, they are used and valued for other reasons as well.

Located in a narrow valley at an elevation of 1507 m, the settlement at Cibecue (from *deeschii' bikoh,* "valley with elongated red bluffs") is bisected by a shallow stream emanating from springs that rise in low-lying mountains to the north. Apache homes, separated by horse pastures, agricultural plots, and ceremonial dancegrounds, are located on both sides of the stream for a distance of approximately 8 km. The valley itself, which is bounded on the east and west by a broken series of red sandstone bluffs, displays marked topographic diversity in the form of heavily dissected canyons and arroyos, broad alluvial flood plains, and several clusters of prominent peaks. Vegetation ranges from a mixed Ponderosa Pine-Douglas Fir association near the headwaters of Cibecue Creek to a chaparral community, consisting of scrub oak, cat's-claw, agave, and a variety of cactus species, at the confluence of the creek with the Salt River. In between, numerous other floral associations occur, including dense riparian communities and heavy stands of cottonwood, oak, walnut, and pine.

Together with Michael W. Graves, I have mapped nearly 104 km^2 in and around the community at Cibecue and within this area have recorded the Western Apache names of 296 locations; it is, to say the least, a region densely packed with place-names. But large numbers alone do not account for the high frequency with which place-names typically appear in Western Apache discourse. In part, this pattern of regular and recurrent use results from the fact that Apaches, who travel a great deal to and from their homes, habitually call on each other to describe their trips in detail. Almost invariably, and in sharp contrast to comparable reports delivered by Anglos living at Cibecue, these descriptions focus as much on *where* events occurred as on the nature and consequences of the events themselves. This practice has been observed in other Apachean groups as well, including, as Harry Hoijer (personal communication, 1973) notes, the Navajo: "Even the most minute occurrences are described by Navajos in close conjunction with their physical settings, suggesting that unless narrated events are *spatially anchored* their significance is somehow reduced and cannot be properly assessed." Hoijer could just as well be speaking of the Western Apache.

Something else contributes to the common use of place-names in Western Apache communities, however, and that, quite simply, is that

Apaches enjoy using them. For example, several years ago, when I was stringing a barbed-wire fence with two Apache cowboys from Cibecue, I noticed that one of them was talking quietly to himself. When I listened carefully, I discovered that he was reciting a list of place-names—a long list, punctuated only by spurts of tobacco juice, that went on for nearly ten minutes. Later, when I ventured to ask him about it, he said he "talked names" all the time. Why? "I like to," he said. "I ride that way in my mind." And on dozens of other occasions when I have been working or traveling with Apaches, they have taken satisfaction in pointing out particular locations and pronouncing their names—once, twice, three times or more. Why? "Because we like to," or "Because those names are good to say." More often, however, Apaches account for their enthusiastic use of place-names by commenting on the precision with which the names depict their referents. "That place looks just like its name," someone will explain, or "That name makes me see that place like it really is." Or, as Benson Lewis (example 4) states so succinctly, "It's name is like a picture."

Statements such as these may be interpreted in light of certain facts about the linguistic structure of Western Apache place-names. To begin with, it is essential to understand that all but a very few Apache place-names take the form of complete sentences. This is made possible by one of the most prominent components of the Western Apache language: an elaborate system of prefixes that operates most extensively and productively to modify the stems of verbs. Thus, well-formed sentences can be constructed that are extremely compact yet semantically very rich. It is this combination of brevity and expressiveness, I believe, that appeals to Apaches and makes the mere pronunciation of place-names a satisfying experience.

By way of illustration, consider the pair of place-names shown in examples 6 and 7 below, which have been segmented into their gross morphological constituents.

6. *tséká' tú yahilíí': tsé-* ("rock"; "stone") + *-ká'* ("on top of it" [a flat object]) + *tú* ("water") + *ya-* ("down"; "downward") + *-hi-* ("in successive movements"; "in regularly repeated movements") + *-líí'* ("it flows").
   Gloss: "water flows downward on top of a series of flat rocks"
7. *t'iis bitl'áh tú 'olíí': t'iis* ("cottonwood"; "cottonwood tree") + *bitl'áh* ("below it"; "underneath it") + *tú* ("water") + *'o-* ("in"; "inward") + *-líí'* ("it flows").
   Gloss: "water flows inward underneath a cottonwood tree"

Notice how thoroughly descriptive these place-names are and how pointedly specific in the physical details they pick out. The two names presented here are not unique in this respect. On the contrary, descriptive specificity is characteristic of most Western Apache place-names, and it is this attribute, almost certainly, that causes Apaches to liken place-names to pictures and to comment appreciatively on the capacity of place-names to evoke full and accurate images of the locations to which they refer. And these images are accurate, as can be seen by matching the place-names in examples 6 and 7 with photographs of their referents (Figures 2 and 3).

Further evidence that Western Apaches value descriptive specificity in place-names comes from a distinction that is drawn between "long names" *(bízhi' ndeez)* and "shortened names" *(bízhi' 'igod).* In this connection, it is important to note that most Apache place-names consist minimally of a noun marking the subject, an imperfective neuter verb that functions as an adjectival modifier, and a perfective neuter verb that describes some aspect of the position, posture, or shape of the subject. However, some Apache place-names lack a perfective neuter verb and consist exclusively of a noun and an imperfective adjectival. In my sample of 296 place-names, 247 names (83 percent) belong to the former type, while 49 (16 percent) belong to the latter. Examples of both types are given below.

Type 1: Place-names containing a perfective neuter verb.

8. *tsé łigai dah sidil:* tsé ("rock"; "stone") + łigai ("it is white") + dah ("located above ground level") + sidil ("three or more objects lie in a compact cluster").
   Gloss: "white rocks lie above in a compact cluster"

Figure 2. tséká' tú yahilį́į́' ("water flows downward on top of a series of flat rocks").

Figure 3. t'iis bitl'áh tú 'olį́į́' ("water flows inward underneath a cotton-wood tree").

9. *goshtł'ish tú bił siką́ą́:* goshtł'ish ("mud") + *tu* ("water") + *bił* ("in association with") + *siką́ą́* ("a container with its contents lies").
    Gloss: "muddy water lies in a concave depression"
    Type 2: Place-names lacking a perfective neuter verb.
10. *nadah nch'íí': nadah* ("mescal") + *nch'íí'* ("it is bitter-tasting").
    Gloss: "bitter-tasting mescal"
11. *ch'o'oł ntsaaz:* ch'o'oł ("juniper"; "juniper tree") + *ntsaaz* ("it is big and wide").
    Gloss: "big wide juniper tree"

I draw attention to this typological difference among Western Apache place-names because it coincides closely with, and probably provides the grammatical basis for, the "long" versus "shortened" distinction that Apaches themselves recognize and comment on. Place-names containing a perfective neuter verb were consistently identified by a group of 12 Apache consultants from Cibecue as belonging to the "long" category of names, while those lacking a perfective neuter verb were consistently assigned to its "shortened" counterpart. In addition, and more revealing still, all but one consultant maintained that the "long names" were "better" than the "shortened" ones because they "told more" or "said more" about the physical properties of their referents. It seems reasonable to conclude, then, that place-names containing a perfective neuter verb are appreciated by Apaches as being more fully descriptive of their referents than place-names in which a perfective neuter verb is absent. And so, in fact, the former usually are. The difference can be easily grasped by comparing a photograph of the referent of a "long name," such as *tsé łigai dah sidil* ("white rocks lie above in a compact cluster"; see Figure 4), with that of a "shortened name," such as *nadah nch'íí'* ("bitter mescal"; see Figure 5).

Given these observations, it should come as no surprise that the large majority of Western Apache place-names present descriptions of the locations to which they refer. All of the place-names considered so far belong to this dominant type, as do 268 (90 percent) of the 296 names in my sample. Apaches observe, however, that some place-names do not describe their referents and are derived from other sources. These include: (1) place-names that allude to activities that were formerly performed at or near the sites in question; (2) place-names that refer to "dangerous" *(bégódzig)* locations; and (3) place-names that allude to historical events that are known to have occurred at or near the sites they designate. Examples of these three types, together with brief descriptions of their sources, are given here.

Type 3: Place-names alluding to former activities.

12. *ndee dah naazįįh:* ndee ("man"; "person"; "Apache") + *dah* ("located above ground level") + *naazįįh* ("three or more animate objects stand about").
Gloss: "men stand about above"
(This name refers to a point on a low ridge that commands an excellent view of the southern portion of Cibecue Valley. Prior to 1872, Apache men were stationed here as lookouts to guard against surprise attacks from Pima, Papagos, Navajos, and troops of the United States Sixth Cavalry.)

12. *gową dahitą́ą́:* gową ("camp"; "wickiup") + *dahitą́ą́* ("crescent moon"; literally, "a slender solid object appears").
Gloss: "crescent moon camp"
(This is the name of a large meadow where a four-day religious ceremonial called *hádndín 'aldee* ("pollen is placed") was formerly performed. The ritual began with the appearance of the first new moon in April or May. The temporary brush dwellings of the participants were arranged side by side in the shape of a crescent.)

Type 4: Place names referring to "dangerous places" *(bégódzig goz'ąą).*

14. *dahzíné sidaa:* dahzíné ("porcupine") + *sidaa* ("an animate object sits").
Gloss: "a porcupine sits"

Figure 4. tsé łigai dah sidil ("white rocks lie above in a compact cluster").

(This name refers to the upper end of a large arroyo near the community of Cibecue where porcupines used to gather in early winter. Western Apaches hold that direct contact with porcupines, or with anything contaminated with porcupine urine or feces or hair, may result in serious illness.)

15. *ma' bichan 'o'áá: ma'* ("coyote") + *bichan* ("its feces") + *'o'áá* ("a solid object sticks up").
    Gloss: "a pile of coyote feces sticks up"
    (This name designates a large meadow where coyotes congregate to hunt field mice and jackrabbits. Like porcupines, coyotes and their excuviae are regarded by Apaches as a source of sickness.)

Type 5: Place-names alluding to historical events.

16. *tá'ke godzig: tá'ke* ("field"; "farm") + *godzig* ("rotten"; "spoiled").
    Gloss: "rotten field"
    (This is the name of a small flat where a group of Western Apaches planted corn many years ago. One spring, after the corn had sprouted, the people left their camps nearby to search for mescal in mountains to the south. They returned to discover that all their corn had been killed by a black, foul-smelling blight.)

17. *łíí' téhitlizh: łíí'* ("horse") + *téhitlizh* ("it fell down into water").

Figure 5. nadah nch'ii' ("bitter-tasting mescal").

Gloss: "horse fell down into water"
(This name refers to a site where a young Apache woman, returning home after gathering mescal, allowed the horse she
was riding to walk too close to a rocky ledge above Cibecue
Creek. The horse lost its balance and fell with its rider into the
stream below. The horse survived; the woman did not.)

Of the 296 Apache place-names in my sample, only 28 (less than 11
percent) were assigned by consultants from Cibecue to the three types exemplified above (Type 3 = 9; Type 4 = 6; Type 5 = 13). This finding
would seem to lend added support to the view that Western Apaches favor
place-names that provide precise and accurate information about observable features of the natural landscape—and the more information the better.[3]

Why should this be so? The reasons, no doubt, are multiple, but one
of them may be closely linked to the stylistic functions served by place-
names in Western Apache storytelling. Place-names are used in all forms of
Apache storytelling as situating devices, as conventionalized instruments
for locating narrated events in the physical settings where the events have
occurred. Thus, instead of describing these settings discursively, an Apache
storyteller can simply employ their names and Apache listeners, whether
they have visited the locations or not, are able to imagine in some detail how
they might appear. In this way, to borrow Hoijer's felicitous phrase, narrated events are "spatially anchored" at points on the land, and the evocative pictures presented by Western Apache place-names become indispensable resources for the storyteller's craft.

"All These Places Have Stories"

When I return to Cibecue in the spring of 1978, Nick Thompson is recovering from a bad case of the flu. He is weak, despondent, and uncomfortable. We speak very little and no mention is made of place-names. His wife is worried about him and so am I. Within a week, however, Nick's eldest son comes to my camp with a message: I am to visit his father and bring with me two packs of Salem cigarettes and a dozen chocolate-covered doughnuts. This is good news.

When I arrive at the old man's camp, he is sitting under the cottonwood tree by his house. A blanket is draped across his knees and he is wearing a heavy plaid jacket and a red vinyl cap with white fur-lined earflaps. There is color in his cheeks and the sparkle is back in his eyes. Shortly after we start to converse, and a propos of nothing I can discern, Nick announces that in 1931 he had sexual intercourse eight times in one night. He wants to know if I have ever been so fortunate. His wife, who has brought us each a cup of coffee, hears this remark and tells him that he is a crazy old man. Nick laughs loudly. Plainly, he is feeling better.

Eventually, I ask Nick if he is ready to resume our work together. "Yes," he says, "but no more on names." What then? "Stories," is his reply. "All these places have stories. We shoot each other with them, like arrows. Come back tomorrow morning." Puzzled once again, but suspecting that the old man has a plan he wants to follow, I tell him I will return. We then discuss Nick's wages. He insists that I pay him more than the year before as it is necessary to keep up with inflation. I agree and we settle on a larger sum. Then comes the predictable farewell joke: a fine piece of nonsense in which Nick, speaking English and imitating certain mannerisms he has come to associate with Anglo physicians, diagnoses my badly sunburned nose as an advanced case of venereal disease.[4] This time it is Nick's wife who laughs loudest.

The next day Nick begins to instruct me on aspects of Western Apache storytelling. Consulting on a regular basis with other Apaches from Cibecue as well, I pursue this topic throughout the summer of 1978.

Western Apache Historical Tales

If place-names appear frequently in ordinary forms of Western Apache discourse, their use is equally conspicuous in oral narratives. It is here, in conjunction with stories Apaches tell, that we can move closer to an interpretation of native claims about the symbolic importance of geographical features and the personalized relationships that individuals may have with them. As shown in Figure 6, the people of Cibecue classify "speech" *(yat'i')* into three major forms: "ordinary talk" *(yat'i')*, "prayer" *('okąąhi)*, and "narratives" or "stories" *(nagoldi'é)*. Narratives are further classified into four major and two minor genres (see Figure 7). The major genres include "myths" (*godiyịhgo nagoldi';* literally, "to tell of holiness"), "historical tales" (*'ágodzaahí* or *'ágodzaahí nagoldi';* literally, "that which has happened" or "to tell of that which has happened"), "sagas" (*nlt'éégo nagoldi';* literally, "to tell of pleasantness"), and stories that arise in the context of "gossip" *(ch'idii).* The minor genres, which do not concern us here, are "Coyote stories" (*ma' highaałyú nagoldi';* literally "to tell of Coyote's travels") and "seduction tales" (*binííma' nagoldi';* literally, "to tell of sexual desires").

Western Apaches distinguish among the major narrative genres on two basic semantic dimensions: time and purpose. Values on the temporal dimension identify in general terms when the events recounted in narratives took place, while values on the purposive dimension describe the objectives that Apache narrators typically have in recounting them (see Figure 8). Accordingly, "myths" deal with events that occurred "in the beginning" *('godiyaaná'),* a time when the universe and all things within it were achieving their present form and location. Performed only by the medicine men and medicine women, myths are presented for the primary purpose of enlightenment and instruction: to explain and reaffirm the complex processes by which the known world came into existence. "Historical tales" recount events that took place "long ago" *(doo 'ánííná)* when the Western Apache people, having emerged from below the surface of the earth, were developing their own distinctive ways and customs. Most historical tales describe incidents that occurred prior to the coming of the white man, but some of these stories are set in postreservation times, which began for the Western Apache in 1872. Like myths, historical tales are intended to edify, but their main purpose is to alarm and criticize social delinquents (or, as the Apache say, to "shoot" them), thereby impressing such individuals with the undesirability of improper behavior and alerting them to the punitive consequences of further misconduct.

Although sagas deal with historical themes, these narratives are chiefly concerned with events that have taken place in "modern times" *(dííjịịgo),* usually within the last 60 or 70 years. In contrast to historical tales, which always focus on serious and disturbing matters, sagas are largely devoid of them. Rather than serving as vehicles of personal criticism, the

Figure 6. Major categories of Western Apache speech.

primary purpose of sagas is to provide their listeners with relaxation and entertainment. Stories of the kind associated with gossip consist of reports in which persons relate and interpret events involving other members of the Western Apache community. These stories, which embrace incidents that have occurred "now" or "at present" *(k'ad)*, are often told for no other reason than to keep people informed of local developments. Not uncommonly, however, narratives in gossip are also used to ridicule and malign the character of their subjects.

Nowhere do place-names serve more important communicative functions than in the context of historical tales. As if to accentuate this fact, stories of the *'ágodzaahí* genre are stylistically quite simple. Historical tales require no specialized lexicon, display no unusual syntactical constructions, and involve no irregular morphophonemic alternations; neither are they characterized by unique patterns of stress, pitch, volume, or intonation. In these ways *'ágodzaahí* narratives contrast sharply with myths and sagas, which entail the use of a variety of genre-specific stylistic devices. Historical tales also differ from myths and sagas by virtue of their brevity. Whereas myths and sagas may take hours to complete, historical tales can usually be delivered in less than five minutes. Western Apache storytellers point out that this is both fitting and effective, because *'ágodzaahí* stories, like the "arrows" *(k'aa)* they are commonly said to represent, work best when they move swiftly. Finally, and most significant of all, historical tales are distinguished from all other forms of Apache narrative by an opening and closing line that identifies with a place-name where the events in the narrative occurred. These lines frame the narrative, mark it unmistakably as belonging to the *'ágodzaahí* genre, and evoke a particular physical setting in which listeners can imaginatively situate everything that happens. It is hardly surprising, then, that while Apache storytellers agree that historical tales are "about" the events recounted in the tales, they also emphasize that the tales are "about" the sites at which the events took place.

If the style of Western Apache historical tales is relatively unremarkable, their content is just the opposite. Without exception, and usually in very graphic terms, historical tales focus on persons who suffer misfortune as the consequence of actions that violate Apache standards for acceptable

nagodi'é
("narrative"; "story")

godiyįhgo nagoldi'   'ágodzaahí   nlt'éégo nagoldi'   ch'idii

("myth")   ("historical tale")   ("saga")   ("gossip")

Figure 7. Major categories of Western Apache narrative.

Narrative Category	Temporal Locus of Events	Purposes
godiyįhgo nagoldi' ("myth")	*godiyaaná'* ("in the beginning")	to enlighten; to instruct
'ágodzaahí ("historical tale")	*doo 'ánííná'* ("long ago")	to criticize; to warn; to "shoot"
nlt'éégo nagoldi' ("saga")	*dííjįįgo* ("modern times")	to entertain; to engross
ch'idii ("gossip")	*k'ad* ("now")	to inform; to malign

Figure 8. Major categories of Western Apache narrative distinguished by temporal locus of events and primary purposes for narration.

social behavior. More specifically, *'ágodzaahí* stories tell of persons who have acted unthinkingly and impulsively in open disregard for "Apache custom" *(ndee bi 'at'ee')* and who pay for their transgressions by being humiliated, ostracized, or killed. Stories of the *'ágodzaahí* variety are morality tales pure and simple. When viewed as such by the Apaches—as compact commentaries on what should be avoided so as to deal successfully and effectively with other people—they are highly informative. What these narratives assert—tacitly, perhaps, but with dozens of compelling examples—is that immoral behavior is irrevocably a community affair and that persons who behave badly will be punished sooner or later. Thus, just as *'ágodzaahí* stories are "about" historical events and their geographical locations, they are also "about" the system of rules and values according to which Apaches expect each other to organize and regulate their lives. In an even more fundamental sense, then, historical tales are "about" what it means to *be* a Western Apache, or, to make the point less dramatically, what it is that being an Apache should normally and properly entail.

To see how this is so, let us consider the texts of three historical tales and examine the manner in which they have been interpreted by their Apache narrators.

18. It happened at "big cottonwood trees stand spreading here and there."

Long ago, the Pimas and Apaches were fighting. The Pimas were carrying long clubs made from mesquite wood; they were also heavy and hard. Before dawn the Pimas arrived at Cibecue and attacked the Apaches there. The Pimas attacked while the Apaches were still asleep. The Pimas killed the Apaches with their clubs. An old woman woke up; she heard the

Apaches crying out. The old woman thought it was her son-in-law because he often picked on her daughter. The old woman cried out: "You pick on my child a lot. You should act pleasantly toward her." Because the old woman cried out, the Pimas learned where she was. The Pimas came running to the old woman's camp and killed her with their clubs. A young girl ran away from there and hid beneath some bushes. She alone survived.

It happened at "big cottonwood trees stand spreading here and there."

Narrated by Mrs. Annie Peaches, this historical tale deals with the harmful consequences that may come to persons who overstep traditional role boundaries. During the first year of marriage it is customary for young Apache couples to live in the camp of the bride's parents. At this time, the bride's mother may request that her son-in-law perform different tasks and she may also instruct and criticize him. Later, however, when the couple establishes a separate residence, the bride's mother forfeits this right and may properly interfere in her son-in-law's affairs only at the request of her daughter. Mrs. Peaches explains that women who do not abide by this arrangement imply that their sons-in-law are immature and irresponsible, which is a source of acute embarrassment for the young men and their wives. Thus, even when meddling might seem to serve a useful purpose, it should be scrupulously avoided. The woman on whom this story centers failed to remember this—and was instantly killed.

19. It happened at "coarse-textured rocks lie above in a compact cluster."

Long ago, a man became sexually attracted to his step-daughter. He was living below "coarse-textured rocks lie above in a compact cluster" with his stepdaughter and her mother. Waiting until no one else was present, and sitting alone with her, he started to molest her. The girl's maternal uncle happened to come by and he killed the man with a rock. The man's skull was cracked open. It was raining. The girl's maternal uncle dragged the man's body up above to "coarse-textured rocks lie above in a compact cluster" and placed it there in a storage pit. The girl's mother came home and was told by her daughter of all that had happened. The people who owned the storage pit removed the man's body and put it somewhere else. The people never had a wake for the dead man's body.

It happened at "coarse-textured rocks lie above in a compact cluster."

Narrated by Mr. Benson Lewis, this historical tale deals with the theme of incest, for sexual contact with stepchildren is considered by Western Apaches to be an incestuous act. According to Mr. Lewis, the key line in the story is the penultimate one in which he observes, "The people never had a wake for the dead man's body." We may assume, Mr. Lewis says, that because the dead man's camp was located near the storage pit in which his body was placed, the people who owned the pit were also his relatives. This makes the neglect with which his corpse was treated all the more profound, since kinsmen are bound by the strongest of obligations to care for each other when they die. That the dead man's relatives chose to dispense with customary mortuary ritual shows with devastating clarity that they wished to disown him completely.

20. It happened at "men stand above here and there."

Long ago, a man killed a cow off the reservation. The cow belonged to a Whiteman. The man was arrested by a policeman living at Cibecue at "men stand above here and there." The policeman was an Apache. The policeman took the man to the head Army officer at Fort Apache. There, at Fort Apache, the head Army officer questioned him. "What do you want?" he said. The policeman said, "I need cartridges and food." The policeman said nothing about the man who had killed the Whiteman's cow. That night some people spoke to the policeman. "It is best to report on him," they said to him. The next day the policeman returned to the head Army officer. "Now what do you want?" he said. The policeman said, "Yesterday I was going to say HELLO and GOOD-BYE but I forgot to do it." Again he said nothing about the man he arrested. Someone was working with words on his mind. The policeman returned with the man to Cibecue. He released him at "men stand above here and there."

It happened at "men stand above here and there."

This story, narrated by Nick Thompson, describes what happened to a man who acted too much like a white man. Between 1872 and 1895, when the Western Apache were strictly confined to their reservations by U.S. military forces, disease and malnutrition took the lives of many people. Consequently, Apaches who listen to this historical tale find it perfectly acceptable that the man who lived at "men stand above here and there" should have killed and butchered a white man's cow. What is not acceptable is that the policeman, another Apache from the same settlement, should have arrested the rustler and contemplated taking him to jail. But the policeman's plans were thwarted. Someone used witchcraft on him and made him stupid and forgetful. He never informed the military officer at

Fort Apache of the real purpose of his visit, and his second encounter with the officer—in which he apologized for neglecting to say "hello" and "good-bye" the previous day—revealed him to be an absurd and laughable figure. Although Western Apaches find portions of this story amusing, Nick Thompson explains that they understand it first and foremost as a harsh indictment of persons who join with outsiders against members of their own community and who, as if to flaunt their lack of allegiance, parade the attitudes and mannerisms of white men.

Thus far, my remarks on what Western Apache historical tales are "about" have centered on features of textual content. This is a familiar strategy and certainly a necessary one, but it is also incomplete. In addition to everything else—places, events, moral standards, conceptions of cultural identity—every historical tale is also "about" the person at whom it is directed. This is because the telling of a historical tale is always prompted by an individual having committed one or more social offenses to which the act of narration, together with the tale itself, is intended as a critical and remedial response. Thus, on those occasions when 'ágodzaahí stories are actually told—by real Apache storytellers, in real interpersonal contexts, to real social offenders—these narratives are understood to be accompanied by an unstated message from the storyteller that may be phrased something like this: "I know that you have acted in a way similar or analogous to the way in which someone acted in the story I am telling you. If you continue to act in this way, something similar or analogous to what happened to the character in the story might also happen to you." This metacommunicative message is just as important as any conveyed by the text of the storyteller's tale. Apaches contend that if the message is taken to heart by the person at whom the tale is aimed—and if, in conjunction with lessons drawn from the tale itself, he or she resolves to improve his or her behavior—a lasting bond will have been created between that individual and the site or sites at which events in the tale took place. The cultural premises that inform this powerful idea are made explicit presently; but first, in order to understand more clearly what the idea involves, let us examine the circumstances that led to the telling of a historical tale at Cibecue and see how this narrative affected the person for whom it was told.

In early June 1977, a 17-year-old Apache woman attended a girls' puberty ceremonial at Cibecue with her hair rolled up in a set of pink plastic curlers. She had returned home two days before from a boarding school in Utah where this sort of ornamentation was considered fashionable by her peers. Something so mundane would have gone unnoticed by others were it not for the fact that Western Apache women of all ages are expected to appear at puberty ceremonials with their hair worn loose. This is one of several ways that women have of showing respect for the ceremonial and also, by implication, for the people who have staged it. The practice of presenting oneself with free-flowing hair is also understood to contribute to the ceremonial's effectiveness, for Apaches hold that the ritual's most basic objectives, which are to invest the pubescent girl with qualities necessary for life as an adult, cannot be achieved unless standard forms of respect are faithfully observed. On this occasion at Cibecue, everyone was following custom except the young woman who arrived wearing curlers. She soon became an object of attention and quiet expressions of disapproval, but no one spoke to her about the cylindrical objects in her hair.

Two weeks later, the same young woman made a large stack of tortillas and brought them to the camp of her maternal grandmother, a widow in her mid-60s who had organized a small party to celebrate the birthday of her eldest grandson. Eighteen people were on hand, myself included, and all of us were treated to hot coffee and a dinner of boiled beef and potatoes. When the meal was over casual conversation began to flow, and the young woman seated herself on the ground next to her younger sister. And then— quietly, deftly, and totally without warning—her grandmother narrated a version of the historical tale about the forgetful Apache policeman who behaved too much like a white man. Shortly after the story was finished, the young woman stood up, turned away wordlessly, and walked off in the direction of her home. Uncertain of what had happened, I asked her grandmother why she has departed. Had the young woman suddenly become ill? "No," her grandmother replied. "I shot her with an arrow."

Approximately two years after this incident occurred, I found myself again in the company of the young woman with the taste for distinctive hairstyles. She had purchased a large carton of groceries at the trading post at Cibecue, and when I offered to drive her home with them she accepted. I inquired on the way if she remembered the time that her grandmother had told us the story about the forgetful policeman. She said she did and then went on, speaking in English, to describe her reactions to it. "I think maybe my grandmother was getting after me, but then I think maybe not, maybe she's working on somebody else. Then I think back on that dance and I know it's me for sure. I sure don't like how she's talking about me, so I quit looking like that. I threw those curlers away." In order to reach the young woman's camp, we had to pass within a few hundred years of *ndee dah naazįíh* ("men stand above here and there"), the place where the man had lived who was arrested in the story for rustling. I pointed it out to my companion. She said nothing for several moments. Then she smiled and spoke softly in her own language: "I know that place. It stalks me every day."

The comments of this Western Apache woman on her experience as the target of a historical tale are instructive in several respects. To begin with, her statement enables us to imagine something of the sizable psychological impact that historical tales may have on the persons to whom they are presented. Then, too, we can see how *'ágodzaahí* stories may produce quick and palpable effects on the behavior of such individuals, causing them to modify their social conduct in quite specific ways. Lastly, and most revealing of all, the young woman's remarks provide a clear illustration of what Apaches have in mind when they assert that historical tales may establish highly meaningful relationships between individuals and features of the natural landscape.

To appreciate fully the significance of these relationships, as well as their influence on the lives of Western Apache people, we must explore more thoroughly the manner in which the relationships are conceptualized. This can be accomplished through a closer examination of Apache ideas about the activity of storytelling and the acknowledged power of oral narratives, especially historical tales, to promote beneficial changes in people's attitudes toward their responsibilities as members of a moral community. These ideas, which combine to form a native model of how oral narratives work to achieve their intended effects, are expressed in terms of a single dominant metaphor. By now it should come as no surprise to learn that the metaphor draws heavily on the imagery of hunting.

"Stalking with Stories"

Nick Thompson is tired. We have been talking about hunting with stories for two days now and the old man has not had an easy time of it. Yesterday, my uneven control of the Western Apache language prevented him from speaking as rapidly and eloquently as he would have liked, and on too many occasions I was forced to interrupt him with questions. At one point, bored and annoyed with my queries, he told me that I reminded him of a horsefly buzzing around his head. Later, however, when he seemed satisfied that I could follow at least the outline of his thoughts, he recorded on tape a lengthy statement which he said contained everything he wanted me to know. "Take it with you and listen to it," he said. "Tomorrow we put it in English." For the last six hours that is what we have been trying to do. We are finished now and weary of talking. In the weeks to come I will worry about the depth and force of our translation, and twice more I will return to Nick's camp with other questions. But the hardest work is over and both of us know it. Nick has taught me already that hunting with stories is not a simple matter, and as I prepare to leave I say so. "We know," he says, and that is all. Here is Nick Thompson's statement:

> This is what we know about our stories. They go to work on your mind and make you think about your life. Maybe you've not been acting right. Maybe you've been stingy. Maybe you've been chasing after women. Maybe you've been trying to act like a Whiteman. People don't *like* it! So someone goes hunting for you—maybe your grandmother, your grandfather, your uncle. It doesn't matter. Anyone can do it.

So someone stalks you and tells a story about what happened long ago. It doesn't matter if other people are around—you're going to know he's aiming that story at you. All of a sudden it *hits* you! It's like an arrow, they say. Sometimes it just bounces off—it's too soft and you don't think about anything. But when it's strong it goes in *deep* and starts working on your mind right away. No one says anything to you, only that story is all, but now you know that people have been watching you and talking about you. They don't like how you've been acting. So you have to think about your life.

Then you feel weak, real weak, like you are sick. You don't want to eat or talk to anyone. That story is working on you now. You keep thinking about it. That story is changing you now, making you want to live right. That story is making you want to replace yourself. You think only of what you did that was wrong and you don't like it. So you want to live better. After a while, you don't like to think of what you did wrong. So you try to forget that story. You try to pull that arrow out. You think it won't hurt anymore because now you want to live right.

It's hard to keep on living right. Many things jump up at you and block your way. But you won't forget that story. You're going to see the place where it happened, maybe every day if it's nearby and close to Cibecue. If you don't see it, you're going to hear its name and see it in your mind. It doesn't matter if you get old—that place will keep on stalking you like the one who shot you with the story. Maybe that person will die. Even so, that place will keep on stalking you. It's like that person is still alive.

Even if we go far away from here to some big city, places around here keep stalking us. If you live wrong, you will hear the names and see the places in your mind. They keep on stalking you, even if you go across oceans. The names of all these places are good. They make you remember how to live right, so you want to replace yourself again.

A Western Apache Hunting Metaphor

Nick Thompson's model of Western Apache storytelling is a compelling construction. To be sure, it is the formulation of one Apache only; but it is fully explicit and amply detailed, and I have been able to corroborate almost every aspect of it with other Apaches from Cibecue. This is not to imply that all Apache people interpret their hunting metaphor for storytelling in exactly the same fashion. On the contrary, one of the properties of any successful metaphor is that it can be refined and enlarged in different ways. Thus, some Apaches assert that historical tales, like arrows, leave wounds—mental and emotional ones—and that the process of "replacing oneself" (a striking concept, that one) is properly understood as a form of healing. Other Apache consultants stress that place-names, rather than the sites to which the names refer, are what individuals are unable to forget after historical tales have done their primary work. But differences and elaborations of this kind only demonstrate the scope and flexibility of the hunting metaphor and do nothing to alter its basic contours or to diminish its considerable force. Neither does such variation reduce in any way the utility of the metaphor as an effective instrument of Western Apache thought.

Although I cannot claim to understand the full range of meanings that the hunting model for storytelling has for Western Apache people, the general premises on which the model rests seem clear to me. Historical tales have the capacity to thrust socially delinquent persons into periods of intense critical self-examination from which (ideally, at least) they emerge chastened, repentant, and determined to "live right." Simultaneously, people who have been "shot" with stories experience a form of anguish—shame, guilt, perhaps only pervasive chagrin—that moves them to alter aspects of their behavior so as to conform more closely to community expectations. In short, historical tales have the power to change people's ideas about themselves: to force them to admit to social failings, to dwell seriously on the significance of these lapses, and to resolve, hopefully once and for all, not to repeat them. As Nick Thompson says, historical tales "make you think about your life."

After stories and storytellers have served this beneficial purpose, features of the physical landscape take over and perpetuate it. Mountains and arroyos step in symbolically for grandmothers and uncles. Just as the latter have "stalked" delinquent individuals in the past, so too particular locations continue to "stalk" them in the present. Such surveillance is essential, Apaches maintain, because "living right" requires constant care and attention, and there is always a possibility that old stories and their initial impact, like old arrows and their wounds, will fade and disappear. In other words, there is always a chance that persons who have "replaced themselves" once—or twice, or three times—will relax their guard against "badness" and slip back into undesirable forms of social conduct. Consequently, Apaches explain, individuals need to be continuously reminded of why they were "shot" in the first place and how they reacted to it at the time. Geographical sites, together with the crisp mental "pictures" of them presented by their names, serve admirably in this capacity, inviting people to recall their earlier failings and encouraging them to resolve, once again, to avoid them in the future. Grandmothers and uncles must perish but the landscape endures, and for this the Apache people are deeply grateful.

"The land," Nick Thompson observes, "looks after us. The land keeps badness away."

It should now be possible for the reader to interpret the Western Apache texts at the beginning of this essay in a manner roughly compatible with the Apache ideas that have shaped them. Moreover, we should be able to appreciate that the claims put forward in the texts are reasonable and appropriate, culturally credible and "correct," the principled expressions of an underlying logic that invests them with internal consistency and coherent conceptual structure. As we have seen, this structure is supplied in large part by the hunting metaphor for Western Apache storytelling. It is chiefly in accordance with this metaphor—or, more exactly, in accordance with the symbolic associations it orders and makes explicit—that the claims presented earlier finally make sense.

Thus, the claim of Annie Peaches—that the land occupied by the Western Apache "makes the people live right"—becomes understandable as a proposition about the moral significance of geographical locations as this has been established by historical tales with which the locations are associated. Similarly, Wilson Lavender's claim—that Apaches who fail to remember place-names "forget how to be strong"—rests on an association of place-names with a belief in the power of historical tales to discourage forms of socially unacceptable behavior. Places and their names are also associated by Apaches with the narrators of historical tales, and Benson Lewis's claim—that a certain mountain near Cibecue is his maternal grandmother—can only be interpreted in light of this assumption. The hunting metaphor for storytelling also informs Ronnie Lupe's claim that Western Apache children who are not exposed to historical tales tend to have interpersonal difficulties. As he puts it, "They don't know the stories of what happened at these places. That's why some of them get into trouble." What Mr. Lupe is claiming, of course, is that children who do not learn to associate places and their names with historical tales cannot appreciate the utility of these narratives as guidelines for dealing responsibly and amicably with other people. Consequently, he believes, such individuals are more likely than others to act in ways that run counter to Apache social norms, a sure sign that they are "losing the land."

Losing the land is something the Western Apache can ill afford to do, for geographical features have served the people for centuries as indispensable mnemonic pegs on which to hang the moral teachings of their history. Accordingly, such locations present themselves as instances of what Mikhail Bakhtin calls *chronotopes*. As Bakhtin (1981:7) describes them, chronotopes are:

> points in the geography of a community where time and space intersect and fuse. Time takes on flesh and becomes visible for human

contemplation; likewise, space becomes charged and responsive to the movements of time and history and the enduring character of a people. . . . Chronotopes thus stand as monuments to the community itself, as symbols of it, as forces operating to shape its members' images of themselves.

Whether or not one is pleased with Bakhtin's use of the term "chronotope" (it is more widely known, but in a very different sense, as a concept in Einstein's theory of relativity), his observations on the cultural importance of geographical landmarks apply nicely to the Western Apache. The Apache landscape is full of named locations where time and space have fused and where, through the agency of historical tales, their intersection is "made visible for human contemplation." It is also apparent that such locations, charged as they are with personal and social significance, work in important ways to shape the images that Apaches have—or should have—of themselves. Speaking to people like Nick Thompson and Ronnie Lupe, to Annie Peaches and Benson Lewis, one forms the impression that Apaches view the landscape as a repository of distilled wisdom, a stern but benevolent keeper of tradition, an ever-vigilant ally in the efforts of individuals and whole communities to put into practice a set of standards for social living that are uniquely and distinctively their own. In the world that the Western Apache have constituted for themselves, features of the landscape have become symbols of and for this way of living, the symbols of a culture and the enduring moral character of its people.

We may assume that this relationship with the land has been pervasive throughout Western Apache history; but in today's climate of accelerating social change, its importance for Apache people may well be deepening. Communities such as Cibecue, formerly isolated and very much turned inward, were opened up by paved roads less than 20 years ago, and the consequences of improved access and freer travel—including, most noticeably, greatly increased contact with Anglo-Americans—have been pronounced. Younger Apaches, who today complain frequently about the tedium of village life, have started to develop new tastes and ambitions, and some of them are eager to explore the outside world. Older members of the community understand this desire and do little to try to stifle it, but they are concerned—and not without good reason—that as younger people learn more and more of the "Whiteman's way," they will also lose sight of portions of their own. Let the pink plastic curlers at the girls' puberty ceremonial stand as a case in point. What can be done to guard against this unsettling possibility? Perhaps, in the long run, nothing. But for now, and probably for some time to come, the landscape is doing a respectable job. It is there, "stalking" people all the time. To the extent that it remains not merely a physical presence but an omnipresent moral force, young Apaches are not likely to forget that the "Whiteman's way" belongs to a different world.

Having pursued Western Apache ideas about the land this far, it is worth inquiring if similar conceptions are held by other groups of American Indian people. Although ethnographic materials bearing on this question are in short supply (I identify some of the reasons for this shortage further on), there is highly reliable evidence from another source—the published work of modern Indian writers—that general similarities do exist. Consider, for example, the following statement by Leslie M. Silko, poet and novelist from the pueblo of Laguna in New Mexico. After explaining that stories "function basically as makers of our identity," Silko (1981:69) goes on to discuss Pueblo narratives in relation to the land:

> The stories cannot be separated from geographical locations, from actual physical places within the land. . . . And the stories are so much a part of these places that it is almost impossible for future generations to lose the stories because there are so many imposing geological elements . . . you cannot *live* in that land without asking or looking at or noticing a boulder or rock. And there's always a story.

A number of other American Indian authors, among them Vine Deloria, Jr. (Sioux), Simon Ortiz (Acoma), Joy Harjo (Creek), and the cultural anthropologist Alfonso Ortiz (San Juan), have written with skill and insight about the moral dimensions of Native American conceptions of the land. No one, however, has addressed the subject with greater sensitivity than N. Scott Momaday (Kiowa). The following passages, taken from his short essay entitled "Native American Attitudes to the Environment" (1974), show clearly what is involved, not only for the Western Apache but for other tribes as well.

> You cannot understand how the Indian thinks of himself in relation to the world around him unless you understand his conception of what is appropriate; particularly what is morally appropriate within the context of that relationship. [1974:82]

> The native American ethic with respect to the physical world is a matter of reciprocal appropriation: appropriations in which man invests himself in the landscape, and at the same time incorporates the landscape into his own most fundamental experience. . . . This appropriation is primarily a matter of imagination which is moral in

kind. I mean to say that we are all, I suppose, what we imagine ourselves to be. And that is certainly true of the American Indian. . . . [The Indian] is someone who thinks of himself in a particular way and his idea comprehends his relationship to the physical world. He imagines himself in terms of that relationship and others. And it is that act of imagination, that moral act of imagination, which constitutes his understanding of the physical world. [1974:80]

"Goodness Is All Around"

The news sweeps through Cibecue like brush fire: Nick Thompson must have purchased a wheelchair because he was seen this morning *racing* in one, against his four-year-old grandson. The little boy, shrieking with glee and running as fast as he could, won the contest, but the old man finished close behind. Nick's wife was horrified and his oldest daughter (the one who hardly ever raises her voice) yelled twice to him to stop. But he kept going, wheeling himself along with his one good arm and paying no attention whatsoever. That old man will do anything! He doesn't care at all what people think! And what if he *crashed!*

Nick Thompson has no intention of crashing. Seated now in his familiar place beneath the cottonwood tree near his house, he says that racing his wheelchair is perfectly safe. He says he plans to do it again; in fact, he has already challenged his six-year-old granddaughter. He says he is tired of the women in his camp telling him what to do. He is also tired of not being able to move around freely, which is why he bought the wheelchair in the first place, and people should understand this and stop making such a fuss. And besides, the old man observes, the wheelchair has good brakes. That's what he likes best—getting up some real speed and jamming on the brakes.

The summer of 1980 is almost gone and soon I must leave Cibecue. I have walked to Nick's camp to tell him good-bye. This is never easy for me, and we spend most of the time talking about other things. Eventually, I move to thank him for his generosity, his patience, and the things he has taught me. Nick responds by pointing with his lips to a low ridge that runs behind his home in an easterly direction away from Cibecue Creek. "That is a good place," he says. "These are all good places. Goodness is all around. I'm happy you know that now."

The old man pauses. Then he reaches beneath the seat of his chair and produces a blue and white cap which he places, slightly askew, on his head. The embossed emblem in front, which is in the shape of a car, reads "Ford Racing Team." We both begin to laugh . . . and laugh and laugh.

Language and Environment

Anthropologists have long been interested in the relationships that link American Indian communities to their ecological settings. In the great majority of cases, however, these relationships have been described and interpreted exclusively in materialist terms; that is, in terms of demographic patterns, subsistence strategies, and forms of social organization that facilitate the exploitation of environmental resources and function in this way to assure the biological survival of native populations (Anastasio 1972; Castetter and Bell 1951; Dozier 1970; Helm 1968; Steward 1955). While this approach is useful for certain purposes, it is clear nonetheless that materialist models are one-sided and incomplete. Such models ignore the fact that American Indians, like groups of people everywhere, maintain a complex array of symbolic relationships with their physical surroundings, and that these relationships, which may have little to do with the serious business of making a living, play a fundamental role in shaping other forms of social activity (Opler 1941; Ortiz 1969; Parsons 1939; Rappaport 1979; Witherspoon 1977). What is ignored, in other words, are the cultural instruments with which American Indians fashion understandings of their environments, the ideational resources with which they constitute their surroundings and invest them with value and significance. We need not go far to seek the reasons for this neglect. Having committed themselves to a search for statistical regularities and functional interdependencies, human ecologists are usually obliged to regard the semiotic dimensions of human environments as "epiphenomena" that lie outside the proper sphere of their concern (Flannery 1972; Vayda 1969). And so, ironically enough, human ecologists have become largely disinterested in what human beings take their environments to mean. This is unfortunate because, as Csikszentmihalyi and Rochberg-Halton (1981:1) have recently written,

> to understand what people are and what they might become, one must understand what goes on between people and things. What things are cherished, and why, should become part of our knowledge of human beings. Yet it is surprising how little we know about what things mean to people. By and large social scientists have neglected a full investigation of the relationship between people and objects.

We should not proceed too hastily, however. There is no doubt in the minds of many anthropologists, including a substantial number who have worked with American Indians, that studies in ecology have made a valuable contribution. In particular, these investigations have shown that indigenous populations may adapt with exquisite intricacy to the physical conditions of their existence (including, of course, the presence of other human populations), and that modifications in these conditions may have a range of dynamic effects on the structure and organization of social institutions. But the fact remains that ecological models have been consistently formulated at a "systemic" level of abstraction that is well removed from the level of the individual—and it is individuals, not social institutions, who make and act on cultural meanings (Geertz 1973; Turner 1969). Here, then, is the problem. Conventional ecological studies proceed on the tacit premise that what people think about the environment—how they perceive it, conceptualize it, or, to borrow a phrase from the ethnomethodologists, "actively construct" it—is basically irrelevant to an understanding of man-land relationships. If this premise is accepted as correct, we must conclude that cultural meanings are similarly irrelevant and that the layers of significance with which human beings blanket the environment have little bearing on how they lead their lives. But the premise is not correct, for American Indians or anyone else; and to suppose otherwise would be a serious mistake.

Accordingly, and by way of illustration, I show here that Western Apache conceptions of the land work in specific ways to influence Apaches' conceptions of themselves (and vice versa), and that the two together work to influence patterns of social action. To reject this possibility—or, as many ecologists would be inclined to do, to rule it out a priori as inconsequential—would have the effect of "removing" the Apache from the world as they have constructed it. This, in turn, would obliterate all aspects of their moral relationship with the land. For reasons that should now be apparent, this relationship is crucial to Apaches—quite as crucial, I expect, as any that deals with subsistence or economics—and for us to lose sight of it could only have damaging consequences.

Societies must survive, but social life is more than just surviving. And cultural meanings are "epiphenomenal" only for those who choose to make them so. I would like to contribute to the development of a cultural ecology that is cultural in the fullest sense, a broader and more flexible approach to the study of man-land relationships in which the symbolic properties of environmental phenomena receive the same kind of care and attention that has traditionally been given to their material counterparts. The Western Apache of Cibecue understand their land, and act on their understandings of it, in ways that standard ecological approaches would overlook. Does this mean that such understandings are unimportant? for the Western Apache? for a stronger and more rounded anthropology? I suggest that on both counts it does not.

Cultural constructions of the environment, whether those of American Indians or of peoples elsewhere in the world, will remain largely inaccessible unless we are prepared to sit down and listen to our native consultants talk—not only about landscapes, which of course we must do, but about talking about landscapes as well. And since spatial conceptions, like temporal ones, are so often found expressed in figurative language, this is almost certain to lead to a consideration of metaphor. Paul Radin (1916:137), writing some years ago of the Winnebago Indians of the Great Lakes, described a particular case that is probably typical of many others:

> Ideas about the habitat are frequently set forth in elaborate similes and metaphors which equate disparate objects in a fashion that at first seems quite unfathomable. Yet once these tropes are uncovered, it can be seen that they rest upon firm assumptions about the workings of nature which, though different from our own, fit together intelligibly.

George Lakoff and Mark Johnson (1980:1) have recently stated that the essence of metaphor is "understanding and experiencing one kind of thing in terms of another." Although this definition departs relatively little from the classical one given by Aristotle ("metaphor implies an intuitive perception of the similarity in dissimilars"), it points to a problem in the study of language and culture that is deeply ethnographic. Where metaphor is concerned, the question always arises, On what *grounds* is one kind of thing understood in terms of another? In other words, what must individuals believe about themselves and their surroundings for their metaphors to "work"?

This question focuses attention on the large body of implicit cultural assumptions that the members of any speech community rely on to interpret instances of situated discourse. Such assumptions, which have been variously described as comprising a speaker's "presuppositions," "background knowledge," or "beliefs about the world," present difficulties for all theories of language which seek to restrict the idea of linguistic competence to a speaker's tacit knowledge of grammatical rules. As I demonstrate elsewhere (Basso 1976), metaphor threatens both the validity of this distinction and the utility of maintaining it, because the ability to interpret even the simplest forms of metaphorical speech cannot be accounted for with grammatical rules alone; presuppositions are also fundamentally involved (Friedrich 1979; Tyler 1978). This is clearly illustrated by Nick Thompson's statement on the Western Apache hunting metaphor for storytelling. As he explicates the metaphor, thereby enabling us to interpret a set of claims that Apaches have made, he articulates the cultural assumptions that make these claims possible in the first place. In other words, he makes presuppositions explicit. Storytellers are hunters for the Western Apache—and stories, arrows; and mountains, grandmothers—by virtue of shared beliefs about the world. Culturally wrought and culturally specific, such beliefs provide the conceptual materials with which competent Apache speakers locate the similarities in metaphorical dissimilars and, in so doing, are able to experience one kind of thing in terms of another. Such beliefs make metaphors "work."

What all of this implies (obviously for many anthropologists, less obvious for many linguists) is that grasping other peoples' metaphors requires ethnography as much as it does linguistics. Unless we pursue the two together, the full extent to which metaphorical structures influence patterns of thought and action is likely to elude us. "To inhabit a language," Samuel Johnson wrote, "is to inhabit a living universe, and vice-versa." That "vice versa" is critical because it suggests, correctly I believe, that linguistics and ethnography are integral parts of the same basic enterprise, one of whose purposes is to construct principled interpretations of culturally constituted worlds and to try to understand what living in them is like. I am not certain where the theoretical line between language and culture should be drawn; there are times, in fact, when I wonder if it can be sharply drawn at all. But this much seems reasonably clear: if anthropology stands to benefit from an approach to cultural ecology that attends more closely to the symbolic forms with which human environments are perceived and rendered significant, so too there is a need for an expanded view of linguistic competence in which beliefs about the world occupy a central place. If it is the meaning of things that we are after—the meanings of words, objects, events, and the claims people make about themselves—language and culture must be studied hand in hand. Our knowledge of one can only enhance our knowledge of the other.

"We Know It Happened"

If the thoughts presented here have a measure of theoretical interest, recent experience persuades me that they can have practical value as well. During the last four years, I have authored a number of documents for use in litigation concerning the settlement of Western Apache water rights in the state of Arizona. Until a final decision is reached in the case, I am not permitted to describe the contents of these documents in detail, but one of my assignments has been to write a report dealing with Apache conceptions of the physical environment. That report contains sections on Western Apache place-names, oral narratives, and certain metaphors that Apache people use to formulate aspects of their relationship with the land.

Preliminary hearings resulted in a judgment favorable to Apache interests, and apparently my report was useful, mainly because it helped pave the way for testimony by native witnesses. One of these witnesses was Nick Thompson; and according to attorneys on both sides, the old man's appearance had a decisive impact. After Nick had taken his place on the stand, he was asked by an attorney why he considered water to be important to his people. A man of eminent good sense, Nick replied, "Because we drink it!" And then, without missing a beat, he launched into a historical tale about a large spring not far from Cibecue—*tú nchaa halį́į́'* ("lots of water flows up and out")—where long ago a man was mysteriously drowned after badly mistreating his wife. When Nick finished the story he went on to say: "We know it happened, so we know not to act like that man who died. It's good we have that water. We need it to live. It's good we have that spring. We need it to live right." Then the old man smiled to himself and his eyes began to dance.

Notes

Acknowledgments. This essay has been several years in the making, and a number of people have contributed to its completion. Michael W. Graves, whose careful work on the Fort Apache Indian Reservation laid an essential cartographic foundation for our research, knows already how grateful I am to him. And so too, though for different reasons, do Priscilla Johnson, William Longacre, Bridget Sullivan, and Jefferson Reid. I presented a preliminary version of the essay to members of the Department of Anthropology at Yale University in March 1982. On that occasion Harold Conklin, Floyd Lounsbury, and M. G. Smith made valuable comments which I incorporated into a second draft. For useful suggestions on how to improve the latter I am pleased to offer my thanks to Judith Aissen, Roger Abrahams, Richard Bauman, A. L. Becker, Karen Blu, Edward Bruner, Roberto DaMatta, Joseph Errington, Larry Evers, James Fernandez, Morris Foster, Bruce Kapferer, William Kelly, Louise Lamphere, Michael Lieber, Ellen Messer, Lita Osmundsen, Gayle Potter, Joel Sherzer, and especially to Dell and Virginia Hymes, N. Scott Momaday, Robert Netting, Alfonso Ortiz, Dennis Tedlock, and Sir Edmund Leach. The prose of the essay was much enhanced by the editorial skills of Sue Allen-Mills and Theresa L. Sears, the photographs that accompany it were generously provided by John Hoffman, and the final manuscript was typed in expert fashion by Elizabeth Kyburg; I thank them, respectively, for their words, pictures, and patience. The Western Apache people of Cibecue have aided and instructed me in countless ways during the last 20 years, and the time has long since passed when I could satisfactorily express in writing my indebtedness to them. So, following the suggestion of Nick Thompson, I shall simply list here the names of those persons with whom I have collaborated most closely: Nashley Tessay, Calvert Tessay, Sr., Darlene Tessay, Robert and Lola Machuse, Morley Cromwell, Roy Quay, Benson Lewis, Annie Peaches, Nelson Lupe, Sr., and Ronnie Lupe. And how, finally, to thank Nick Thompson himself? Reluctantly, I shall comply with his request and say nothing. There is, he says, no need.

Note on Western Apache Texts. Statements 1, 3, 4, 18, 19, and 20 were recorded in Western Apache and translated by the author. Interested readers may contact the author for copies of the original Western Apache texts.

1. A prominent figure in Western Apache oral literature, Slim Coyote is appreciated by Apache people for his keen and crafty intelligence, his complex and unpredictable personality, and his penchant for getting himself into difficult situations from which he always manages to extract himself, usually with humorous and embarrassing results. Short collections of Western Apache Coyote tales may be found in Goddard (1919) and Goodwin (1939).

2. One consequence of this neglect is that few Native American groups living today in the United States and Canada possess maps representing the lands that formerly belonged to them. This has become a source of major concern to Indian people. As Vine Deloria, Jr. (personal communication, 1981) observes, "To name the land was for many Indians a way of claiming it, a way that proved more than adequate until Europeans arrived and started to claim the land with more harmful methods. Now, in litigation over the land, Indian claims can be disputed (and sometimes rejected) because many of the old names that marked tribal boundaries have been forgotten and lost."

3. Other aspects of the Western Apache place-name system are described and discussed in Basso (in press).

4. Jokes of this type are intended to poke fun at the butt of the joke and, at the same time, to comment negatively on the interactional practices of Anglo-Americans. An extended treatment of this form of Western Apache humor is presented in Basso (1979).

References Cited

Anastasio, A.
 1972 The Southern Plateau: An Ecological Analysis of Group Relations. *In* Northwest Anthropological Research Notes, No. 6. pp. 109–229. Seattle.
Bakhtin, M.
 1981 The Dialogic Imagination: Four Essays. M. Holquist, ed. Austin: University of Texas Press.
Basso, K.
 1976 "Wise Words of the Western Apache": Metaphor and Semantic Theory. *In* Meaning in Anthropology. K. Basso and Henry Selby, eds. pp. 93–123. Albuquerque: University of New Mexico Press.
 1979 Portraits of the "Whiteman": Linguistic Play and Cultural Symbols among the Western Apache. New York: Cambridge University Press.
 in press Western Apache Place-name Hierarchies. *In* Naming Systems. 1981 Proceedings of the American Ethnological Society. H. Conklin, ed. Washington, DC: American Ethnological Society.
Boas, F.
 1901–07 The Eskimo of Baffin Land and Hudson Bay. Bulletin of the American Museum of Natural History, No. 15, New York.

1934   Geographical Names of the Kwakiutl Indians. Columbia University Contributions to Anthropology, No. 20. New York.
Castetter, E., and W. Bell
1951   Yuman Indian Agriculture. Albuquerque: University of New Mexico Press.
Csikszentmihalyi, M., and E. Rochberg-Halton
1981   The Meaning of Things: Domestic Symbols and the Self. New York: Cambridge University Press.
de Laguna, F.
1972   Under Mount St. Elias: The History and Culture of the Yakotat Tlingit.
Smithsonian Contributions to Anthropology, No. 7. Washington, DC: Smithsonian Institution Press.
Dozier, E.
1970   The Pueblo Indians of the Southwest. New York: Holt, Rinehart and
Winston.
Flannery, K.
1972   The Cultural Evolution of Civilization. Annual Review of Ecology and
Systematics 3:399–426.
Friedrich, P.
1979   Poetic Langue and the Imagination. *In* Language, Context, and the
Imagination: Essays by Paul Friedrich. A. S. Dil, ed. pp. 441–512. Stanford:
Stanford University Press.
Geertz, C.
1973   Thick Description: Toward an Interpretive Theory of Culture. *In* The In-
interpretation of Cultures: Selected Essays by Clifford Geertz. New York:
Basic Books.
Goddard, P. E.
1919   Myths and Tales from the White Mountain Apache. Anthropological Pub-
lications of the American Museum of Natural History, No. 24. New York.
Goffman, E.
1974   Frame Analysis: An Essay on the Organization of Experience. New York:
Harper & Row.
Goodwin, G.
1939   Myths and Tales from the White Mountain Apache. Memoir No. 39,
American Folklore Society. Manasha, WI.
Harrington, J.
1916   The Ethnogeography of the Tewa Indians. Annual Report of the Bureau
of American Ethnology, No. 29. Washington, DC.
Helm, J.
1968   The Nature of the Dogrib Socioterritorial Groups. *In* Man the Hunter.
R. Lee and I. DeVore, eds. pp. 118–125. Chicago: Aldine.
Kluckhohn, C.
1949   Mirror for Man. New York: McGraw-Hill.
Lakoff, G., and M. Johnson
1980   Metaphors We Live By. Chicago: University of Chicago Press.
Lounsbury, F.
1960   Iroquois Place-names in the Champlain Valley. *In* Report of the New

York–Vermont Interstate Commission on Lake Champlain Basin. New York
Legislative Document, No. 9. pp. 21–66. Albany.

Momaday, S.
    1974 Native American Attitudes to the Environment. *In* Seeing With a Native
    Eye: Essays on Native American Religion. W. Capps, ed. pp. 79–85. New York:
    Harper Forum Books.

Opler, M.
    1941 An Apache Life-way. Chicago: University of Chicago Press.

Ortiz, A.
    1969 The Tewa World. Chicago: University of Chicago Press.

Parsons, E.
    1939 Pueblo Indian Religion. 2 vols. Chicago: University of Chicago Press.

Radin, P.
    1916 The Winnebago Tribe. Annual Report of the Bureau of American Ethnol-
    ogy, No. 37. Washington, DC.

Rappaport, R.
    1979 Ecology, Meaning, and Religion. Richmond, CA: North Atlantic Books.

Sapir, E.
    1912 Language and Environment. American Anthropologist 14:226–242.

Silko, L.
    1981 Language and Literature from a Pueblo Indian Perspective. *In* Opening
    Up the Canon. L. Fiedler and H. Baker, transls. and eds. pp. 54–72. Baltimore:
    Johns Hopkins University Press.

Steward, J.
    1955 Theory of Culture Change: The Methodology of Multilinear Evolution.
    Chicago: University of Chicago Press.

Turner, V.
    1969 The Ritual Process: Structure and Anti-Structure. Chicago: Aldine.

Tyler, S.
    1978 The Said and the Unsaid: Mind, Meaning, and Culture. New York: Aca-
    demic Press.

Vayda, A.
    1969 Introduction. *In* Environment and Cultural Behavior. A. Vayda, ed.
    pp. xi –xvi. Austin: University of Texas Press.

Witherspoon, G.
    1977 Language and Art in the Navajo Universe. Ann Arbor: University of
    Michigan Press.

2
Dialogic Narration and the Paradoxes of Masada

Edward M. Bruner
University of Illinois, Urbana-Champaign
and
Phyllis Gorfain
Oberlin College

Dialogic Narration

Occasionally, a story becomes so prominent in the consciousness of an entire society that its recurrent tellings not only define and empower
storytellers but also help to constitute and reshape the society. Such a story
is the 1900-year-old account of a first-century seige, resistance, and defeat
at the mountain fortress Masada on the shores of the Dead Sea.[1] In our
view, what is particularly significant about the dramatic Masada narrative
and similar cultural texts is that they are frequently national stories and
rarely remain monologic. They do serve to integrate the society, encapsulate
ideology, and create social order; indeed, the story may become a metaphor
for the state, and poetic means may be used for political purposes. But
because these narratives are replete with ambiguity and paradox, an inherent versatility in interpretation arises that allows for conflicting readings
and dissident, challenging voices. Despite the forces toward authority and
monologic certitude, the semiotic openness in the Masada narrative, as in
all great stories (see Rabkin 1967:13–28), creates the potential for contradictory explanations of world order and generates an arena for ideologies at
war.

An ongoing discourse emerges from the exchange of authoritative
and challenging tellings and, in turn, supports a historically situated debate
over the interpretation and uses of the story. Authoritative voices attempt
to fix meanings and stabilize order, whereas challenging voices question
established meanings and tend to be deconstructive. Taken together, the
various tellings and interpretations lead to what we call a process of dialogic
narration.

Many of our ideas about dialogic narration are derived from the powerful insights of Mikhail Bakhtin (1981). In using this term, we argue that a story cannot be viewed in isolation, as a monologic static entity, but must be seen in a dialogic or interactive framework; that is, all stories are told in voices, not just in structuralist oppositions or syntagmatic functions of action. A story is told in a dynamic chorus of styles which voice the social and ideological positions they represent. Stories are polyphonic—they voice the narrative action, the reported speech of characters, the tellers' commentary, evaluative remarks, interpretive statements, and audience acknowledgments. This dialogic freedom creates in storytelling a field for the contesting of views and of power. For us, the term dialogic is not restricted to a two-way binary interchange but calls attention to multiple languages, to plural voices, and to the heterogeneity of speech acts, genres, and styles.

A similar view of language as the interaction of formal givens and spontaneous utterances is held by Bakhtin (1981:276), who points to the interactive embeddedness and dialogic orientation of any utterance or story:

> It is entangled, shot through with shared thoughts, points of view . . . enters a dialogically agitated and tension-filled environment of alien words, value judgements and accents, weaves in and out of complex interrelationships, merges with some, recoils from others, intersects with yet a third group: and all this may crucially shape discourse, may leave a trace in all its semantic layers, may complicate its expression and influence its entire stylistic profile. The living utterance, having taken meaning and shape in a particular historical moment in a socially specific environment, cannot fail to brush up against thousands of living dialogic threads, . . . cannot fail to become an active participant in a social dialogue.

Bakhtin writes primarily about language, which for him is alive. There is an "uninterrupted process of historical becoming that is characteristic of all living language" (1981:288), and there is no static representation of reality. Further, language is stratified and heteroglot, and there are "socio-ideological contradictions" between different historical epochs and between various contemporary groupings. For Bakhtin (1981:293) there is no such thing as a language but rather many overlapping, intersecting, contradictory languages: "All words have a taste of a profession, a genre, a tendency, a party, a particular work, a particular person, a generation, an age group, the day and hour. Each word tastes of the context and contexts in which it has lived its socially charged life."

We take Bakhtin's ideas about language and apply them to narration. As we focus on the play of voices in the Masada tradition, our concept of dialogic narration recognizes that no story is "a" story or "the" story but rather a dialogic process of many historically situated particular tellings. In our theoretical perspective, narration refers to a process rather than to an entity; to discourse rather to a text; to interpretation and feeling rather than to the abstract sequence of events. Narration includes voice, point of view, and the positioning of a narrative within a discourse. In sum, we do not conceive of narration as monologic in voice or monolithic in structure since we find that within any narration the elements of style, rhetoric, point of view, plot, interpretation, evaluation, and performance choices are not necessarily concordant or isomorphic. At the end of a story, for example, one may have incomplete and unresolved styles and points of view, as expressed by dialogues among characters, whereas the plot itself may be totally resolved (see Bakhtin 1981:349).

Relationship to Other Narrative Studies

Identifying ourselves with the work on narration and performance, style and power currently being advanced by folklorists and anthropologists such as Barbara Kirshenblatt-Gimblett, Richard Bauman, Dell Hymes, Barbara Meyerhoff, Victor Turner, Clifford Geertz, and the contributors to the 1983 AES Proceedings volume, we reconceptualize the narrative process beyond the narrow confines of either structuralism, on the one hand, or pure emergence, on the other. The difference between our more processual and contextual approach and the extremes of structuralism or pure emergence may be seen if we examine the relationship between the basic story and its variable manifestations (Genette 1980; Chatman 1978).

Some approaches to narrative privilege the basic story as the primary object or goal of research. Historicism, for example, analyzes a series of stories or tales in space and time to reconstruct an archetype or Ur-type; the basic story is conceived of as the single original source of all later versions and variants. Structuralism also isolates a basic story but as an ahistorical deep structure, a model of the underlying relationships which produces the various surface manifestations through a set of transformational rules. The difficulty with historicism and structuralism is that as they isolate "the story," they also strip away all the uniqueness, spontaneity, and cultural-historical relevance of narratives to individuals and societies. A narrative core becomes monolithic; stories become static artifacts with rules unto themselves.

In reaction to these paradigms, other approaches to narration (e.g., Herrnstein-Smith 1980) focus so intensely on the presentness of the narrative act and on the responsiveness of form to situation and speaker that they end in pure emergence, thereby diminishing the importance of history and tradition. Our perspective, on the contrary, acknowledges that a story may exist prior to any narration—Masada does refer to a series of incidents and a configuration of recurrent themes—but we also insist that a story can only occur in a particular situated telling.

Authority and Power in Dialogic Exchange

Bakhtin's notions of hierarchy in language and of authoritative voices are especially significant in understanding dialogic processes. The "authoritative" in this view is not inherent in some authoritative version of the story but in the authoritative positions of tellers within a community, in the interaction between a performance situated within a locus of power and one offered on the boundaries of public structures. In Bakhtin's words, the "authoritative" is the "already uttered"; it is "prior discourse," backed by legal, political, and moral authority. Authoritative tellings of national stories thus enjoy a privileged position: they dominate official public performances. Challenging voices must be uttered through the channels available to them and must employ different genres and forms, such as questions, interruptions, back-channel commentary, or argumentation in underground publications. Authoritative tellings occupy the dominant positions and sound like the words of fathers, adults, leaders, and teachers; they represent the "official line" and are sponsored by or associated with the state. The authoritative voice expresses the established position and sees itself as giving the correct interpretation. The challenging voices cannot be so easily characterized, for they remain individualized and bear a metaphorically "marked" quality; they are "other" and are always uttered in reaction to the dominant tellings.

In one sense, the power of authoritative versions derives from the power of the state, but in another, deeper sense each authoritative telling of a national story constitutes the power of the state. Accordingly, it follows that each critical, challenging telling may be perceived as an attack on the authority of the state, on the authority of the official tellers, and on the authority of "the story." The dialogue of ideolects and ideologies embodies more than a conflict over power; the dialogue also tests the way power is defined, displayed, recognized, and changed—through narration. Every performance, then, not only expresses power but also creates it. This treatment of power is derived from Foucault's (1978) idea that power is constituted from the bottom up rather than emanating in some divine manner from the top down.

For many stories, no authoritative version exists or assumes dominance through state sponsorship. This kind of dominance does obtain in the case of Masada, however. When an official government function, such as a formal military induction, is held at Masada and the story is told or referred to by government officials, this is an authoritative telling, in our sense. When the National Parks Authority, a state agency, issues tourist literature on the meaning of Masada, this is also an authoritative version.

Bakhtin writes that speech is basically polemical. So it is with narration. Authoritative and challenging tellers constantly struggle for supremacy over the interpretations and uses of a story, over rights and powers of narration. Every dissident telling may be seen as an invasion of the establishment position, every commentary on the authoritative version as a critique. Competition emerges for narrative space in the discourse (Foucault 1973), for the right to tell one's story. Just as speech is shaped in dialogic interaction, so is the narrative process.

Three Levels of Dialogic Narration

In this paper we show that in dialogic narration the interaction between voices occurs in at least three domains. First, a story may be dialogic with itself, insofar as a story generates inquiry and resists a single definitive interpretation. Some stories, of course, are more dialogic than others, but we suggest that great national stories tend to be more open-ended, ambiguous, and paradoxical; hence, more inherently dialogic. They raise questions about themselves for which no obvious resolution can be found.

Second, stories may be dialogic with culture and history. Any given telling takes account of previous and anticipated tellings and responds to alternative and to challenging stories. The Freudian narrative (see Schafer 1980), for example, is dialogic insofar as it developed historically in response to the alternative methods of psychiatric treatment of its era, as well as to direct challenges and criticisms. Serious literature and parental choices in the 20th century were vastly changed by this Freudian narrative tradition. In this second sense of dialogic, every telling responds to and helps to condition its cultural and historical context.

Third, in any given telling there is a dialogic relationship between self and society. Tellers and listeners do not take passive roles in a superorganic process of storymaking but actively engage in an interpretive act to make "the story" meaningful to themselves and relevant to their own life situations. In this third sense, there is a dialogue between autobiography and history as each person is aligned with the prevailing cultural tradition; or, to put it in other terms, the national self is constituted through national stories. If we ask where the dialogic is located, the answer is in the discourse, in the discourse about the story, about society, and about the self.

Our aim, then, is to develop the concept of dialogic narration, to contribute to narrative theory by introducing a processual perspective, and to root the narrative process in society without reducing it to a mere reflection of society. Let us turn now to the story of Masada, and then to further discussion of the three dialogic domains of the intrinsic, the historical, and the experiential.

Masada

It should be relatively easy to give an account of Masada, the mountain fortress near the Dead Sea, as there are so many occasions for tellings. Masada is simultaneously a tourist attraction (MacCannell 1976), a pilgrimage site (Turner and Turner 1978), an archaeological excavation (Yadin 1966), the idiom of political debate (Alter 1973), the topic of a novel (Gann 1981), a scholarly dissertation (Zerubavel 1980), a television spectacular (CIS 1981) and, for some, a national symbol of the state of Israel. New recruits to the Armoured Corps of the Israel Defence Force take their oath of allegiance at the top of the fortress and repeat the words of the poet Lamdan, "Masada shall not fall again." Israeli school children visit Masada as part of their school curriculum, families from Israel and other countries hold bar/bat mitzvah ceremonies at the synagogue on top of Masada, and there is a Masada stamp and even a commemorative coin, the "Official Israel Masada Medal." On all these occasions the story is told or referred to. Which one shall we tell here?

In scholarly articles one usually tells a story by presenting a plot summary, a supposedly objective kernel narrative, based on the facts of the case. Here is such a version of the Masada tale.

> The Jewish revolt against Roman rule led to the conquest of Jerusalem and the destruction of The Temple in A.D. 70. However, a group of 960 Jewish zealots continued the fight from the fortress at Masada built years earlier by King Herod. In A.D. 73, after a three-year siege, the Roman Tenth Legion advanced up a stone ramp to the mountain top only to find that the zealots had committed mass suicide.

One of the difficulties with this account is that it adopts a rhetorical stance of assumed objectivity, as if the facts were established, which is not the case. Also, it is told in such a flat style that it makes one wonder about the point of the story!

How about this version, excerpted from the guide to the television series (CIS 1981):

> In the first century A.D., Palestine was part of the vast Roman Empire. . . . Sporadic uprisings by the populace against Roman oppression were held in check until the year A.D. 66 when a large-scale revolt broke out. Rome sent the famous general Vespasian to quell the rebellion. Victory seemed assured when, in A.D. 70 his son Titus conquered Jerusalem, burning the Second Temple. . . . One group of freedom fighters escaped across the desert to Masada. From the mountain fortress, these zealots conducted raids on Roman camps. In A.D. 72 the Roman Tenth Legion, under the command of Flavius

Silva marched on Masada. In A.D. 73, 960 Jewish men, women and children made their last stand against 5,000 Roman soldiers. . . . The Jewish leader, Eleazar, presents the alternatives to his followers, "The choice is yours. You can choose to fight them in the morning. They'll kill you or enslave you. You can choose to hide from them. They'll find you. Or you can choose to take their victory from them. They will remember you." The next morning when the Roman commander Silva discovers that all the Jews have committed suicide he says, "The victory—we have won a rock. In the middle of a wasteland. On the shore of a poisoned sea."

Or this telling, from a tourist advertisement in the *New York Times Magazine* (26 April 1981, p. 83):

You're standing on a massive mountain of stone, some 1300 feet above the Holy Land. It's an awesome sight with a breathtaking view of the Dead Sea and the sweeping sands of the Judean desert. You feel a sense of power standing high among the remains of King Herod's palace. Are there ancient spirits here? Or is the wind playing a game with your imagination? Perhaps it's the fearless Eleazar ben Yair shouting commands to his courageous band of Jewish patriots. It was on Masada that 960 men women and children fought off the mighty Roman Tenth Legion. It was on this very spot 1900 years ago that these freedom fighters took their own lives—choosing a death of glory to a life of slavery.

The television version makes the home audience a spectator to a historical and narrativized conflict between the two generals, the Roman Silva and the Jewish Eleazar, the two heroic protagonists. The tourist ad places the lone reader at the abandoned site and suggests the kernel stories the reader as tourist will hear as dim memory at Masada itself.

So, which story should we tell to tell "the story of Masada"? With Derrida (1980:55), we find that any telling forces us "to choose among several interpretative [and we would add rhetorical] options." A story, he writes, forms "an open and essentially unpredictable series . . . an account without edge or boundary" (1980:73).

Our tellings thus far are derived from American as opposed to Israeli accounts and popular as opposed to scholarly literature. If there were sufficient space, we would analyze the tellings of the Masada story by the first-century historian Josephus Flavius or by the Israeli archaeologist and army general Yadin, as well as those by religious and political critics. The vast literature on the subject testifies to the extensive discourse generated by the story. Our purpose in this paper, however, is to demonstrate how all these tellings, including ours, are dialogic. And so we turn to our first domain, the story itself.

The Intrinsic Dialogue

Authoritative tellings view the mass suicide at Masada as a courageous act, a symbol of freedom (Livneh and Meshel ca. 1970:2). But using the story to celebrate freedom and continued life, when the events end in death, produces a paradox. The meaning of death must be taken in the Masada narrative as a victory over death. Suicide is paradoxically hailed as a victory over external forces, as an assertion of determination. As Israelis tell the story of Masada, they manipulate the paradox; they recall the story of mass suicide to avoid the story's ending of suicide. The story is told in order to say, "Never again." But such a telling cannot be so monologically directed and raises semiotic or interpretive dilemmas (Syrkin 1973).

With the Masada story no telling can fully ignore, even if it suppresses, the question, How are we to interpret mass suicide? Was it heroism or madness, an acceptance or denial of reality? As a definitive and irrevocable act, suicide forces others to consider alternatives, since suicide is so obviously an absolute choice. Multiple possibilities arise, yet the meaning of suicide remains ambiguous, our cultural and social judgments often ambivalent. Freedom of choice in living and in interpreting stories becomes all the more evident when viewed against the final act which precludes all such choices. Audiences can ask about alternatives: Could the zealots have escaped from Masada? Was accommodation with the Romans possible? Could the besieged have fought to the last and still been as heroic? In the made-for-TV movie, in a kind of reflexive way, Eleazar is portrayed in his final speech as saying, "They will remember us," in effect asking his compatriots to exchange life for memory, for the construction of a story. This is only one of many arguments he uses in the movie and in the novel. In Josephus's (1936:853–854) first-century account, the eloquent Eleazar concludes,

> Let us therefore make haste, and instead of affording them so much pleasure, as they hope for in getting us under their power, let us leave them an example which shall at once cause their astonishment at our death, and their admiration of our hardiness therein.

The aim of mass suicide, like all acts of martyrdom, is to leave a message, to communicate meaning and stimulate exchange. The zealots' choice was death in exchange for remembrance. And Israelis choose to use that remembrance in alternative ways. Jewish rabbinical tradition ignored or suppressed the Masada story for 20 centuries because the commentators disapproved of suicide and the secularity of the story's values (Zerubavel 1980:95–116). Suicide may take control over death and leave a legacy of memory, but suicide cannot control the uses of that legacy—the interpretations or evaluations of the action; or the response of future readers or generations. Ironically, suicide, like authoritative readings, attempts to fix meaning but produces inquiry instead, a story full of implication and one that remains intrinsically open-ended. Paradoxically, no act seems more final than suicide, but the act itself confounds finality: mass suicide may end life, but it cannot end the story.

Paradox generates dialogic meanings because of its self-contradictory structure. As Colie (1966:6) writes, paradox equivocates, "it lies, and it doesn't. It tells the truth, and it doesn't." Paradox speaks with two voices; it always exists in two universes of discourse. In a failed paradox, one truth becomes evident, one voice predominates. But in a true paradox, one meaning must always be taken "with respect to the other," so that paradox produces meanings in dialogue, "infinitely mirrored, infinitely reflected, in each other." Paradoxes involve reflexivity in their self-referentiality (Babcock 1980:5), they "play with human understanding" (Colie 1966:7) and comment on themselves, for what they ultimately refer to is the interpretive process itself. Precisely because in paradox one meaning is not dominant, interpretation not singular, and truth not apparent, paradox operates as a figure of thought which foregrounds the multiplicity of meaning, interpretation, and truth.

Even as suicide poses a semiotic problem about endings, it also generates a problem of beginnings, a question about authoritative sources—an epistemological enigma. By eliminating its own protagonist, a suicide story precludes any definitive account. Who is left to tell the tale and how do we know what actually happened? Even suicide notes fail to explain the choice fully or to describe the final act, for they are written, however close to the end, at a distance from it. If there were witnesses we wonder, "Why did they fail to intervene? The problems simply multiply with tales of heroic last stands. All "last-stand" stories must have a source, and nearly all of these narratives derive from "a lone survivor" (Rosenberg 1974). But these accounts strike us as necessarily suspect and partial, for questions emerge about "lone survivors": Why didn't they die with the rest? Were they insufficiently courageous or did they lack full solidarity with the group?

In the case of Masada, Josephus claims, the story comes to us from one person among a small group of survivors, two women and three children. They supposedly hid in the bottom of a dry well, in the conduits that brought drinking water to the zealots. The waterwork technology responsible for the remarkable survival of the zealots in the desert becomes a new means for survival—now against both the forces of suicide and of invasion. The semblance of burial in an underground well creates parallels between a return to life and the telling of the story. Both become resurrections, yet both feats remain merely symbolic restorations. The emergence from the grave is not from actual death, only its likeness; the story is not the redemption of the dead, only the symbolic means for that through creating memory. The neatness of the concordance between survival and storytelling adds power to this story, but the artificiality is also more evident. The symbolic relationship between survival and narration is both causative and analogic. And this doubling qualifies the tale as a possible fabrication; at the least, it highlights it as a construction, whatever its "truth." Such artful narratives move us, but they may also remind us how they stand at a remove from the shadowy events they illuminate.

Our sense of the fictionality of Josephus's account is further enhanced when we examine his biography, for Josephus epitomizes the unreliable narrator. He did not witness the events at Masada; he wrote the account years later, when he, a Jewish general who defected to the Roman side, wrote his history of the Jewish wars in Rome, under the protection of the emperor Titus. A further question arises about his motives, for in an earlier incident at Jotapata, Josephus, then a commander, participated in a suicide pact following the defeat of his forces. The difference from Masada is that Josephus chose not to commit suicide but to become, eventually, a storyteller. After 40 of his comrades died at Jotapata in a procedure similar to the one Josephus describes at Masada, he chose not to take his own life; he betrayed his pledge and turned himself over to the Roman conquerors. The contrived plan for suicide, the casting of lots to determine the last suicide, appears in both cases. Josephus invented this device at Jotapata, and the reappearance of this motif in his account of Masada suggests that he laminated his personal story over that of the zealots. He did so, we could argue, both to expiate his own guilt through valorizing their bravery and, by denigrating the zealots' act, which he does in some of the rhetorical exchange, to excuse his own cowardice, admitted to in his autobiography.

We do not aim to criticize Josephus, only to highlight some of the enigmas which produce an epistemological dilemma about the authority of the text. In the case of Masada, the problems about suicide, endings, and Josephus produce an ongoing dialogue. The literature is vast and the resulting Masada discourse is reflexive—a stance which is also dialogic, since reflexivity speaks in two voices, just as paradox does. Reflexivity paradoxically requires the subject to look at itself as object, the speaker to speak about the process of speaking (Babcock 1980; Ruby 1980). Any narration of Masada, at some level, must not only tell the Masada story but also address the narrative process, even if indirectly: How does one know the story? How does one understand and use the story?

Performances of legends—narratives which purport to be true accounts of real events—abound in claims to authority and authenticity. Authenticating devices such as voices quoted, speech reported, and narrator commentary create a fictive and dialogic quality which betray the inherent problems of belief in storytelling. The play of uncertainty in narrative accounts for the elasticity in the readings.

Every story can be reinterpreted at a later date or retold in a different context, and new meanings will emerge. Universally, in all narration an inevitable gap opens between the original event and the telling, but here we refer to something more specific. We claim that the story of Masada, because of its incidents of resistance and suicide, is especially riddled with paradox, reflexivity, and inquiry. There is no guarantee, of course, that the story will necessarily be told. Narration depends on historical circumstances. But once the Masada narrative is told, we suggest that the potential for variable interpretation is inherent.

The Historical Dialogue

The cultural and historical aspects of the Masada story crystallize in a struggle over meaning that takes place between authoritative and challenging versions in Israeli political and moral discourse. In the current heroic version, Masada represents militancy, resistance, freedom, and an ancient claim to the land. Such tellings see the zealots surrounded by the mighty Roman legions; in the present, Israel is surrounded by hostile Arab neighbors. For General Yadin, Masada is an inspiring story of the resistance of the few against the many, a story of David fighting Goliath. This Biblical narrative, used by Yadin and others in analogy to Masada, also is used in the Middle East to characterize a variety of asymmetrical contests.

Establishment stories emphasize the martyrdom of the zealots, who give their blood in the desert for the freedom of Zion. They are seen against a tradition of Jewish martyrdom from the Babylonian captivity up to the first national Israeli hero, Trumpeldor, whose defeat produced the national motto, "It is good to die for our country" (Zerubavel 1980:182–216). Whatever the analogy, the Masada story is seen in relation to other known stories and narrations. In this interaction of tellings, the dialogic quality of the story is heard against history and its characterizations in narrative.

For the youthful generation in Israel during the 1930s and 1940s the zealots were seen as Jewish militants who defied the religious and political majority to fight the Romans vigorously, cleverly, and indefatigably. At that time, Masada served as a challenging narrative set against the traditional image of the Eastern European Jews who maintained tradition through the Diaspora, but only (according to the folk idea) by means of prayer, study, accommodation, and retreat (Hrushovsky and Ben-Amos, 1982 personal communications). After World War II, the apparent failure of assimilation and piety led young people to turn away from their European heritage with its honored folk image of the Jewish male as Talmudic scholar, finding fulfillment through knowledge. Further setting themselves against the alternative of emigration to America, youthful Israeli idealists saw themselves choosing the rigors and perils of pioneering a new, beseiged, and collective society, like the zealots who together survived the rigors of desert life instead of choosing survival in the cities under Roman occupation.

In the challenging political reading "from the left," Israel is seen as a fortress state, isolated from the rest of the world, creating its own doomed Masada. The story is retold to warn of the outcome of such absolutist and isolationist choices. Orthodox religious readings "from the right" question the glorification of suicide. These critics chafe against the defiantly secular embrace of Masada and its lesson of fighting, rather than prayer, as the method for Jewish survival. Both types of criticism call into question the authority of Josephus, undermine the archaeological evidence as support for the Josephus story, and use scholarly, religious, historical, and other texts to counter the authoritative readings. The challenging readings introduce into the dialogic discourse a multiplicity of other texts, voices, and alternative authorities. Both challenging tellings emphasize the ending of the Masada story, the mass suicide, whereas the establishment tellings emphasize the middle of the story, the heroic resistance (Zerubavel 1980).

Professor Yehoshafat Harkabi writes that those leaders who dragged Judea into futile military struggles 2000 years ago were irrational, as the ancient Jewish state was destroyed in the process and a terrible price was paid in human life and suffering. Harkabi warns that in glorifying Masada and the Bar Kochba revolt "we are forced into the position of admiring our destruction and rejoicing over a deed amounting to national suicide." Yehoshua Sobol, a dramatist, claims that the Jews under the Romans "were given much more freedom and autonomy than we give the Palestinians today in the occupied territories." Through the idiom of the Masada story, Harkabi and Sobol argue against the present Israeli government policies and against such contemporary nationalistic-religious groups as Gush Emunim, which they equate with the zealots of the first century (all quotes from *The Jerusalem Post Magazine,* 7 August 1981, pg. 9).

The authoritative version claims that stability exists in narration, as if the 1983 interpretation of Masada is the same as the A.D. 73 interpretation. It tells the story as objective truth, tries to stabilize meaning, and uses poetic and inspirational rhetoric. These tellings tend to be monologic—one voice, one story, one truth. Challenging versions present alternative interpretations, locate tellings within history, and claim to be more realistic. They characterize establishment versions as romantic, political, mythical, poetic, and the like (Alter 1973). Alternative versions set the voice of Josephus in his autobiography against the voice of Josephus in his historical writings; they discriminate between archaeological fragments and archaeological inference. Their tellings tend to be deconstructive and delegitimizing. Indeed, in order to place a different interpretation on Masada, they first must attack and unhinge the authoritative account. They do so by explicitly exposing the constructed nature of storytelling. In the process of the attack, critical tellings are metacommunicative, for they openly question the act of narration as they attempt to reconstitute the sites of power.

Although we stress the distinction between the authoritative and the challenging, they are not two independent stories but rather multiple stances toward a story told in dialogic relationship. The authoritative story as the dominant narrative (Bruner in press) provides the social matrix for dissident voices and secondary tellings.[2] There may be a struggle over meaning, but one meaning is always taken with reference to the other. And all interpretations derive from the paradoxes, enigmas, and ambiguities inherent in the Masada story.

We need to clarify the distinction between dialogue and dialogic, for the two are not the same. First, an example of a dialogue that is also dialogic. When one of the authors (Bruner) was at Masada, the tour guide told the standard story, the one from the tourist literature. One member of the tour group (all professors) asked, "How do we know that Josephus was correct?" The guide replied, "The archaeologists have proved it. Everything that Josephus wrote was absolutely correct." Another question: "Were the zealots like terrorists today?" "No, they were freedom fighters," answered the guide. This interplay, a dialogue between separate speakers, was also dialogic in that the story was being told in response to mildly challenging voices.

Now, for an example that shows dialogic exchange but not dialogue. Before going to Masada, the same group had visited other tourist sites, including the Museum of the Holocaust, which conveys the message, "Let us never forget," and the Museum of the Diaspora, which demonstrates that many kinds of Jews in the world have survived and preserved Jewish tradition. These metonymic sites on a guided tour stand in a dialogic relationship to each other in that they create a multivocal discourse about the fate and alternatives available to Jews in different historical eras and cultural contexts. No face-to-face dialogue occurs, however. More than mere tourist attractions, Masada, the museums of the Holocaust and the Diaspora, and other sites, when taken together, form a larger dialogic story that the Israelis choose to tell about themselves.

Dialogic narration is not simply a dialogue or a debate but a polyphonic discourse based on tellings, retellings, or references to important cultural narratives. Any particular telling of the Masada story then resonates against previous and future tellings, against its own past centuries of silence, against metonymic sites, against analogic stories of Jewish resistance (the Warsaw Ghetto), and against stories that embody alternatives. The latter become particularly fascinating from our theoretical perspective because alternatives to the Masada story almost never appear in the authoritative texts but are present in the consciousness of Israelis and remain an inherent part of the Masada discourse.

At the time of the destruction of Jerusalem in A.D. 70, when the zealots were in the fortress at Masada, Rabbi Johanan ben Zakkai asked permission of the Romans to establish an academy of learning at Yavneh. He realized the helplessness of the struggle against Rome and founded an academy to preserve traditions in the absence of a functioning priesthood in Jerusalem. Today, ben Zakkai is called the "Savior of Judaism," and frequently in Israeli discourse Masada is opposed to Yavneh in a dual set of metaphors for the two types of response they represent. Such alternative stories are taken account of but not necessarily voiced in the authoritative tellings. From an examination of the text itself, one would never appreciate the cultural significance of the alternative stories.

Yet such alternative stories figure implicitly in dialogic narration and become explicit when critical voices tell the story. For example, such accounts claim that the present-day Israelis are not descendants of the zealots who died but of those, like the people of Yavneh, who made peace with the Romans and lived. The two stories, Masada and Yavneh, serve as alternative guides for Israeli policy and also offer alternative social roles, the warrior versus the scholar. Thus, in their lives as in their stories, the Israelis live out a dialogic reality (Handelman, 1982 personal communication). Their stories resonate not only against Israeli political options in the Middle East but also, more broadly, against Jewish historical experience throughout the world. In their stories, they formulate basic questions about their past and their future.[3] Shall we follow the people of Masada or Yavneh? Fight or accommodate? Resist militantly and in nationalistic terms? Or survive culturally through preserving traditions?

Having established more clearly the distinction between dialogue and dialogic, we note the remarkable dialogic narration in the poem that renewed the Masada story. The famous motto, "Masada shall not fall again," derives from the poem "Masada," written by Isaac Lamdan in 1923–24 after he had migrated to Palestine from postrevolutionary Russia. In the first part of the poem, he contrasts four options available to Jews in the bloody aftermath of the Russian Revolution. These options appear dialogically and polyphonically in the poem, for they are spoken by four different, unnamed personae. Each alternative is really an ideolect, the voice of an ideology. The first option is to seek vengeance; the alternative Masada is only a fiction for this speaker. The second option is to be passive, to wait for the end; the alternative Masada is only an illusion. The third option is communism, to join the revolution and make a new world; the alternative Masada is a "ruined fortress" that failed against Rome in A.D. 73 and will fail again. The fourth option, which Lamdan selects, is Masada, which now represents a commitment to a new life in Palestine and to Zionism.

This poem, written long before the Holocaust and the establishment of the state of Israel, places the Masada story within the contemporary alternative courses of action available at a particular historical moment. Moreover, because Masada is viewed in a variety of ways—as fiction, illusion, a ruined fortress, the promised land—the poem gives voice to the choices inherent in the Masada story. Yudkin (1971), for example, asks why

Lamdan chose to write about Masada, a mass suicide, a "symbol of defeat," to celebrate a new life in Palestine, rather than to select another story from a more successful period in Jewish history, such as one from the Biblical era. In this very question and in the poem itself we see aspects of the intrinsic dialogue—what are the options?—and the experiential dialogue—how does this relate to Lamdan's personal vision and life situation?

In its historical dialogic dimension, the Masada story furnishes multiple uses and many variant readings. The discourse about Masada evolves over time and moves in and out of history. After Josephus, with a few scattered exceptions, the story dropped out of Jewish literature for 1800 years. The Josephus account remained intact, of course, but the story was rarely told by Jews and the location of the site was forgotten until redis-covered in the 19th century. The Masada story was resurrected with the rise of Jewish nationalism, with Lamdan's poem, with youth movement expedi-tions to Masada, and later with the official 1963–65 archaeological excava-tions. In a sense, the dialogic narration of Masada frames the state; its beginning commemorates the destruction of the old Jewish state in A.D. 73, and its resurrection foreshadows the emergence of the new Jewish state in 1948.

Masada may have reached its peak significance in Israeli society by the 1960s, for some observers now see a shift to the Western Wall as a favored symbol (Shargel 1979). The Western Wall stands as the last rem-nant of The Temple destroyed in Jerusalem in A.D. 70 and signifies Israel's continuity with the past. In the words of one Israeli, "Even the mighty Romans couldn't knock the Wall down completely." The Western Wall has become associated with Jewish spiritual resistance and with a claim to the disputed city of Jerusalem. As a site it offers something different than the double-edged sword of Masada: it furnishes a more hopeful and optimistic symbol, better suited to the present government's expansionist claims based on both nationalistic and religious grounds.

We see, then, how a dialogic discourse changes over time, with changing circumstances, with the evolving relationship between what stands as authoritative and what stands as challenging. Masada was once the challenging story, opposed to the European narratives. Now that story is under attack.

We might instructively compare Masada with the Alamo to see how such stories change. If the story of Masada has begun to decline, the story of the Alamo has declined so far that it has lost much of its resonance in the contemporary world, primarily because the history of Texas is resolved, at least with regard to Mexican or American boundary claims. When the Roman hegemony was complete, the Masada story was "over," only to be resurrected when needed in a new historical context. If lasting peace were established in the Middle East and no threats endangered the security of Israel or Diaspora Jews, then Masada might become a historical relic. What keeps the story alive is that the survival of the present state of Israel is not yet resolved. In 1942, after the Japanese attack, a popular song told us to "remember Pearl Harbor as we did the Alamo." In times of upheaval, dialogic stories such as Masada and the Alamo achieve renewed prominence.

Not only do the Masada and Alamo stories possess similar historical dialogic qualities, both also have similar intrinsic features. They cite a defeat in order to incite victory. Masada and the Alamo serve as national shrines and tourist attractions, both marking the sites of heroic last stands. The defenders of Masada and the Alamo died for freedom and for a memory. The mottos of the two are similar and paradoxical. Both were sites of resistance to authority in that the zealots were marginal to the Jewish defenders and, at the Alamo, Travis acted against his official orders, which were to destroy the Alamo. The Alamo defenders were not part of the regular army, Travis being the only person in the fortress who wore an army uniform. In both Masada and the Alamo, marginal revolutionaries became national heroes, but retrospectively. The defenders of both Masada and the Alamo subverted not only the authority of the Romans and the Mexicans, but also the authority of their own governments' resistance to their enemies. Only later did history redeem their subversion.

In both cases ambiguities arise over the authenticity of the "original" event. If you visit the Alamo today, for example, you see a display about the defender James Butler Bonham, including both descriptive information and a picture. Under the picture a small inscription states that this is not really a picture of Bonham but rather a portrait of his nephew who "resembled" Bonham, presented so viewers may know the "appearance" of the man who died for freedom. The original is known by a representation of a representation. At the Alamo the Bowie knife is prominently displayed but the curator does not claim that the knife now placed under glass is the original; it is only a reproduction, a representation, to show what the Bowie knife looked life—it is a presence to mark an absence. During a visit to the Alamo we also learn that the story of the Alamo comes from Moses Rose, the lone survivor who escaped from the fort on 3 March 1836. A plaque relates his account of the events of the Alamo defense, but it also explains that this is not really Moses Rose's account. We learn instead that Rose stayed with the Zuber family, to whom he told his story, and they produced an account which was not published until 1873, a full 37 years later. The plaque is an account of an account of an account, a story without edge or boundary. Shades of Derrida!

Historic last stands offer magnificent examples of dialogic narration because they present problems of authority, closure, and interpretation. The ambiguities and paradoxes inherent in the original serve to make the story versatile and powerful; the story responds to shifting cultural and historical contexts; and meanings reside not in the original but in present tellings. Because the inevitable gap between the event and its tellings becomes so apparent in these narratives, the constructed nature of all narrative processes is exposed.

The Experiential Dialogue

The fluidity of interpretation and the elusive meaning of Masada is attached to the most solid of sites, to an immovable mountain, an eternal fortress. Masada is massive—1300 feet high and 29 acres on top. To attach such a mutable story to such an immutable site makes use of a device to fix meaning, to lend stability to authority and interpretation. Masada is a mountain fortress located in the Judean desert, but the dialogic narration is used for mobility. Masada becomes all of Israel; A.D. 73 becomes all time; an ambiguous mass suicide becomes a universal symbol of freedom; events in history attain meaning beyond their context. At the same time, the context is given meaning by the story.

Whereas the names of sites provide coordinates in space, stories about sites provide coordinates in both space and time, giving sites a historical as well as a geographic alignment. Stories about the landscape identify persons and time—and allow the imagination to rest and wander, to become a stage for memory or a bridge for making connections. At Masada, the attachment between story and site gives the legend the permanence of the mountain, as if the Masada story itself were unchanging.

The physical products of archaeological excavations—artifacts, utensils, coins, and other objects—that can be seen and displayed serve a similar function. It is not simply that scientific archaeology "proves" Josephus correct, as the tour guide claimed, but that the sheer materiality of the results of archaeology confer credibility to the authoritative interpretation, as if the story itself could be touched and handled. In effect, Yadin excavated for the artifacts to authenticiate meaning, as if digging in the ground, digging deep, would reveal the true original meaning of Masada. The height of the site lends awe; the depth of the excavation supplies symbolic verification. Both are used to enforce belief, finalize meaning, produce knowledge, and make knowledge itself appear as if an artifact.

An El Al advertisement touts Masada as "the mountain that will move you." The story is transformative, processual, and moving to the extent that it is experienced by persons moving processually through the site. How can we experience a story? We can resurrect that buried past by a visit to the "setting," by seeing artifacts belonging to the "characters," and by participating in the discourse. Many tourist-pilgrims who go to Masada begin by climbing up the Roman ramp, roaming the mountaintop with the zealots, and then taking the Israeli cable car down the other side. The story of Masada is simulated in the tourist-pilgrim experience, not passively contemplated from afar, and dialogic narration occurs on site. We move through the story as we move through the site, using all channels of communication—we hear the story, read the literature, talk about it with other tourists, see the site, photograph it, and touch it. More hardy souls—groups of young people and the military—climb or run up the winding snake path to the top of Masada, an exhausting two-hour trek, best started in the early hours to avoid the desert heat and to arrive at the summit in time to witness the sunrise. The physical exertion maximizes the experience.

Stories, like ritual, are transformative insofar as they are experienced and performed (Turner 1982). Just as a story is never actualized except in a particular telling, the full power of a story is never felt unless it is realized in an experience. The interpretive process works in a similar way. We never remain just the passive recipients of an interpretation, mechanically transmitted. Interpretation requires that an active self engage in it. At Masada, tourists climb the mountain; pilgrims celebrate Hanukkah; the Armoured Corps is inducted; adolescents engage in a rite of passage; and school children, office groups, and families enjoy outings together. For religious retreats and camp groups, Masada becomes theater, where children take the parts of Romans and zealots and reenact the story.

What is so crucial about the experiential aspect of dialogic narration is that we return not just with *the* story of Masada but rather with *my* experience of Masada. An event is personalized and made relevant to our own life situation. The story of Masada becomes utterly present, fresh, and unique. A historical narrative is transformed into a personal narrative as we gain the right to tell the story. The consequence is to align individual biography with tradition, to incorporate national stories within the self. Meaning is individualized; culture becomes autobiography.

Narration, then, is not just dialogic with reference to texts or storytellers. It is equally dialogic with reference to readers of the texts or listeners of the story. As the story of Masada is told and retold, it reverberates not only through history and society but through ourselves.

Conclusion

We advance the concept of dialogic narration as a contribution to narrative theory to show that stories are responsive to and interactive with themselves, with communities and their histories, and with the self. This perspective enables us to examine the narrative process in three domains: intrinsically, as the polyphony of voices and ideologies in a text; historically, as the dialogue between text and contexts; and experientially, as the alignment of self and history. We do not view stories as monologic entities reducible to a basic formula, as do some structuralists, but we see narration as ever changing, without edge or boundary. Our readings do not end in the nihilism of radical relativity, with no meaning possible; rather, we see any given telling as situated in the real world, in a particular context, and told in a voice that takes account of other voices either by suppressing, denying, acknowledging, or responding to them. Our perspective does not have an a priori conception of privileged referents—Israel as Masada; youth as zealots; resistance as doom; resistance as Israeli indomitability. Rather, we let indigenous voices tell us what is important and how meanings are chosen and how they compete. We focus on narration as a process, always in production, in dialogic interplay, emergent and indeterminate, which exists in and helps to create a social world of virtuality, potentiality, and inquiry.

Notes

Acknowledgments. The order of authors' names is alphabetical and indicates no precedence in authorship. We wish to acknowledge the help of Nina Auerbach, Dan Ben-Amos, Peter Garrett, Jack Glazier, Linda Taranik Grimm, Güneli Gün, Don Handelman, Benjamin Hrushovsky, Keiko Ikeda, Diana Grossman Kahn, Cary Nelson, Isaac Neuman, William Schroeder, Stephen Sniderman, Victor Turner, Ana Cara Walker, Sandra Zagarell, and Yael Zerubavel.

1. The authors, an anthropologist and a folklorist, are not Middle East specialists and do not read Hebrew. Fortunately, many of the primary texts, such as Josephus (1936) and Yadin (1966), have been translated into English, and we have relied on such excellent secondary sources as Yudkin (1971), Shargel (1979), and Zerubavel (1980).
2. We are indebted to Hayden White for this phrasing.
3. That the Israelis conduct a national debate and inquiry through the idiom of the Masada story is not an original idea; many others have stressed this important concept (e.g., Alter 1973; Zerubavel 1980). Our emphasis is on the way those uses of the story constitute a dialogic discourse in narration and how that process can be generalized.

References Cited

Alter, Robert
   1973   The Masada Complex. Commentary 56:19–24.
Babcock, Barbara A.
   1980   Reflexivity: Definitions and Discriminations. Semiotica 30(1/2):1–14.
Bakhtin, M. M.
   1981   The Dialogic Imagination. Michael Holquist, ed. Austin: University of
      Texas Press.
Bruner, Edward M.
   in press   Ethnography as Narrative. *In* The Anthropology of Experience. Victor
      Turner and Edward M. Bruner, eds. Urbana: University of Illinois Press.
Chatman, Seymour
   1978   Story and Discourse. Ithaca: Cornell University Press.
CIS
   1981   A Viewer's Guide to Masada, an ABC Novel for Television. New York:
      Cultural Information Service.

Colie, Rosalie
  1966   Paradoxica Epidemica. Princeton: Princeton University Press.
Derrida, Jacques
  1980   The Law of Genre. Critical Inquiry 7:55–81.
Foucault, Michael
  1973   The Order of Things. New York: Vintage Books.
  1978   The History of Sexuality. New York: Pantheon.
Gann, Ernest K.
  1981   Masada. New York: Jove.
Genette, Gérard
  1980   Narrative Discourse. Jane E. Lewin, transl. Ithaca: Cornell University
         Press.
Herrnstein-Smith, Barbara
  1980   Narrative Versions, Narrative Theories. Critical Inquiry 7:213–236.
Josephus, Flavius
  1936   The Works of Flavius Josephus. Philadelphia: Porter & Coates.
Livneh, Micha, and Ze'ev Meshel
  ca. 1970   Masada. Jerusalem: National Parks Authority.
MacCannell, Dean
  1976   The Tourist. New York: Schocken.
Rabkin, Norman
  1967   Shakespeare and the Common Understanding. New York: Macmillan.
Rosenberg, Bruce A.
  1974   Custer and the Epic of Defeat. University Park: Pennsylvania State Uni-
         versity Press.
Ruby, Jay
  1980   Exposing Yourself: Reflexivity, Anthropology, and Film. Semiotica
         30(1/2):153–180.
Schafer, Roy
  1980   Narration in the Psychoanalytic Dialogue. Critical Inquiry 7:29–53.
Shargel, Baila R.
  1979   The Evolution of the Masada Myth. Judaism 28:357–371.
Syrkin, Marie
  1973   The Paradox of Masada. Midstream 19:66–70.
Turner, Victor
  1982   From Ritual to Theatre. New York: Performing Arts Journal Publications.
Turner, Victor, and Edith Turner
  1978   Image and Pilgrimage in Christian Culture. New York: Columbia Univer-
         sity Press.
Yadin, Yigael
  1966   Masada: Herod's Fortress and the Zealot's Last Stand. New York: Ran-
         dom House.
Yudkin, Leon T.
  1971   Isaac Lamdan: A Study in Twentieth-Century Hebrew Poetry. Ithaca:
         Cornell University Press.
Zerubavel, Yael
  1980   The Last Stand: On the Transformation of Symbols in Modern Israeli

Culture. Ann Arbor, MI: University Microfilms.

Appendix

While preparing a professional paper, most scholars engage in a series of exchanges with their students and colleagues. They may present preliminary versions of the paper in class, seminar, or at meetings; discuss the paper informally with close friends or colleagues; or elicit critical evaluation from knowledgeable specialists in the field. While engaging in this process, we received letters from two Israeli social scientists, Dan Ben-Amos and Don Handelman, which were thoughtful, sophisticated, highly interpretive, and very personal reactions to the Masada story. The problem of what to do with these letters became, for us, a theoretical as well as a moral issue.

Usually, an author changes the text to incorporate such comments and acknowledges the colleague's assistance. This we have done. But we cannot simply subsume their independent voices, for that would mask the dialogue. Our article would thereby gain the illusion of being monologic and authoritative. Instead, we decided that it is appropriate to our theory to reproduce both letters, lightly edited and with the authors' permission, in the form of an appendix, so as to make them part of the "text."

When Ben-Amos and Handelman wrote to us, they did not know that their letters would eventually appear in this form, and so their letters were not written with this purpose in mind. The significance of these letters for us, however, goes beyond their perceptive commentaries on the article as such. Their letters offer other tellings of the Masada story, told in particular voices and situated historically, analytically, and experientially. The commentaries form an inherent thread in the ongoing discourse we analyze, the dialogic narration of Masada, and constitute further evidence that although the formal paper ends, the dialogue in which it participates continues, without edge or boundary. . . .

UNIVERSITY OF PENNSYLVANIA
Philadelphia, PA 19104

Faculty of Arts and Sciences
Folklore and Folklife
Room 415, Logan Hall CN

18 February 1983

Dear Ed and Phyllis,

It is fun to be on the other side of research, that is, as the "informant." I always wonder how much or how little we are able to understand the "other societies" which we study, and I have always looked for those people who will be able to fill in the gaps that I have in understanding the culture and the traditions that I study. I do not know whether I'll be able to fill those "gaps" for you, but I definitely feel that I am one of those people that have a corner in their biography in which the dialogic narration of Masada takes place. Therefore, upon receiving your paper, I put aside all other "pressing" work, and I am writing this letter.

For a person who grew up in Israel in the forties and fifties, and for whom, at the time, Masada was a dynamic symbol, your paper comes at the tail end of the vitality of this symbol. When Masada became a tourist attraction (with restored archaeological finds and a cable car) and a subject of a television series, it became impoverished as a cultural symbol for the "country" itself. These phases of the symbol provide, it seems to me, a waning glow of a flame that was once vigorous. The dialogue in this dialogic tension is a denouement of the drama Masada was in the lives of people of my generation, and of two or three generations before that.

Dates are important. Lamdan wrote his poem in 1923-24. The major heroic event that preceded these years was the fall of Tel-Hai in the Upper Galilee, in which Trumpeldor died. At that time, before his death, he allegedly uttered a phrase every child in Israel since learned: *"Tov la-mut be'ad artzenu,"* that is, "It is good to die for the sake of our country." Trumpeldor captured the imagination even of his own times. Unlike most Jews in Eastern Europe, he did not avoid military service, but rather joined the army and even achieved the rank of an officer, and then lost his arm on the battlefield. At the time he was seen as a commander, the Masada Eleazar who would fight, and who would be ready to die for the sake of his people. You have to see the development of this image in the light of the 1880s and the 1905 pogroms on the Jews that the Russian government encouraged. During those pogroms, and in their aftermath, Jewish defense began to get organized, and the European Jewish population began to shift from rabbinical Judaism to secular-military Judaism. The Masada narration is the model, in some ways a newly created archetype of this tension (as you point out) between rabbinic Judaism and militant Judaism, and it was a powerful image not so much in relation to the holocaust, but rather in relation to the whole previous Jewish existence in the diaspora that continued the Yavneh tradition.

The Masada story, you have to remember, is not only a story about suicide but also a story about a prolonged battle that lasted three years in which a small group of people (the perennial Jewish symbol of David battling Goliath) are able to engage in combat many Roman soldiers. There is, if you wish, a dialogic tension in the story itself, not only in the narrations of this story by different groups of people and different periods. You have also to remember that in the popular version of Josephus, known as *The Josippon,* (recently David Flusser published an excellent critical edition, alas, in Hebrew) the Masada story ends with all the males killing their wives and daughters, and the next day they plunge into the last war in which all of them are killed on the battlefield.

I feel that your argument will be more powerful if you take the dialogic narration of the Masada story not so much in terms of the postindependence (of Israel) history of the story, but rather, in terms of its emergence in Zionistic consciousness in the twenties and thirties. This was the era of fermentation of this narration. When Jewish militancy was institutionalized in statehood it lost, in my mind at least, its symbolic effectiveness. The army ceremonies on the top of Masada, the tourist-guide accounts, and the television programs are futile attempts to capture a spirit of Masada that they (i.e., these institutions or channels of popular culture) killed.

Probably my comments are not very helpful. I suspect that they add to the confusion and the frustration that you probably feel. Perhaps I voice another aspect that can be added to the dialogic narration of Masada. Most of the events and history to which I refer is available in English, I think; at least so much of Jewish history is. Now there is a growing literature about the history of the Jewish immigration to Israel (Palestine, if we talk about the period before statehood), and you probably can glean the sentiments I have expressed here in some of this literature. No doubt I agree with you completely that the Masada story is one of the best examples of dialogic narration in modern society; perhaps I would like to implore you to examine even more aspects of this dialogic process than you already did.

Best,
Dan Ben-Amos

UNIVERSITY OF MINNESOTA   Department of Anthropology
Twin Cities   215 Ford Hall
                                                                        224 Church Street, S.E.
                                                                        Minneapolis, MN 55455

6 March 1983

Dear Ed and Phyllis,
        I've been a few days (after Baton Rouge I swung through Duke, Chapel Hill, and Harvard) and have had a chance to read the Masada paper. It is fine, as far as it goes, but the paper indicates that its primary emphasis is on a discussion of dialogic narration, and that the Masada story is used primarily as illustrative of this. I would change the title to use the Masada theme as a subtitle.
        Of the three dialogues discussed in the paper, my greatest difficulty is with the "historical" one: there are two points that any student of Israel should take into account: first, that Israelis sense, even if they do not enunciate, that the shape of Israel is still being molded, and that they are taking an active part (and have an active voice) in this shaping of the character of the state. Therefore it is likely an error to write of an authoritative telling of the Masada story, and of alternative versions, since ongoing happenings were, and probably are, retelling and interpreting this story. One doesn't need Derrida to tell Israelis that "texts" are open-ended, without boundaries. Or that texts contextualize themselves and expand upon themselves. They are reminded often enough that they are living (not just reliving) the multiple texts of Masada, the Holocaust, the Diaspora, the Wall, and so forth. And in living these texts they are not only interpreting them, but are also acting through them to effect their development and emergence. I believe that such texts, in the Israeli context, are more metonymic than metaphoric. Their retelling is also their making, and their making shifts and pulls the emerging shape of the nation this way and that.
        The second point is that Israelis are highly politicized. We write that certain preliterate societies should not be subdivided into religious, political, economic, and other institutions—or that we should recognize that these are analytical distinctions. The same holds true for Israel—there most events have political import, and most public acts are explicitly political, as of course are the stories of Masada. The symbolism of Masada flourished so long as labor zionism was at the helm of the state—with an emphasis on quite strict separation of "church" and state, and the importance of developing a secular Jewish-Israeli culture with a martial *and* a moral character. The tellings of Masada were political ones, in the Israeli context. And political tellings and other acts shaped, and shape, the emerging nation.
        Is it an accident that Masada stands on the periphery, isolated, almost

diasporic, speaking to a center that perhaps was partially hollow, unformed, and amorphous, still in the process of being formed? And is it accidental that the Six-Days War eclipsed Masada and made it redundant—the miracle of the "terrible swift sword" (the title of Herzog's book on that war) provided Israel with a symbolic center—the whole of Jerusalem and the Western Wall at its center. The whole of Jerusalem and of Israel swirled and re-formed around this centrist solidity and stability.

It is easy to see how the Western Wall supplanted Masada as *the* symbol of the Israeli nation-state: the Wall synthesizes the alternative versions of Masada and Yavneh, superceding and encompassing both—the martial and the learned, adaptation and last stand—within its own unbroken continuity growing out of the Land of Israel, something built, and not built on, a signpost for both secular historicity and religious yearnings. At the center, for Jerusalem is an earth navel for Jews (and for Christians, in the Holy Sepulchre; and for Muslims in the Dome of the Rock), and a traditional place of pilgrimage.

And yet, the Wall is also a terrible symbol, in a sense that Masada is not. Masada may teach that it will not fall again, but the Wall evokes the words of the Lord to Moses, most evocative to Jews, that he would behold the Holy Land, but he, that most righteous of men, would never enter it. The Temple Mount remains in Muslim hands and, looking down from the Jewish Quarter, one sees that terrible double vision contained within one glance, the Wall that abuts the Mount dominated by mosques—the contiguity of confrontation, yet separation; the Wall that caresses the final centricity, yet shows an incomplete coalescence. But a continuity that incites to confrontation—the stasis of Wall and Mount evoke the dynamic that lurks within their relationship, and strongly suggests that this text cannot be complete. This place, then, is pregnant with alternative potential future story-lines, as Masada is not.

Well, perhaps I'll write about the Kotel.

Yours,
Don Handelman

3
Stories at Work:
Play in an Organizational Context

Helen B. Schwartzman
Northwestern University

Organizations keep people busy, occasionally entertain them, give them a variety of experiences, keep them off the streets, provide pretexts for storytelling, and allow socializing. They haven't anything else to give.

—Karl Weick (1979:264)

Until recently, organizational researchers (including anthropologists) have assumed that formal organizations are stable, concrete, objective, and essentially unproblematic entities. The existence of organizations has been taken for granted and the behavior that occurs within them has been thought to be dominated by rational, goal-directed and instrumental behavior (it is work, after all, not play). Almost all of the models that researchers have constructed to explain organizational behavior accept this objectivist view. But the stories that researchers, as well as organizational actors, tell about organizational life consistently contradict these models. The analysis that I present in this paper disregards these models and starts with the stories. I suggest that story themes and the story form itself may be the best model to use to study the organization as a social construction. When stories are approached from this perspective, they can no longer be treated as simple expressive activities that occasionally appear in work settings. It is argued here that stories are a pervasive social form in these contexts that can generate organizational activity (not just comment on it) and interpret and sometimes transform the work experience. The significance of stories in a community mental health center is examined. I suggest that stories work for individuals and organizations in a variety of unexpected ways.

Midwest Community Mental Health Center:
Stories in an Organized Anarchy[1]

Midwest Community Mental Health Center (MCMHC) was studied by a team of researchers from the Institute for Juvenile Research between January 1975 and July 1976. We did not intend to study stories at the Center, although I must admit that one of the reasons I wanted to study the organization was because of the stories I had heard about it.[2] Our research was designed to study the Center's implementation of a community paraprofessional model for the treatment of chronically mentally ill patients, but it was hard to miss the fact that in interviews our informants always discussed their activities by telling stories. "Tell me about your work as a paraprofessional?" I would ask in an interview, and invariably I would be told a story—about specific events or happenings, about individuals, and about the organization in general. My observations suggest that staff members tell each other the same stories over and over again.

Storytelling, in fact, is much more than a pastime at the Center, for stories both shape and sustain the staff's image of the organization and their work within it. In this context, stories become an important form that individuals use to interpret to each other their experience of work at the Center. In the process, stories (especially certain stories) play an important role in the constitution of organizational reality for all participants. Before presenting an analysis of these stories at work, it is necessary to more fully describe the nature of the organization which they have come to represent and also to transform.

The early 1970s saw a rise in the number of alternative organizations (such as free clinics, free schools, collectives, and communes) that were a response to the radical cultural and political movements of the 1960s (Swidler 1979:vii). These organizations were often developed in direct opposition to public service agencies that were perceived to be overly bureaucratic, generally inaccessible, and very ineffective. MCMHC is a creature of these times; it was formed specifically as an alternative mental health treatment agency for residents in a community located in a large midwestern city, referred to here as West Park. West Park is a low-income, multiethnic community made up of numerous "at-risk" populations, including a large number of former mental patients who had been "deinstitutionalized" into the community during the 1960s. The presence of this population on city streets sometimes gives West Park the appearance of a back ward in a state mental hospital. In fact, many residents refer to this community as a "psychiatric ghetto."

MCMHC was enthuiastically intitiated in 1971 as a new solution to the mental illness/social problems of the West Park area, and it was felt that this was the *community's* mental health center (although funding for the Center was provided by the National Institute of Mental Health). It soon became clear, however, that each word in the Center's name reflected ambiguity about the Center's goals, techniques, and mode and focus of operation. Who represented the community (staff, board, patients, community interest groups)? What was mental health and how did one promote it? Who should treat mental illness and how should they do it? And finally, what was the Center, how should it be organized, and who was in charge of it (the board, the director, the funding sources)? These ambiguities, and the fact that more than 30 different organizations combined to form the original service consortium, quickly translated into a pattern of individual and group conflict. By the time we began our research in 1975, the dominant image used by almost all participants to describe the organization was that it was like a "crazy house."

Organizations such as MCMHC that experience severe ambiguity in all areas of their operation have been usefully described by March and Olsen (1976) as "organized anarchies."[3] Such organizations are characterized by: (1) ambiguous or inconsistent goals; (2) unclear or fuzzy technologies; (3) fluid participation of members; (4) unpredictable environments; and (5) confusing histories. In other words, individuals working in these organizations do not have a clear or consistent view of what they are trying to do, how they should do it, who should be doing it, where they are doing it, or what they have already done (see Padgett 1980).

An organized anarchy has very few products to offer to organizational actors as evidence of organizational action. What it does have, in abundance, is talk. The social form that structures most of this talk at MCMHC is "the meeting"; however, individuals talk in a variety of other contexts as well, including therapy sessions, coffee breaks, chats in the hall or office, and parties. In these settings, talk is often structured by the story form, but it is important to point out that these stories are triggered by everyday conversation (as well as the researchers' interviews). These are everyday stories told in ordinary settings, which is one reason why researchers have overlooked them.[4]

Stories at Work

Only a few ethnographers and folklorists have pointed to the significance of storytelling in work settings or during work activities. These researchers, for the most part, have examined stories as expressive activities that relieve the tedium of work (especially manual labor). For example, the stories that accompany the performance of tasks such as harvesting, herding, and especially spinning and weaving have been collected and analyzed (see e.g., Newall 1980; Pellowski 1977). Recently, however, the role of stories in contemporary organizational settings has come to the attention of a few researchers in social psychology and organizational behavior (see Clark 1980; Martin 1980; Martin, Feldman, Hatch, and Sitkin 1983) in conjunction with an emerging interest in the symbolic systems of organizations. These studies are more compatible with the analysis offered here because they seek to understand how stories constitute organizational reality. Recent work, especially by Pacanowsky and O'Donnell-Trujillo (1982), has focused on how stories typify organizational experience for actors by weaving a historical texture into the organization which participants come to recognize and reshape in their continual narration (1982:125–126).

At MCMHC, stories make their appearance in conversations, interviews, informal discussions, and so on, in a variety of ways. A story in this setting can be an account of something that happened in the distant past or only a few minutes earlier. It is important to remember that these stories are always situated in ordinary turn-by-turn talk. In general, something is said in a conversation which reminds a participant of a specific story, and the story is then introduced into the conversation by a variety of techniques which signal the start of the story and also attempt to display a relationship between the story and prior talk (Jefferson 1978:220). For example:

Jan:　How long are they going on? (referring to a meeting)
Bill:　Don't know.
Jan:　I remember one time [STORY].

In general, these stories are presented as if they depict real events, and they are heard and repeated as representations of real events. In some instances, however, the stories are more elaborate and appear in conversation as more obviously "storied" descriptions. The presentation and style of these stories make it clear that they are depicting imaginary events.

Four specific features of the stories at MCMHC should be mentioned. First, the storytellers are often the stories' heroes, heroines, victims, and villains. Second, the story texts invariably describe behavior that is the inverse of expected and "proper" organizational (especially therapeutic) behavior. Third, the stories treat everyday organizational events as momentous and sometimes life-or-death issues. And fourth, the stories are almost always used by tellers, and heard by listeners, as illustrations of the "crazy" (a favorite term) nature of the organization and/or individuals in the organization.

I classify the stories into three general types: (1) stories about meetings, (2) stories about individuals, and (3) stories about the organization. Obviously these are arbitrary divisions, but they are based on the teller's emphasis in relating the story to me or to someone else.

Stories about Meetings

Stories about meetings are extremely common because meetings are ubiquitous at the Center. There are literally dozens of meetings occurring at any one point in time—staff meetings, unit meetings, cabinet meetings, supervisors' meetings, board meetings, and so on. Everyone who works at MCMHC spends a significant portion of each working day in meetings. I estimate, based on my fieldnotes and the daily time that I spent in meetings while conducting fieldwork, that the staff spends an average of 50 percent of their day in meetings, while Center management spends over 80 percent of their time in this activity. Meetings at MCMHC frequently last between three and five hours and elicit a high degree of involvement from almost all participants. In general, these meetings produce what Kuper (1971) has called unauthoritative decisions, or else they produce no decision (except, of course, for the decision to have another meeting). It is also common for meetings at the Center to be the context for emotionally charged social dramas (see Turner 1981).

In one sense, meetings in this organization are like stories in that the format allows participants to engage in a type of collective storytelling (like Geertz's Balinese cockfights), where they are both the subjects and objects of the process. The participants refer to this activity as "dancing" (see Schwartzman 1978, 1981). Dancing involves a complicated system of saying one thing in terms of something else in order to define "reality" one way, or to comment on or redefine a situation. Meetings facilitate this process because they are a context wherein one set of subjects (e.g., the social relationships of participants) can always be talked about in terms of another set of subjects (e.g., the ostensible purpose of the meeting).⁵ In a meeting in which dancing takes place, specific problems, crises, solutions, or even simple requests (as in the example below) are quickly incorporated into the dance routines of specific individuals or into a collective group dance. In this way the "reality" or seriousness of the problem is transformed into the "unreality" of the dance—which is itself a comment, at another level, on the "realities" of life at the Center. Because meetings in which dancing takes place are themselves "good stories," jokes and tales about the length and "craziness" of specific meetings are quite common. These stories simultaneously create, transform, and comment on the realities of Center life. A staff member told this story about his last board meeting in an interview.

> You won't believe the last board meeting I went to, it was one of those coalitions of community control. . . . This young woman . . . delivers a sensible, a little bit adolescent in the sense that she wasn't

as articulate as she could have been, request to become a member of the Council and there is a member of the board who you might have thought they were talking about recognizing the People's Republic as opposed to Formosa. . . . I was unable to follow the thought/cognitive function that she was laying down verbally, even given the fact that it was not germane to [the other woman's request]. . . . Mary [another member of the board] was trying to say slow down . . . this doesn't make any sense. Then Mary made a motion, which was weird enough, so they had to discuss it for 15 to 20 minutes. And sure enough when that woman left [the one making the membership request] she didn't have any idea where she had been and she walked out without her coat and purse. Five minutes later out on the street she realized she left her clothes behind. It was like that woman must have felt like she was on a teeter-totter that not only was going up and down, but was being spun at some tremendous rate because that was one of the craziest [meetings] I've ever been to.

Meetings frequently "spin" people around, because when dancing occurs any actions that do take place are always confusing and often unpredictable. It is this sense of "unreality" or "craziness" that the meeting stories always emphasize and that leads to the feeling that things "are not quite right at the Center." But this feeling always leads to more meetings, which lead to more dancing, which lead to more "crazy meeting" stories, and so on. In this way, meetings and stories are systemically related to one another, and this relationship ultimately reframes everyone's view of what it is they are doing. The stories suggest (and the meetings "prove") that this is not an ordinary group of people working in an organization, attending meetings, seeing clients, drinking coffee, and gossiping in the halls. Instead, the stories suggest (and the meetings "prove") that this is an extraordinary group of people involved in a bizarre and "Alice in Wonderland-like world" (as one informant expressed it). This is a world, the stories suggest, that could be quite dangerous. But just how dangerous can a meeting be? To understand how this question is answered at the Center, it is necessary to consider the second common story type, stories about individuals.

Stories about Individuals

At the time of our fieldwork, the Center employed approximately 100 staff members; another 40 individuals were involved with the organization as board or council members. Almost all of these individuals told stories, but only a few staff/board members appeared as recurring characters in the stories everyone told. The two "characters" who appeared most frequently in the stories were the Center's director (David) and assistant director (Paula). These stories almost always focused on the power that David or Paula exercised over individuals at the Center (generally as displayed in the context of meetings). One frequently repeated saying, used to describe the relationship between David and Paula, illustrates this view. It was said that "David makes the bullets, and Paula shoots them." "Bullets" were almost always "shot" in meetings, and one of the more dramatic stories we heard was always told to illustrate the power and effect of Paula's "shots."

> One day in a training meeting the topic was death and dying. It was supposed to help the fieldworkers [paraprofessionals] to be able to deal with dying clients. A book on the subject was being discussed and Paula said that she thought the author was wrong about her ideas. Ed [a staff member in substance abuse] disagreed with Paula about this and she fired back at him—how did he know that this author was right, he hadn't ever died and hadn't ever been dying. Two weeks later he killed his wife, killed himself, and sent the suicide note to Paula. Paula got the suicide note in the mail at the Center. The stationery was from a motel, and it was postmarked Dayton, Ohio. Paula called the police and asked them to check this particular place out. The police called back later, after having gone to this motel, and confirmed that they found the bodies of both Ed and his wife in the motel room. The first line of the note said, "The author was right. . . ."
>
> Paula did another training meeting on death and dying the day that she got the suicide note from Ed. No one knew about the note before the meeting and during the discussion Paula kept using Ed's name as an example of a person who was either dead or dying. Then, at the end of the meeting, she pulled out the note and read it to everyone.

This story confirmed everyone's view of Paula as an extraordinary, powerful person whose behavior could even provoke a suicide/murder ("and God knows what else," as one staff member suggested). Several versions of this story exist (in some, Ed only kills himself, in others he only threatens to kill himself and his wife), but all of my attempts to uncover the "facts" behind the story only produced more stories. However, by checking all of the stories that we heard, and by rechecking with some of our informants about particular stories, I was able to determine that a staff member named Ed did commit suicide while employed at the Center. The primary circumstance that led to this suicide appears to have been Ed's chronic physical illness. Of course, what is interesting about the "suicide stories" that we heard is that this information was left out and only the relationship between Paula's statement in a meeting and Ed's suicide is specifically emphasized.

It was exactly this type of story that generated "work" in the form of meetings for the Center. An accumulation of what came to be known as "Paula stories" produced an investigation committee charged with the task of examining "all of the problems at the Center." This committee met for approximately one year, sometimes two or three times a week, and these meetings sometimes lasted between five and six hours. This committee and its behavior produced a new set of "crazy meeting" stories, which in turn led to the creation of a subcommittee charged with the task of establishing fair and understandable guidelines and procedures for the investigation. To my knowledge, these guidelines were never produced.

According to the stories (e.g., Ed's suicide story), work at MCMHC can be quite dangerous, but it is also quite exciting. Along with actually generating work for the Center, stories also generate a series of recurring images for individuals to use to depict their activities and relationships, especially their conflictual relationships. The stories specifically offer a number of images of death, killing, and warfare which participants use in a variety of contexts:

1. to describe their relationship to their work (e.g., during a board meeting, a secretary angrily announced her refusal to work: "I will not give one more drop of blood to this place until these problems are resolved");
2. to comment on their relationships to each other (e.g., a staff member described his relationship to the clinical director by saying, "I stand behind her with a knife at her throat");
3. to depict their relationship to the Center itself (e.g., a staff member filed a grievance against the director and assistant director because he believed that they "were trying to kill the organization or at least not let it be born").

The images everyone employs support the view that extraordinary events are happening in what appears to be ordinary contexts. Meetings are not really meetings but instead become battlegrounds for individual and group hostilities, which are created and perpetuated in part by the stories everyone tells. At the Center the principal competing groups are staff and board members who become locked in a struggle over what the goals and aims of the Center can and must be. These differences are looked on as matters of historic importance, as a memo written by one of the Center's "grandparents" (a board member and founder of the organization) illustrates. This particular memo was written in reaction to the deliberations of the investigation committee discussed earlier; it should be recalled that this committee was created in part as a response to "Paula stories." The memo uses examples from the organizational history of the Catholic church as a way to describe and interpret differences between the board and David and Paula.

TO: Bill McCoy, Chairman
           Investigation Committee
FROM: Jean Bell
SUBJECT: Committee Deliberation of May 23

During the time I was present at the meeting of May 23 (not the whole time I concede) the discussion revolved around possible reorganization of the Board. To me, it seemed like a record (not a very good one) being played for the umptieth time. Now, on thinking it over this morning, let me add I also feel that such efforts are a rather stupid cop-out on the real problem.

Let me cite, in a seemingly diversionary tactic, some of the experience of the Roman Catholic Church in its long organizational history for an example I find enlightening. During the twelfth and thirteenth centuries the Church really began to get organized, and several major religious orders were founded. Why not just one order for one Church? Well, it is, after all a Catholic Church—in the sense of universal, something for everyone—and one order would not be able to suit all people, given their diverse cultures and personalities. So we see the founding of an order by a guy I think David resembles: Ignatius of Loyola. An elite group, highly trained and maneuverable, intellectually skilled, dedicated and loyal. Willing to submit to the discipline of not being respected until they proved themselves to the other members of the order. A group both Ignatius and the Pope could depend on in any kind of situation. Not always lovable, but effective as the devil himself.

Then you find another order, which I think the grandparents and the community probably had more in mind: the Franciscans. Sloppy by Jesuit standards, not worldly, the opposite extreme, in fact. They were poor people who ministered to poor people. Not bookish, but simple, practical in an impractical way: empathic, familiar with the paradoxes of life that can make a rich man miserable and a poor man happy. Spending a minimum amount of time in study and the pursuit of books, and a maximum time in addressing themselves in any way they could to the needs of the poor. Lovable for seven centuries.

Here, I think, is the heart of our problem: what shall the spirit of our Center be like? Which of these alternatives shall we choose? We obviously cannot have both, at least not with David and Paula, Jesuits both, in charge. If they stay, their ideal stays. Do we want it? Or can we even settle for it? Might it be better than the one we had? This is the question we must answer, not how the Board can be reorganized, in the vague hope of "controlling" David. I do not wish to exercise great control over the director, I want him to control himself in a way that is congruent with our aims. We must now decide which to adjust: our aims or our leadership.

Documents such as this (and the story presented below) illustrate how individuals at the Center interpret their own conflicts and activities to each other. These differences are never perceived as ordinary differences that one might expect to occur between board and staff members in such an organization, because the images that everyone uses to describe their activities suggest that they are extraordinary individuals acting out historically important differences between groups who are living in very unusual times. For many participants, David really was Ignatius of Loyola (or the devil), and the board really represented the Franciscan order. These transformations make life at the Center seem very exciting, and stories that specifically describe this life and become metaphors for the organization as a whole are also quite frequently told. Therefore, the third category of stories described here is stories about the Center.

Stories about the Center

The stories that appear in conversations as very obvious stories are those that have as their principal subject the Center and its fate. These stories are elaborate, often amusing, and very clearly framed, and they often compare events at MCMHC to specific historical eras or to current international crises. In the following story, the Center is depicted as a boomtown on the verge of destruction.

It's 1850 and the wild, wild West and what happened is that Uncle Sam and Washington said, "hey man, thar's gold in them thar hills," and everybody rushed right over to get the gold and the organizers came along. The state and the feds came along with it and said, "Well, you have this boomtown but you really need somebody to build the houses and things like that." So they built these shacks and shanties and they got somebody from Washington to be the mayor of the town, to run it and everybody was happy ever after. And it was really gaudy too, they had all kinds of saloons and houses of ill-repute and everybody had the God-damnedest good time you've ever seen. But what they forgot to do, of course, was to build sewage systems and provide adequate law enforcement to keep certain things, banks, solvent and all the other things that a place needs; they just neglected it, forgot about it totally which meant no fire department, one day one of the shacks goes up and then the whole town. Also the gold is running out "in them thar hills" and now it's becoming unreal.

This story encapsulates the Center's history: (1) by focusing specifically on the organization's relation to its funding sources, founders, and leaders (the "gold" provided by "Uncle Sam and Washington," i.e., NIMH; and the "mayor from Washington," i.e., David); and (2) by using the imagery of the boomtown to comment on the Center's constitution as an organized anarchy (building "shacks and shanties" and forgetting "to build sewage systems and provide adequate law enforcement"). The individual and organizational advantages (life is fun) and disadvantages (life is precarious) of life in an organized anarchy are cleverly presented in this narrative. The story, however, also contains a moral message that seems quite clear—boomtowns may be fun, "but you can't just enjoy yourself without having to pay for it." And so the Center as boomtown burns up.

The idea that the organization can self-destruct at any moment is an extremely powerful and pervasive view held by participants. It is therefore not surprising to find that individuals describe working in such an agency as an especially intense experience. Not one of the 70 individuals interviewed in our research described their working experience in neutral terms. For some, "it was totally involving and extremely intense"; "it was undignified, unprofessional, just plain craziness, but it was fun in a way"; or "when the place got started we were so into the whole process, it became your life . . . and it used to be fun, that was the great part." For other staff members, working at MCMHC was often frustrating, sometimes "unreal," and in some instances, very traumatic. One ex-staff member reported having nightmares about the Center two years after he resigned from the organization. Other ex-staff members described their present work as "just a job," as "much less intense," or as "a place where you can keep your sanity intact, but not as much fun."

How Stories Work

In most organizations, life is not very exciting. In some organizations, however, life seems to be very exciting and these are the organizations to which researchers (especially anthropologists) should direct their attention, because the social forms that individuals use to construct and "organize" the organization, and their work within it, are specifically revealed in these settings. The two forms that stand out at MCMHC—the meeting and the story—are discussed here. Meetings, in this context, are a form for group interaction, for interpretation and construction of events; stories are a form for individual interpretation, construction, and reconstruction of events.[6] Both of these forms provide individuals and the organization with a way to create and then discover the meaning of what it is they are doing and saying. In this way meetings and stories, and the systemic relationship that exists between them, allow individuals "to talk in order to discover what they are saying, [to] act in order to discover what they are doing" (Weick 1977). In an organized anarchy these activities are essential because they are the only way available for the organization to constitute itself to its members and for the members to legitimate their actions to each other. I assume that meetings and stories play this constitutive role in all organizations, but their importance has been missed by most researchers who take the existence of organizations for granted and treat them as concrete, objective, and essentially unproblematic entities.

In conclusion, perhaps the most important aspect of the stories (and meetings) at MCMHC is that they provide individuals with something to do in a system where everyone is unclear about what it is they should be doing. In this way, these events *work* for the organization, and the individuals in the organization, because they generate activity which in turn generates interpretations of this activity, which suggests that it is not what it seems to be. What more can we ask from a story?

Notes

Acknowledgments. My thanks to both the members of this research team— Anita Kneifel, Don Merten, and Gary Schwartz—for their collaboration on this project and to all of the individuals involved with MCMHC for their participation and interest in this study. Edward Bruner and Don Handelman provided extremely useful comments on this paper. I would also like to thank Barb Schalk, Joan Stahl, and Andrea Dubnick for typing various versions of this manuscript.

1. In keeping with anthropological convention, fictitious names are used for the Center and the community in which it is located, as well as for all of the individuals referred to in this paper. The social system and culture of Midwest Community Mental Health Center are discussed in more detail in Schwartzman, Kneifel, and Krause (1978) and Schwartzman (1980). The conflictual and "crazy" aspects of the Center are specifically examined in these discussions as well. Merten and Schwartz (1982) offer a similar interpretation of life in this organization.

2. Material for this research project was collected from several sources, including: participant observation; in-depth interviews with a cross section of individuals involved with the early formation as well as current operation of the Center; transcripts of meeting tapes; and collection and content analysis of documents (e.g., grant proposal, legislation, guidelines, memos, job descriptions).

3. For a more specific application of the concept of an "organized anarchy" to the understanding of events at MCMHC, see Schwartzman (1981). For an application of this concept to the understanding of a large federal bureaucracy—the National Institute of Education—see Sproull, Weiner, and Wolf (1978).

4. The part that the story form plays in everyday discourse is something that very few researchers have investigated. This topic is specifically considered in several of Harvey Sacks's unpublished class lectures. Jefferson (1978) builds and expands on this work.

5. A more detailed analysis of the metaphoric quality of meetings is offered in Schwartzman (1981).

6. I would like to thank Don Handelman for suggesting this distinction to me.

References Cited

Clark, B. R.
  1980   The Organizational Saga in Higher Education. *In* Readings in Managerial Psychology. H. J. Leavitt, L. R. Pondy, D. M. Bohe, eds. pp. 604–613. Chicago: University of Chicago Press.
Jefferson, Gail
  1978   Sequential Aspects of Storytelling in Conversation. *In* Studies in the Organization of Conversational Interaction. J. Schenkein, ed. pp. 219–248. New York: Academic Press.
Kuper, Adam
  1971   Council Structure and Decision-Making. *In* Councils in Action. A. Richards and A. Kuper, eds. pp. 13–28. Cambridge: Cambridge University Press.
March, James G., and Johan P. Olsen, eds.
  1976   Ambiguity and Choice in Organizations. Bergen, Norway: Universitetsforlaged.
Martin, Joanne
  1980   Stories and Scripts in Organizational Settings. Research Paper No. 543, Graduate School of Business, Stanford University.
Martin, Joanne, Martha Feldman, Mary Jo Hatch, and Sam Sitkin
  1983   The Uniqueness Paradox in Organizational Stories. Paper presented at the Organizational Folklore Conference, Santa Monica, California, 10–12 March.
Merten, Don, and Gary Schwartz
  1982   Metaphor and Self: Symbolic Process in Everyday Life. American Anthropologist 84:796–810.
Newall, V.
  1980   Tell Us a Story. *In* Not Work Alone. J. Cherfas and R. Lewin, eds. pp. 199–213. Beverly Hills, CA: Sage.

Pacanowsky, Michael E., and Nick O'Donnell-Trujillo
  1982 Communication and Organizational Cultures. The Western Journal of
    Speech Communication 46:115–130.
Padgett, John F.
  1980 Managing Garbage Can Hierarchies. Administrative Science Quarterly
    25:583–604.
Pellowski, A.
  1977 The World of Storytelling. New York: Bowker.
Schwartzman, Helen B.
  1978 The Dichotomy of Work and Play. *In* Play: Anthropological Perspectives.
    M. A. Salter, ed. pp. 185–187. West Point, NY: Leisure Press.
  1980 The Bureaucratic Context of a Community Mental Health Center: The
    View from "Up." *In* Hierarchy and Society: Anthropological Perspectives on
    Bureaucracy. G. M. Britan and R. Cohen, eds. pp. 45–59. Philadelphia: ISHI
    Press.
  1981 Hidden Agendas and Formal Organizations or How to Dance at a Meeting.
    Social Analysis 9:77–88 (special issue on "Administrative Frameworks and
    Clients." D. Handelman and J. Collman, eds.).
Schwartzman, Helen B., Anita W. Kneifel, and Merton S. Krause
  1978 Culture Conflict in a Community Mental Health Center. Journal of Social
    Issues 34:93–110.
Sproull, Lee, Stephen Weiner, and David Wolf
  1978 Organizing an Anarchy: Belief, Bureaucracy, and Politics in the National
    Institute of Education. Chicago: University of Chicago Press.
Swidler, Ann
  1979 Organization without Authority. Cambridge: Harvard University Press.
Turner, Victor
  1981 Social Dramas and Stories about Them. *In* On Narrative. W. J. T.
    Mitchell, ed. pp. 137–164. Chicago: University of Chicago Press.
Weick, Karl
  1977 Re-punctuating the Problem. *In* New Perspectives on Organizational Ef-
    fectiveness. P. S. Goodman and J. M. Pennings, eds. pp. 193–225. San Fran-
    cisco: Jossey-Bass.
  1979 The Social Psychology of Organizing. Reading, MA: Addison-Wesley.

4
Religion and Life History: An Exploration in Cultural Psychology

James L. Peacock
University of North Carolina, Chapel Hill

Religion and *life history* are both familiar notions in anthropology. Religion I take to mean something like a system of symbols that express or embody a relation between world and spirit. A life history is a story of an individual's life. The study of religion is central to the study of culture, that is, a system of symbols that is public, collective, and tends toward logical and aesthetic coherence. The study of life history is generally considered more of a psychological matter. Most of us share a commonsense Western view of the life history, that it reveals a process experienced by the individual. "He led a life," we say, implying both that the individual was in control and that he moved in a direction: he led.

Religion, then, is seen as a collective structure, life history as an individual process. Yet a life history is also a collective, public structure—a narration, shared with an audience, possibly even a congregation or nation. Actually, it follows that both religion and life history are cultural structures. Religion, though, points toward the spiritual, life history toward the natural—processes through which the organism moves from birth to death. Analysis of the relationship between religion and life history should contribute to understanding the perennially puzzling yet fundamental relationships between collective and individual, culture and nature, structure and process, text and experience.

If anything is distinctive about the approach employed here, it is the endeavor to treat the life history as a narrative form having its own structural integrity. Life histories are usually treated reductionalistically, cannibalized as sources of data to reveal psychological traits or mechanisms, cultural categories, or social relationships; the patterning of the life history as narrative is not sufficiently grasped.

Religion, of course, can be treated also as a narrative form as well as a cultural structure. At least this treatment is appropriate for such narrative forms as testimonies and parables that express religious views and experience. But religion is conceived here as a pattern or structure that the analyst and, to an extent, the actor abstract from a variety of particular forms and actions, including narrative but also ritual and other modes of behavior, and summarize in a style more propositional than narrative, such as a "belief system," a "creed," or a "world view." Accordingly, when we speak of exploring the relationship between religion and life history we refer to a relationship not between two distinct and discrete things or events but to analytically separable patterns, the one fairly concrete—a narration of a life—the other more abstract—a summation of a religious orientation drawn from myriad sources, including narrations of lives. We treat a relationship of part to whole, but not simply that.

Before proceeding to the texts, a few words should be said about the place of narrative study within anthropology and of life histories within narrative study. At an American Ethnological Society symposium held in 1969 (then, too, in Louisiana), I presented a paper entitled "Society as Narrative." I criticized social anthropology for failing to accord narrative analysis a proper place within social analysis, and I proposed an alternative model at two levels, both of which went beyond typical structural-functional models of that day. Most concretely, I emphasized the need to analyze the texts and immediate contexts of narration (as opposed to the structural-functional tendency to submerge both to the wider patterning of society). More generally and whimsically, I suggested consideration of the narrative patterning of society itself—that societies were organized not only around such functional exigencies as integration and adaptation to the environment, but also around the motive of constructing a story; as we say, making history. I suggested some implications of seeing society in this way. While this latter argument was not developed further by anyone, so far as I know, similar emphases have surfaced recently in anthropology. A view of society as oriented toward making history, in some sense constructing a story through its playing out of events, can be seen in recent writings that call for a new historical anthropology (e.g., Sahlins 1981). Increased emphasis on the immediate text and context of narration is evidenced by numerous recent anthropological writings of the last decade, including those of this seminar.

Anthropological interest in narration is doubtless due to the influence of structuralism and of such humanistic fields as literary criticism, folklore, and phenomenology, with which anthropology has renewed contact after a period of positivism and sociologism. Aside from interdisciplinary cross-fertilization, though, the greater attention to narration must have come simply from the endeavor to work carefully through texts, as opposed to the older functionalist concern with context. Leach's (1961, 1969) structuralist analyses of the Bible are a case in point. Claiming inspiration from Lévi-Strauss, Leach's structuralist analyses of Scripture in fact differ from those originally proposed by Lévi-Strauss (1967[1958]) in taking more account of patterns of narration per se rather than ignoring narrative structure in order to move directly to allegedly deeper structures (see Baggett 1982).

Such a trend brings symbolic studies in anthropology into resonance with many other approaches; for example, the performance-oriented study of narrative exemplified by linguistic, folklorist, and literary models associated with the scholars at the University of Pennsylvania (see Hymes 1971; Herrenstein-Smith 1978; Abrahams 1980; Labov 1977); with form-criticism in scriptural studies (Bultmann 1934); and with Burke's (1962) "dramatism."

Despite enhanced attention to narrative, no anthropologist known to me has gone to the lengths of such phenomenologists as Ricoeur (1979, 1981, 1982a, 1982b) to assert that experience itself, in its most fundamental aspect, is narrative in patterning. The anthropologist's objection to such an assertion would likely be threefold. First, we would suspect cultural provincialism—that a view of experience as quintessentially narrative reflects a sense of history and time peculiar to Western, Judeo-Christian-Islamic, or modern culture. Second, despite all the discrediting of stereotyping non-literate societies as viewing reality as timeless, we might still believe that some such world view is more pervasive in the full span of human experience than is the historical sense. And third, we might hew to the common assumption that analysis must ultimately reduce event to structure—a methodological principle that reflects an ontological assumption of the existence of a set of principles or categories, a deep structure, which underlies narration of events seen merely as a surface structure.[1] This is not the place to challenge such assumptions, but they must be acknowledged.

We find that the life history has received a treatment by anthropology parallel to that accorded other narrative forms; that is, life histories have been treated not so much as forms whose narrative patterning is significant in its own right, but instead have been cannibalized to feed analyses at other levels, such as the psychological and sociological. Psychological anthropology has given the most explicit and coherent attention to life histories within anthropology and has stressed one of two approaches. Either the life history is treated as a statement about reality, a history of a life, in which case attention is drawn to the life that is presumably being narrated (and away from the narration itself). This life then becomes the object of analysis, perhaps in terms of stages of the life cycle, and the study becomes developmental psychology. Or, the life history is treated as a projection of inner states, in which case attention is drawn to those subjective dispositions presumed to lie behind that expression, and the study then becomes one of clinical psychology. In neither case is the narrative itself of more than passing interest, for one dives beneath the surface to bring up the deeper psychological reality, which is, of course, data screened through the categories of psychological theory. While truer, perhaps, of older approaches in psychological anthropology, this characterization would seem to remain broadly true even of the rich assortment of recent studies of the life history surveyed by Langness and Frank (1981).

What, then, would proper analysis of life history entail? Hermeneutical vagaries aside, elementary empiricism dictates that we attend properly to the narration itself. The narration is, after all, what the native places before us; he himself organizes his experience into a form with its own integrity and force. Unforgivable is a psychological, sociological, or any other kind of reductionism that ignores this form to go straight for some allegedly deeper structure, which of course also reflects the abstracted categories of that frame of reference selected for emphasis. This is not to say one should end with the narrative form, but one should start with it.

One cannot end with the narrative form because the narrative is not self-contained. To abstract it as a text and treat that part only is, as Ricoeur (1979, 1981, 1982a, 1982b) puts it, "methodological asceticism." The life history narration does, after all, purport to narrate a *life;* it is narrated by a person, as a process, in a context. From all this the text is abstracted. Further, and this is the point Ricoeur and other phenomenologists would emphasize, it is narrated *to* someone—even to the readers of this paper. Our act of reading, hearing, and interpreting the life history becomes part of the history of that life history and therefore must itself be interpreted; this interpretation then must be interpreted, and so on, so that no interpretation is conclusive and the text is placed in ever more ramified and convoluted contexts.

Accepting this lack of limits on the unit of analysis, one may nevertheless keep one's sense of proportion. How much weight should be given the experience of the interpreter as opposed to that of the narrator, the interpretation as opposed to the narration? Is it not arrogant (and tedious) to give as much attention to us as to the story? Here is psychological reductionism in a new guise, a hedonism that begs for methodological asceticism. Granted, the narration is distilled from life; still, it *is* distilled and it is the native's distillation. An ethnographer should, one would think, accord proper recognition to the native form's objective integrity.[2]

The life histories analyzed here are of three religious leaders, with whose organizations I have had fairly recent field experience: Kijahi Hadji Achmad Dahlan, founder of the Indonesian Muslim reformist movement,

Muhammadijah, among whom I did fieldwork in 1970; Reverend J. C.
Clyde (a pseudonym), a preacher in the Christian Pentecostal movement,
among whom I have done fieldwork in North Carolina (jointly with Professor Ruel Tyson, Department of Religion, University of North Carolina,
Chapel Hill) intermittently during 1975–80; and Pak Nyata (a pseudonym),
a teacher or "guide" *(pamong)* in the meditation group Sumarah, in Java,
with whom I had a month's contact during summer 1979 (while working
with Mr. David Howe, whose 1980 Ph.D. dissertation provides detail to
buttress my own limited observations). To compare life histories from such
varied places and groups, expressed, as will be seen, in varied forms, may
seem less comparative method than madness. Probably, I should issue some
methodological disclaimer; instead, I simply assert that what is done is adequate for illustrative purposes.

The Life Histories

Dahlan

*K. H. A. Dahlan, Amal dan Perdjoanganja, Riwajat Hidup (K. H. A.
Dahlan, His Actions and Struggle, Life History)* is the official biography of
Muhammadijah's founder, written by Solichin Salam and published in 1962
by Muhammadijah. *Riwajat hidup* (life history) is actually only one section
of the book, the others being devoted to such matters as the history of Islam
and Muhammadijah. The life history is divided into five seemingly straight-
forward sections: childhood and youth; education; as father and husband;
struggle; the end of his life.

After setting the scene in Yogyakarta, Central Java, Indonesia,
birthplace of both Dahlan and Muhammadijah, the author describes the
ancestry of Dahlan: "In the nineteenth century there lived a religious
teacher named Kijahi Hadji Abubakar bin Kijahi Hadji Salaiman" (Salam
1962:6). *Bin* means "son of," reflecting a patrilineal emphasis among these
pious Muslims, which contrasts with the bilateral balance of most Javanese.
The patrilineal stress is shown, too, in Salam tracing Dahlan's ancestry for
11 generations on his father's side and only 4 on his mother's side.

The biographer gives the year of Dahlan's birth (1868, Christian
calendar; 1285, Muslim) but apologizes because he does not know the date.
This again contrasts with the wider Javanese pattern, where often one
knows the day of one's birth but not the year. The pious Muslims are seemingly more concerned with the passing of unrepeatable years—in a word,
linear time-history—while the syncretist Javanese stress the repeatable day,
which bears a relation to cosmic cycles. Essentially nothing is said of
Dahlan's childhood, but a list is given of his siblings; he was number four.

The section on education provides two more lists: his books and his teachers. And it relates that he was "ordered" by his father to go to Mecca, for pilgrimage and study. When he returned, his name was changed from Darwisj to Dahlan. "As Husband and Father" picks up the story after Dahlan returned to Yogyakarta. He is described as "replacing his father" by becoming an official of the Great Mosque of the Sultan of Yogyakarta, a position he occupied for the rest of his life. At the same time, he was a traveling merchant. He married his mother's brother's daughter, Siti Walidah, then four additional wives, divorcing each after a short time but retaining Siti. These wives and his children by each also are listed.

"Struggle" *(perdjuangan)* is a standard category in Indonesian narration of history and life history. This section tells how Dahlan came to found Muhammadijah, on 18 November 1912, when he was approximately 44 years old. As is often the case in Indonesian movements, the early nucleus was the leader's pupils and the setting, a school. Note that as Dahlan was "ordered" to go to Mecca, so he is "urged" to found Muhammadijah. Perhaps the other-directedness reflects both a prophetic notion of being called and a Javanese de-emphasis of individual initiative and decision.

"The End of His Life" contains one of the two efforts at dialogue in the life history. Dahlan became ill from overwork, his wife begged him to rest, and he replied,

> I must work hard, in order to lay the first stone in this great movement. If I am late or cease, due to my illness, there is no one who will build the groundwork. I already feel that my time is almost gone, thus if I work as fast as possible, what remains can be brought to perfection by another. [Salam 1962:13]

He summoned friends and a brother-in-law to delegate tasks, and then died on 23 February 1923 at his home, Kauman 59, Yogyakarta.

Salam summarizes the character of K. H. A. Dahlan as *sepi ing pamrih* (Javanese for "tranquil in silencing self-interest") yet *rame ing gawe* (Javanese for "active in work"). Dahlan is described as *ichlas* (stoic, devoted, steadfast) and as a doer *(manusia amaliah)* rather than an intellectual *(manusia ilmiah)*. Toward the end of the book are two sections, "Pearls of Wisdom" and "Several Anecdotes." "Pearls" cites 25 aphorisms from Dahlan, "Anecdotes" records 26 events. The aphorisms emphasize the need for salvation, for example, "We humans are given as a wager only one life in the world. After you die will you be saved or damned?" (Salam 1962:50). The anecdotes include tales of Dahlan's generosity and humility, as well as the one incident in which he directly protested against the Yogyakarta

authorities in the name of reform, when he objected to the incorrect placement of the Great Mosque, a protest that reportedly caused him to be exiled
for a time.

This is the material. What are the patterns? Consider the structure of
the text. At first glance, this is a developmental account like those
customary in Western biography. Childhood leads to education, which
leads to adulthood and finally death. On closer examination, the pattern is
as much classificatory as developmental.

No developmental psychology leads from one phase to the next.
Most prominent in each section of Dahlan's biography is a list: a list of siblings, a list of books and teachers, a list of wives and children. The prominence of lists and the absence of dialogue are an indication of the lack of a
processual narration from "formative years" to "private life," to take two
familiar phrases from the bourgeois Western biographical genre. The two
last sections on "struggle" and "end of his life" are more narrative and include the only two instances of dialogue, but they are schematic.

The 25 "pearls" and 26 "anecdotes" relegated to the end of the
book contain raw material that could flesh out this narrative. Why was it
not so used? Partly, I think, because the author's conception of life history
is somewhere between the developmental and the classificatory. Life is imagined as sequential, as history, but the concern is not so much to show how
individual experience unfolds psychologically as to exemplify by each phase
a category of culture. Hence the numbered lists, ordered not dynamically
but thematically.

Now a few words about the content. Like many reformists and revolutionaries—all, if we believe Erik Erikson—Dahlan began his struggle after
a moratorium, a period of separation from his familiar setting, namely, the
pilgrimage. But this pilgrimage was, as Victor Turner notes about traditional pilgrimages, securely within the traditional social framework, as was
his return. Unlike Luther, who violated his father's wish by entering the
monastery, Dahlan took the pilgrimage at his father's command and then
returned to replace his father in familial, occupational, and religious categories. By his 30s, he had family, position, and students. In contrast to the
Christian biographical tradition of celibacy and isolation while changing the
world (think of Christ and Paul, or for that matter, Luther), Dahlan could
follow Muhammad's example of polygyny and community in the midst of
reform, and his reform never shattered his status in the Yogya hierarchy.

Absent from the biography of Dahlan is the account of intense inner
struggle known in Christian writings, which depict a person obsessed by the
need to achieve justification or salvation by purging himself of guilt and sin.
The surface result of Dahlan's reformism was not unlike that of a Luther, a
Calvin, or a Zwingli: the stripping of ritual to its essentials, delivery of ser-

mons in the vernacular, reliance on the book instead of the priest. But the formulation of a Luther, meaningful only in a culture imbued with the notion of original sin, was also an inner solution to a torment peculiar to himself. Less subjective, the reformation of Dahlan was a legalistic attempt to impose a Middle Eastern ethic on a Malayo-Indonesian society. The method was a stoic, dedicated, tranquil, systematic, unquestioning application of received creed.

In the biography, initiation into a vocation and the vocation itself, the struggle, are separated. After education and pilgrimage, Dahlan changed his name then dutifully applied what he had learned (the doctrine of reformism, especially from Egypt's Mohammad Abduh). No description is given of further thought or spiritual experience during the struggle; Dahlan had completed his initiation and now he undertook his vocation, in a highly bureaucratic manner, what Weber (1978:218) would term "rational-legal."

The end of Dahlan's life is depicted in the same bureaucratic way. Western biographers are fond of dramatic last words. The classic paradigm is the account of Christ's cry as he died on the cross. More trivial but typical patterns are illustrated by two personal favorites: Robert E. Lee is said to have shouted, "Strike the tents!" and Stonewall Jackson quietly remarked, "Let us pass over the river and rest on the other side." Max Weber, according to his wife, died singing a Wagnerian aria! Dahlan simply arranged for the organization to continue.

Clyde

Reverend J. C. Clyde tells his life story during an interview and elaborates it during nightly sermons for two weeks at a revival in a Pentecostal church in a place I call Tarville, North Carolina. "I didn't have a very illustrious life coming up, we were just poor folk," he begins. "My dad was just a common laborer, saw mill. My mother was just a housewife. As far as I know she was always a Christian." Clyde grew up in rural Mississippi, near Booneville, moving with his father from one sawmill to another. At age 12 he left home, riding a freight train to Memphis. By 15 he was running a farm for a widow. By 20 he was a country singer in Nashville, the country music capital of the South. Nashville led to that other mecca for country singers and assorted types, Los Angeles.

Clyde gives no account of his schooling, doubtless because he had little; but, also, omission of an account of formal education is typical in Pentecostal narration of life history, while inclusion of it is customary for Muhammadijans. Pentecostals, however, always include their conversion experience, while Muhammadijans never do. Clyde's conversion account is quoted here from the interview:

I thought I had it made. But it was always just in front of me. It took everything I made for advertising, I never made it then. But my mother never would attend any of our dances, shows or anything, although she lived here in Tennessee at this time. I thought why wouldn't she attend those shows, or any of our dances, but she visited me at the radio station one Sunday afternoon. I dedicated her one of the few gospel songs I do, my mother sat and cried audibly there and I was embarrassed, two months later the call came saying my mother has passed away. I was so glad she never mixed with the world. She lived for God, I knew where she was. From that hour on I never had a minute's rest, till in Los Angeles, California, about two or three years later I was sitting in a club there waiting to talk to a man about playing, and God spoke to my heart. I got up, walked out of that club, I don't know how He spoke to me, I just know He did, I walked up and down the street and didn't know which way to turn. I got on the street car and I started home. Right in front of me said a sign, REVIVAL. And I didn't know what kind of church it was. It didn't make any difference, I just knew I wanted to go to church. I went home and told my wife, and she said I'll go with you. And that night I knelt at the altar and gave my heart to God. I turned to my wife before I went to the altar, after the minister got through preaching. She said she would go with me. Our little boy who was just two years old at that time, he didn't know what was with daddy, but when I knelt at the altar he knelt with me there, but he didn't know what it was all about, but today he pastors our church at Los Angeles. I've got a son-in-law that pastors in Atlanta, Georgia, another daughter that is an organist in my son's church and also sings with the Freedom Singers in Southern California. Got another daughter that teaches in the college in Chico, California. God's been so good to me to watch my children grow up to live for God. But I never thought about going into the ministry, I didn't want to go into the ministry.

In his sermons Clyde stresses that he is a new person as a result of his conversion. A woman telephones him, "Is this Cowboy Clyde?" "No ma'am, he's dead," replies Clyde. Cowboy Clyde was dead; Reverend Clyde is a new creature, born again. Some Muhammadijans would seem to be, from an objective standpoint, as radically changed as Clyde: former Christians or Hindu-Buddhists, for example, who are now committed Muhammadijans. But never does a Muhammadijan life history so radically or dramatically separate pre- and postinitiation phases as does the Pentecostal. Muhammadijans, however, more firmly separate initiation and postinitiation phases. As noted, Dahlan's initiation (i.e., education) is sharply separated from his vocation (i.e., struggle). When Dahlan's education is finished, it is not repeated or continued, though the concept derived from it (reformism) is applied. Clyde's initiation, his conversion experience, *is* repeated in his vocational phase. In fact, much of his preaching consists of reliving dramatically his conversion so that others can experience their own conversion.

"More gospel to be preached, more souls to be reached," sings Clyde in his deep, rough country voice. He once had a church in Los Angeles, but for eight years has been on the road in a van, preaching revivals such as this one in Tarville. "Brother Clyde is a God-filled man," remarks Sister Carole. But Clyde's conversion did not lead directly to his preaching. He ran an automotive body repair shop in Los Angeles while active as a layman in the Pentecostal church, but he did not preach "because I didn't have the education, didn't have the words." The step from being saved to being called to preach came through his daughter's healing. She was 18 months old, had bronchial pneumonia, and the doctors had given up. Clyde prayed, "God heal my baby, I'll preach." God healed her and Clyde preached a revival that Saturday night.

While preaching part-time he worked for a body shop, commuting 240 km every night. After six years, he himself developed pneumonia. The day before Christmas he was in a hospital, broken physically, financially, and spiritually, wondering how he would get presents for his children. Then, "Jesus walked through that door. . . . God healed me that day." He responded ecstatically: "That was the spell to end all spells. I had the time of my life. From that day to this I have never had to work another job." And he sings:

> I've had to walk through that valley of Pain
> I've tried to pray when it seemed so in vain.
> But I'll not walk through that valley again.

The call to preach typically comes as life reaches a crisis, and the linkage between the pledge to preach and someone being healed or some other crisis being resolved is also common. In retrospect, it may seem that circumstances force the individual to accept the call; nevertheless, it is a decision, sometimes a momentous and difficult one. To be in a crisis when much hinges on your decision, and then to *decide*—this is a pattern prominent in Pentecostal life history, not in Muhammadijan accounts. After decision comes ecstasy: "I had the time of my life." Here, by that revealing cliche, Clyde singles out a particular time, a unique ecstatic moment, *"the* time of my *life"* (my emphasis). No parallel accounts occur in Dahlan's story, which portrays time as flat though progressive: each moment is like the last, except that it is an advance.

Brother Clyde is less organizationally engaged than was Hadji Dahlan. For Dahlan, conversations are mentioned only when they resulted in establishing a new branch of the organization. Clyde quotes only those conversations associated with the saving of souls, or such homely matters as eating his supper. He has given up his body-shop work, then his church, and now "goeth where the spirit listeth," in his van, harnessing his craggy face, square physique, and rough-hewn magnetism to night after night of revival preaching. The truck driver-song leader at this church contrasts the saved, who awaken and say brightly, "Good morning, Lord," with the unsaved, who stare bleary-eyed and mutter, "Good Lord, morning." Clyde never refers to his life in terms reflecting the daily routine of the working man; he speaks instead of nights in his van spent meditating on the gospel, agonizing over his failure to bring the revival to a culmination. He does not mention his days. Conversion and the calling have transformed his daily routine from that of the farmer and worker to the performer, and his life rhythm has become geared to the draining rhythms of the revival, which in its crises and culminations repeats the paradigm of the individual drama of salvation.

Hadji Dahlan's bureaucratized struggle is embedded in kinship. He derived from a patrilineal ancestry, replaced his father in the religious hierarchy, established his own family described by a numbered list of wives and children. Brother Clyde gives himself no ancestry; his father provides nothing for him to replace (and, in fact, disappears from Clyde's story after the second sentence). Clyde's mother moves him into his vocation, not by establishing a social structure but by symbolizing a Christian virtue that makes him feel love, shame, and guilt. The invisible father coupled with the sentimentally inspiring religious mother appear in the life histories of other Pentecostal preachers. Clyde is creating something of a dynasty, consisting of his children and protégés who carry the word. In his preaching he is working through the theme of a family of God baptized in the blood of Christ, all somehow partaking of ancestry drawn from the chosen people of Israel. But, as suggested in the terms "brother" and "sister" by which Pentecostals refer to each other, that church resists the model of the patriarchial hierarchy, whereas such a model sets a framework for Dahlan.

One day, while in his study reading scripture, Clyde had a vision. He found himself on the road to Calvary and the guide told him a certain spot was where Jesus stumbled under the weight of the cross. Clyde knelt, prayed, and wept, then awoke depressed because he interpreted the vision as meaning that he was seeking an easy path to Calvary instead of climbing where Jesus climbed. Years later, two days before the Seven Days' War,

Clyde visited Jerusalem and in real life repeated the vision; but this time he climbed Calvary, even though guards tried to prevent him.

Clyde's life here imitates Christ's. No similar imitation of Muhammad is mentioned for Dahlan. Dahlan's guide is Muhammad's law, not his life, and the linkage is legal rather than dramatic and metaphorical. Dahlan concludes his life by delegating tasks. Clyde hopes to conclude his by the Rapture, when the dead and the living are changed in a twinkling of an eye and all shall rise in the air to meet Christ.

Nyata[3]

Pak (meaning "father" or "papa") Nyata, a prominent teacher in the Sumarah meditation group of Surakarta, Java, does not recount either education or conversion as leading to his practice and teaching of meditation. He does mention a time of near-insanity, when he was tormented by visions of the dead in their graves and worked through these images by meditation and self-analysis. He also outlines programs of spiritual development and refers to his own spiritual progress. But he does not separate his life into such clear and definite phases as either Dahlan's education and struggle or Clyde's conversion and preaching. In fact, Nyata emphasizes the *continuity* of experience; his teaching is still learning. He states, "You find out which of your tools have not yet conformed by giving service, that is by Guiding."

Now a mature guide in his mid-40s, thick-limbed, bass-voiced, vigorous in movement—rather the Bima type of Javanese—Nyata guides the Sumarah meditation and self-analysis sessions with great power, yet also fluidly and sensitively. He is capable of shifting from guide to guided, as when he asks someone to "check" (by empathetic meditation) his own spiritual state. He also continues to consult his own guide, Pak H of Yogyakarta, who advises him on such matters as whether to have more children, how he must psychically release his dead mother-in-law, and how to subdue his attraction to women. Dahlan is portrayed as completing an education, after which he ceased to learn but spent his life implementing what he had learned. Clyde had a conversion experience at a certain date, then spends his life replicating it in others. Nyata's life is represented by him as not so sharply divided into phases, as more fluid, continuous, and dialectical: he continuously enriches his own spiritual state through experiences that deepen his guiding, which in turn is experience.

Nyata is active. He runs a private bank, he has a cottage batik industry, and he is constantly traveling on his motor scooter to the villages surrounding Solo to hold spiritual meetings. Objectively, his life seems a bit frantic, but subjectively he characterizes his great energy as flowing naturally and effortlessly from his resonance with the widest ground of existence, *alam,* which is nature but also, he says, God. He describes the apparently draining hours of guiding Sumarah sessions as effortless; what he says comes not from his consciousness but from the deeper source, *alam.* What he tries to avoid is "pulling," that is, striving toward a goal, such as Dahlan's or Clyde's salvation. Even a meaningful experience can become a goal, he warns, if you try to repeat it, and this "pulling" must be avoided. Thus, his life, which we might characterize as "productive," he represents as an inevitable expression of energies flowing from the reality with which he is in resonance.

What of his eschatology? The contrast between his view and that of salvation religion is illustrated by the following bit of dialogue, paraphrased here from a Sumarah session at which Nyata was questioned by a young Chinese woman whose Christian affiliation was indicated by the cross on her necklace:

> SHE: What is the source of life? If it goes, can it return?
> HE: If it's gone, it's not life.

Nyata then dropped into a low-toned mumbling, grumbling conversation with the men about life being tough—this *ngoko* Javanese style of *ngomong* and *ngobrol* sometimes termed *ngomel,* an earthy form that debunks the abstract and idealistic. He then shifted to elevated Krama Javanese language, speaking resonantly about meditation being a way of accepting life's sadness, a way to address reality *(nyatane).* Finally, he completed his rhetorical disarming of the girl by turning to us visitors and saying, sotto voce in the Indonesian language she used, "She doesn't accept my teachings, even though she is silent." She, however, comes back at him: "Pak, again, what is the source of life?" He replies, "The source matters less than life writ small—the daily experience of reality. What is the source?" She points upward, presumably indicating God. He lights a match and watches the smoke, then says, "Life is like *that* [presumably implying that life has no certain end, path, or source; it just exists and dissipates, returning to *alam*]."

The Religious Systems

What does this add up to? Three characters in search of a plot, you may say, or an analyst in search of a point. Let us turn to the three religious systems, focusing on the pattern by which symbols mediate between spirit and world.

Muhammadijah

Above all symbols is God, pure spirit. God is transcendent, not to be experienced directly (Sufist mysticism is not welcome in Muhammadijah). He is to be worshiped by the *salat,* erroneously translated as prayers but in fact not communications with God, as are Christian prayers. *Salat* are collective, ritual affirmations of the greatness of God: *Allah akbar.*

God's will is embodied in his word, the Qur'an, from which is elaborated prescriptions that guide life in the world, including prescriptions for ritually organizing the life cycle—rituals of birth, circumcision, marriage, and death. God's will is also expressed through his Prophet, Muhammad, to whom he dictated the Qur'an. Although Muhammad's life is known, it does not bear the mystical relationship to the Muslim that Christ's life bears to the Christian. Muhammad did not die that believers could be mystically reborn, and Muhammad's birth and death do not constitute a symbolic paradigm as do Christmas and Easter. In fact, to be ruthlessly structuralistic, the belief that Muhammad was born and died on the same day implies that his life had no history. His role is to transmit God's command through the Scripture, to be, if a crude comparison is permitted, lawgiver rather than life-liver.

Opposed to God's will is man's desire *(nafsu). Nafsu* includes lust, ambition, and other self-will, based in nature, and it must be controlled by ethical prescription *(achlak)* and rationality *(akal).* Women are peculiarly evocative of *nafsu,* hence their natural sensuality must be controlled by segregation, covering of head and body, and subordination. If the ethical prescriptions are correctly followed, one can look forward to salvation.

Pentecostalism

As with Muhammadijah, God is a transcendent spirit; but God is also three persons, the Blessed Trinity. In his person as Holy Ghost, God can possess and be directly experienced. "If God is dead, what is this in my soul?" sings a Pentecostal minister. To "get the Holy Ghost" is to manifest the gifts of the spirit, to speak in tongues, to be healed, to dance in the spirit, to run up and down the aisles shouting; in short, in Clyde's words, to "have a spell." Outsiders tend to see this psychologically, as emotionalism, ecstasy, altered states of consciousness. From a Pentecostal standpoint this view is incorrect; Pentecostalism is not so much God psychologized as man theologized. The believer lives in the spiritual instead of in what Pentecostals term "the natural," in the word instead of in the world.

Like Muhammadijans, Pentecostals are fundamentalists insofar as they regard the Scripture as the literal word of God. But where the Muhammadijans interpret the Qur'an legalistically, the Pentecostals recreate the biblical epic dramatically. For Muslims, the culmination of the Qur'anic vision would be institutional, Islamic law and the Islamic state. For Pentecostals, the biblical word implies not so much legal, political, and institutional construction, as dramatization—bringing the word to life, certainly in preaching but also in one's own life. "Jesus walked here," said a Lumbe Indian preacher of the land on which his concrete-block church was built, and Clyde tells of his vision of Christ climbing Calvary. The word is made flesh.

Pentecostal ritual is honed toward having the spirit descend or toward raising the spirit. To maximize openness to the spirit, forms are reduced. Services are not guided by printed programs or set liturgy, and the minister is supposed to "move as the spirit listeth" in the service as in life.

In this ritual, music has a special place, certainly by comparison with Muhammadijan services where instrumental music and singing are absent, and even by comparison with the more institutionalized churches. If Christian services are categorized according to the extent to which music, preaching, and congregation are differentiated, Pentecostalism would be at the integrated pole. Choir and congregation are one when the choir is not singing, for the singers come down and sit in the congregation. Preaching and singing are interwoven, too. The preacher sings solos, probably accompanying himself with a guitar; and even when he preaches his sermon, which he typically introduces with a song, he is periodically accompanied by an organ. In some black and Native American Pentecostal churches, testimonial is introduced by the testifier singing, and in some urban white churches, the conclusion of testimonial is celebrated by striking up a band. One could note the common observation that music is a form suited for representing the patterning of emotion, while other forms specialize in representing the external world; thus, music is well suited for a religion of "enthusiasm."

As with Muhammadijah, spirituality is opposed to natural impulse and desire. Pentecostals discourage sensuality in the form of dancing and drinking and, for women, makeup and the cutting of hair. Where Muhammadijans *prohibit* illicit sensuality, Pentecostals *replace* sensuality with spirituality—of a rather sensual type. Drinking spirits and dancing in the flesh on Saturday night are exchanged for getting filled with the spirit and dancing in the spirit on Sunday night. By coming to live in the spirit rather than in the world—religiously, not socially, for monasticism is as absent from Pentecostalism as it is from Muhammadijah—one is set for salvation, the Rapture.

Sumarah

Ultimate reality is Kainiki, rather like Brahma. Kainiki is spirit but also nature and self; it is reality. Through the practice of Sumarah, which entails meditation, self-analysis, discussion of experiences with a guide at meetings, and other religious actions, one endeavors to resonate with Kainiki and thus deepen and broaden awareness. To reach this state, one must transcend thought, emotion, and judgment, getting in touch with one's deeper consciousness/unconsciousness *(rasa)*. To guide the seeker of Kainiki, Sumarah provides no fixed forms: no scripture, no set ritual, not even a mantra or model figure such as Buddha. For Sumarah, as for the Western mystic Meister Eckhart, reality is "regarding forms, formless," and so is the path toward it, at least in theory.

As in Muhammadijah and Pentecostalism, natural impulses such as lust must be transcended by spirituality, but Sumarah adds an apparent ambiguity: spirituality is also nature, part of the *alam*. However, the spiritual state idealized by Sumarah is a deeper nature, while emotions such as lust are ephemeral and must be neutralized if one is to reach the deeper reality. The neutralization is achieved by contextualizing. Nyata tells how he was infatuated with a former girlfriend who caused him to have an erection each time he saw her, a matter that troubled his wife. He meditated about her, subordinating her image to a wider frame of awareness so that she became less an obsession and more an aesthetic form as she ceased to dominate his perceptual field.

Afterlife is not commonly discussed in Sumarah. Although occasional allusions to reincarnation can be heard, no Hindu-Buddhist, and certainly no Islamic-Christian, notion of salvation is central to Sumarah belief. Recall Nyata's example of the diffusing smoke. Sumarah's concern is less with future life than with resonance with ultimate reality here and now.

The Structure of Religious Experience in Relation to the Structure of Life History

While many particular relationships between religious patterns and those of life histories have doubtless suggested themselves and, indeed, have been suggested, I shall endeavor now to summarize a general parallel of structures (see Table 1). For Muhammadijah, God is transcendent and his relationship to man is rather bureaucratic, in that God dictated his command to His Prophet, who codified it in Scripture, which was then elaborated into law, which should control all action in the world, including natural desire *(nafsu)*. Spirit, form, and world compose a hierarchy in which the top level

Table 1
*Structure of Life Histories in Relation to Structure
of Religious Systems*

| | Life History | | |
	Dahlan	Clyde	Nyata
Initiation	education	conversion	experience
Vocation	bureaucratic application of education	dramatic replication of conversion	experience
Termination	continuing application	continuing dramatization	experience
Relationship	bureaucratic/ causal	dramatic/ metaphorical	unity

| | Religious System | | |
	Muhammadijah	Pentecostal	Sumarah
Spirit	transcendent	personal	immanent
Form	scriptural/ritual application of spiritual norms	dramatic manifestation of spiritual personality	negated
World	controlled by spirit and form	transformed into dramatized spirit	encompassed by larger reality
Relationship	bureaucratic/ causal	dramatic/ metaphorical	unity (as part seen to fuse into whole)

ideally controls the lower ones by a chain of command. Dahlan's life history can be viewed as a hierarchy. It connects three entities: initiation, vocation, and termination. The first controls the next two. Dahlan's initiation, by formal education, established his guiding concept, Islamic creed, with reformist tenor. His life consisted of an application, in a rather bureaucratic way, of that concept—throughout his vocation and to the point of death.

In Pentecostalism, spirit is translated into form and then world dramatically rather than bureaucratically. The Holy Ghost is manifested in the experience of conversion and then in other dramatizations, such as healing, speaking in tongues, and testifying or preaching, all of which are believed to make the spirit live in the world. Clyde's life history can be viewed as dramatically motivated as well. His initiation is the drama of the conversion experience. This drama becomes the metaphor, or script, which is recreated in his vocation, that of evangelical preaching. It is recreated, finally, in the Rapture.

In Sumarah, spirit, form, and world are conceived as more a unity than in either Muhammadijah or Pentecostalism. These three entities are not so much a hierarchy as manifestations of a single ground of being, Kainiki. Accordingly, neither bureaucratic chain of command nor dramatic recreation is required to unite the three. Spirit is immanent in the world, and world is, when properly perceived, a limited manifestation of spirit. Forms are narrower still, limited efforts at concretizing and grasping the wider and deeper reality. Nyata's life, as self-described, is likewise a unity. While vaguely distinguishing between passage into and out of his life work, he would not distinguish, as do the life histories of Dahlan and Clyde, any single initiation pattern that determines the rest of his life. Instead, initiation, vocation, and termination are all part of the whole experience, and progress through life consists in part of growing awareness of that whole.

Cases Again: Healing

Before concluding, a brief return to the concrete is instructive. The comparison can be made more pointed by examining how each of the three men responded to the same situation: the illness of his child. In each life history such an incident is mentioned, and each is called on to invoke spiritual healing. Such healing is an especially powerful encounter of world by spirit, for in healing spirit becomes flesh and transforms flesh. And when it is the healer's own child, it is his own flesh that is to be transformed. Clyde's experience has already been described. His daughter's pneumonia built to a crisis, which he resolved by his decision: "God, heal my baby. I'll preach!"

Dahlan was teaching one day when he was summoned by his wife, who said that his son was very ill. He went home, asked nothing of God himself, but spoke to his son, saying, "Son, pray to God that you will be given health, but if your time has come, with God's will we shall meet in heaven. Quieten your heart, and be patient." He then said to his wife, "Do not believe that my child's life depends on my vigilance. Whether he lives or dies is in God's hands" (Salam 1962:59). Then he returned to his teaching.

During a discussion with a mother who could not sleep because of worry about her child's illness, Nyata said:

> This was my experience. My son had typhus fever. We had been to the doctor. What should we do? I was quiet, but I treated him myself . . . so he drank water [often used to impart energy, after being meditated upon]. . . . I gave him over to the doctor, but we had already gotten the fever down. My own body was feverish, but that was all right.

Nyata then discerned that the woman felt impatient that her child return to health. He advised her that her feeling of "bearing" (carrying the child spiritually) was right, but that her desire to "lighten the load" by speeding the process of recovery was wrong. "You must suffer," he said. The woman complained about the heat she felt while bearing and asked if it could be relieved by special breathing. Nyata warned her, "If you get all pumped up with the breathing hoping they'll get well quicker, it doesn't work that way."

All three men, then, appear to believe that spirit and flesh can interact so that disease is cured. But the mode of relationship envisioned differs. For Dahlan, the hierarchy is maintained even in crisis; dramatic urgency cannot disrupt the chain of command established by God. For Clyde, the dramatic urgency that provokes human decision is a catalyst for healing, though the background to his plea to God must be considered. Pentecostals believe that it is Christ's original sacrifice which purified humans, establishing the condition for them to be healed: by his stripes we are healed (Isaiah 53:5). Humans need merely claim the healing; but still, to claim is to choose. For Nyata, a dramatic pattern which pushes or pulls toward a climax must be avoided; healing is obtained only by the healer bringing his own being into resonance with the deeper reality, then acting as a vessel between that reality and the patient. Reality absorbs the forces of disease and radiates the forces of health through the healer to and from the patient. Nyata goes on to explain how, at first, because he was insufficiently in tune with reality, he would himself be ill after healing: "It was because I had been pulling. . . . The character of my *rasa* was not yet clean." Purifying his *rasa* was difficult, "like getting excrement off your shoe," but finally "the healing force now just went direct and didn't really involve me. But my duty was the same. I must still be willing." As he says elsewhere, "Existence is a duty."

Conclusion

This exercise serves to explore a relationship of which everyone is aware but which is not usually made explicit—the relationship between cultural structure and the structure of the life history. It should be noted that both of these "structures" are abstracted from public forms—narrated life histories, on the one hand, and statements about belief (including narrative statements), on the other. In this way, the analysis differs from a psychological study, which would infer from the life histories private states and dispositions. I do not intend to denigrate such inferences, which can be ingenious and fascinating (see, e.g., Steven Marcus's [1974] interpretation of the private experiences that lay behind Freud's narration of the life history of

Dora). The point is simply to locate my more "cultural" or "structural" psychology in relation to the individualistically psychological.[4]

It should be noted also that certain kinds of narrative analysis are not deployed, for example, microtextual analysis of such "literary" devices as metaphor or allegory. Emphasis is placed instead on the overall structure of the narration of life and the structure of the lives narrated.[5] A simple outline of the three "plots" in terms of the sequences of phases and the kinds of logic linking these phases serve as dual purpose. On the one hand, the approach attends to the thrust of the narratives, both in form (the mode of narration) and content (the pattern of life narrated); on the other hand, the patterns elucidated can be directly paralleled to patterns of belief, while parallels between belief and the more refined aesthetic techniques are often difficult to draw. In short, the analysis is couched at a level that could—admittedly with some forcing and schematizing—relate narration to culture.

The reader may feel that he has met Dahlan, Clyde, and Nyata before. Indeed, the three sets of beliefs more or less exemplify familiar patterns, which we could gloss as Islamic, Christian, and Buddhist, while the three life histories exemplify rather standard religious careers, the legalistic, shamanic, and mystical. At this level, the study may be seen as illustratively explicating psychocultural types that are widely distributed in world religion. The substantive contribution is then one of illustrative explication of such a typology, by setting forth ethnographically certain regular relationships between the logic of life narration and the logic of religious patterning.

At a methodological level, the exercise reminds us that narration is bound to cultural context and psychological experience in a deeper sense than is usually realized. Cultural and psychological patterning is embodied in narrative structure as well as in content. Hence, to grasp cultural and psychological patterning through narration (and in a broad sense, cultural patterning is revealed by no other means) requires that one take account of the structure of narration as well as the content—a simple admonition, but one rarely followed.

Some of these points can be illustrated by brief reference to the literature of psychology and anthropology to suggest ways both fields could push further toward recognition of the structure of life-history narration in relation to cultural and psychological patterning. Reference has already been made to the study of life history in psychological anthropology, but consider the field of psychology itself. One popularized recent theory of life history that centered around the notion of "mid-life crisis" (Levinson 1978) proclaims as universal a pattern which is, in fact, based on such provincial data as that derived from urban, Northern middle-class males—data laundered through screens of psychological theory and method, with little explicit attention to the patterning and structure of the subjects' own narrations of their lives. Narrative as well as cultural analysis can inform psychology.

In anthropology, it is inevitable that cultural or structural analysis would turn to the individual life, now seen as a cultural form. A suggestive essay is Geertz's *Islam Observed* (1968), which depicts the history and patterning of two cultures as embodied in the lives of certain paradigmatic individuals. A more recent insightful example of the approach is J. M. Taylor's *Eva Peron: The Myths of a Woman* (1978). But even in these works, little is made of the *structure* of the life history. Some consideration of such a structure would seem useful to clarify the vexed relationship between culture and experience, history and life.

Notes

Acknowledgments. Grateful acknowledgment is made to the Guggenheim Foundation, which generously supported a research visit in association with All Souls College, Oxford University, during which a draft of this paper was written.

1. An example of this assumption is provided by a colleague's remark during a recent department colloquium. It happened that I asked the visiting speaker a question about the patterning of certain narratives she had described. My colleague proposed that we now move to "deeper issues," which for him turned around structures of thought and belief, as opposed to narration.

2. I have in mind here experiments performed in Java while studying ludruk plays in 1962 (see Peacock 1968). I remain impressed with the fact that the Javanese and I, despite vast cultural differences, constructed similar plot outlines of ludruk performances. At a gross level, the objective force of a form or text may override differences among the perceivers, and we are wrong to ignore this force in recognizing the interplay between perceiver and object.

3. The form of this life-history narration differs from the first two. Analysis of Dahlan centers around a written biography, analysis of Clyde around a kind of oral autobiography. Perhaps in keeping with his world view, but also simply because I never asked him to do so, Nyata did not formally narrate to me a life history. The account given here is my summary drawn from myriad statements and observations during a month's conversation and participation in his Sumarah meetings. I assume the role of narrator as well as commentator. Variation in form among the three life histories is not critically important for the structuralist argument of this paper, although such variation would require careful consideration for an argument depending more strongly on style of narration.

4. The level of analysis followed here is at a rather surface level outlining patterns of belief stated in "official" contexts and patterns of life history that were narrated in the initial interviews or printed as an official book. Probing for more subtle levels obviously dissolves the structures presented here into more complex configurations, but the official, public, "surface" level has its own integrity.

5. It is important to distinguish the sequence of the narration from the sequence of the life narrated. Thus, in narration, some Pentecostals mentioned their sanctification before mentioning their salvation. In the construction of their lives as portrayed through the narrative, however, they would designate salvation as coming before sanctification. Since doctrine decrees the latter sequence, it is suggestive to consider why some narrations followed the former. But the point is not relevant to the particular Pentecostal life history analyzed here.

References Cited

Abrahams, Roger
   1980   Bringing Down the House at St. Vincent. Ms. Files of the author.
Baggett, John
   1982   The Hermeneutics of Biblical Mythology: A Comparison of the Structural Analysis of Edmund Leach with the Historical Demythologizing of Rudolf Bultmann. M.A. thesis. Department of Anthropology, University of North Carolina, Chapel Hill.
Bultmann, Rudolf
   1934   Form Criticism. New York: Harper & Row.
Burke, Kenneth
   1962   A Grammar of Motives and a Rhetoric of Motives. New York: World Publishing Co.
Geertz, Clifford
   1968   Islam Observed. Chicago: University of Chicago Press.
Herrenstein-Smith, Barbara
   1978   On the Margins of Discourse. Chicago: University of Chicago Press.
Howe, David
   1980   Sumarah: A Study of the Art of Living. Ph.D. dissertation. Department of Anthropology, University of North Carolina, Chapel Hill.
Hymes, Dell
   1971   The "Wife" Who Goes Out Like a Man. *In* Structural Analysis of Oral Tradition. Pierre Maranda and Elli Köngas Maranda, eds. pp. 49–80. Philadelphia: University of Pennsylvania Press.
Labov, William
   1977   Therapeutic Discourse: Psychotherapy as Conversation. New York: Academic Press.
Langness, Lewis L., and Geyla Frank
   1981   Lives: An Anthropological Approach to Biography. Novato, CA: Chandler and Sharp Publishers.
Leach, Edmund R.
   1961   Lévi-Strauss in the Garden of Eden: An Examination of Some Recent Developments in the Analysis of Myth. Transactions of the New York Academy of Sciences (Series 2) 23:386–396.
   1969   Genesis as Myth and Other Essays. London: Jonathan Cape.

Lévi-Strauss, Claude
  1967[1958] The Structural Study of Myth. *In* Structural Anthropology. C. Jacobson and B. Schoepf, transls. pp. 206–231. Garden City, NY: Anchor Books.
Levinson, Daniel
  1978 The Seasons of a Man's Life. New York: Knopf.
Marcus, Steven
  1974 Freud and Dora: Story History, Case History. Partisan Review 41:12–23, 89–108.
Peacock, James
  1968 Rites of Modernization: Symbolic and Social Aspects of Indonesian Proletarian Drama. Chicago: University of Chicago Press.
  1969 Society as Narrative. *In* Forms of Symbolic Action. 1969 Proceedings of the American Ethnological Society. June Helm, ed. pp. 167–177. Seattle: University of Washington Press.
Ricoeur, Paul
  1979 The Rule of Metaphor. Toronto: University of Toronto Press.
  1981 Hermeneutics and the Human Sciences. John B. Thompson, ed. and transl. Cambridge: Cambridge University Press.
  1982a Narrative and Hermeneutics. Ms. Files of the author.
  1982b Mimesis and Representation. Ms. Files of the author.
Sahlins, Marshall
  1981 History as Myth. Ann Arbor: University of Michigan Press.
Salam, Solichin
  1962 K. H. A. Dahlan, Amal dan Perdjoanganja, Riwajat Hidup. Yogyakarta: Pimpinan Pusat Muhammadijah.
Taylor, J. M.
  1978 Eva Peron: The Myths of a Woman. Chicago: University of Chicago Press.
Weber, Max
  1978 Economy and Society. Berkeley: University of California Press.

5

The Origins of Fiction and
the Fictions of Origin

Brian Sutton-Smith
University of Pennsylvania

The interpretive turn in social science, which seeks to make human meaning the central focus of scholarly endeavors rather than, or as well as, lawfulness and predictability (Bernstein 1978; Gadamer 1982; Habermas 1983), has increasingly turned toward uniquely human institutions such as drama, games, and narratives as "metaphors" for its own systems of cultural interpretation (Geertz 1973). In this paper the focus is in general on the use of "narrative" as an interpretive metaphor and in particular on the way in which children in our own culture acquire the power of narrating. If, as has been said, the mind is by nature a narrative happening (Schafer 1981; Foulkes 1982), then any inquiry into the origins of narrative in childhood should serve to test this assumption and should illuminate our social science use of narrative metaphors for cultural interpretation.

The Genesis of Narrative Structures

The first and skeptical question to be asked of this paper and of me is whether my analyses of how children create stories can be of any value in understanding some of the uses of narrative as a social science metaphor. Most of what is written here is based on samples of stories elicited from Anglo-American children, who by and large no longer tell stories as a part of their spontaneous lore, having been disfranchised by literacy from that kind of oral tradition—although obscenities and rhymes and jokes still flourish among them. The full account of sources can be found in *The Folkstories of Children* (Sutton-Smith 1981a).

Naturally, I began my own studies with no such skepticism in mind and proceeded early to the kinds of plot analysis that have dominated the parsimonies of psychologists in this field over the past decade (see Winner 1982). Borrowing from Köngäs Maranda and Maranda (1970), who in turn had borrowed from Lévi-Strauss, my colleagues and I were able to show various stages in which conflicts are only stated (under five year olds), to those in which there is some reaction that fails (seven year olds), to those in which the threat of villainy is nullified (nine year olds), to those in which the original situation is completely transformed (eleven year olds). What we had achieved for the genre of hero narratives, we thought, was the kind of Piagetian sequence that takes you from some infant state to some adult state while showing how the early precursors of plot become transformed into later-stage more complex and profound operations (Botvin and Sutton-Smith 1977).

While it is not unsatisfying to discover some such paleolithic to neolithic transformation in one's data, with hindsight one realizes that he has fallen into that pallid latter-day "evolutionism" that dominates most current developmental psychology. Throughout that discipline, adult stages are privileged, in much the same way as complex civilizations have been privileged through the history of culture evolution studies. Thus, there is seldom any question that it is preferable to be at the adult stage than at the infant or childhood stages of almost anything that is studied. It is better to be capable of formal operations (after Piaget), compassionate morality (after Kohlberg), personal integrity (after Erikson), and even self-actualization (after Maslow), than to be fixated at the early stages of these phenomena. It is not far-fetched, however, to suggest that this conclusion is a scholarly vestige of earlier evolutionism and that developmental psychologists, despite their useful work in tracing developments that occur normatively within our own culture, are beset by such an unexamined anthropological presupposition. In short, they have themselves swallowed the Western hero tale and unwittingly hailed the child who proceeds appropriately and speedily through their own accounts of child development into a hero with formal operations, compassion, integrity, and self-actualization. This might not be quite as good as getting the fairy princess, but it is not far off.

Let us now look at two of the best stories from *The Folkstories of Children* and reevaluate what we are about here.

1. Once upon a time there was a monster named King of Beasts and King of Beasts went out for a walk
   he walked for a hundred and two years and he died
   his bones said "wake up, wake up"
   and then his bones died and then his spirit said "wake up, wake up"
   to his bones

the house became haunted
and then a person went in and the person got scared away and
   his brother bit the body part
his brother died
and then the other brother died in the same house
and then the same thing happened
and then often the same thing happened the same thing happened
   to both of them again and they were really dreaming that
   they died
after they woke up they really died
and then the skeleton said "wake up, wake up" and the spirit
   said "wake up, wake up" to the skeleton
the end

[Sutton-Smith 1981:112–113]

2. *Chapter 1:* Mr. Hoot and the Married Lady
One night Mr. Hoot was sitting in his house thinking why he
never had any fun. He said to himself, "Maybe I'm too shy." So
he said to himself again that he was going to go out and get into
mischief. He got on his coat and put on his contact lenses and he
was off. There he was strolling from bar to bar. At his fifth bar,
he decided to have a drink. He pounded on the table and said two
martinis on the rocks. While he was waiting for his two drinks, he
took off his shoes and socks and picked his feet. Then he got his
drinks and chug-a-lugged them down the hatch. After his drinks,
he saw a beautiful lady in the corner of the bar. So he went over to
her and said, "Can I buy you a drink?" She replied, "No, thank
you. I'm not finished with this one." Then she said, "Anyway,
please sit down and we will talk."
   A big guy walking out the men's room came over to Mr.
Hoot and said, "Are you fooling with my wife? How dare you,"
and picked Mr. Hoot up and threw him on the ground. The moral
of the story is—you can't tell a married lady from a single lady.

Chapter 2: Mr. Hoot and the Stewardess
Once Mr. Hoot was sitting in the bar with his friend Bobby the
Baboon. They were discussing going to Hollywood. Mr. Hoot
said to Bobby, "Let's go next week." So they made all the arrangements and before they knew it they were on the airplane going to Hollywood. While they were on the airplane, Mr. Hoot saw
this very attractive stewardess. So Mr. Hoot called her over and
said, "Hi, what's your name?" She said, "Laura Sinch, what's
yours?" "Harold Hoot," he said. Then he said, "How long have
you been working for the airlines?" She replied. "Two years and

seven months.'' Then they started talking about where they lived and other things like that. Then a little baboon said, "Hey, would you stop it with the lady and let her do what she's supposed to be doing.'' Then Harold got mad and said, "Shut up, you little baboon.'' Then Bobby said "Hey, are you sounding on my kind? How dare you.'' "Oh, Bobby, butt out of this,'' Harold replied. Then the little baboon said, "Shut up, you overgrown owl.'' Then they really started at it. They were throwing pillows and suitcases at each other and cursing at each other. Then Harold gave him a good sock in the face and that was the end of the adventure.

Chapter 3: Mr. Hoot Gets Married
Once Harold was sitting in a restaurant at a table all by himself. Then he noticed there was a female owl sitting down by herself. Mischievously he walked over and asked her what her name was. She said, "Mary Gline.'' Then Harold thought for a moment and said, "Are you the girl that broke her wing when you were nine years old?'' Then she said, "What's your name and how did you know about my wing?'' "Well,'' said Harold, "I knew about your wing because your name sounded very familiar so I thought back to my childhood and remembered a girl named Mary broke her wing, and my name is Harold Hoot.'' Then she said, "You were the kid they called Hoot the Toot.'' "Oh yeah,'' Harold replied. "I forgot about that.'' Then they started to talk about their childhood and ate dinner together. After that night they went out to dinner, to movies and did lots of other things like that. After about a year, they told their parents they were going to get married. Their parents agreed and they had a wedding. They had the most beautiful wedding you can imagine. Then after that they settled down in a nice house in Poughkeepsie and had boys named Bobby and Peter. Last and not least, they lived happily ever after.

[Sutton-Smith and Sutton-Smith 1974:208–210]

If you pay attention only to plot structure in these two stories, what you see from one to the next is a clear improvement both in framing and plot structure. The first story (by a four year old) has no resolution; the last story (by a ten year old) has a clear resolution, as well as subplots and chapter frames. But is the last story really a "better" story? Isn't that really like saying that the structured, satirical drolleries of Pieter Bruegel are better than the looser, mordant fantasies of Hieronymus Bosch—and wouldn't that be a rather pointless statement? We know that in general younger children's stories have more poetry in them, just as their artwork has more free form and vivid color contrasts. And there is also the question of genre.

We assume that the hero story is the story to be discussed, but there are other genres. The first story (example 1) is a monster story; and younger children find their greatest excitement and storytelling skill in those (Rubin and Gardner 1977). It has been shown likewise that if the trickster stories are taken from this corpus, the earlier, under-seven-year-old ones are actually as remarkable as the later ones (Abrams and Sutton-Smith 1977), and the same is true of the "fucker" genre (Sutton-Smith and Abrams 1978).

Consider, for example, the two stages in the following trickster tale told by the same child over a period of several years. In the first the trickster loses and in the second the trickster wins. Is the latter therefore "better"?

3. Once there was two babies and they hung from the ceiling naked and their weenies was so long their mother needed 300 and 20 rooms to fit half of it in. But they had to chop half of it off. And the baby had to go to the bathroom. So, since they didn't have no bathroom big enough for his weener to fit, so he put his weener out of the window and Nixon happened to be walking along. And he said, "Flying hotdogs, I never heard of it." And then he said, "Well, I might have one, it looks good." So the baby had to go to the bathroom and Nixon took a BIG BITE. And there was a trampoline, because he was in the circus, and he went through the ceiling. And then by accident he went so fast and he was holding on to the weener so hard that he went straight smack into the middle of the ocean. And then—all of a sudden—he saw a giant sea spider. And his hair standed straight up. And the baby was coming so fast he landed on Nixon's head and made the long straight-up hair into bushy curls. And then he went, "I'm going to get out of here real quick, man." And um, and then the baby saw this giant anchor and he was holding onto it. And he stretched the baby's weener so far that it was four thousand times the size it was. The end.

[Sutton-Smith and Abrams 1978:532]

4. Once upon a time there were two babies. They loved, they hated spinach. So once their mother gave them a big pot of spinach, each with one fried egg on it. And they hated it *so much,* they threw it at their mother. She gave them another pot of spinach with *two* eggs on it this time and they were even madder and they threw it at their father this time. Then their mother gave them two pots of spinach with six fried eggs on it. They threw it at their sister. Then, when Nixon heard of this, he called them "The Fried Egg Family." But the baby was angry at Nixon. So when Nixon came to their house, they did nothing to him. But as he was walking out the door, the baby saw him and they stuck out their

weenies and then they put their weenies to work. And when Nixon saw these things, he flipped. But then, they pulled in their weener and put 2 buns on top of them and put some catsup and spinach and then Nixon got right back up and he started to bite. All of a sudden, the babies went pissing and shot their X-Y-Z. And Nixon was so upset he almost, his heart almost cracked. But then, they had more strategy.

So when he was walking over the mountain, they made flying hamburgers and then Nixon screamed, "We're being invaded by flying hamburgers!" And then the babies made flying hamburgers shoot out missile hotdogs and then Nixon had a very good idea! And he ate it—the hotdogs. But Nixon was so dumb, those hotdogs were solid metal and when he bit on them, they cracked his teeth and he was so upset. And then a lady came and said, "Will you help me across the street?" And Nixon said, "Whaaaaaaah." You are weird, Man," the lady said. And then the babies had little bit more strategy. They started shooting spinach with fried eggs on top. And then New York called Nixon "The Fried Egg President." That's all. The end.

[Sutton-Smith and Abrams 1978:534]

When it is realized that the first tale (example 3) is more like American Indian trickster tales of self-defeating clumsiness and obscenity and the second (example 4) is more like African trickster tales of cleverness (Abrahams 1968), is there much point in seeing these only in terms of the age differences of the storytellers and the plot complexity as modeled after the kinds of steps taken toward resolution that characterize the Western hero tale? Perhaps the time has arrived for psychologists to concede that cultural relativity applies to children as well as to the peoples of the globe. Younger children under the age of seven are not simply "preoperational" or the "last primitives." They live, perhaps, in their own Dionysian universe, but that should not be obscured by Western adult Apollonian needs to socialize them into more public-technical norms and to think of them dominantly in terms of their cognitive maturity.

Elsewhere, Shirley Heath and I have argued that similar injustices are done when one applies cross-culturally a one-genre concept of narrative as a standard (Sutton-Smith and Heath 1981). For some peoples, the major line of narrative development is in personal narrative and personal fictions; for others, it is in fictional narrative. Because fictional narratives are the dominant Western form, we tend to downgrade other forms that do not show this kind of fictional "imagination." What I am discussing here shows that when we go to the origin of children's stories in our own culture to discover implicit assumptions for our own metaphoric use of narrative, we find paradoxically that the interpretations of that childhood domain already tend to be conceptualized in a unidimensional way in terms of the Western hero narrative.

Child psychology, or developmental psychology, is itself cast within a hero paradigm, and one must struggle beyond it to see that other material exists there, which the above stories exhibit and which permit quite other sorts of narrative. As Bruner (in press) shows so cogently of the changing American historical views of Indians, unless we are careful we are caught in the circularity of our own stories and cannot even see there are yet other possible stories. We know that the description of young childhood as a subculture of its own with a more starkly Freudian or Boschian or Dionysian view of the universe, and as a series of emergent crises without resolution, without internal locus of control, and without the view that persistence and need achievement are virtues, is something that certainly makes adults uncomfortable. Yet these fictions may be as appropriate a source of narrative as those we usually choose. Gilgamesh, of the original Mesopotamian hero myth, was only a success in the earlier stages of his saga. In the later stages, as he faced his own mortality despite his struggle for immortality, there was finally nothing he could do to stop his own death. Young children tend to tell stories in which there are crises but there is nothing they can do about them. And while that typically Third World view is often abhorrent to the Western ear, it also has its wisdom.

The lesson to be learned from children's stories in general, however, is that they do not contain simply one kind of plot, nor are they of one genre. If one makes the argument in social science, as some have, that the mind occurs in a narrative form or that culture is best interpreted in narrative form, it is important to realize that the structure and character of that narrative form is not automatically deriveable from some universal childhood experience. Childhood permits the derivation of a number of kinds of narrative forms, only two of which are sketched here. Childhood is not a safe and self-evident source for our narrative metaphors. As the case of developmental psychology shows, these metaphors tend to be imposed on childhood rather than derived from it.

Three Ethnographic Studies of Children's Narrative

My earlier narrative studies, and those of others, were carried out within a largely "structural" frame of mind and implicitly assumed the existence of the same kind of normative developmental laws that are criticized above. It is not that such evolving structures cannot be found among certain samples of children but that the expectation of finding such structures, explicitly justified in terms of normative natural science, is implicitly based on a hero narrative view of modern society. As natural science, there is some worth to saying that as children develop in this group they will do A before B and B before C and C before D. This is a predictive statement, of some use to those who read stories to children of particular ages and teach them how to write stories. To realize, however, that this is not simply a "science" but a Western prejudice in favor of resolved endings is to see that the science in this case is a vehicle of a certain myth. That myth, in turn, has disadvantages (as well as advantages) because it tends to give a lower value to the more elementary forms of plot analysis. It makes the main point that they are more "primitive" and neglects a whole variety of other virtues they may have.

Subsequent to my structural studies, and very much under the influence of the ethnographic tradition of the Graduate School of Education at the University of Pennsylvania (Dell Hymes as dean), I turned toward studies that were concerned more specifically with the uses and origins of narrative in the lives of particular children. All of these were further attempts to discover how "natural" was the functioning of narrative in childhood, as it worked out, in particular well-described cases. To what extent was narrative an inherent quality of the child's mind?

The first of these studies, carried out on her own initiative by Diana Kelly-Byrne (1982), was a year-long study of a seven-year-old girl's use of narrative in her spontaneous play. To the best of my knowledge, Kelly-Byrne undertook the first systematic scholarly study of adult-child play in which the major aim of the adult was to be a playmate and support the child in whatever direction he or she wished to proceed. While this kind of coparticipation is hinted at in child play therapy (Erikson 1951; Axeline 1954), it has never been carried out with any duration and with freedom from the usual psychodynamic paradigms of interpretation.

Given that children's play is their most spontaneous and persistent medium of activity, it is possible to ask of Kelly-Byrne's data (some 50 hours of play activity during 14 sessions over 12 months), to what extent this play was guided by narrative concerns. The answer is very clear. In the first third of their play sessions, narrative exercised at best a schematic control over events, that is, there was some minor narrative discussion of the events that would follow. Most of the content of these early sessions occurred in the midst of dramatic enactments. This finding is very much in accord with an emerging literature on the play of the very young (which also shows that in the first several years of life the most constant framing device is itself a play gesture, or play transformation (Corsaro 1979; Goncu and Kessel 1983). By exaggerating an action, by making iconic sounds (e.g., automobiles), one child immediately signals a play episode to another and is usually imitated by the other, thus confirming the existence of the separate frame. Even when narrative was well known by this child (she was well read and well acquainted with Greek and Biblical myths), she did not use it as her most spontaneous device for the control of her symbolic actions.

In the second third of their year together, the child devoted herself to the endless telling of the anticipatory narrative of that play in which she was about to be engaged but which seldom actually happened. In other words, narrative had become the event in itself, an outcome very much affected by the child's awareness of and delight in performing before the tape recorder. In the earliest stages she had wanted to have only the play tape recorded, not the narrative and stage-setting anticipation of the play. The child introduced yet another shift during the last third of their year together. She was no longer centrally concerned with narrative but was more concerned with using the sessions for a direct discussion of the problems of her own life and her relationships to her parents, to her own growth, to boy friends, and so on. Thus, in her guidance of symbolic action in these sessions, play had given way to narrative, which in turn had given way to intimate dialogue.

Far from concluding that narrative was the major way in which the child formed and framed her deepest concerns, we must say it was only one of her genres. In fact, looking at her control of the total situation, it is possible to see it as Victor Turner (1974) might, as a miniature social drama in which conflicts about growth and conflicts with her parents became acted, narrated, and conversed in the liminoid area of her play with the investigator, who then became her closest friend and, as such, a real-life substitute for her mother—a person to whom the child could divulge and express feelings not permissible within the primary group; a person who gradually became a real-life agent, removing the need for liminoid indirections. In this case, both play and narrative were masks for other, more intimate concerns (Sutton-Smith and Kelly Byrne 1983). But the total situation could also be conceptualized as a series of self-presentations used by the child to control the ongoing events (Goffman 1959). The child insisted on playing only in her own private space, the bedroom; on always being the most powerful actor; on putting the investigator through a series of initiations (mainly, expecting her to imitate play acts and secret languages). In the beginning, she also imposed on the investigator the interdiction that there would be no discussion of her private dreams, secrets, secret languages, or superheroes (Kelly-Byrne 1983). What actually happened, however, was a ludic display of her dreams, secrets, secret languages, and superheroes, a kind of Batesonian paradox in which what was first forbidden in reality was made manifest in play; that is, meaning the opposite of what you say (the interdiction) by saying the opposite of what you mean (let's share my dreams). What all of this adds up to is that at least by seven years of age this child was using "blurred genres" (Geertz 1980), just as much as social scientists do.

The second study, by Ellen Brooks (1981), followed a group of mentally retarded seven to ten year olds with audio and video tape recording during a year in which every endeavor was made to teach them how to tell stories. What was remarkable about this group (each with a mental age of four to six years) was that in the beginning they had no storytelling competence at all. Their initial narratives, as they emerged like those of most two and three year olds, were personal narratives about daily events rather than fictional narratives. That is, their first narratives were "scripts." Their first attempts at portraying fictional stories, however, were through playful enactment, as in the case of Kelly-Byrne's study. Somewhat later, there were the retellings of tales already told to them, though only partially recaptured. But perhaps most remarkable about this group were the tales they sometimes created with elaborate framing devices. This is remarkable because in other records of much younger, two-year-old children, stories usually appear prior to the emergence of verbal-centered framing devices ("once upon a time," etc.). Here we find an example of one story wherein the major preoccupation is with framing and another wherein fictional and personal narratives are mixed together.

> 5. This story is called about Cinderella
>   Pictures by Jimmy
>   Pictures by Paddy
>   Once upon a time there was a little girl called Cinderella
>   Once upon a time there was a nice little girl called Cinderella
>   By Timmy
>   The End.
>
> [Brooks 1981:83]

> 6. Once upon a time
>   I go kill robbers
>   And I kill them
>   And I put them in jail
>   And I put them in the truck
>   I kill the bad robbers
>   I kill the bees
>   And I went to the dentist yesterday
>   My name is Jimmy
>   1979.
>
> [Brooks 1981:83]

This account emphasizes the wide variability in the acquisition of narrative. Given that such variability also exists in the acquisition of the more basic and underlying communication device of language, this outcome should perhaps not be surprising. It is only surprising if one holds fairly universalistic or innate notions of the structure of narrative, as some do (Winner 1982:271–272).

The third study, with Mary Ann Magee, drives this same point home even more subtly (Magee and Sutton-Smith 1983). In this case, a year-long effort was made to record storytelling time in the home of a 23 month old. Some 28 sessions were recorded, the longest including about 37 minutes of narrative discourse, and the shortest about 1 minute. Using a 50-category system, a factor analysis of adult and child responses yielded some 20 factors covering 75 percent of the variance, 8 for the adults and 12 for the child. The parents took up approximately 75 percent of the talking time. Unlike the one other similarly documented case in the literature, that of a British child (Ninio and Bruner 1976), this child was much more wildly and enactively participatory from the very beginning, her largest category of response being playful enactments. This nicely replicates the finding in the other two studies discussed above. More importantly for our present purposes is that each kind of adult storyteller (father, mother, investigator) and each kind of genre of telling (picture book, story, personal narratives, made-up stories) lead to a different grouping of adult and child responses.

The intricacy of context and text interactions is emphasized by these findings, which to the best of my knowledge involve the most detailed analysis of a series of narrative encounters in the child development literature. In the case now under discussion, the father was more authoritarian but the child's response to him was more emotional and playful; the mother

Table 1

Variation in Adult and Child Response as a Function
of Narrator, Expressed as Correlations

Adult Behavior		Child Behavior	
Father as narrator			
Reversal of roles	(−.47)	Reverses roles	(−.35)
Repetitions	(−.34)	Ask questions	(.34)
Length of session	(−.33)	Laughter at text	(.32)
Affective responses	(.29)	Nonsense	(.32)
Dramatizing text	(.29)	Anticipates	(.31)
Mother as narrator			
Cotelling	(−.29)	Laughter at text	(−.43)
Reversal of role	(.29)	Anticipates	(−.42)
Terminal framing	(.27)	Intense affect	(−.35)
Questions on what child has said	(.25)	Exclamatory response	(−.34)
Teacher as narrator			
Questions on text	(.39)	Enacts characters or actions	
Volunteered explanations	(.36)	from text	(.41)
		Assumes regular storyteller	
		role	(.33)

Table 2
Variation in Child Response as a Function
of Genre, Expressed as Correlations

Picture books shown by adult	
Emotional responses	(.56)
Playful transformations	(.48)
Invents emotions suggested by pictures	(.41)
Story books read by adult	
Answers to questions	(.38)
Becomes own storyteller	(−.40)
Made-up story by adult	
Becomes storyteller with character impersonations	(.53)
Tells story of own	(.40)
Contributes to story role with parent	(.36)
Personal narrative by adult	
Child tells own personal narrative	(.66)
Talks out of context	(.33)

was more educational but the emotional level was more neutral. In addition, each kind of genre tended to evoke differential child reactions, usually modeled after the parents' role. The child was more playful with the picture book probably because that was her oldest narrative vehicle and the easiest for her. She was more attentive to story reading, which was always more novel for her, and she herself became a storyteller or personal narrator after the parent did either of those things.

By the end of the study year, when the child was almost three years old, we were able to detect that she herself had made up a recognizable story of her own (Magee and Sutton-Smith 1983:4). After thousands of repetitions by the parent and thousands of imitations and transformations of pieces of their activity by the child, she finally was capable of staging her own storytelling event. Her parents had assiduously framed it for her, and at last she was able to capture the appropriate frame and form. But if this study is representative (and here my colleague and I concur with Ninio and Bruner 1976), there is nothing very innate about any of this. The learning activity was exhaustive and the form of response quite variable. For example, this child's first own original story was about biting others, an activity for which she had gotten into trouble at nursery school. It was not a story ever read to her by her parents but was a projection of her own deep emotions onto the stage that they had so carefully scaffolded for her throughout this year. This finding sustains the view derived from our earlier normative work (Sutton-Smith 1981a) that the first forms of narrative originated by young children tend to be concerned with what they feel are crises. Fictional narratives are in the first place about "something *critical* that happened," to paraphrase and extend B. H. Smith (1980). It is what presumably gives the child's word some of its nightmarish quality.

It seems a fair conclusion to this study of both normative and ethnographic work with children's stories that there is no given, innate, or universal narrative form in childhood from which we might implicitly derive a "structure" for use in social science interpretation. Children take a considerable time to acquire the narrative forms of their own culture, and these forms themselves are quite variable. Furthermore, having acquired the forms, they become only one part of the way in which children make their own lives meaningful, their play being a more central expressive genre for them.

Narrative Reflexivity

When we become involved with the use of narrative metaphors for social science interpretation, there must always follow, as further instances of reflective narrative self-consciousness, the issue of the way in which we make a narrative report of our concerns. (Kelly-Byrne and Sutton-Smith in press) and the way in which our own biographical narrative enters into and inflects that report (Ruby 1982). For example, in this paper a story is told about a series of structural and ethnographic studies in order to convince the reader that childhood cannot be used as a simplistic or automatic source of any narrative paradigms we might wish to generate for social science interpretations. Its conclusion is clearly that from a genetic epistemological point of view, the mind does not begin as a text—or at the very least, not as the kind of hero text that we find very comfortable in Western civilization. This does not, of course, prevent the social scientist from arguing that culture is a text to be interpreted. That may well be the case, although I indicate here a preference for blurred genres.

Again, although it is difficult to ever be sure of the extent or the manner in which one's own biographical story enters into presentations, it is perhaps worth reporting that my present involvement in narrative and my skepticism toward narrative contentions have clear origins in my life and works. The "story" reported here is founded on lifelong biographical themes. It was my childhood experience to have a raconteur father (who had had a raconteur father) who nightly told bedtime stories to my brother and me in a vivid and histrionic manner. My father was a participant in local amateur theater companies and good at storying. Unfortunately for him, and perhaps for me, when he left the room my brother, who was four years my senior and rebellious in nature, would then parody those same well-told stories in obscene and violent terms. I grew up, it seems, both with a belief in the relevance of storying and in its destruction. My own novels written for children (Sutton-Smith 1975a [1950], 1975b [1961], 1976) were both lauded as "realistic" accounts of New Zealand child life and abominated as teaching immorality to children; they were considered in the New Zealand Parliament, at one stage, as being connected with the decay of modern civilization, or at least that part of it induced by the other parliamentary party (Gilderdale 1982). The parallel between my enthusiasm for stories and my antithetical attitude toward them is to be found also in my work on play and games as order and disorder (Sutton-Smith 1978a), as caricature (Sutton-Smith 1978b), as cruel play (Sutton-Smith 1981b), and as masks of play (Sutton-Smith and Kelly-Byrne 1983), throughout which I treat play as a dialectical phenomenon (Sutton-Smith 1978a).

In sum, it is not hard to make a case that my own biographical narrative has played a heavy hand in the direction of the present analysis and its conclusions, slanting the analysis toward the appreciation of the nonnormative aspects of this segment of cultural expression. It is a part of modern interpretive science to recognize that personal influence by the interpreter is an inevitable part of the "interpretations"; that biographical narrative and narrative documentation become intertwined and are an inevitable part of one's science. With sufficient effort at self-consciousness and continued reinterpretation by others, it should become possible for the biographical posture to be sorted out, the hidden agendas to become explicit and kept in mind during the presentation of the report. The report is not invalidated by such self-consciousness: it is simply given one more layer of significance. With many such layers there develops both an increasing consensus and a laminated variety that contributes to our sense that what has been placed before us is indeed the way in which things happen, at least from one perspective.

The final argument of this article, therefore, is that the epistemology of a narrative account of culture requires us to look over the shoulder of the narrator and know something about his own chosen genres as well as about those he lays before us. In this interpretation, a narrative account of culture relies very much on a narrative account of the narrator. When culture is seen as a text or a set of blurred genres, we must also know the genetic narrative epistemology of the reader. The origins of fiction and the fictions of origin are of the same cloth.

References Cited

Abrahams, R. D.
  1968   Trickster, the Outrageous Hero. American Folklore 81:196–199.
Abrams, D. M., and B. Sutton-Smith
  1977   The Development of the Trickster in Children's Narratives. Journal of American Folklore 90:29–47.
Axeline, V. M.
  1954   Dibs in Search of Self. New York: Ballantine.
Bernstein, R. J.
  1978   The Restructuring of Social and Political Theory. Philadelphia: University of Pennsylvania.

Botvin, G. J., and B. Sutton-Smith
1977   The Development of Structural Complexity in Children's Fantasy Narratives. Developmental Psychology 13:377–388.
Brooks, E.
1981   A Description of the Development of Story Telling Competence in Educable Mentally Retarded Children, Ages 7–10. Ph.D. dissertation. Graduate School of Education, University of Pennsylvania.
Bruner, E. M.
in press   Ethnography as Narrative. *In* The Anthropology of Experience. V. Turner and E. M. Bruner, eds. Urbana: University of Illinois Press.
Corsaro, W.
1979   "We're Friends, Right?" Children's Use of Access Rituals in Nursery School. Language in Society 8:315–336.
Erikson, E.
1951   Childhood and Society. New York: Norton.
Foulkes, D.
1982   Children's Dreams: Longitudinal Studies. New York: John Wiley and Sons.
Gadamer, Hans-George
1982   Text and Interpretation. Paper presented at the conference on the Philosophy of Human Studies, Philadelphia.
Geertz, C.
1973   The Interpretation of Cultures. New York: Basic Books.
1980   Blurred Genres: The Refiguration of Social Thought. The American Scholar, Spring:165–179.
Gilderdale, B.
1982   A Sea Change: 145 Years of New Zealand Junior Fiction. Auckland, NZ: Longman Paul.
Goffman, E.
1959   The Presentation of Self in Everyday Life. New York: Doubleday.
Goncu, A., and F. Kessel
1983   "Are We Pretending?" An Observational Study of Imaginative Play Communications. Paper presented at the annual meeting of the A.E.R.A., 12 April, Montreal.
Habermas, J.
1983   Hermeneutics and Critical Theory. Paper presented at the conference on the Philosophy of Human Studies, Philadelphia.
Kelly-Byrne, D.
1982   A Narrative of Play and Intimacy: A Seven Year Old's Play and Story Relationship with an Adult. Ph.D. dissertation. Graduate School of Education, University of Pennsylvania.
1983   A Narrative of Play and Intimacy. *In* The World of Play. F. E. Manning, ed. pp. 160–169. West Point, NY: Leisure Press.
Kelly-Byrne, D., and B. Sutton-Smith
in press   Narrative as Social Science. The Quarterly Newsletter of the Laboratory of Comparative Human Cognition.
Köngäs Maranda, Elli K., and P. Maranda
1970   Structural Models in Folklore and Transformational Essays. The Hague: Mouton.

Magee, M. A., and B. Sutton-Smith
  1983 The Art of Storytelling: How Do Children Learn It? Young Children
        38:4–12.
Ninio, A., and J. Bruner
  1976 The Achievement and Antecedents of Labelling. Journal of Child Lan-
        guage 5:1–15.
Rubin, S., and H. Gardner
  1977 Once upon a Time: The Development of Sensitivity to Story Structure.
        Ms. Project Zero, Graduate School of Education, Harvard University.
Ruby, J., ed.
  1982 A Crack in the Mirror: Reflexive Perspectives in Anthropology. Philadel-
        phia: University of Pennsylvania Press.
Schafer, R.
  1981 Narrative Actions in Psychoanalysis. Worcester, MA: Clark University
        Press.
Smith, B. H.
  1980 Narrative Versions, Narrative Theories. *In* On Narrative. W. J. T.
        Mitchell, ed. pp. 209–232. Chicago: University of Chicago Press.
Sutton-Smith, B.
  1975a[1950] Our Street. New Zealand: Price-Milburn.
  1975b[1961] Smitty Does a Bunk. New Zealand: Price-Milburn.
  1976 The Cobbers. New Zealand: Price-Milburn.
  1978a Die Dialektik des Spiels. Schorndorf: Verlag Karl Hoffman.
  1978b Initial Education as Caricature. Keystone Folklore 22:37–52.
  1981a The Folkstories of Children. Philadelphia: University of Pennsylvania
        Press.
  1981b A History of Children's Play. Philadelphia: University of Pennsylvania
        Press.
Sutton-Smith, B., and D. M. Abrams
  1978 Psychosexual Material in the Stories Told by Children: The Fucker.
        Archives of Sexual Behavior 7(6):521–543.
Sutton-Smith, B., and S. B. Heath
  1981 Paradigms of Pretense. The Quarterly Newsletter of the Laboratory of
        Comparative Human Cognition 3(3):41–45.
Sutton-Smith, B., and D. Kelly-Byrne
  1983 The Masks of Play. West Point, NY: Leisure Press.
Sutton-Smith, B., and S. Sutton-Smith
  1974 How to Play with Your Children. New York: Hawthorn Books.
Turner, V.
  1974 Dramas, Fields and Metaphors. Ithaca: Cornell University Press.
Winner, E.
  1982 Invented Worlds: The Psychology of the Arts. Cambridge: Harvard
        University Press.

II
Shaping the Text

6
Biography of a Sentence: A Burmese Proverb

A. L. Becker
University of Michigan, Ann Arbor

There are three kinds of mistakes: those resulting from lack of memory, from lack of planning ahead, or from misguided beliefs.

—Burmese proverb

I call this essay "Biography of a Sentence" in order to evoke Wittgenstein's way of thinking about language as a form of life, a mode of being in the world, and so to depart from an atomistic picture of language and meaning and to move toward a contextual one. In using language one shapes old words into new contexts—*jarwa dhosok,* the Javanese call it, pushing old language into the present. All language use is, in this sense, translation to some degree; and translation from one language to another is only the extreme case. I argue here that translation for the philologist—one who would guide us across the terra incognita between distant languages—is not the final goal but only a first step, a necessary first step, in understanding a distant text; necessary because it opens up for us the exuberancies and deficiencies of our own interpretations and so helps us see what kinds of self-correction must be made. And so the goal of this essay is to begin with a Burmese proverb, a simple sentence, a minimal text, and to move step by step from a translation (provided by a bilingual Burmese) closer to the original. Each step is a correction of an exuberance or a deficiency of meaning as presented to us in the English translation.

In moving from an atomistic mode of interpretation to a more contextual one, new kinds of questions appear just as old ones lose their force. One asks not how some phenomenon is built up in a rule-governed way out of minimal bits but rather in what ways context constrains particular language—real text (i.e., remembered or preserved language). There are many ways to answer that question, depending on how one defines context. One way to see context is as sources of constraints on text. Linguists and language philosophers could agree on five or six sources of constraints, although they would group and name them differently, I suspect. Let me for present purposes identify these six kinds of contextual relations, none of which seems to me to be reducible to another:

1. *structural relations,* relations of parts to wholes;
2. *generic relations,* relations of text to prior text;
3. *medial relations,* relations of text to medium;
4. *interpersonal relations,* relations of text to participants in a text-act;
5. *referential relations,* relations of a text to Nature, the world one believes to lie beyond language;
6. *silential relations,* relations of a text to the unsaid and the unsayable.

There is nothing particularly original about these six, and there has been a great deal of work on each, except perhaps the last one. Together they define context. A text is the interaction of the constraints they provide.

The terms have one great weakness: they are all too categorial—too "nouny," too liberally neutral. As Kenneth Burke might say, their "improvisational" quality is weak. The life of a text is in the weighting and balancing and counterbalancing of the terms and figures and in the conceptual dramas they evoke. To transcend these neutral terms, one can make them active—as a text strategy—and say that a text has meaning because it is structuring and remembering and sounding and interacting and referring and not doing something else . . . all at once. The interaction of these *acts* is the basic drama of every sentence.

The sentence—simple or complex—is, in any language, the minimal unit in which all these actions are happening, in which the drama is fully staged. Only with sentences—and larger units—are there speakers and hearers and times and worlds; that is, particular speakers, particular hearers, particular times, and particular worlds. Paul Ricoeur (1981) calls sentences the "minimal units of discourse," the "minimal units of exchange." Jan Mukarovsky (1977:15) wrote of the sentence as "the component mediating between the language and the theme, the lowest dynamic (realized in time) semantic unit, a miniature model of the entire semantic structuring of the discourse."

Words and phrases are *staged* only as sentences. Much of our language about sentences overlaps with our language about drama, an iconicity we share with many other languages. That is, in both there are actors or agents, goals, undergoers, instruments, accompaniments, times, and settings—all bound into an act or state, or just plain *being,* and all shaped to a context in subtle ways. To see the drama of a sentence requires only a bit of contemplation: stepping back (as a friend puts it) to take a closer look. To hide that drama with neutral terms—what Burke (1964) calls "bureaucratizing" knowledge—is to lose the essential liveliness and excitement of that contemplation. And it is to miss the considerable aesthetic pleasure one gets in contemplating a text and seeing the drama of terms and figures unfold, a good deal of it at the level of sentences.

Not all sentences are whole texts in themselves. Most are parts of larger texts. Yet there are sentences free enough of lingual context to be treated as texts. Proverbs, perhaps, which are not really self-sufficient texts but rather small texts used to evaluate (give value to) new situations. They are recurrent evaluatory statements, part of whose job is to sound like proverbs, language in the public domain. Proverbs are a mode of sounding, referring, interacting, remembering, and shaping which are small enough to be discussable in an essay (a ratio of 1 sentence of text to 320 sentences of commentary, in this case). In larger texts, one is forced to sample.

Contemplating single sentences or very small texts brings one into the world of the grammarian, the world of delicate parsing. It thus brings one up against a very large, wildly ill-defined grammatical terminology: all the names for the categories, processes, and relations that grammarians talk about, often very intimidatingly. One can get the feeling that from grammar school to graduate school the prime use of grammar has been some variety of intimidation.

However, the *pleasures of the text* (one of the phrases Roland Barthes left us) are too important not to encourage people to enter as amateurs and to experience the whole of the journey to a distant text. There is a skill in parsing which a good linguist can be led to display on small persuasion, but it should be only inspiring to the amateur, not intimidating—like Billie Holiday's singing.

There are two basic ways to think about grammar (as a prelude to the contemplation of a small text). One view leads us to think of the field of study as a system of rules that somehow map abstract and a priori semantic categories and relations onto phonic substance—or in different terms, map a logical deep structure onto a surface structure. Language in this structural sense is "rule governed," and the task of the grammarian is to find the most economical, least "subjective" formulation of the rules. Theory is exclusively formal. In this view the computer is a natural metaphor for the language-processing mind. Grammars—or tiny fragments of unfinished grammars—tend to be written as rules accompanied by examples, illustrating problems of theory shaping (Geertz 1983:19).

There is another kind of grammar, based on a different perspective on language, one involving time and memory; or, in terms of contextual relations, a set of prior texts that one accumulates throughout one's lifetime, from simple social exchanges to long, semimemorized recitations. One learns these texts in action, by repetitions and corrections, starting with the simplest utterances of a baby. One learns to reshape these texts to new context, by imitation and by trial and error. One learns to interact with more and more people, in a greater and greater variety of environments. The different ways one shapes a prior text to a new environment make up the grammar of a language. Grammar is context-shaping (Bateson 1979:17) and context shaping is a skill we acquire over a lifetime. We learn it essentially by continual internal and external corrections, in response to change and lack of change in the environment. From the first point of view, constraints common to all languages tend to be structural (or logical); from the second, pragmatic (or rhetorical). What I call philology might also be called a rhetorically based linguistics.

The ways one shapes a text to new contexts include such operations as substitution of words or other larger or smaller lingual units, rearrangements, repetition, expansion, inflexion, and embedding. These are all things one can do with a word or a sentence or a larger text, all general strategies, which one learns to do more and more skillfully and which become (potentially) more and more complex. The problem with stating them all as rules is that the constraints on shaping are not entirely structural; and they are not a closed system but open to context. We are not so much compositors of sentences from bits as reshapers of prior texts (the self-evident a prioris of language). The modes of reshaping are in large part conventional, but also in some unpredictable part innovative and unpredictable—except for the most formulaic of utterances. Language interaction is not a closed system (i.e., rule-governed).

Even very formulaic utterances have interesting histories. The strange imperative greeting that has blossomed (along with the three-piece smiling face) in the currency of noetic exchange over the past few years in American English has been, "Have a nice day." The reader is invited to notice how many different shapings of that formula he or she encounters over the next few days. This morning, in good New Jersey accent, I got, "Have one, y'hear," from an exuberant gas station attendant. "I will," I answered, not knowing what I was saying. In all language, there are prior norms and present deviations going on constantly.

Proverbs tend to be slower changing than nonproverbs, since they are public language and not private language and depend on recognition as proverbs in order to work. But there are a whole range of things we recognize as proverbs—not just wise, comfortable ones, but also banal clichés and even original evaluations not yet fully in the public domain. Here are a few:

> He who hesitates is lost.
> Well, it takes all kinds. . . .
> Sometimes a man just has to stand up for his rights.
> We're all in it for the money.
> He leaped before he looked.

Here are some not yet in the public domain, perhaps never to be:

> Progress: that long steep path which leads to me.
> *Jean-Paul Sartre*

> Contextual shaping is only another term for grammar.
> *Gregory Bateson*

> Art and the equipment to grasp it are made in the same shop.
> *Clifford Geertz*

> Do not be overwhelmed by all that there is to know. It is a myth of the oppressor.
> *Kenneth Koch*

Public evaluatory sentences are of many sorts. One need only look through the *Oxford Dictionary of Proverbs* to see the great variety in even so small a sample. But the goal here is not to provide a classification scheme for proverbs (as Burke 1964:108 writes in his short essay on proverbs, "The range of possible academic classifications is endless"—a good and useful candidate for the public domain). They are sometimes "generic" sentences, in two senses: they are often marked by indefinite subjects and indefinite tense and thus meant to refer to a large class of phenomena; but they are also generic in the sense that they are quite overtly drawn from the past and help to identify a present text as belonging to a *genre,* a set of prior texts. They are meant to stand apart. Their power comes from one's recognition of them as shared public opinion, and one is not supposed to argue with them in situations that call for politeness. They are part of the credit of society on which one lives.

As prevailing opinions, public opinions are uttered differently than private opinions are. They need no support, since they do not depend on the adherence of individuals, and are not presented as hypotheses to be proved. They are there, to be reckoned with, as authoritative as law. We sometimes think of public opinion as a collection of private opinions (polls operate on this fallacy), rather than as a collection of evaluatory statements, there in the language—like proverbs—on which we are free to draw (Ortega y Gasset 1957:266). This collection is not identical for each of us and like much of language is broader in recognition than in use. The closer we are to people, in a communal sense, the more we share evaluations—and the less we seem willing to tolerate evaluatory differences.

There is a continuum of evaluatory utterances from those, like proverbs, which we share exactly (i.e., with identical wording) to those which we recognize as having some family resemblance with our own evaluatory stock sufficient to be accepted as equivalent or nearly so. For example, "He who hesitates is lost" is always said in just those words—even when referring to women. Here, context shaping is minimal, a matter only of one's voice, its qualities, pitches, and rhythms. By contrast, the cynical observation, "We're all in it for the money" is less frozen and more likely to be reshaped—softened or strengthened—each time it is used.

These small texts—proverbs, semiproverbs, and clichés—are a form of speaking the past. But uttering them—even with all the controls over rhythm, pitch, and voice quality that music can provide—is also to some extent speaking the present. They evoke a norm and to some degree, however small, deviate from it.

Utterances with a family resemblance to, for instance, the cliché "We're all in it for the money" include those utterances that can be seen to have a connection with it via substitution, rearrangement, repetition, expansion, inflexion, and/or embedding. As a figure, the cliché sets up points of substitution:

> We are all in it for the money.
> They were partly in it for the money.
> He was in it because of his interest.

The sentence is a frame for the substitution of words, affixes, phrases, and whole clauses—all the levels of lingual units.

Besides substitution, context shaping can involve rearrangement and the consequent readjustments, which contribute much of the complexity to syntax (Givón 1979:235ff.):

> It's the money that we're all in it for.
> Money is what we're all in it for.

Or expansion:

> We're all—you me and everyone—in it right now for the money we can get out of it.

Or repetition:

> We're all in it for the money . . . for the money.

Or inflexion:

> He's in it for the money.

Or the whole can be embedded:

> I don't believe that we're all in it for the money.
> Our all being in it for the money disturbs me.

(One can reduce these modes of context shaping by considering inflexion a structural type of substitution and by considering repetition and some embedding as types of expansion.) Mostly one uses combinations of these strategies to shape prior text into new contexts—and to recognize someone else's shaping.

The important thing here is not whether one can describe all the shapings that are possible, singly and in combination, and all the remedial strategies that they entail, in some formalism, but rather where family resemblance fades in the reshaping that keeps lingual strategies alive. Most people—our cousins and aunts—are not often aware of the extent to which one constantly reshapes old language into new contexts. The process is rapid, and only if there is a breakdown do we normally become conscious of it—when something doesn't *sound* right (under analysis, as Wittgenstein [1958] put it, language is on holiday).

The difference between looking at grammar as rules which map logical categories and relations onto a medium and looking at it as ways of reshaping old language to new contexts is, primarily, that in the first case one begins with a priori or "universal" categories as being common to all languages, while in the second case what is common are pragmatic or rhetorical situations—common features of the context—and what is a priori is prior text. To assume a universal logic seems to be to take very abstract representations of the categories and relations of Indoeuropean languages as inherent in all languages (see Benveniste 1971). One learns, of course, to confront all new experience in one's own language, including experience of another language. It is not difficult to assume that these categories and relations are "there" *in* the phenomena, a priori to language. However, it seems more conducive to cross-cultural understanding that one not assume an abstract realm of absolute categories and relations—some kind of extra-lingual logic—as a ground for all languages, but rather start in language, with actual remembered texts (however they are preserved). Recall Wittgenstein's (1958:114) caution: "One thinks that one is tracing the outline of the thing's nature over and over again, and one is merely tracing round the frame through which we look at it."

The meaning of a word, then, is not a combination of atomic categories and relations or underlying features or properties, but the past and present contexts it evokes. Then how do grammars and dictionaries of distant languages work? They work as abductions: one language in terms of another. A grammar of Burmese in English is an English version of certain aspects of Burmese—that is, those having English analogs. A Burmese grammar of English does not yet exist, except as a translation into Burmese of an English grammar of English; but if it did, it would be a Burmese interpretation of English in which, for instance, the simplicity of our numeral classifiers and verb particles might be noted. Grammars and dictionaries are as much cultural artifacts as newspapers or shadow plays.

In understanding a distant text, even for the writer of the most formal of grammars, there is an essential first step—a gloss or rough word-for-word translation. It is always present and is always meant to be invisible, like the invisible man, dressed in black, in the Japanese Noh drama, who moves props, adjusts costumes, and generally keeps things tidy on stage. The gloss, rather than the abstract representations of categories, features, and relations, is the underlying vehicle for understanding. The only mode that we have of understanding a distant text is first to jump to an interpretation, to guess (or have someone guess for us), and then to sort out the exuberancies and deficiencies of one's guess. One's own language is the initial model for another language, a metaphor of it (Pike and Pike 1977:69).

A philologist does well to be always self-conscious that his understanding of another language is initially metaphoric and not "pure" meaning. To do otherwise is to add to the exuberancy of thinking of logical categories as reified "things," the further exuberancy of assuming that they are the categories of one's own language. It is at this point that grammatical explanation becomes political: when we assume that there is one grammar for the Greek and the Barbarian—and it is Greek. To ask, for instance, what the passive is in Burmese is to assume (1) that "the passive" exists a priori to any language, and (2) that "it" has an English name or an English function in shaping context, whatever one calls it. To translate some Burmese clause as an English passive, however, is both necessary and reasonable.

A methodology for parsing should be a lightly held thing, as one confronts the distant text with it. When methodology and text conflict, it is the methodology that should give way first. In thise sense, one's discipline is the text. Methodologies come and go, but the discipline of the text and its language remain. Perhaps a particular experience can illuminate this point.

On arriving in Burma in 1958, I began to learn Burmese from a very kind and patient old teacher, U San Htwe. As I had been taught to do, I would ask him words for things and then write them down. He watched me writing for a while and then said, "That's not how you write it," and he wrote the word in Burmese script. For the word evoked by English "speak," I wrote /pyɔ/ and he wrote ၆ၐၢ ၁. I insisted it made no difference. He insisted it did and told me I was hurting his language. And so I began, somewhat reluctantly, to learn to write Burmese: /p—/ was a central ∪ , and /-y-/ wrapped around the ∪ to make ၐ and the vowel /၆—ၢ/ fit before and after it:၆ၐ ၁.

This difference in medial representation made a great difference, on at least two levels. For one thing, I could not segment the Burmese syllable into a linear sequence, as I could /pyɔ/, as one can see clearly by studying the two representations. But segmentation into linear sequence is a prerequisite for doing linguistics as most of us have been taught it: normally, sounds string together to make morphemes and words, and words string together to make phrases, and so on. We analyze strings, with analog phenomena relegated to super- or subsegmental status. To write my kind of grammar I had to violate his writing.

At first it seemed to me a small price to pay, to phonemicize his language. But over the years—particularly 20 years later, in Java and Bali—I learned how that kind of written figure (a center and marks above, below, before, and after it; the figure of the Burmese and Javanese and Balinese syllable) was for many Southeast Asians a mnemonic frame: everything in the encyclopedic repertoire of terms was ordered that way: directions (the compass rose), diseases, gods, colors, social roles, foods—everything (see Zurbuchen 1981:75ff.). It was the natural shape of remembered knowledge, a basic icon.

As Zurbuchen (1981) has shown us, this notion of the syllable is the ground even of the gods: it is evoked at the beginning of every Balinese shadow play. Even though the shadow play is taught and performed orally, it begins with an invocation of the written symbol as a source of power.

> Just as the boundaries of awareness become perceptible,
> There is perfect tranquility, undisturbed by any threat,
> And even the utterances of the gods subside.
> It is none other which forms the beginning of my obeisance to the Divine.
> Greatly may I be forgiven for my intention to call forth a story.
> And where dwells the story?
> There is a god unsupported by the divine mother earth,
> Unsheltered by the sky,

Unilluminated by the sun, moon, stars, or constellations.
Yes, Lord, you dwell in the void, and are situated thus:
You reside in a golden jewel,
Regaled on a golden palanquin,
Umbrellaed by a floating lotus.
There approached in audience by all the gods of the cardinal direc-
    tions. . . .

[1981:vi]

These last lines, after locating the written symbol outside of time and space, describe metaphorically the shaping of the written symbol as a focal point for natural order. Zurbuchen's (1981:vi–vii) translation continues, describing the implements of writing:

There, there are the young palm leaves, the one *lontar,*
Which, when taken and split apart, carefully measured are the
    lengths and widths.
It is this which is brought to life with *hasta, gangga, uwira, tanu.*
And what are the things so named?
Hasta means "hand"
Gangga means "water"
Uwira means "writing instrument"
Taru means "ink."
What is that which is called "ink"?
That is the name for
And none other than
The smoke of the oil lamp,
Collected on the bark of the kepuh-tree,
On a base of copper leaf.
It is these things which are gathered together
And given shape on leaf.
"Written symbol" is its name,
Of one substance and different soundings. . . .

The translation, which I have taken the liberty of arranging in lines (mainly to slow down the reader), goes on slowly to evolve the story from the written symbol.

My point, however, is not to explore this image further, or to retell Mary Zurbuchen's fascinating stories, but to try to understand why U San Htwe had insisted on my learning Burmese this way. I think it was that the traditional learning was organized around that shape, that it was a root metaphor (see Lakoff and Johnson 1980), the stuff that holds learning together—just as our sequential writing lines up so well with our sequential tense system or our notions of causality and history. That is a great deal to ask anyone to give up—the metaphoric power of his writing system. And I had tried to argue with that wise old man that it did not matter.

One of the most subtle forces of colonialism, ancient or modern, is the undermining of not just the substance but the framework of someone's learning. As Gregory Bateson put it, in his oft-quoted letter to the other regents of the University of California, "Break the pattern which connects the items of learning and you necessarily destroy all quality." I see now that what I had been suggesting to my teacher, though neither of us could articulate it, was that we break the pattern which connects the items of his learning. When methodology and language conflict, it is the methodology which should give way first.

The proverb that serves as an epigraph to this paper comes from a small book my teacher gave to me just before I left Burma in 1961, after studying with him for three years and mostly reading Burmese classics, after I had grasped a bit of the language. I read with a great deal of what Keats called "negative capability": Keats spoke of Shakespeare as one who was "capable of being in uncertainties, mysteries, doubts, without any irritable reaching after fact and reason" (quoted in Dewey 1934:33). I read with half-understanding the children's histories, poems, plays, chronicles, and *jataka* tales he brought me, and heard with half-understanding his commentaries and corrections of me. I taught English to children in the morning—funny, uninhibited Burmese children—and studied Burmese in the late afternoon, at twilight, at U San Htwe's house. Just before I left, he gave me a small notebook, a child's copybook with a picture of a mountain on the front, in which he had copied lists of sets: the two thises, five thats, and fifteen whatevers. I had asked him how I might continue studying Burmese without him and this book was his solution and gift. I stared at it for years, and with the help of a Burmese friend, U Thein Swe, began to understand some of it, much later.

In the book, written in U San Htwe's fine hand, are all classes of things, abstract as well as concrete, in this world and out of it—a syllabus for study. It begins with sets of twos and grows, as if paralleling the growing complexity of one's experience, to larger and larger sets. The initial sets are sometimes obvious, like the two parents and the two strengths (strength of arm and strength of heart), but are sometimes more exotic pairs like the two worlds (the zero world—in which Buddhas, monks, supernatural beings, and so on, do not appear, exist, or flourish—and the nonzero world—in which the above appear, exist, and flourish). The sets in my book continue to sets of eighteen. (I learned later that other lists go on to bigger sets and that my teacher may have censored a bit.) To understand the sets, he said, is to understand the world, both inner and outer, seen and unseen. They represent, taken together, a taxonomy of the phenomenal and noumenal universe of at least some traditional Burmese.

Each set is itself a kind of plot from a universal plot book, around which to build a discourse. For example, a sermon can be built around, say, the four cardinal virtues (love, attention, happiness, detachment), or a political speech around those three kinds of mistakes mentioned in the epigraph (resulting from lack of memory, from lack of planning ahead, or from misguided beliefs). Or a play might be constructed around some other appropriate set, perhaps the four false hopes (hoping to get rich by reading treasure maps, hoping to get healthy by reading medical literature, hoping for wisdom by following a learned man, and hoping for a girlfriend by dressing up). These sets are assumed a priori to any discourse as impersonal frames to which nature, both human and nonhuman, properly and appropriately corresponds. A true sermon, a wise foreign policy, or a well-constructed drama can be rooted in one or more of them. One can contemplate these sets with continual fascination and increasing insight, as one learns to see things in new ways. Like a good poem, a new set can defamiliarize one's world.

The proverb used as the epigraph to this paper appears in my copybook as in Figure 1. U San Htwe copied this from a manuscript book that one of his teachers had given to him. Similar books were common in traditional Buddhist monastic education. They were learned first then gradually understood over the years, like most things in traditional Southeast Asian education. Memory preceded understanding, an order practiced by few in our culture other than classical pianists. The closer one gets to nonliteracy

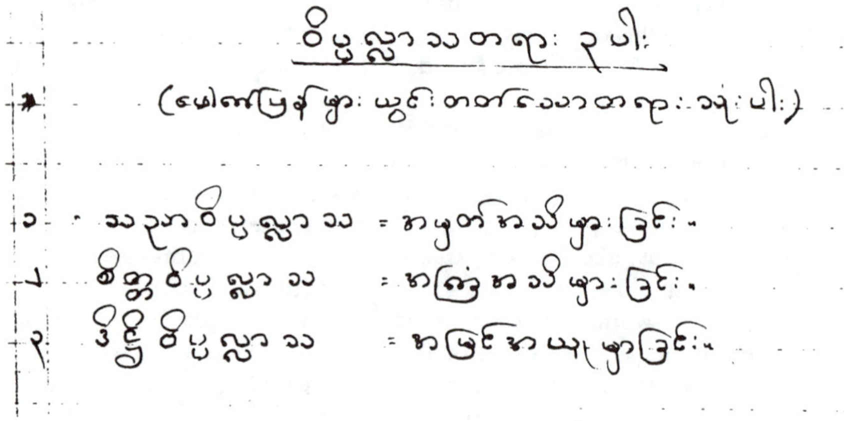

Figure 1.

(and a chirographic culture is, in this sense, less literate than a print culture), the more a student seems to be expected to *perform* the past like a classical pianist. Language classes in traditional schools were not so much the acquiring of a neutral tool as a set of prior texts, serious cultural wisdom.

Neither had writing come to Burma, as it never does anywhere, as a neutral tool. It had come with content: a religion, a calendar, and a new set of cultural prior texts in Pali, the language of Buddhism. The new writing was, first of all, access to those Pali texts, the real sources of knowledge. Only gradually did the local language begin to be written in the new writing, at first only for translation. Later, this translation language—far from the language acts and strategies of everyday discourse (the vernacular)—began to be used for creating local texts and replacing individual memory. Very much later, some bold innovator began to write the vernacular. In a very general way, that is what happened throughout Southeast Asia under the noetic impact of Sanskritic languages.

And so this set about mistakes is not a proverb in our sense but rather Buddhist categories indicating natural laws of human nature, stated first in Pali and then in Burmese. Phrase-by-phrase translation of this sort is also common in Southeast Asia, and no doubt elsewhere, as a way of *performing* a translation. It has had profound effect on literary styles and performance techniques, where translating is a very common speech act (Okell 1965). These traditional styles make most foreigners feel that about half the words should be crossed out: we get impatient with that extra step of glossing so many words.

In order to parse the Burmese passage, we must first transliterate it, or else learn Burmese writing. Taking the former, faster course means both addition and loss of meaning: what is lost is the powerful iconicity of the image of the Burmese syllable, the visual gesture and pace of reading it and sounding it, and the aesthetic possibilities of the shaping and combining of syllables. Using a Burmese typewriter, even, is like decorating a Christmas tree: the central symbol is struck and the carriage does not automatically jump ahead but just sits there, while one adds things above, below, before, and after the central syllable. One focuses on syllables, not phonemes.

Figure 2 gives an interpretation (meant to be read slowly) of the Burmese text in Roman letters, a transliteration, with rough glosses in English, taken from dictionaries and bilingual Burmese friends.

wippallāthạ	*ta ya:*	*thoñ:*	*pa:*				
error	law	3	classifier				

(*hpau'*	*pyañ*	*hma:*	*ywiñ:*	*ta'*	*thaw*	*ta yạ*	*thoñ: pa:*)
(perforate	return	error	misplace	do	connective	law	3 classifier)

1	*tha̧ nya*	*wippallātha̧* =	*a̧ hma'*	*a̧ thi*	*hma:*	*hkyiñ:*
	perceive-mark	error	sign-mark	know-witness	error	doing

2	*sitta*	*wippallātha̧* =	*a̧ kyañ*	*a̧ thi*	*hma:*	*hkyiñ:*
	mind-thought	error	plan	know-witness	error	doing

3	*ḑiti*	*wippallātha̧* =	*a̧ myiñ*	*a̧ yu*	*hma:*	*hkyiñ:*
	opinion-doctrine	error	appear-ance	belief	error	doing

Figure 2.

With this, let us go back to the original English translation (the epigraph of this paper) and remove from it all the exuberance we can by taking out everything that has no counterpart in the Burmese (in this passage):

three kind mistake

error memory   error plan   error belief

Everything else in the English is there because of the demands of English: existential frame ("There are. . . ."), tense, number, *of,* deictics, prepositions, connective. Nearly none of the things that give the English passage its cohesion by relating the parts to each other is left. What remains is that thin, sparse wordscape that characterizes "literal" translation. It might be argued further that only one of the English words comes reasonably close to the range of meaning of its Burmese counterpart: three, (၃).

The cohesion of the Burmese passage comes from grammatical phenomena that we do not have in English or that we have but do not exploit in the way Burmese does. One deficiency, one of the things missing from the English, is *classification.* It occurs twice, once in the top line (*pa:*) and again in the parenthetical explanation in the second line. It is used in counting, but it also has several other grammatical-rhetorical functions in Burmese. It evokes a universe of discourse, that is, a particular perspective on the word classified (Becker 1975). It marks, by its special prominence, a discourse topic, and therefore shares some of the function of the English existential sentence ("There be . . ."). The classifier *pa:* is one of a paradigm of classifiers that mark the status of beings and some things associated with them. There are five categories, which might be conceptualized as a center and four concentric rings radiating from that center. In the center are Buddhas, relics, images, and the Buddhist Law. In the next ring, closest to the center are the things classified as *pa:*: deities, saints, monks, royalty, scriptures, and Pali terms. The word *pa:* itself is felt to be related to the term for "close" by some Burmese friends, while others are skeptical about that etymology. In the next orbit are things associated with the head, metaphorically: people of status, teachers, and scholars. And next are ordinary humans, followed by an outer realm of animals, ghosts, dead bodies, depraved people, and children. A classifier is a locus on a conceptual map, not the name of a genus, all members of which have some attribute. Animate beings are ordered according to their distance from Buddhahood: spiritual progression is a movement from animality to Buddhahood. The three mistakes as a set are Buddhist wisdom and so are closest to the center in this conceptual map.

Classifiers almost seem to add another level of reality to the world as seen through Burmese. We are accustomed to quantifiers, like two pounds of something or three yards of something else, but we do not regularly and obligatorily classify everyone and everything with the same unconscious thoroughness that, by contrast, we mark relative times in our tense-aspect system. Classifiers give special salience to terms as they are introduced, marking out the topics of a discourse. What linguists call "zero anaphora" (marking a discourse role as unchanged by *not* mentioning it) indicates the domain of a term in a Burmese discourse. My own Burmese was always very confusing because I kept overmentioning things, a particular form of exuberance to which English conditions us.

Most other terms a foreigner usually undermentions. These are the so-called elaborate expressions (Haas 1964:xvii–xviii; Matisoff 1973:81ff.). Although words are almost all monosyllabic in Burmese (with the exception of foreign terms like *wippallāthạ* and the other Pali terms in the text), they are used in pairs. There are examples in lines 2 through 5:

1. *hpau' pyañ*   "perforate-return" meaning to "fall-away" (as from a religion)
2. *hma: ywiñ:*   "error-misplace" meaning "mistake"
3. *a hma' a thi*   "mark-know" meaning "perceiving and remembering" (no English term of this scope)
4. *a kyañ a thi*   "intent-know" meaning "planning ahead," "intending"
5. *a myiñ a yu*   "appearance-belief" meaning "belief" in a broad sense.

There are no precise English equivalents for any of these pairs of terms, but via their Burkean dialectic they help us to imagine what they might mean. Like the classifiers, they tend to make phrases double-headed. Few foreigners manage this very well and so speak very *thin* Burmese, while we find them, as our name for this phenomenon suggests, elaborate.

The rhythm of good Burmese seems to demand these expressions, and rhythm is probably the most basic and powerful cohesive force in language. When two people speak comfortably to each other, they both join in the creation of a rhythm, marked by stresses, nods, grunts, gestures, and sentence rhythms. On the basis of this created rhythm they exchange words. If the conversation is not going well, the discomfort will be manifested in arhythmic responses and repairs, until they get rolling again. Speaking a language requires skill in those background rhythms, which are not the same in all languages. Our basic, elusive unease in speaking to foreigners is in large part inexplicable because it is often in large part rhythmic (Erickson and Shultz 1982; Scollon 1981). Here, the rhythmic elaborate expressions mark the parallelism of the three pairs of terms, perhaps also bringing the Burmese terms into balance with the heavier Pali terms.

Slowly, by a process of self-correction after a ventured glossing, the Burmese passage is emerging: the drama of the classifiers and the elaborate expressions. This slow emergence is the aesthetic of philology. It emerges in all the dimensions of meaning: as a structure, as a genre, as an exchange, as a sounding, and as a potential reference to (or evaluation of) an appropriate event.

If we look at the overall syntax of the text, we can clearly identify two strategies. One is the strategy of the title and its paraphrase, which might be interpreted as:

X law   three   "close"   things
X *taya: thoñ: pa:*

Here the X represents the variable term, the difference between the first and second lines. This is a particular classifier strategy, to give it a name based on its final constituent. By comparing other sets in the little book, we might make a more general formula for classifier strategies, but that would be to move away from understanding how this strategy is shaped in this context. A strategy is not an abstract pattern but an actual bit of text, used as a point of departure, either across texts or in a single text. Here, the first line is a frame for the second, in which the Pali term is paraphrased in Burmese. To give the most generalized formulation of the strategy is to move too far from the text in separating formal meaning from the four other kinds of meaning. It is possible to do so, as a long period of structural analysis has proved, yet it is also a movement away from understanding.

The second strategy is what we might call (after the distinctive sign =) an equative strategy, and it might be interpreted as: NUMBER Y *wippallātha* = Z error-ing. This is the strategy of the final three lines. In this small text, a system has been established in which certain slots in a frame are varied, others kept unchanged (other entries in the little book almost all use variants of these strategies). These repeated strategies give *structural coherence* to the text and provide a ground for thematic coherence.

By looking at the relation of the three slots (*X, Y,* and *Z*), we find a further pattern. The fillers of *X* are modifiers of *taya* (law). In the first line the filler is the Pali term (Burmanized) *wippallāthạ,* and this term becomes part of the *frame* of the second strategy (i.e., the term which *Y* modifies). In the second line, the paraphrase, the filler of *X* is *"hpau' pyañ hma: ywiñ: tat thaw"* (a modifying clause: "perforate-return error-misplace doing + connective term and clause particle"—a Burmese paraphrase of *wippallāthạ,* the Pali origins of which are discussed later in the paper.) Part of this Burmese paraphrase (the word *hma:* [error]) is the key framing term in the second part of the equative strategy (i.e., the term which *Z* modifies). The two fillers of *X* are Pali and Burmese, respectively, while the fillers of *Y* and *Z* are also, respectively, Pali and Burmese. Furthermore, each filler of *Y* is structurally parallel, as is each filler of *Z*. And, one might add, the number *three* of the first two lines constrains the number of equative figures in the list. The structural figure might be represented as in Figure 3.

X law three revered things
(X law three revered things)

1 *Y wippallāthạ* = *Z* error-ing
2 *Y wippallāthạ* = *Z* error-ing
3 *Y wippallāthạ* = *Z* error-ing

Figure 3.

As a structure, the text is very elegant. Each part is tightly bound into a very symmetrical overall pattern. At the lower levels of structure in this text are the varieties of relations of modifier terms to modified terms and the internal structure of the elaborate expressions:

ạ hma'	*ạ thị*	"mark know"
ạ kyañ	*ạ thị*	"plan know"
ạ myiñ	*ạ yu*	"appearance belief"

Here, the particle *ạ* marks a noun derived from a verb (Okell 1969:243). However, what phonological and semantic constraints there are on the order of these constituents is still unclear.

Probably, it takes a close parsing to make us aware how tightly structured this figure is. It is a structure used throughout the book U San Htwe gave me, and hence quite appropriately called a frame for a certain kind of language—a coherence system, a language-game, an episteme.

The kind of knowledge that these frames "contain"—to use our English metaphor for the relation of knowledge to language (Lakoff and Johnson 1980:92)—or better, that these "frames" are the formal meaning of—is for the most part originally in Pali and is being shaped into Burmese in these figures. There are two lingual interfaces here, from English back to Burmese and from Burmese back to Pali. These can be seen as two sets of prior texts, although the relations are not that simple, if we consider, for instance, the curious use of the equal sign—the source of which in Burma may well have been English—or the intrusion of Burmese into the Pali words— where a Burmese writer's possible confusion over long and short vowels in Pali led to the "misspelling" of *wippallāthạ* (only one *p* in Pali). Or, both these things may be U San Htwe's own deviations. One of the hardest things to know in reading a distant text is what is stereotypic and what is innovative.

The term *wippallāthạ* is a Burmese interpretation of Pali *vipallasa* from Sanskrit *viparyasa*. Edward Conze (1957, 1962a, 1962b) translates it as "perverted views." The noun *viparyasa* is from a root *as,* which means, roughly, "to throw." The whole term is used for the "overthrowing" of a wagon, or even, as a Sanskrit pundit told me, "turning a pancake." It has been translated as "inversion," "perverseness," "wrong notion," "error," "what can be upset," or "missearches"—that is, looking for permanence in the wrong places. I think it quite appropriate to call them "mistakes of interpretation" and so underscore their special relevance for philologists. "The Scriptures," writes Conze (1957:314 and 1962a:40) "identify the *viparyasas* with 'unwise attention' *(ayoniso manasikaro)*—the root of all unwholesome dharmas—and with ignorance, delusion, and false appearance." In another place, he writes, "The *viparyasa* are sometimes treated as psychological attitudes, sometimes as logical propositions, and sometimes even as an ontological condition" (1962b:39). When considered as features of the world they distort, the *viparyasas* are four in number; but when considered as *locations* in the mind they are three:

samjna	(Pali-Burmese *thanya*)	=	"perception"
citta	(Pali-Burmese *sitta*)	=	"thought"
drṣṭi	(Pali-Burmese *diṭi*)	=	"theoretical opinions"

All of these mistakes of interpretation lead us to habitually act as if things were different from what they are. Perception (blending in Burmese with what we might call memory) is perverted when we forget that what we perceive is impermanent, ultimately unpleasant, and not us (not to be seen ego-fully). And so we meditate on the rise and fall of the thing, breaking it down into dharmas. Thought (blending in Burmese with planning) is perverted by our wishes and fears. Both fear and hope make us overstress the permanence of things, make us close our eyes to suffering and exaggerate the importance of our own existence. Belief is perverted when we formulate a theory that the world contains permanent objects, with permanent properties, or that good outweighs suffering, or that there is a self.

These are all empirical mistakes, summarized in the formula that these views lead one to seek "the Permanent in the impermanent, Ease in suffering, the Self in what is not the self." As Conze (1962a:41) writes,

> All this we can see quite clearly in our more lucid moments—though they be rather rare and infrequent. The techniques of Buddhist meditation aims at increasing their frequency, and innumerable devices have been designed with the one purpose of impressing the actual state of affairs on our all too reluctant minds.

Even yet there remains what Ricoeur has called a "surplus of meaning"—an open-endedness about what I first saw as a proverb (translated for me by a non-Buddhist Burmese) but later came to see as a translated bit of Buddhist philosophy. We have sampled each of the contextual sources of meaning—the interpersonal uses of public language, the metaphoric power of the medium, the kinds of references the proverb might be appropriate with, the tight symmetry of its structure, and the prior (and posterior) Buddhist texts it evokes. We have moved back from translation toward the original text, and beyond. The text was our discipline and the unfinished process has been one of self-correction: removing exuberancies of interpretation, filling in deficiencies. The Burmese text eventually overtakes us, as a Buddhist injunction to philologists.

> There are three kinds of perversions of interpretation, three kinds of mistakes of philology:
> 1. Perversions of perception, including memory = perversions of the past, of prior texts
> 2. Perversions of thought . . . fore-thought, planning, hopes and fears = perversions of the future
> 3. Perversions of appearances and beliefs = perversions of theory.

Notes

Acknowledgments. The author is grateful to Madhav Deshpande and Luis Gomez for help with the Pali terms; to Michael Aung Thwin and U Thein Swe for help with the Burmese; and to Clifford Geertz and others at the Institute for Advanced Study, Princeton, for many valuable suggestions when a version of this essay was presented there in March 1982. This paper is dedicated to Saya San Htwe, my teacher in Taunggyi, Burma, 1958–61.

References Cited

Bateson, Gregory
   1979   Mind and Nature. New York: E. P. Dutton
Becker, A. L.
   1975   A Linguistic Image of Nature: The Burmese Numerative Classifier System. International Journal of the Sociology of Language 5:109–121.
Benveniste, Emile
   1971   Categories of Thought and Language. *In* Problems in General Linguistics. pp. 55–64. Coral Gables: University of Miami Press.
Burke, Kenneth
   1964   Literature as Equipment for Living. *In* Perspectives by Incongruity. pp. 100–109. Bloomington: Indiana University Press.
Conze, Edward
   1957   On "Perverted Views." East and West 7(4):313–318.
   1962a   The Three Marks and the Perverted Views. *In* Buddhist Thought in India. pp. 34–46. London: George Allen & Unwin.
   1962b   The Maháyána Treatment of the Viparyāsas. Orientemus Jk. 1:34–46.
Dewey, John
   1934   Art as Experience. New York: G. P. Putnam's Sons.
Erickson, Frederick, and Jeffrey Shultz
   1982   The Counselor as Gatekeeper: Social Action in Interviews. New York: Academic Press.
Geertz, Clifford
   1983   Blurred Genres: The Refiguration of Social Thought. *In* Local Knowledge: Further Essays in Interpretive Anthropology. pp. 19–35. New York: Basic Books.
Givón, Talmy
   1979   On Understanding Grammar. New York: Academic Press.
Haas, Mary R.
   1964   Thai-English Student's Dictionary. Palo Alto: Stanford University Press.
Lakoff, George, and Mark Johnson
   1980   Metaphors We Live By. Chicago: University of Chicago Press.
Matisoff, James A.
   1973   The Grammar of Lahu. Berkeley: University of California Press.
Mukarovsky, Jan
   1977   The Word and Verbal Art. John Burbank and Peter Steiner, eds. New Haven: Yale University Press.
Okell, John
   1965   Nissaya Burmese. *In* Indo-Pacific Linguistic Studies. G. B. Milner and Eugenie J. A. Henderson, eds. pp. 186–227. Amsterdam: North-Holland Publishing Company.

1969   A Reference Grammar of Colloquial Burmese. London: Oxford University Press.

Ortega y Gasset, José
1957   Man and People. New York: W. W. Norton & Company.

Pike, Kenneth L., and Evelyn G. Pike
1977   Grammatical Analysis. Arlington: Summer Institute of Linguistics and University of Texas.

Ricoeur, Paul
1981   The Model of the Text: Meaningful Action Considered as a Text. *In* Hermeneutics and the Human Sciences. John B. Thompson, ed. and transl. pp. 197-221. Cambridge: Cambridge University Press.

Scollon, Ronald
1981   The Rhythmic Integration of Ordinary Talk. *In* Georgetown University Round Table on Language and Linguistics, 1981. pp. 335-349. Washington, DC: Georgetown University Press.

Wittgenstein, Ludwig
1958   Philosophical Investigations. New York: Macmillan.

Zurbuchen, Mary S.
1981   The Shadow Theater of Bali: Explorations in Language and Text. Ph.D. dissertation. University of Michigan, Ann Arbor.

7
Folly, Bali, and Anthropology, or Satire Across Cultures

James A. Boon
Cornell University

In sum, no society, no union in life, could be either pleasant or lasting without me. A people does not for long tolerate its prince, or a master tolerate his servant, a handmaiden her mistress, a teacher his student, a friend his friend, a wife her husband, a landlord his tenant, a partner his partner, or a boarder his fellow-boarder, except as they mutually or by turns are mistaken, on occasion flatter, on occasion wisely wink, and otherwise soothe themselves with the sweetness of folly . . . you owe these choice blessings of life to Folly, and—what is the cream of the jest—you reap the fruits of a madness you need not share.
—Erasmus (1941[1511]:28, 35; Folly speaking)

There are parodic books. Are there parodic cultures? parodic disciplines? These are questions I raise in a parodic paper. Parody-books are legion. To name the most biting: Swift, *Max Havelaar;* to name the most ludic: Rabelais, Twain; to name the most ambiguous: Melville, *Tristes Tropiques.* But what about cultures?

Certainly there are parodic components of cultures. As Paul Radin (1972:168–169) reminds us: "Every generation occupies itself with interpreting Trickster anew. No generation understands him [*sic*] fully but no generation can do without him . . . he became and remained everything to every man—god, animal, human being, hero, buffoon. . . . If we laugh at him, he grins at us." An early, thoroughgoing analysis of trickster components in their full institutional complexity is Bateson's (1958[1936]) *Naven,* which conveys the buffoonish character of a ritual setting plus its social structural apparatus. Bateson ends by saluting travesty, exaggerated "meta-" role playing, and the apparent necessity in Iatmul life and culture for all values and actions to pull the rug out from under each other. With *Naven,* both through Bateson's excruciating self-conscious method and through the Iatmul themselves, lampoon successfully entered the comparative study of society and ritual.

Thanks to Victor Turner and a host of recent interpreters and celebrators of serio-ludic forms—rites, performances, institutions, texts—Bateson's brand of insight, long rejected in standard functionalist anthropology, has become something of an industry. Parody has been busting out all over: once Trickster is unshackled or Folly unleashed, he/she doesn't know where to stop. And rightly so.

Is Wayang a Parodic Form?

A. L. Becker's (1979) recent, challenging article on "Javanese Shadow Theater" employs a rhetorical, ludic leitmotif. "Where," he ponders, "in Western literary and dramatic traditions with their Aristotelian constraints" would we find "Jay Gatsby, Godzilla, Agamemnon, John Wayne, and Charlie Chaplin" (1979:219) appearing in the same plot? Becker feels that such potpourris of protagonists—both *sublimitas* and *humilitas,* both fantastic and realistic—flourish in the "epistemology" of wayang, which requires no temporal-causal sequences, no classical unities of place, time, or action, indeed no "linearity" whatsoever. I want to take Becker's question seriously and almost literally, and intensify matters by adding to the list "Jesus Christ, Moses, or Mohammed." Where in the West do we encounter in one form, wayang-like, a riot of types: "Jay Gatsby, Godzilla, Agamemnon, John Wayne, Charlie Chaplin, Jesus Christ . . ."?

The answer I propose may be unexpected, in light of the East/West contrast implicit in Becker's study and necessary to its healthy polemic. I suggest we find such concoctions *everywhere* in Western performance and literary genres *except* a narrow segment of bourgeois novels, neoclassical dramatic conventions, reformist religious creeds, Augustan standards of prosody, and other areas of enforced, homogenized *bienseance,* Jamesian unified point of view, or insistent monotheism. The remainder is, to say the least, impressive: miracle plays, masques, *Trauerspiele,* follies, carnivals and the literary carnivalesque, everything picaresque, burlesque, or vaudevillian, *Singspiele,* gestes, romances, music drama, fairy tales, comic books, major holidays (Jesus cum Santa; Christ plus the Easter Bunny), Disney, T.V. commercials, the history of Hollywood productions, fantastic voyages, sci-fi, travel*liars'* tales, experimental theater, anthropology conferences, proceedings of anthropology conferences. . . .

So what are we doing contrasting shadow plays *(wayang)* to Aristotelian proprieties in the first place, considering the slight range of performative and textual traditions the latter have influenced? Why not at once place wayang alongside *Anthony and Cleopatra, Pericles,* or *The Tempest* rather than oppose it to overorderly *Bérénice?* Both Henry Thoreau and Clifford Geertz (cf. Agamemnon and Charlie Chaplin!) have wondered whether it is worth it when travelers (or ethnographers) go around the world to count the cats in Zanzibar. Similarly, need we engage the theatrical epistemologies of the shadowy East simply to rediscover aesthetic, dramatic, and cultural principles that have lurked just off-Aristotelian-stage in the history of Western (I would rather say Indo-European) religion, literature, philosophy, and theater? YES!

Becker's generalizations about Javanese wayang performance have been expertly documented for neighboring Bali as well by Mary Zurbuchen (1981) and others. We enter a theatrical world of paradigmatic, associational links shaping cycles into nested structures playing description, dialogue, and action off against each other in shifting paces, tonalities, and hierarchies. As many commentators have stressed (e.g., Brandon 1970), realms of sensual demons, dignified ancestor heroes, distant deities, and pragmatic clowns coexist and bring the timeless and the timely into conversation. This aesthetic of plural voices is clearly demonstrated by the multiple languages activated in every performance, with their stylistic and cosmographic correlates, all conjoined in the clowns (and necessarily in the *dalang* puppeteer):

> A wayang includes within it, in each performance, the entire history of the literary language, from Old Javanese, pre-Hindu incantation and mythology to the era of the Sanskrit gods and their language, blending with Javanese in the works of ancient poets (the *suluks*), adding Arabic and Colonial elements, changing with the power of Java to new locations and dialects, up to the present Bahasa Indonesia and even a bit of American English (in which one clown often instructs another): I do not just mean here vocabulary, syntax, and phonological variation. That is also true of modern Javanese. The difference is that in the shadow play, the language of each of these different eras is separate in function from the others; certain voices speak only one or the other of these languages and dialects, and they are continually kept almost entirely separate from each other. One could even say that the content of the wayang is the languages of the past and the present, a means for contextualizing the past in the present, and the present in the past, hence preserving the expanding text that is the culture [Becker 1979:232].

Performatively, then, wayang is poly-; but it is polythematic, indeed polycyclic, as well. James Brandon's (1970:16) *On Thrones of Gold* discloses how wayang revises and fractures epic components that constitute its episodes: "In the *Reincarnation of Rama* the god Guru explicitly commends the incarnation of Wisnu's authority and truth to Kresna and Ardjuna, thus passing on to the Pandawas the rights of kingship previously held by Rama and Leksmana (an idea not found in the Indian epics)." Everywhere, wayang allows the frameworks of the *Ramayana* and the *Mahabharata* (plus Panji and other cycles) to disturb each other in performance as they have actually done throughout the literary and political history of Java and Bali. Such juggling makes it difficult to construe the epics in terms of Good/Evil (cf. Rassers 1959; Held 1935). Consider how the contrast between Kosala/Videha parties is displaced to heroes/Raksashas. Is Bhima in part the clown-factor projected onto the Pandawa brothers, much as Panji represents the Indonesian indigenization of the cyclic cum heroic and Menak represents its Islamization? Does the *Ramayana* conform more to principles of creation myths wherein clowns are integral factors of divinity and nobility, while the *Mahabharata* appears more chroniclelike, with clowns providing a foil to divinity and nobility (see Boon 1977:190–205; 1982a:191–200; in press)?

For the sake of argument, and ultimately of assessing more precisely wayang's distinctive qualities, what Western genres display similar devices: juxtaposing different languages and dialects, ideally separate; connoting diverse times and social and cosmological strata; inclining to etymologize and reetymologize; fracturing and coalescing themes and cycles; employing all acoustical registers; setting in gear paradox and coincidence; all to "expand the text that is the culture"? Several examples come to mind, most of them parodic, or what Northrop Frye (1957) is prone to call "apocalyptic": liturgy (the less reformist, the more apposite); Scripture, together with its commentaries; Menippean satire, a literary and performative genre based on multiple voices and viewpoints, plural languages, obsessive quotation, pastiche, etymology, blather, and always imbued with a flavor of fragmented parody; multilingual bazaar or "commercial" cultures (versus centralized, territorial cultures) and their characteristic genres; 16th-century humanism, rooted in Lucianic satire . . . for a start. Like wayang, these genres disturb the boundary between written texts and oral renditions; their spirit is accumulative; they strain toward plenitudes rather than routines; and their generators (authors, readers, actors) share the dalang's penchant for explicating proper names, and all words, as if they were "motivated" rather than "arbitrary." Western equivalents for the dalang include punsters from More and Erasmus to Melville and Twain, to Joyce and his re-joicer, Hugh Kenner. Thus, the text-building strategies that Becker discloses in wayang are not unknown in the West; yet they are seldom performed in those noncompulsive settings—"more like a Western sports event than serious theater" (Becker 1979:230)—that characterize Indonesian shadow theater. (Of course, compulsive "audiencehood" versus free-for-all spectatorship is relatively recent in the West as well). Western genres that most resonate with wayang are ironic rather than reformist; they too manage, in Northrop Frye's sense, "to incorporate the demonic."

Becker's own rhetorical strategy is artfully to pose wayang against everything it isn't: sequential; decorous; unified in space, time, authorial vantage; monolingual. This procedure helps to heighten the question, If that's what wayang isn't, what is it? We might attempt to answer this from within: wayang as lived (but from the perspective of the dalang? one audience member? another audience member? the puppets themselves, and which one? a camera and tape recorder?). And/or we might turn to other anti-Aristotelian genres in an effort to appreciate the spirit of nonsequential, nondecorous, nonunified performance and textual traditions. We could designate such contrary, heterodox dimensions of Western dramatic and cultural performances by what Mikhail Bakhtin (1968) terms "the grotesque," "carnivalization," "languages of the marketplace."[1] But I think an earlier proponent of ludic extremes should suffice. Reenter, Erasmian Folly:

> For what merry pranks will not the ramshackle god, Priapus, afford? What games will not Mercury play, with his thefts and deceits? And is it not the custom for Vulcan to act as jester at the banquets of the gods, and partly by his lameness, partly by his taunts, partly by his silly sayings, to enliven the community drinking? . . . The half-goat satyrs act out interludes. Stupid Pan moves the laughter of all by some ballad, which the gods prefer above hearing the Muses themselves. . . . Such foolish things, so help me, that sometime I, though I am Folly, cannot keep from laughing. [Erasmus 1941:22]

As in wayang, clowns and laughter (hilarious, nervous, teary) are keys to an epistemology of folly.

I am inclined to be suspicious of any moralistic interpretation of folly-forms, whose protagonists (whether heroes, gods, demons, or clowns) are designed to transgress conventions, to "problematize" proprieties. Exemplary characters, or apt models *for* conduct, are as elusive here as they are in, say, *Hausmärchen*. Yet, paradoxically, many commentators construe follies in moralistic ways. In the case of wayang such interpretations may come from the domestic-right (e.g., Mulyono 1978a, 1978b, 1979a,

1979b) or from the foreign-left (e.g., Anderson 1965). Ironically, both extremes of the political spectrum (more strange bedfellows!) wish to discover in playful, perhaps subversive, epistemologies patent codes for conduct—those very things that the forms themselves would undermine. I wonder, Can performances that set in motion any and all voices, languages, moral values, character traits, and ethoses be construed ultimately as disguised codes for conduct? Or ought their multiple voices be allowed to subvert and therefore to sustain each other by canceling themselves out, thus producing a field of motives (in Kenneth Burke's sense), with any partisan or ethical direction left to other forms or to readings narrowed to certain partisan interests?

Scholars have been willing to celebrate the servant-clowns in wayang and related genres, to applaud their controlled disruptiveness, and to appreciate the insulated satire they sometimes create from the margins. Geertz's (1973:139–140) influential portrait of Semar, for example, discloses his conjunction of spiritual refinement plus rough-hewn comportment, his blend of god-clown opposites, and his championing of non-absolutism:

> Like Falstaff, Semar is a symbolic father to the play's heroes. Like Falstaff, he is fat, funny, and worldly-wise; and like Falstaff, he seems to provide in his vigorous amoralism a general criticism of the very values the drama affirms. . . . Semar reminds the noble and refined Pendawas of their own humble, animal origins. He resists any attempt to turn human beings into gods and to end the world of natural contingency by a flight to the divine world of absolute order, a final stilling of the eternal psychological-metaphysical struggle.

Other scholars have gone on to assess the social and political uses to which satire, topsy-turvydom, and ritual reversal are put, as in James Peacock's (1968) analysis of the functions of the ludic in *ludruk* (Javanese proletarian dramas). Recent performers (e.g., Jenkins 1980) have adapted the skills of Balinese clowning to enrich their own theatrical repertoire and to achieve a variety of participant empathy and understanding. But are we ready to approach wayang itself (and related performances and certain aspects of the cultures sustaining them) as altogether subversive, not just *partially* subversive in the name of one social stratum, some particular ideology, or other brand of interest? Could the subversiveness of wayang—like the subversiveness of art, whether right, left, or center—be an end and not a means? Could this subversiveness underlie Becker's "expanding text that is the culture"?

Is Topeng *a Menippean Satire? Is Bali?*

F. A. Payne (1981) has recently characterized Menippean satire as a
"medley": it weaves together genres, abruptly shifts between prosody and
prose, pastes together writing into collages of narrative and artifact, avoids
any reliable authorial "authority," obliterates absolutes, amalgamates languages and dialects, and disturbs every boundary it must rely on. Menippean satire is in a sense the original "blurred genre" (cf. Geertz 1980). The
number of Western works that slip into this pervasive tradition is
astonishing. I'll name only Lucian's satires (since one of them lends the
genre its name); More's *Utopia; Don Quixote;* Rabelais; Burton's *Anatomy
of Melancholy; Tristram Shandy;* Hoffman's *Kater Muur;* Grandville's *Un
Autre Monde;* Carlyle's *Sartor Resartus;* Melville's *Mardi, Moby Dick,
Pierre,* and *Confidence Man;* Flaubert's *Bouvard et Pecuchet;* Multatuli's
Max Havelaar; much of Mann; and a great deal of modern literature in the
wake of Joyce (leaving aside Scripture). These examples occupy the margins
between drama, or romance, or history, or autobiography, and the *book* as
a self-conscious material item. They are like plays that weave stage directions, multiple voices, several levels of commentary, and the physical and
"spiritual" conditions of possibility of their own production into a package
of print.

A modern critic who has insisted on the importance of the genre is
Northrop Frye, whose *Anatomy of Criticism* (echoing Burton's *Anatomy*)
is a Menippean satire of Menippean satires. Frye (1957:225, 234–235) first
salutes parody and the comic:

> Most fantasy is pulled back into satire by a powerful undertow often
> called allegory, which may be described as the implicit reference to
> experience in the perception of the incongruous. . . .

> This type of fantasy breaks down customary associations, reduces
> sense experience to one of many possible categories, and brings out
> the tentative *als ob* basis of all our thinking. Emerson says that such
> shifts of perspective afford "a low degree of the sublime," but ac-
> tually they afford something of far greater artistic importance, a
> high degree of the ridiculous. And consistently with the general basis
> of satire as parody-romance, they are usually adaptations of
> romance themes: the fairyland of little people, the land of giants, the
> world of enchanted animals, the wonderlands parodied in Lucian's
> *True History.*

He eventually isolates Menippean satire itself:

It deals less with people as such than with mental attitudes. Pedants, bigots, cranks, parvenus, virtuosi, enthusiasts, rapacious and incompetent professional men of all kinds, are handled in terms of their occupational approach to life as distinct from their social behavior. The Menippean satire thus resembles the confession in its ability to handle abstract ideas and theories, and differs from the novel in its characterization, which is stylized rather than naturalistic, and presents people as mouthpieces of the ideas they represent. [1957:309]

Frye (1957:310) is primarily concerned with Menippean satires in texts: "The Alice books are perfect Menippean satires, and so is *The Water-Babies,* which has been influenced by Rabelais. The purely moral type is a serious vision of society as a single intellectual pattern, in other words a Utopia." But the texts can be construed as cues for performance, even as idealized filled-out scripts. Consider *The Compleat Angler:*

An anatomy because of its mixture of prose and verse, its rural *cena* setting, its dialogue form, its deipnosophistical interest in food, and its gentle Menippean raillery of a society which considers everything more important than fishing and yet has discovered very few better things to do. In nearly every period of literature there are many romances, confessions, and anatomies that are neglected only because the categories to which they belong are unrecognized. [1957:312]

It is perhaps disputable whether wayang is an example of Menippean satire performed; but certainly *topeng* is. John Emigh's (1982) stimulating account of *topeng pajegan* in contemporary Bali highlights several relevant dimensions. Unlike wayang, topeng plays are appropriate at a cremation (because, I suspect, they are oriented to ancestors and clowns more than to heroes or Hindu deities). Like danse macabre and other satirical forms, topeng embeds the grandiose and sublime in the actual and earthy. Emigh makes interesting observations about theatricalized visitations; the past being ushered into current contexts; and the skills of a topeng virtuoso, who matches in dancing, masking, and vocalizing the dalang's achievement with puppets. A sole performer becomes king, beast, hero, rogue, and buffoon, blending martial arts and magical mantras. All is set to the "multiples" of the gamelan "musical pulse" to achieve a synesthetic experience, as the dancer "plays with the dynamics of the performance situation" to enact proud *patihs* and their "antic opposites" (Emigh 1982:25–29; see also Young 1982).

We can safely call topeng a parodic view of court life and of the in-
gredients of quasi-historic chronicles *(babad)*. Babad values appear one way
on palm leaf manuscripts *(lontar),* another way in social action (see Boon
1977:70–92, 145–164), and yet another way in open-air theater: script, institutions, and dance "ironize" each other. Emigh (1982:26) outlines com-
edic structures of topeng:

> As with any good comedy team, the 'brothers' have contrasting
> styles. The Penasar Kelihan is the straight man, full of self-
> importance and bound to the world of the past by word and gesture.
> The Penasar Cenikan, on the other hand, has the freedom from con-
> straints of a comic innocent. . . . His speech is almost always in con-
> temporary Balinese. When he does sing a *kidung* selection or quote
> *kekawin* poetry, the result is often parody. In his light, nasal voice,
> he often makes light of the pretentiousness of his older sibling. . . .

But Emigh (1982:26) makes the important point that "the Penasar Cenikan
does not mock the heroic values espoused by the Penasar Kelihan—he
speaks as an outsider to the heroic world that supports those values." It
may be more accurate still, I suspect, to say that all the worlds of topeng are
made *outside* to each other. Of course, the audience at large most readily
identifies with the low-popular, or low-mimetic, components. But the tone
is less interestedly satirical than disinterestedly parodic—"satiric" in the
Menippean sense.

Several other features of topeng suggest Menippean satire: it plays
out the antitheses in rhetoric between heroic, high-caste eloquence and
everyday colloquial talk. Yet in the very act of undercutting vainglorious
language and comportment (recalling the braggadocious stock types of
comedy), topeng preserves a sampler of the gamut of language and etiquette.
By subverting it catalogs. The particular play Emigh summarizes inclines
toward, indeed progresses toward, the values of Si Mata Mata, the
Sganarelle-like jokester who sneezes when he should compliment and who
debunks all status puffery. But just when the vernacular, human, and contemporary have gained ascendancy, the stage-space reverts to Sidha Karya,
the high-caste Brahmana personage whom legend credits with estabishing
proper cooperation between raja and priest *(bagawanta)* and with creating
the authority of *pedanda*s in many areas of Balinese ritual and performance.

One last aspect of topeng's context, which Emigh (1982:35) alludes
to as a "bewildering and intriguing paradox," fits the Menippean satire
mold:

> Kakul can only take on the role of priestly mediator because of his skills as a dancer and storyteller. A priest cannot perform the Sidha Karya ceremony himself and Kakul would not perform it without previously doing the rest of the performance. . . . . The village of Tusan, with a large Brahmana population, must bring in an outside performer, a Sudra, in order to complete successfully a ceremony attending the cremation of a high priest.

This feature of topeng concerns the situation of performance specialists in the "division of labor" in Balinese society and culture. The performing arts join various priesthoods and interlocal temple networks in the cross-cutting specializations at the local and pan-Bali levels: under specific circumstances performers are substituted for priests; moreover, locales engage in exchanges of respective talents, tasks, and often trancers (see Boon 1977: 100–102). Beyond the properly Balinese context, these conventions call to mind the festival forms, carnivals, and "languages of the marketplace" addressed by scholars of communicative events from Mauss to Bakhtin (see Boon 1982a:175, 278–279). In light of their insights into the social and historical circumstances yielding Menippean satire, I would surmise that the genre's most characteristic context is where *sacrament and dramaturgy become playful replacements of each other.* One might then even wonder whether Bali "itself" represents a prolonged case of this grotesque genre and its particular social and historical conditions.[2]

These questions point toward important institutional and historical components of Bali's interpretive "scene," beyond those contextual dimensions of Balinese activities saluted in Geertz's (1973:412–453) notion of "deep play." The endless cross-commentary between social and performative genres, and the prevalence of forms like wayang and topeng, may relate to the restricted place of specialized interpretation within Balinese traditions. Compared to other Southeast Asian and Indic areas, Bali has developed few institutions of formal, cumulative exegesis. Here, priests and scribes tend ritually *to do* rather than exegetically *to interpret*—hence Geertz's label of (and for?) Balinese religion as an orthopractice rather than an orthodoxy. Although Geertz's label was resisted by philologists of Bali (cf. C. Hooykaas 1976; Geertz 1976), it is not difficult to substantiate his claim. Innumerable frustrated investigators of meanings behind Balinese performances have reported anecdotes like the following one by J. Hooykaas (1960:426) in her enthralling study of changeling children in local folklore and life-crisis rites, including the three-month birthday:

> There also a *bajang cholong* is used. The word *cholong* means something like "stealthy;" *bajang cholong* is, therefore, fairly well trans-

lated by "changeling" since it conveys the idea of the child exchange being done with stealth.

    The treatment of the changeling in Bali is exactly the same as that which obtained for it in Europe. In Bali the changeling is regarded as unclean and is treated as such. A Brahmin lady, well known as a maker of offerings, was shocked when I asked her for details of the *bajang cholong.* "We leave that to *sudras,*" she said scornfully.

But the Sudras, we can be sure, would in turn have deferred to still other parties, although for different ostensible reasons. Knowledgeable investigators can guess that the interpretive buck would ultimately be passed back to the ancestors. It goes without saying that the ancestors themselves do not speak, although their desires (but not their interpretations) are made known through performers in trance. Hence, in Bali, like so many other cultures, ancestral "exegesis" answers all impertinent "whys" with a silent, sacrosanct, untranslatable "because."

    My point is that Bali displays few occasions for disembodied reference or ritually neutralized commentary that one would readily call exegetic. Members of reading groups *(sekaha bebasan)* do sometimes discuss texts appropriate to particular rituals; but such activity (like wayangs, topengs, and similar performances) serve more as additional ritual ingredients. To enact, cite, or even refer to a text is to activate its power. Moreover, Bali sports many varieties of priest and textual expert, whether high caste or commoner, heavenly or netherly, lettered or less lettered (including pedanda Siva, pedanda Bauddha, sengguhu, pemangku, dalang, obscure dukuh). But no such specialist is precisely a professional exegete. Although Balinese value ascetic withdrawal from procreative life after completing social tasks, neither monasticism, liberation through renunciation, nor ultimate extinction of the social self have become dominant themes for particular institutional sectors. There is less formal *institutional remove from life in society,* from the dense regulations organizing and perpetuating the social system, than we find in those Southeast Asian and Indo-European traditions supporting full-fledged monasticism or ascetic specialization in textual knowledge and recitation. Similarly, in Bali there is less *institutional remove from writings* that could make texts the subjects of exegetical reflection rather than powerful words of efficacity in the entire ritual scheme. The Balinese case, then, helps give edge to a vexed issue in the historiography of "manuscript cultures" in both European and Asian variations of Indo-European institutional and textual arrangements: Are principles of *ascetic remove from society* and what one might call *exegetic remove from texts* (and ritual performances) intrinsically connected?[3]

    Bali's writings range over Indic mythology and epic; assorted cycles

from indigenous, Hindu, Islamic, and Chinese sources; chronicles of court-
ly expansion and collapse; and manuals for the ritual regulation of etiquette
and of cures in the event of etiquette's dangerous lapse. Yet these writings
are not precisely texts *about* their contents. They are more like performances *in script*, just as wayang is a performance *in puppets* and topeng is a
performance *in persons* (or actor-dancers). The complexities behind Bali's
dedication to exponential performance coordinated with ritual processes are
vast. They involve the island's entrenched position vis-à-vis Islam: the Islam
that displaced antecedents of Hindu-Buddhism in Java, the Islam practiced
by the portion of Lombok that Balinese never managed to conquer; and the
Islam of enclaves in North and West Bali. Indonesian Islam itself contains
many strains, including mystical, rationalist, and puritan-reformist. And
just how Islamic doctrines and practice came to penetrate Javanese court
centers is an intricate, disputed topic (see J. Peacock 1978; Boon 1977:
205–214). But one general contrast prevails in relations between religions
like Islam and cultures like Bali (or perhaps Majapahit Java) in matters of
ritual, performances, and texts. Islam tolerates with difficulty theatrics,
totalized drama, ambiguous myth, and elaborated ritual categories of
male/female, divine/demonic, and microcosm/macrocosm formulae such
as proliferate in Bali. Islam prefers the pure "letter," the direct moralistic
word. Like Protestantism and like Augustan movements in literature (see
Boon in press), indeed like all reformist developments in the interconnected
histories of religion, literature, and philosophy and method, Islam
diminishes the *wayang*ish properties of cultures. Viewed historically, then,
Bali's exegesis-resistant performances may have intensified partly as an
allegory of antithesis to Islam.

Regardless of such hazy historical reasons, exegesis has remained
muted in contemporary Balinese religion and drama. Ideally, exegesis seeks
to centralize and standardize meanings (it was the Dutch philological mission to institute such exegesis in Balinese letters); this much exegesis has in
common with reformist traditions. Unlike ideal-type reformism, however,
exegesis necessarily implies no thorough rationalization, such as univocality
of referents, moralistic monotheism, or universalistic ethic for true
believers. It is important to remember that in contrast to many other
"manuscript cultures," Balinese textual experts (even *pedanda* priests) have
traditionally not inclined to exegesis in the strict sense. What Bali has lacked
in exegetical motives (that tend to pose the whys and wherefores of ritual
and belief *at a remove*) it has made up for in multiple performances (that
transpose one set of values into some related set). The characteristic
Balinese way of commenting on one performance is by producing another:
like wayang, like a folly.

Bali's proclivity to exponential performance and the dilemmas it pre-

sents to hard-nosed philologists or somber-minded exegetes helps to explain
the distinctive flavor of Balinese studies and the occasional rivalry between
philological enterprises and more contextual (including anthropological)
approaches to the island's cultural forms. Part of Becker's (1979) effort in
the abovementioned article is to snatch wayang from the clutches of uni-
vocal philology and to advance a refreshed philology cum anthropology in
the name of linguistics and contextualized performance. He helps us sense
what has been routinely expurgated from methods for studying the epistemology that wayang represents. From here we even go on to appreciate
how the history of interpreting a form like wayang, or indeed a culture like
Bali, itself smacks of Folly, in the positive, Erasmian sense.

Take, for example, certain laughter-provoking items from the
history of efforts to document Balinese performances. In the long list of
methodological devices none seems less appropriate than Margaret Mead's
routine of stopwatch timing to plot sequences and coincidences of trances,
dances, and everything else (splitting seconds in the land of *jam karet*—rub-
ber time!). Other methodological devices have been just as arbitrary, even
gimmicky, but more productive and inescapable for purposes of comparison: Colin McPhee's (1966) confinement of Balinese music in Western
notation, for example; or Becker's own phrase-diagrams of options in a
dalang's text building (shifted to Bali by Mary Zurbuchen [1981]). Indeed,
the philological collection, standardization, and translation of texts is such
a device on the grand scale (see C. Hooykaas 1970 for a nonironic review of
this commendable accomplishment). To acknowledge as much is not to
undermine the desirability or the necessity of cataloging, transcribing, and
translating Balinese manuscripts; but it is to resist reducing Balinese performances to the contents of manuscripts, or their meanings to the standard
glosses once initiated arbitrarily in philology and controlled in a proprietary
way ever since. Now, interweaving Bali and Erasmian Folly is itself a gimmick, but one conceivably truer to certain spirits of wayang than would be
the folly-less rigidification of Balinese manuscripts and performances in a
library of books. Folly joins Becker in interpreting wayang-like components
of cultures in light of not just how they can be recorded and collated but
how they happen.

Several fresh devices have recently graced Balinese studies. One appears in a translation of a topeng play by J. Emigh and I Made Bandem
(1982): they employ eight (count them, eight) different typefaces to distinguish voices sounding in Sanskrit, Kawi, Middle Javanese, High Balinese,
"Medium Balinese," Low Balinese, modern Indonesian, and stage directions. This delightful gimmick is much more helpful than a stopwatch; a
sense of Menippean satire begins to emerge in/as translation. Other scin-
tillating "soundings" of Balinese performances appear in Zurbuchen's (1981)

detailed account of the dalang's art, his languages, and their context. She employs Walter Ong's concept of "noetic" to accentuate Bali's "multiple code situation" plus its aesthetic (ethic?) of translation, transposition, or paradoxical juxtaposition of multiple languages. We can trace wayang's own reflexivity in its symbolic classification that turns back on itself to classify its own classification: for example, the contrasts among *wayang lemah, wayang sudamala,* and *wayang sapuleger* that match Heaven/World/Underworld schemes of completeness implicit in many Balinese rituals, myths, and institutions (see Boon 1982b). Zurbuchen stresses the activation of script in and as sound. She adds to this emphasis on performative practice keen insights into cosmology. Examples include poets who liken their works to architectural split-gates *(candi)* and ideals of voluntary associations *(sekaha)* of words. She finds a material, craftlike sense of sounded words; actual manuscripts as utilized seem less like play-books or illusionistic narratives than script-scores, perhaps even lettered notations in the musical sense, there for the sounding. Following Zurbuchen and Becker, we might ponder whether wayang forms world as gamelan orchestra forms sound; indeed, within wayang (with its gamelan accompanying), is world shaped *like* sound or *as* sound, recalling the Menippean dilemma of the world *like* book or *as* book? On the linguistic side, it is important to recall that the languages of wayang are never languages *of* but only languages *to:* Sanskrit is language not of the gods but to the gods; Kawi is language to the ancestor heroes; high Balinese is language to the raja or pedanda priest; and so on. Everything is already, in the parlance of recent Western critical discourse, "de-centered," or perhaps centerless (Boon in press).

It may be worth intensifying speculations about wayang and world by adapting a *Panji*esque epistemology to comparative questions, by directing a wayang state of mind and method across wayangs themselves. One might, for example, compare not Javanese wayang and Balinese wayang but Javanese wayang and Bali. One might consider the situation of wayang in each culture: unsurprisingly, wayang is desired at a Balinese temple and forbidden in a Javanese mosque; yet in Bali, wayang is generally disallowed (although exceptionally permitted, and thus conceivable) at cremations, while in Java, wayang is traditionally inconceivable at burials. In both islands, wayang enjoyed court favor and often patronage; the political domain shifted allowed/disallowed wayangs contrasting Bali-Hinduism and Islam to different rituals. Thus, although less explicitly parodic than wayang, Balinese cremation festivities may be seen as an implicit parody of Sasak circumcision (in neighboring Lombok) and vice versa, especially when we recall that each served as the principal ceremony of state for courts that in other respects were organized similarly. By opening performances and institutions to such comparative parodic possibilities, we reinstate Bateson's (1958:266) policy of leavening his mixture in *Naven* "with a little Hegelian dialectic." Clearly, to investigate Balinese culture as parody we must address not just the island's native life as lived but its historical situation in Indonesia and its "subversive" place in the variations of Indonesian, Southeast Asian, and even Indo-European configurations.

Conclusion: Is Anthropology a Parodic Pursuit?

In a recent book, *Other Tribes, Other Scribes* (Boon 1982a), I imply that the twin questions, Is Bali a parodic culture and is anthropology a parodic discipline? have something to do with each other. If we consider relevant cultural history, institutional complexities, comparative religion and mythology, and fundamentals of ethnological writing, we begin to suspect that both Balinese culture and cultural anthropology have emerged as discursive heterodoxies, designed to counter more standardized, reformist traditions of belief and practice. With no space here adequately to demonstrate the fact, let me conclude with a fragmentary list (parodic papers, too, are obsessively "listy") of rhetorical properties behind ethnological discourse. Anthropology may, like Bali, partake of the nature of Menippean satire.

1. Consider the GN category in the library stacks; notice its outlandish, globe-circling, multilanguaged contents.

2. What could better guarantee obliterating any absolute (the role Geertz attributes to wayang's clowns) than a doctrine of cultural relativity?

3. Ponder the peculiar assemblage that counts as an anthropological text: the continual displacements of reportage and citation or paraphrase, documentation and indirect discourse, interlinear translations, folk etymologies, polyglot glossaries and appendixes (see Tedlock 1979). What is an ethnographic "monograph" if not a grotesque, or in the word of Julia Kristeva (1980), a *polylogue?* If we acknowledge that any ethnography is a more or less disguised collage, certain ethnographic mysteries may speak (see Clifford 1981).

4. Where do we locate ethnography's "authority"? In the native point of view, and if so, which one? in the expert fieldworker, and if so, which of his or her facets? in comparativist dislocation from any authoritative presence? in the arts of exaggeration and typology which no ethnography can altogether avoid? This kind of paradox may inhibit "science" but it animates "anthropology."

5. Ethnographers, like Menippean satirists, convert the complexities of historical cultures into packages of print, and they know it.

Perhaps cultural anthropology is most Menippean when it keeps readers attuned to heterodoxies resisted by conventionalized, standard canons of rationality. Whether this persistent subversiveness serves the political left or the right (if either) remains an open question. A recent article by Allon White (1982) on "the politics of transgression" contrasts two arguments: (1) Bakhtin's and Kristeva's assumption that subversive overplay is inevitably radical; and (2) anthropological demonstrations by Balandier (and, I would add, many of the scholars in this proceedings volume) that such play can be conservative, indeed restorative (cf. Turner 1974; Boon 1982d). As White (1982:60) expresses the issue: "How far does carnivalesque transgression remain complicit with the rules and structures which it infringes, and how far does it really subvert and radically interrogate those rules and structures?"

But are the alternatives mutually exclusive? Perhaps Menippean satire occurs wherever the would-be subversive and the wished-for conservative recognize each as complicit in the other (pace Luther; vive Erasmus!). Still, I subscribe to the cautions of White (who follows Natalie Z. Davis): any ritual transgression must be situated in its historical and cultural context before we rush to declare it Nietzsche-esque (poststructuralists beware!). I would add that Erasmus's wisdom beckons whenever the same transgressive carnivalizations are simultaneously restorative in some respects and subversive in others: for example, those wayang-style social and ritual forms that both serve Bali's hierarchical status quo and subvert varieties of reformism represented by Islam and rival forces of Indonesian national centralization.

Does a similar complexity and ambivalence characterize the play of anthropology itself, a discipline that is inherently transgressive, or as Erasmus might have put it, the cream of the academic jest? If so, cultural anthropology is not alone in its (conservative? radical? both?) subversiveness. Rather, it contributes to a vital discourse of the *longue dureé* that investigates, questions, even celebrates humanity's polyglot circumstances. This fact ensures Menippean irony a place among anthropology's many mirrors and voices; and it also ensures that the voice of irony will be only one among others.

Anthropological texts thus join a panoply of parodic, doubting works. In *Other Tribes, Other Scribes* I allude to many members of this unlikely chorus and draw on their example to orchestrate a cross-cultural history of discourses. To take only one case from an impossibly copious list of thousands, consider Melville's *Mardi* (Agamemnon and Charlie Chaplin; Thoreau and Geertz; Christ cum Santa; Bali and *Mardi*!). I wish I had the space to subvert this paper on folly, Bali, and anthropology into a paper on Melville's mock-fantastic *Mardi;* but there is room only to hint. In *Mardi*, Melville consolidated Near Eastern and Malayo-Polynesian terminologies into an imaginary nomenclature more convincing than vocabularies from the real Marquesans and the real Tahiti he had visited. He spun his traveler's tale around Sir William Jones's influential fourfold division of the history of world mythology (Franklin 1963; cf. Boon 1983), and he produced a visionary "world's language" whose cosmopolitan sea-goers established for all nations a "lingua-franca of the forecastle." Along the way to Mardi, Melville achieved resplendent parodies of mid-19th-century ethnological writing as well. The following example, called "How Teeth were Regarded in Valapee," requires delivery in the style of a bad, a very bad, Shakespearean actor (read it as Folly herself would):

Now human teeth, extracted, are reckoned among the most valuable ornaments in Mardi. So open wide they strong box, Hohora, and show thy treasures. What a gallant array! standing shoulder to shoulder, without a hiatus between. . . . something farther needs be said concerning the light in which men's molars are regarded in Mardi.

As in all lands, men smite their breasts, and tear their hair, when transported with grief; so, in some countries, teeth are stricken out under the sway of similar emotions. To a very great extent, this was once practiced in the Hawaiian Islands, ere idol and altar went down. Still living in Oahu, are many old chiefs, who were present at the famous obsequies of their royal old generalissimo, Tammahammaha, when there is no telling how many pounds of ivory were cast upon his grave.

Ah! had the regal white elephants of Siam been there, doubtless they had offered up their long, hooked tusks, whereon they impale the leopards, their foes; and the unicorn had surrendered that fixed bayonet in his forehead; and the imperial Cachalot-whale, the long chain of white towers in his jaw; yea, over that grim warrior's grave, the mooses, and elks, and stags, and fallow-deer had stacked their antlers, as soldiers their arms on the field.

Terrific shade of tattooed Tammahammaha! if, from a vile dragon's molars, rose mailed men, what heroes shall spring from the cannibal canines once pertaining to warriors themselves!—Am I the witch of Endor, that I conjure up this ghost? Or, King Saul, that I so quake at the sight? For, lo! roundabout me Tammahammaha's tattooing expands, till all the sky seems a tiger's skin. But now, the spotted phantom sweeps by; as a man-of-war's main-sail, cloud-like, blown far to leeward in a gale.

Banquo down, we return. . . .

From the high value ascribed to dentals throughout the archipelago of Mardi, and also from their convenient size, they are circulated as money; strings of teeth being regarded by these people very much as belts of wampum among the Winnebagoes of the North; or cowries, among the Bengalese. So, that in Valapee the very beggars are born with a snug investment in their mouths; too soon, however, to be appropriated by their lords; leaving them toothless for the rest of their days, and forcing them to diet on poee-pudding and banana blanc-mange. [Melville 1970(1849):205–206]

Tattooed Generalissimo Tammahammaha, or MacBeth? Who could say, in a world of poee-pudding and banana blanc-mange, where all cultures, histories, and languages theatrically, parodically, and apocalyptically converge.

So Melville wrote; and so anthropologists write, or more of us than we conventionally acknowledge. The very jargon of our discipline recalls Melville's lingua-franca, his hybrid Sailor-*sprache*. Our oft-derided technical vocabularies sustain motives of and for inscribing the world's rarities and varieties in a world language: totem, taboo, *fétiche,* tattoo, hapu, mana, orenda, amok, *dan lain lain;* taking care to preserve classical-sounding complements as well: anima, connubium, exogamy, *et cetera.*[4]

With our polyglot vocabularies anthropology pursues multivalent, relativist, subversive concerns; in our somber, disenchanted age, we champion heterodoxies, at least of others. Like Melville, anthropologists inscribe values contrary to our rational order. How does this enterprise differ from the view Melville alludes to in a probable parody of Christian apologists who reconciled exotic mythologies and theological orthodoxy?

All things form but one whole; the universe a Judea, and God Jehova its head. . . . Away with our stares and grimaces. The New Zealander's tattooing is not a prodigy; nor the Chinaman's ways an enigma. No custom is strange; no creed is absurd; no foe, but who will in the end prove a friend. In heaven, at last . . . [Melville 1970:12; cf. Boon 1982a:150–151].

Might anthropologists, too, be emboldened explicitly to ask the question that wayang, Melville, and comparable follies often implicitly ask of themselves? Are we, anthropologists, the apologist or the parodist? And might we (Folly speaking) answer "YES!"

Notes

Acknowledgments. Portions of this paper (Boon 1982c) were first prepared for a Wenner-Gren conference organized by Richard Schechner and Victor Turner in

August 1982; another version was prepared for delivery at the American Ethnological Society symposium on "Text, Play, and Story" in 1983. I thank Edward M. Bruner for reactions to an earlier draft and Ivan Brady and Masao Yamaguchi for conversations that contributed to the spirit of the study. This paper forms part of a projected collection of essays revolving around Bali, in which documentation and acknowledgments will be more adequate.

1. See particularly Bakhtin (1968); relevant translations of Bakhtin and recent works on Bakhtin, particularly by Michael Holquist, are too copious to list (see other references to Bakhtin in several articles in this proceedings volume). A recent Bakhtin-informed study of all manner of "grotesque" is Harpham (1982); several views of anthropology and carnivalization appear in Babcock (1978); carnival logics (contrasted to their absence: Lent) pervade Lévi-Strauss (1973).

2. I broach related issues in Boon (in press). "Sacrament" is intended here in the most general sense of sanctified custom, as employed by Hocart (1952, 1954); allusions to sacrament and dramaturgy as replaceables will be developed in a future paper.

3. "Manuscript cultures" refer to the historical circumstances of societies with a rapidly expanding role for scribes, before a thoroughly rationalized "print culture" comes to dominate. "Print culture" is a slogan used by Frances Yates (1979) in a review of Eisenstein (1979); equally relevant are the works of W. J. Ong (1967, 1977). While Zurbuchen (1981) ties Balinese language in performance to the idea of a "manuscript culture," I am more concerned with the institutional arrangements implied in the concept and in prolonged lags, even disjunctions, between the rise of print technologies and the fall of "manuscript cultures." This, too, is the subject of current research regarding contemporary Bali and similar cultures.

4. I would have celebrated this fact with extra relish at the American Ethnological Society meetings in Baton Rouge, for which this paper was prepared, because participants there had the opportunity to bow to that man among them who made *mayu/dama* household words!

References Cited

Anderson, Benedict R. O'G.
   1965   Mythology and the Tolerance of the Javanese. Data Paper No. 27. Ithaca: Cornell University Southeast Asia Program.
Babcock, Barbara A., ed.
   1978   The Reversible World. Ithaca: Cornell University Press.
Bakhtin, Mikhail
   1968   Rabelais and His World. H. Iswolsky, transl. Cambridge: M.I.T. Press.
Bateson, Gregory
   1958[1936]   Naven. Stanford: Stanford University Press.
Becker, A. L.
   1979   Text-building, Epistemology, and Aesthetics in Javanese Shadow Theater. *In* The Imagination of Reality. A. L. Becker and A. Yengoyan, eds. pp. 211–243. Norwood, NJ: Ablex.

Boon, James A.
1977   The Anthropological Romance of Bali, 1597–1972: Dynamic Perspectives in Marriage and Caste, Politics and Religion. New York: Cambridge University Press.
1982a   Other Tribes, Other Scribes: Symbolic Anthropology in the Comparative Study of Cultures, Histories, Religions, and Texts. New York: Cambridge University Press.
1982b   Incest Recaptured: Some Contraries of Karma in Balinese Symbology. *In* Karma: An Anthropological Inquiry. C. F. Keyes and E. V. Daniel, eds. pp. 185–222. Berkeley: University of California Press.
1982c   In Praise of Bali's Folly: Remarks on the History of Interpreting Performance in a Parodic Culture. Paper presented at the Wenner-Gren Conference on Theater and Ritual, New York.
1982d   Introduction. *In* Between Relief and Transgression. M. Izard and P. Smith, eds. pp. v–xiii. Chicago: University of Chicago Press.
1983   Birds, Words, and Orangutans: Divinity and Degeneracy in Early Indonesian Ethnology. Ms. Files of the author.
in press   Symbols, Sylphs, and Siwa: Allegorical Machineries in the Text of Balinese Culture. *In* The Anthropology of Experience. V. Turner and E. Bruner, eds. Urbana: University of Illinois Press.
Brandon, James
1970   On Thrones of Gold: Three Javanese Shadow Plays. Cambridge: Harvard University Press.
Burke, Kenneth
forever.   His corpus.
Clifford, James
1981   On Ethnographic Surrealism. Comparative Studies in Society and History 23(4):539–564.
Eisenstein, Elizabeth
1979   The Printing Press as an Agent of Change: Communication and Cultural Transformation in Early-modern Europe. Cambridge: Cambridge University Press.
Emigh, John
1982   Playing with the Past: Visitation and Illusion in the Mask Theatre of Bali. The Drama Review/T82:11–36.
Emigh, John, and I Made Bandem, transls.
1982   Jelantik Goes to Blambangan: A Topeng Pajegan Performance by I Nyoman Kakul. The Drama Review/T82:37–48.
Erasmus, Desiderius
1941[1511]   The Praise of Folly. H. H. Hudson, transl. Princeton: Princeton University Press.
Franklin, H. Bruce
1963   The Wake of the Gods: Melville's Mythology. Stanford: Stanford University Press.
Frye, Northrop
1957   Anatomy of Criticism. Princeton: Princeton University Press.

Geertz, Clifford
  1973   The Interpretation of Cultures. New York: Basic Books.
  1976   Reply to Hooykaas (1976). Archipel 12:219–225.
  1980   Blurred Genres. American Scholar 49:165–182.
Harpham, Geoffrey Galt
  1982   On the Grotesque: Strategies of Contradiction in Art and Literature.
         Princeton: Princeton University Press.
Held, G. J.
  1935   The Mahabharata: An Ethnological Study. London: Kegan Paul, Trench,
         Trubner.
Hocart, A. M.
  1952   The Life-giving Myth. London: Methuen.
  1954   Social Origins. London: Watts.
Hooykaas, C.
  1970   The Treasure of Bali. *In* R. C. Majumdar Felicitation Volume. H. B.
         Sarkar, ed. Calcutta: K. L. Mukhopadhyay.
  1976   Social Anthropology, A "Discipline" of Theories and Hear-say? Archipel
         11:237–243.
Hooykaas, J.
  1960   Changeling in Balinese Folklore and Religion. Bijdragen tot de Taal-,
         Land-, en Volkenkunde 116:424–436.
Jenkins, Ron
  1980   The Holy Humor of Bali's Clowns. Asia 3(2):28–35.
Kristeva, Julia
  1980   Desire in Language. L. S. Roudiez, ed. New York: Columbia University
         Press.
Lévi-Strauss, Claude
  1973   From Honey to Ashes. John and Doreen Weightman, transl. New York:
         Harper & Row.
McPhee, Colin
  1966   Music in Bali. New Haven: Yale University Press.
Melville, Herman
  1970[1844]   Mardi and a Voyage Thither. Evanston: Northwestern University
         Press and the Newberry Library.
Mulyono, Ir. Sri
  1978a   Wayang: Asal-usul, Filsafat dan Masa Depannya. Jakarta: Gunung
         Agung.
  1978b   Wayang dan Karakter Wanita. Jakarta: Gunung Agung.
  1979a   Wayang dan Karakter Manusia. Jakarta: Gunung Agung.
  1979b   Simbolisme dan Mistikisme dalam Wayang. Jakarta: Gunung Agung.
Ong, Walter J.
  1967   The Presence of the Word. New Haven: Yale University Press.
  1977   Interfaces of the Word. Ithaca: Cornell University Press.
Payne, F. Anne
  1981   Chaucer and Menippean Satire. Madison: University of Wisconsin Press.

Peacock, James L.
   1968   Rites of Modernization. Chicago: University of Chicago Press.
   1978   Muslim Puritans: Reformist Psychology in Southeast Asian Islam. Berkeley: University of California Press.
Radin, Paul
   1972   The Trickster. New York: Schocken Books.
Rassers, W. H.
   1959   Panji, the Culture Hero. The Hague: Martinus Nijhoff
Tedlock, Dennis
   1979   The Analogical Tradition and the Emergence of a Dialogical Anthropology. Journal of Anthropological Research 35:387–400.
Turner, Victor
   1974   Dramas, Fields, and Metaphors. Ithaca: Cornell University Press
White, Allon
   1982   Pigs and Pierrots: The Politics of Transgression in Modern Fiction. Raritan 2(2):51–70.
Yates, Frances
   1979   Print Culture. Encounter 52(4):59–64.
Young, Elizabeth F.
   1982   The Tale of Erlangga: Text Translation of a Village Drama Performance in Bali. Bijdragen tot de Taal-, Land- en Volkenkunde 138(4):470–491.
Zurbuchen, Mary
   1981   The Shadow Theater of Bali. Ph.D. dissertation. Department of Linguistics, University of Michigan, Ann Arbor.

8

Grief and a Headhunter's Rage: On the Cultural Force of Emotions

Renato I. Rosaldo
Stanford University

In what follows I want to talk about how to talk about the cultural force of emotions. *Emotional force* refers to the kinds of feelings one experiences on learning, for example, that the child just run over by a car is one's own and not a stranger's. One must consider, in other words, the subject's position within a field of social relations in order to grasp their emotional experience. This approach of showing the force of a simple statement taken literally instead of explicating culture through the gradual thickening of symbolic webs of meaning can widen our discipline's theoretical range. The vocabulary for symbolic analysis, in other words, can expand by adding the term *force* to more familiar concepts, such as *thick description, multivocality, polysemy, richness,* and *texture.*[1] The notion of force, among other things, opens to question the common assumption that tt e greatest human import always resides in the densest forest of symbols and that cultural depth always equals cultural elaboration. Do people always, in fact, describe most thickly what to them matters most?

If you ask an older Ilongot man of northern Luzon, Philippines, why he cuts off human heads, his answer is a one-liner on which no anthropologist can really elaborate: he says that rage, born of grief, impells him to kill his fellow human beings. The act of severing and tossing away the victim's head enables him, he says, to vent and hopefully throw away the anger of his bereavement. The job of cultural analysis, then, is to make this man's statement plausible and comprehensible. Yet further questioning reveals that he has little more to say about the connections between bereavement, rage, and headhunting, connections that seem so powerful to him as to be self-evident beyond explication. Either you understand it or you don't. And, in fact, for the longest time I simply did not.

It was not until some 14 years after first recording this simple statement about grief and a headhunter's rage that I began to grasp its overwhelming force. For years I had thought that more verbal elaboration (which was not forthcoming) or another analytical level (which remained elusive) could better explain the kinds of things these older men, when enraged by grief, can do to their fellow human beings. It was not until I was repositioned through lived experience that I became better able to grasp that Ilongot older men mean precisely what they say when they describe the anger in bereavement as the source of their desire to cut off human heads. This statement, taken at face value and granted its full weight, reveals much about how Ilongots can find headhunting so compelling.

The Rage in Ilongot Grief

The Ilongots number some 3500. Living in an upland area some 150 km northeast of Manila, they subsist by hunting deer and wild pig and by cultivating rain-fed gardens (swiddens) and rice, sweet potatoes, manioc, and vegetables. Their kin relations are bilateral. Due to uxorilocal postmarital residence, parents and their married daughters live in the same or adjacent households. Sibling ties among married couples in the senior generation link the dispersed houses within local clusters. The largest unit within the society, a largely territorial putative descent group called the *bērtan,* is manifest primarily in the context of headhunting feuds. Headhunting, for themselves, for their neighbors, and for their ethnographers, stands out as the Ilongots' most salient cultural practice.

When Ilongots told me, as they often did, how the rage in bereavement could impel men to headhunt, I brushed aside their one-line accounts as too simple, thin, opaque, implausible, stereotypic, or otherwise unsatisfying. Probably, I was naïvely equating grief with sadness. Certainly no personal experience allowed me to imagine the force of rage possible in bereavement for older Ilongot men. Such seemingly simple Ilongot statements thus led me to seek out another level of analysis that could provide deeper explanations for the older men's desire to headhunt.

In a representative foray along these lines, I pursued the deeper explanation by trying to use exchange theory, perhaps because it had informed so many celebrated ethnographies, to solve the analytical problem. One day in 1974, I explained the anthropologist's model to an older Ilongot man named Insan. What did he think, I asked, of the idea that headhunting resulted from one death (the beheaded victim's) cancelling another (the next of kin). He looked puzzled, so I went on to say that the victim of a beheading was exchanged for one's own dead kin, thereby, so to speak, balancing the books. Insan reflected on this for a moment and then replied that he imagined somebody could think such a thing (a safe bet, since I just had) but that he and other Ilongots did not think any such thing. Nor was there any indirect evidence for my exchange theory in ritual, boast, song, or casual conversation.[2]

In retrospect, then, these efforts to impose exchange theory on one aspect of Ilongot behavior appear feeble. Suppose I had discovered what I sought? Although the notion of balancing the ledger does have a certain elegant coherence, one wonders why such bookish dogma could inspire any man to take another man's life at the risk of his own.

My life experience had as yet not provided the means to imagine the rage that can come with devastating loss. Nor could I therefore fully appreciate the acute problem of meaning that Ilongots faced in 1974. Shortly after Ferdinand Marcos declared martial law in 1972, rumors reached the Ilongot hills that firing squads had become the new punishment for headhunting. In past epochs when headhunting had become impossible, Ilongots had allowed their rage to dissipate in the course of everyday life as best they could. In 1974, they instead began to consider conversion to Evangelical Christianity as an alternative means of coping with their grief. Accepting the new religion, people said, implied abandoning their old ways, including headhunting. It also made coping with bereavement less agonizing because they could believe that the deceased had departed for a better world. No longer did they have to confront the awful finality of death.

The force of the dilemma faced by Ilongots at that time eluded me. Even when I correctly recorded their statements about grieving and the need to throw away their anger, I simply did not grasp the weight of their words. In 1974, for example, while Michelle Rosaldo and I were living among the Ilongots, a six-month-old baby died, probably of pneumonia. That afternoon we visited the father and found him terribly stricken: "He was sobbing and staring through glazed and bloodshot eyes at the cotton blanket" covering his dead baby (R. Rosaldo 1980:286). The man suffered intensely, for this was the seventh child he had lost. Just a few years before, three of his children had died, one after the other, in a matter of days. At the time, the situation was murky as people present talked both about Evangelical Christianity and about their grudges against lowlanders as they expressed their anger and perhaps contemplated headhunting forays into the surrounding valleys.

Through subsequent days and weeks, however, the man's grief moved him in a way I had not anticipated. Shortly after the baby's death the father converted to Evangelical Christianity. Altogether too quick on the inference, I immediately concluded that the man believed that the new religion could somehow prevent further deaths in his family. When I pursued this line of thought, an Ilongot friend sharply corrected me, saying that

> I had missed the point: what the man in fact sought in the new reli-
> gion was not the denial of our inevitable deaths, but a means of cop-
> ing with his grief. With the advent of Martial Law, headhunting was
> out of the question as a means of venting his wrath and thereby les-
> sening his grief. Were he to remain in his Ilongot way of life, the
> pain of his sorrow would simply be too much to bear [R. Rosaldo
> 1980:288].

Taken verbatim from my own monograph, this description now seems so
apt that I wonder how I nonetheless could have failed to appreciate the
weight and power of the man's desire for "venting his wrath and thereby
lessening his grief."

Another anecdote makes all the more remarkable this failure to imagine the rage possible in Ilongot bereavement. On this occasion Michelle
Rosaldo and I were urged by Ilongot friends to play the tape of a headhunting celebration we had witnessed some five years earlier. No sooner had we
turned on the tape recorder and heard the boast of a man who had died in
the intervening years than did people abruptly tell us to shut off the
machine. Michelle Rosaldo (1980:33) reported on the tense conversation
that ensued:

> As Insan braced himself to speak, the room again became almost un-
> cannily electric. Backs straightened and my anger turned to nervous-
> ness and something more like fear as I saw that Insan's eyes were
> red. Tukbaw, Renato's Ilongot "brother," then broke into what was
> a brittle silence, saying he could make things clear. He told us that it
> hurt to listen to a headhunting celebration when people knew that
> there would never be another. As he put it: "The song pulls at us,
> drags our hearts, it makes us think of our dead uncle." And again:
> "It would be different if I had accepted God, but I still am an Il-
> ongot at heart; and when I hear the song, my heart aches as it does
> when I must look upon unfinished bachelors whom I know that I will
> never lead to take a head." Then Wagat, Tukbaw's wife, said with
> her eyes that all my questions gave her pain, and told me: "Leave off
> now, isn't that enough? Even I, a woman, cannot stand the way it
> feels inside my heart."

From my present position it now is evident that the tape recording with the
dead man's boast spontaneously revived among those listening powerful
feelings of bereavement, particularly rage and the impulse to headhunt. At
the time I could only be frightened and sense the force of the emotions experienced by Tukbaw, Insan, Wagat, and the others present.

The dilemma for Ilongots grew out of a set of cultural practices that, when blocked, were agonizing to live with. This blockage called for painful adjustments to other modes of experiencing their bereavement. One could compare this dilemma with Radcliffe-Brown's notion that ritual, particularly when not performed, can create anxiety. In this case the notion that to throw away a human head is also (by a metaphoric principle of sympathetic magic) to cast away the excessive anger in one's grief itself, creates a problem of meaning when headhunting seems out of the question. Indeed, the classic Weberian problem of meaning is precisely of this kind. On a logical plane the doctrine of predestination seems flawless: God has chosen the elect but his decision can never be known by mortals. If a group's ultimate concern is salvation, however, this coherent doctrine proves impossible to live with for all but the religious virtuoso. The problem of meaning, for Calvinists and Ilongots alike, involved practice, not theory. At stake for both groups were practical matters concerning how to live with one's beliefs, rather than logical puzzlement produced by an abstract doctrine.

How I Found the Rage in Grief

One burden of this paper concerns the claim that it took some 14 years for me to grasp what Ilongots had told me about their grief, rage, and headhunting. During all those years I was not yet in a position to comprehend the force of anger possible in bereavement, and now I am. Introducing myself into this account requires a certain hesitation both because of the discipline's taboo and because of its increasingly frequent violation by essays laced with trendy amalgams of continental philosophy and autobiographical snippets. The vice of the latter trend, of course, is that reflexivity leads the self-absorbed Self to lose sight altogether of the Other. Despite this risk, as the ethnographer I must enter the discussion at this point to elucidate certain issues of method.

The key concept in what follows is that of the positioned (and repositioned) subject. In routine interpretive procedure, according to the methodology of hermeneutics, one can say that ethnographers reposition themselves as they go about understanding other cultures. One begins with a set of questions and subsequently revises them in the course of inquiry. Thus, ethnographers emerge from fieldwork with a different set of questions than those they posed on initial entry. Ask a question, in other words, and through surprise at the answer you'll revise your question until lessening surprises or diminishing returns indicates a stopping point. This approach has been most influentially articulated within anthropology by Clifford Geertz (1974).

This view of interpretive method usually rests on the axiom that gifted ethnographers learn their trade through a broad course of preparation. In order to follow the meandering course of ethnographic inquiry, fieldworkers require wide-ranging theoretical capacities and finely tuned sensibilities. After all, one cannot predict beforehand what one will encounter in the field. Clyde Kluckhohn even went so far as to recommend a double initiation: first the ordeal of psychoanalysis and then that of fieldwork. All too often, this view is extended so that certain prerequisites of actual field research appear to guarantee an authoritative ethnography. Eclectic book knowledge and a range of life experiences, edifying reading and self-awareness, supposedly vanquish the twin vices of ignorance and insensitivity.

Although the doctrine of preparation, knowledge, and sensibility contains much to admire, one should work to undermine the false comfort it can convey. At what point, for example, can people say that they have completed their learning or their life experience? The problem with taking too much to heart this mode of preparing the ethnographer is that it can lend a false air of security, an authoritative claim to certitude and finality that our analyses cannot have. All interpretations are provisional; they are made by positioned subjects who are prepared to know certain things and not others. Good ethnographers, knowledgeable and sensitive, fluent in the language and able to move easily in an alien cultural world, still have their limits, and their analyses always are incomplete. Thus, I began to fathom the force of what Ilongots had been telling me about their losses through the accident of my own devastating loss and not through any systematic preparation for field research.

My own understanding had been prepared a little over a decade earlier with my brother's death in 1970. By experiencing this trying ordeal with my mother and father, I gained a measure of insight into the trauma of a parent losing a child. This insight informed my account, partially described earlier, of an Ilongot man's reactions to the death of his seventh child. At the same time, my bereavement was so much less than that of my parents that I could not then imagine the overwhelming force of rage possible in such grief. My former position probably obtains rather generally in the discipline. One should recognize that ethnographic knowledge tends to have the strengths and limitations given by the relative youth of fieldworkers who, for example, could have no personal knowledge of how devastating the loss of a long-term partner can be for the survivor.

In 1981 Michelle Rosaldo and I began field research among the Ifugaos of northern Luzon, Philippines. On October 11 of that year, Shelly was walking along a trail with two Ifugao companions when she lost her footing and fell to her death some 20 m down a sheer precipice into the swollen river below. Immediately on finding her body I became enraged. How could she abandon me? How could she have been so stupid as to fall? I tried to cry. I sobbed, but rage blocked the tears. Earlier lived experience, on the fourth anniversary of my brother's death, had taught me to recognize heaving sobs without tears as a form of anger. This anger, in a number of forms, has swept over me on many occasions since Shelly's death, lasting hours and even days at a time. Such feelings can be aroused by rituals, but more often they emerge from unexpected reminders (not unlike the Ilongots' experience of their dead uncle's recorded voice).

Lest there be any misunderstanding, bereavement should not be reduced to anger, neither for myself nor for anyone else. Powerful visceral emotional states swept over me, at times separately and at other times together. Among other things, I felt in my chest the deep cutting pain of sorrow almost beyond endurance, the cadaverous cold of realizing the finality of death, the trembling beginning in my abdomen and spreading through my body as a form of wailing, the mournful keening that started without my willing, and frequent tearful sobbing. My present purpose of revising earlier understandings of Ilongot headhunting and not a general view of bereavement thus grants centrality to the anger rather than the other emotions in grief.

One should probably add that writings in English especially need to emphasize the emotion of anger. Although grief therapists routinely encourage awareness of the anger in bereavement, American culture in general ignores the rage that devastating losses can bring. Paradoxically, cultural wisdom denies the anger in grief even though members of the invisible community of the bereaved can be encouraged to talk obsessively about their anger. My brother's death in combination with Ilongot teachings about anger (for them, a publicly celebrated rather than a hidden emotion) allowed me immediately to recognize the experience of rage.

Writing in my journal some six weeks after Shelly's death, I noted: "If I ever return to anthropology by writing 'Grief and a Headhunter's Rage. . . .' " It seems, as I discovered only a week before completing the initial draft of this paper, that I had made a vow to myself about how I would return, if I did so, to writing anthropology. Reflecting further on death, rage, and headhunting, my journal goes on to describe my "wish for the Ilongot solution; they are much more in touch with reality than Christians. So, I need a place to carry my anger—and can we say a solution of the imagination is better than theirs? And can we condemn them when we napalm villages? Is our rationale so much sounder than theirs?" All this was written in despair and rage.

This paper itself, in fact, has been cathartic, though perhaps not in the way one would imagine. Not until some 15 months after Shelly's death was I able to write anthropology. In the month before beginning this paper, I was ill with a fever and felt diffusely depressed. Then one day an almost literal fog lifted and words began to flow. Thus, the experience of catharsis enabled the writing to proceed, rather than the reverse.

By invoking lived experience as an analytical category, one risks easy dismissal. Unsympathetic readers could reduce this paper to an act of mourning or to a report on a personal discovery of the anger possible in bereavement. Frankly, this paper is both and more. An act of mourning *and* a personal report, it simultaneously involves a number of distinguishable processes no one of which cancels out the others. Indeed, in what follows I make precisely this argument about ritual in general and Ilongot headhunting in particular. The paramount claim made here, aside from revising the ethnographic record, concerns the ways in which my own mourning and consequent reflection on Ilongot bereavement, rage, and headhunting raise methodological issues of general concern in anthropology.

Death in Anthropology

Symbolic anthropology in particular has privileged interpretations that ground their understanding in cultural elaboration and deeper levels of analysis. In practice, many analyses favor restricted spheres where formal and repetitive events take center stage. Consider, for example, Victor Turner on ritual process or Clifford Geertz on deep play in the Balinese cockfight. Studies of word play, in the same vein, are more likely to focus on jokes as programmed monologues than on the less-scripted, more free-wheeling improvised interchanges of witty banter. Symbolic anthropology often focuses on rituals, ceremonies, games, and other activities played out in visibly bounded arenas. These events have definite locations in space, with centers and outer edges. Temporally, they also are well defined, with fixed beginnings, middles, and endings. Historically, they appear to repeat identical structures. These qualities of fixed definition have liberated such events from the untidiness of everyday life so that they can be read like articles, books, or, as we now say, *texts*.

These remarks can take on more substance in the context of particular studies of death and its rituals. Take, for example, William Douglas's book, *Death in Murelaga: Funerary Ritual in a Spanish Basque Village* (1969). Notice that the title equates death and "funerary ritual." The objective, Douglas (1969:209) says, is to use death and funerary ritual "as a heuristic device with which to approach the study of rural Basque society." The author begins his analysis by saying that "death is not always fortuitous or unpredictable" (1969:19). He goes on to describe how an old woman, ailing with the infirmities of her age, welcomed her death. The description itself largely ignores the perspective of the most bereaved survivors and instead vacillates between those of the old woman and a detached observer.

Undeniably, certain people do live a full life and suffer so greatly in their decripitude that they embrace the relief death can bring. Yet the problem with making such an easy death (I use Simone de Beauvoir's [1969] title, as she did, with irony) the paradigm case of dying is that it makes death appear as routine for the survivors as this one apparently was for the deceased. Douglas (1969) captures only one extreme in the range of possible deaths. It seems exemplary, not in describing how people cope with death but in being as routine as possible and thereby fitting neatly with the author's view of funerary ritual as a mechanical, programmed unfolding of prescribed acts. "To the Basque," says Douglas (1969:75), "ritual is order and order is ritual."

Putting the accent on the routine aspects of ritual conveniently conceals the agony of such unexpected early deaths as parents losing a grown child or a mother dying in childbirth. Concealed in such descriptions are the agonies of the survivors who muddle through shifting, powerful emotional states. Although Douglas acknowledges the distinction between the bereaved members of the deceased's domestic group and the more public ritualistic group, he writes his account primarily from the viewpoint of the latter. He masks the emotional force of bereavement by reducing funerary ritual to orderly routine.

In a more recent compendium of the wisdom of the discipline, Richard Huntington and Peter Metcalf's *Celebrations of Death: The Anthropology of Mortuary Ritual* (1979) takes another tack in dismissing the force of emotions.[3] They admit the presence of emotions but deny their explanatory power for understanding ritual in a line of argument made classic by Emile Durkeim and Claude Lévi-Strauss. Their argument begins by using Radcliffe-Brown to assert that "crying at funerals is not merely tolerated, it is required by custom, and at predetermined moments the entire body of mourners will burst into loud and piercing cries. Just as suddenly, the weeping halts and the tears that had just been running so profusely cease" (Huntington and Metcalf 1979:24). They go on to applaud Radcliffe-Brown's notion that "the sentiment does not create the act, but wailing at the prescribed moment and in the prescribed manner creates within the wailer the proper sentiment" (1979:26). Thus far, the argument on emotions seems as standard as it is sensible, but note well that conventional wisdom defines ritual and obligatory behavior as one and the same. Collapsing the two eliminates the space for improvisation and spontaneous sentiment within ritual.

When Huntington and Metcalf (1979:31) discuss Durkheim, they extend their argument on ritual weeping by saying, "We cannot assume that people actually feel the sorrow they express." Certainly, the obligatory acts in ritual do not arise from spontaneous sentiment, but neither should one assume that people do or do not "feel the sorrow they express." One could reasonably assume, along these lines, that certain people just go through the motions while other people's ritual wailing is heartfelt. Even here, however, one could not simply say that those most attached to the deceased most feel the emotions they express, whereas those most distant least feel them. A death can touch one deeply because of its resonance with other personal losses, rather than because of one's intimate ties with the deceased. The point, in any case, is that analysis can assume neither that individuals do nor do not feel the sentiments they express during a funeral.

Huntington and Metcalf (1979:44) complete their dismissal of emotions in mortuary ritual by saying, "Though often intense, emotional reactions to death are too varied and shifting to provide the foundation for a theory of mortuary ritual." Thus far I am with them, but they go on:

> The need to release aggression, or break ties with the deceased, or complete any other putatively universal psychic process, does not serve to explain funerals. The shoe is on the other foot. Whatever mental adjustments the individual needs to make in the face of death he or she must accomplish as best he or she can, through such rituals as society provides [1979:44].

Their claim that "in the face of death" individuals rely entirely on "such rituals as society provides" makes a crucial mistake: it collapses the ritual process and the process of mourning.

Surely, human beings mourn both in ritual settings and in the informal settings of everyday life. Consider, for example, the following passage from a paper Huntington and Metcalf cite, "Nyakyusa Conventions of Burial" by Godfrey Wilson (1939:22–23):

> That some at least of those who attend a Nyakyusa burial are moved by grief it is easy to establish. I have heard people talking regretfully in ordinary conversation of a man's death; I have seen a man whose sister had just died walk over alone towards her grave and weep quietly by himself without any parade of grief; and I have heard of a man killing himself because of his grief for a dead son.

Note well that all the instances Wilson has witnessed happened outside the circumscribed sphere of ritual where people simply conversed among themselves, walked alone, or more impulsively committed suicide. The work of grieving, probably universally, occurs both within obligatory ritual acts and in more everyday settings where people find themselves alone or with close kin.

The general argument that Huntington and Metcalf make can easily be turned on its head. Just as the intense emotions of bereavement do not explain obligatory ritual acts, so obligatory ritual acts do not explain the intense emotions of bereavement. It is no more true that all intense emotional states are obligatory (as Huntington and Metcalf seem to claim) than to assert that all obligatory emotional states are intense. The approach to ritual advocated by these authors works to deny the socially consequential force of emotions that can overwhelm the bereaved, especially the chief mourners. Even in the face of volatile rage and sorrow, such analyses allow the comfort of denial through their focus on the elegant order often found in prescribed cultural elaboration.

Among the Nyakyusa, to return to Wilson's account, men danced the passions of their bereavement. They described their feelings in this manner:

> "This war dance *(ukukina),*" said an old man, "is mourning, we are mourning the dead man. We dance because there is war in our hearts. A passion of grief and fear exasperates us *(ilyyojo likutusila)*." . . . *Elyojo* means a passion of grief, anger or fear; *ukusila* means to annoy or exasperate beyond endurance. In explaining *ukusila* one man put it like this: "If a man continually insults me then he exasperates me *(ukusila)* so that I want to fight him." Death is a fearful and grievous event that exasperates those men nearly concerned and makes them want to fight. [1939:13]

Descriptions of the dance and subsequent quarrels, even killings, provide ample evidence of the emotional intensity involved. The articulate testimony by Wilson's informants makes it obvious that even the most intense sentiments can be studied by ethnographers (see M. Rosaldo 1980).

Whether resulting from notions of objectivity or dogmas about the indeterminacy of inner states, ethnographies that eliminate such qualities as anger, lust, and tenderness both distort their descriptions and remove potentially key variables from their explanations. My use of personal experience as a point of departure in characterizing the rage of grief for Ilongots has been, among other things, a vehicle for enabling readers to apprehend the force of emotions in another culture. Ilongot anger and my own, of course, only overlap in a significant respect, but they are not identical. Fantasies about life insurance agents who refused to recognize Shelly's death as job related did not, for example, lead me to kill them, cut off their heads, and celebrate afterward. Stating in such concrete terms the modest truism that any two human groups must have certain things in common can appear to fly in the face of a once-healthy methodological caution that warns against the reckless attribution of one's own categories and experiences to members of another culture. Such warnings against facile notions of universal human nature can be carried too far and harden into the equally pernicious doctrine that, my own group aside, everything human is alien to me.

Thus, in most anthropological studies of death, analysts simply eliminate the emotions by assuming the position of a most detached observer. Their stance also equates the ritual with the obligatory, ignores the relation between ritual and everyday life, and conflates the ritual process with the process of mourning. The general rule, despite such exceptions as Wilson's account, seems to be that one should tidy things up as much as possible by wiping away the tears and ignoring the tantrums.

When analysts equate death and funerary ritual, they assume that rituals encode and store encapsulated wisdom as if it were the formalized microcosm of the informal workings of everyday life in a culture. Johannes Fabian (1973:178), for example, found that during the decade of the 1960s the four major anthropological journals carried only nine papers on death, and most of those "dealt only with the purely ceremonial aspects of death." The bias that so privileges ritual risks assuming the answers to the questions that most need to be asked. Do rituals, for example, always reveal cultural depth? Huntington and Metcalf (1979:1) simply reflect the received wisdom as they confidently begin their work by affirming that rituals embody "the collective wisdoms of many cultures." Surely this assertion requires investigation.

At the polar extremes, rituals could either display cultural depth or be brimming with platitudes. In the latter instance, rituals could, for example, act as catalysts that precipitate processes whose unfolding occurs over subsequent months or even years. My own experience fits the platitudes and catalyst model better than the model of microcosmic deep culture. Even a careful analysis of the language and symbolic actions during the two funerals for which I have been a chief mourner could reveal precious little about the lived experience of bereavement.[4] This statement, of course, should not lead anyone to derive a universal from somebody else's personal knowledge. Instead, it should encourage ethnographers to ask whether a ritual's wisdom is deep or conventional and whether its process is immediately transformative or but a single step in a lengthy series of ritual and everyday events.

In attempting to grasp the cultural force of rage and other powerful emotional states, one should look both to formal ritual and to the informal practices of everyday life. Symbolic analysis, in other words, can be extended from formal ritual to the inclusion of myriad cultural practices less elaborate and circumscribed. Such descriptions can seek out force as well as thickness.

Grief, and Rage, and Ilongot Headhunting

Allow me now to sketch how considerations of cultural force apply to Ilongot headhunting. Perhaps we should begin by viewing headhunting as the ritual enactment of piacular sacrifice. The raid begins with calling the spirit of the potential victim, moves through the rituals of farewell, and continues with seeking favorable omens along the trail. Most Ilongots speak about hunger and deprivation as they take days to move slowly toward the place where they will set up an ambush and await the first person who happens along. Once the raiders kill their victim, they toss away the head rather than keep it as a trophy. Before a raid, men describe their inner state by saying that the burdens of life have made them heavy and entangled, like a tree with vines clinging to it. After a successful raid, they say that they become light of step and ruddy in complexion. The collective energy of the celebration with its song, music, and dance is said to give the participants a sense of well-being. This ritual process involves cleansing and catharsis.

The view just outlined gains analytical power by regarding ritual as a self-contained process. Without denying the insight in this approach, we should also consider its limitations. Suppose, for example, we view exorcism rituals as if they are complete in themselves and never consider them as parts of larger processes unfolding before and after the ritual period. What can we say about the state of being demented through possession? Through what processes does someone recover or continue to be afflicted when rituals fail? Failure to consider these questions can rob the force from the afflictions and therapies only partially actualized during the formal ritual. Still other questions could apply, not only to the person afflicted but also to such differently positioned subjects as the healer and the audience. In all cases the problem involves the delineation of processes that occur before and after, as well as during, the ritual moment.

If the position just outlined critically can be called the *microcosmic view,* I should like to propose an alternative called *ritual as a busy intersection.* Rather than a self-contained sphere of deep cultural activity, ritual can be seen as a place where a number of distinct social processes intersect. The crossroads simply provides a space for distinct trajectories to traverse rather than containing them in complete encapsulated form. From this perspective, Ilongot headhunting can be seen as standing at the confluence of three analytically separable processes.

The first process concerns whether or not it is an opportune time to raid. In the past, historical conditions have determined raiding patterns ranging along a spectrum from frequent to likely to unlikely to impossible. These conditions, for example, have included American colonial efforts at pacification, the Great Depression, World War II, revolutionary movements in the surrounding lowlands, feuding among Ilongot groups, and the already cited declaration of martial law in 1972. Ilongots themselves speak of such historical contingencies by analogy with hunting. Hunters say that one's opportunities lie beyond one's control, for who can say whether game will cross one's path or whether one's arrow will strike its target. My book on Ilongot headhunting explores these historical factors at some length (R. Rosaldo 1980).

Second, young men coming of age undergo a protracted period of personal turmoil during which they desire nothing so much as to take a head. It is a time when they seek a life partner and contemplate the traumatic dislocation of leaving their families of origin and entering their new wife's household as a stranger. Young men weep, sing, and burst out in anger because of their intense, fierce desire to take a head and wear the coveted red hornbill earrings that adorn the men who have, as Ilongots say, arrived *(tabi)* before them. Volatile, envious, and passionate, at least according to their own cultural stereotype of the young unmarried man *(buintaw),* they constantly lust to take a head. During the initial period of Ilongot fieldwork, Shelly and I only the year before had abandoned our unmarried youths; hence our ready empathy with late-adolescent turbulence. Her book on Ilongot notions of self explores the passionate anger of young men in considerable depth (M. Rosaldo 1980).

Third, older men are rather differently positioned than their younger counterparts. Because they have already beheaded somebody, they can wear the red hornbill earrings so coveted by youths. Thus, their desire to headhunt grows less from chronic adolescent turmoil than from more intermittent acute agonies of loss. After the death of somebody to whom they are closely attached, older men often vow to punish themselves until they participate in a successful headhunting raid. These deaths can cover a range of instances from literal death through natural causes or beheading to social death where, for example, a man's wife runs off with another man. All these cases share the rage born of devastating loss. This anger at abandonment is irreducible in that nothing at a deeper level explains it. Although symbolic analysis often argues against the dreaded last analysis, the linkage of grief, rage, and headhunting has reached rock bottom.

It is evident that my earlier understandings of Ilongot headhunting missed the full significance of how older men experience loss and rage. The position of older men proves critical in this context because they, and not the youths, set the processes of headhunting in motion. Their rage is intermittent, whereas that of youths is continuous. Thus, in the equation of headhunting, older men are the variable and younger men are the constant. Culturally speaking, older men are endowed with knowledge and stamina that their juniors have not yet attained, hence they care for *(saysay)* and lead *(bukur)* the younger men when they raid.

In a preliminary survey of the literature on headhunting, I found that the lifting of mourning prohibitions frequently occurs after taking a head. Compared with reported notions, such as that men cut off human heads in order to acquire either soul stuff or personal names (see McKinley 1976; Needham 1976; M. Rosaldo 1977), this account of youthful anger and

older men's rage born of devastating loss lends greater human plausibility
to the notion that headhunters can find their cultural practices compelling.
Because the discipline correctly refuses to say that by nature headhunters
are bloodthirsty, it must construct convincing explanations of how
headhunters create an intense desire within themselves to cut off human
heads. Hence, the significance in seeking an account of the passions that
animate human conduct by exploring the cultural force of the emotions.

Emotion, Ritual, and the Positioned Subject

Of the four major assertions made in this paper, the initial two concern
problems that emerge from assuming a correct answer instead of raising a
question that requires investigation; the latter two outline certain
methodological consequences of speaking about the positioned subject.

    1. Does cultural depth always equal cultural elaboration? Think
simply of the speaker who is filibustering. The language used can sound
elaborate as it heaps word upon word, but surely it is not deep. Depth, in
other words, should be separated from the presence or absence of elaboration. By the same token, one-liners can be vacuous or pithy.

    The concept of force calls attention to an enduring intensity in
human conduct which can occur with or without the dense symbolic
elaboration conventionally associated with cultural depth. Although
relatively without elaboration in speech, song, or ritual, the rage of older Ilongot men who have suffered devastating losses proves enormously consequential in that, foremost among other things, it leads them to behead their
fellow humans. Thus, the notion of force involves both affective intensity
and significant consequences that unfold over a long period of time.

    2. Do rituals always encapsulate deep cultural wisdom? Could they
instead contain the wisdom of Polonius? Certain rituals, of course,
manifest and indeed create ultimate values, key cultural conceptions, and
the bases of group solidarity. In other cases, however, they bring people
together and deliver a set of platitudes that enable them to go on with their
lives rather than offering them insight.

    Rituals can thus serve as the vehicles for processes that occur both
before and after the period of their performance. Funeral rituals, for example, do not contain the entire process of mourning. It is a mistake to collapse the two because neither ritual nor mourning fully encapsulates or fully
explains the other. In such cases the ritual process can be only a resting
point along a number of longer processual trajectories; hence, the image of
ritual as a crossroads where distinct life processes can intersect.

    3. The ethnographer, as a positioned subject, can grasp certain
ethnographic phenomena better than others. Most simply, the concept of
position refers to a structural location from which one has a particular angle

of vision. Consider, for example, how age, gender, being an outsider, and association with a neocolonial regime can influence what one learns.

Position can also refer to how one's lived experience both enables and inhibits particular kinds of insight. Nothing in my own experience, for example, had equipped me even to imagine the anger possible in bereavement. It was not until after Shelly's death in 1981 that I was in a position to grasp the force of what Ilongots had repeatedly told me about grief, rage, and headhunting.

4. Natives, as positioned subjects, also have their insights and blindness. This paper considers both the structural positions of older versus younger men and how lived experience positions chief mourners differently from those less involved. In reviewing anthropological writings on death, I often simply shifted the analysis from the position of those least involved to that of the chief mourners.

From this perspective the positions of the ethnographer and the native should be considered in conjunction with one another. The following remarks by Pierre Bourdieu (1977:1), despite his unforgivable use of the masculine pronoun, seem apposite here:

> The anthropologist's particular relation to the object of his study contains the makings of a theoretical distortion inasmuch as his situation as an observer, excluded from the real play of social activities by the fact that he has no place (except by choice or by way of a game) in the system observed and has no need to make a place for himself there, inclines him to a hermeneutic representation of practices, leading him to reduce all social situations to communicative relations and, more precisely, to decoding operations. . . . And exaltation of the virtues of the distance secured by externality simply transmutes into an epistemological choice the anthropologist's objective situation, that of the "impartial spectator," as Husserl puts it, condemned to see all practice as spectacle.

Similarly, most anthropologists write about death as if they were positioned as uninvolved spectators who have no lived experience that could provide knowledge about the cultural force of emotions.

Notes

Acknowledgments. Field research among the Ilongots, conducted over 30 months during 1967–69 and 1974, was financed by a National Science Foundation predoctoral fellowship, by National Science Foundation Research Grants GS-1509 and GS-40788, and a Mellon Award for junior faculty from Stanford University. A Fulbright Grant financed a two-month stay in the Philippines during 1981. This paper has benefitted from the comments of Jane Atkinson, Edward Bruner, Roberto DaMatta, Louise Lamphere, Rick Maddox, Kirin Narayan, Emiko Ohnuki-Tierney, Mary Pratt, Amelie Rorty, and Maidi Rosenblatt.

1. Force and related concepts, particularly those concerning emotions, have long been part of the anthropological vocabulary (see, e.g., H. Geertz 1959). In *Islam Observed* (1968), Clifford Geertz found it necessary to distinguish the force of cultural patterning from its scope as he delineated the contrasts between Moroccan and Javanese forms of mysticism. He states the distinction between force and scope in this manner:

> By "force" I mean the thoroughness with which such a pattern is internalized in the personalities of the individuals who adopt it, its centrality or marginality in their lives. . . . By "scope," on the other hand, I mean the range of social contexts within which religious considerations are regarded as having more or less direct relevance. [1968:111–112]

In his later works, Geertz develops the notion of scope more than that of force. My use of the term "force" differs from that of Geertz in stressing the concept of the positioned subject rather than processes of internalization within individual personalities.

2. Lest the hypothesis Insan rejected appear utterly implausible, I should mention that among the Berawan of Borneo "death has a chain reaction quality to it. There is a considerable anxiety that, unless something is done to break the chain, death will follow upon death. The logic of this is now plain: The unquiet soul kills, and so creates more unquiet souls" (Metcalf 1982:127). The Berawan, in other words, link a version of exchange theory to headhunting.

3. Like Douglas, Huntington and Metcalf conflate death and mortuary ritual by announcing the former in their title and specifying the latter in their subtitle.

4. Arguably, ritual works differently for those most affected versus those least affected by a particular death. Funerals may distance the former from overwhelming emotional states, whereas they may draw the latter closer to strongly felt sentiments (see Scheff 1979). Such matters can be investigated through the notion of the positioned subject.

References Cited

Bourdieu, Pierre
  1977   Outline of a Theory of Practice. Cambridge: Cambridge University Press.
de Beauvoir, Simone
  1969   A Very Easy Death. Harmondsworth, UK: Penguin.
Douglas, William A.
  1969   Death in Murelaga: Funerary Ritual in a Spanish Basque Village. Seattle: University of Washington Press.
Fabian, Johannes
  1973   How Others Die—Reflections on the Anthropology of Death. *In* Death in

American Experience. A. Mack, ed. pp. 177–201. New York: Schocken.

Geertz, Clifford
1968 Islam Observed. New Haven: Yale University Press.
1974 The Interpretation of Cultures. New York: Basic Books.

Geertz, Hildred
1959 The Vocabulary of Emotion: A Study of Javanese Socialization Processes. Psychiatry 22:225–237.

Huntington, Richard, and Peter Metcalf
1979 Celebrations of Death: The Anthropology of Mortuary Ritual. Cambridge: Cambridge University Press.

McKinley, Robert
1976 Human and Proud of It! A Structural Treatment of Headhunting Rites and the Social Definition of Enemies. *In* Studies in Borneo Societies: Social Process and Anthropological Explanation. G. Appell, ed. pp. 92–126. DeKalb, IL: Center for Southeast Asian Studies, Northern Illinois University.

Metcalf, Peter
1982 A Borneo Journey into Death: Berawan Eschatology from Its Rituals. Philadelphia: University of Pennsylvania Press.

Needham, Rodney
1976 Skulls and Causality. Man (NS) 11:71–88.

Rosaldo, Michelle
1977 Skulls and Causality. Man (NS) 12:168–170.
1980 Knowledge and Passion: Ilongot Notions of Self and Social Life. Cambridge: Cambridge University Press.

Rosaldo, Renato
1980 Ilongot Headhunting, 1883–1974: A Study in Society and History. Stanford: Stanford University Press.

Scheff, T. J.
1979 Catharsis in Healing, Ritual, and Drama. Berkeley: University of California Press.

Wilson, Godfrey
1939 Nyakyusa Conventions of Burial. Johannesburg: The University of the Witwatersrand Press.

III
Performance and Inversion

9

Convivial Attitudes: The Ironic Play of Tropes in an International Kayak Festival in Northern Spain

James W. Fernandez
Princeton University

Just as in the case with respect to persons in whom the reasoning power is absent, the figurative imagination of crowds is very powerful, very active and very susceptible to being keenly impressed. . . . A crowd thinks in images and the image itself immediately calls in a series of other images having no logical connection with the first. . . .

—Gustave Le Bon, *The Crowd*

The progress of human enlightenment can go no further than in picturing people not as vicious but as mistaken. When you add that people are necessarily mistaken, that all people are exposed to situations in which they must act as fools, that every insight contains its own special kind of blindness, you complete the comic circle returning again to the lesson of humility. . . .

—Kenneth Burke, *Attitudes towards History*

The focus of discussion in this paper is an international kayak festival and race held in the seaside mountains of northern Spain, and particularly the folklore parade *(desfile folklorico)* held just before the race. The paper is motivated by enduring Durkheimian interests in the "laws of collective ideation" and in the problem of the creation of moral order in community. But this paper also bears relevance to the work of two thinkers of inescapable concern to students of the human condition: Kenneth Burke, and particularly his concern with viable *Attitudes towards History* (1937), and Ivan Illich (1975), and his repeated attention to the problem of conviviality in the "technological iron cage" of modern society.

The race takes place from Arriondas to Ribadesella in the Province of Asturias, northern Spain, and the parade takes place in Arriondas. In

this parade, to borrow and rephrase W. L. Warner's (1961) observation on
a similar American event, the citizens of Arriondas and Asturias collectively
state what they do not really believe themselves to be and thus leave open
what they can become. Locating the parade within a simple typology of
northern Spanish street events, I also attempt to locate its historical position. The most instructive comparison for this time and place—immediate
postauthoritarian democratic Spain—is with the military parade. Rather
than the military "instruments of violence," we might say, the folklore
parade displays "instruments of conviviality." But the parade is also a
playful counterstatement to the exaltation of national culture. The consequence of such playfulness is a potentiality for a wider collectivity of human
relations.

Knowledge from work in the behavioral sciences on collective behavior and crowd formation is employed to understand the phases of the
festival. But fundamentally, it is a theory of the role of figurative predication in behavior—the play of tropes—that is explanatory and helps us to account for the "convivial attitudes" of this kayak festival. The basic trope
considered here is "reflexive irony"; and we must think about its place in
historical process. This mix in the inquiry leads to a theory of "transcendent
humanization" in behavior. The play of tropes is shown, essentially, to be
the play of collective mental processes of classification and collection. In
briefest formulation, this paper deals with the relation between collective
ideation and historical processes of human enlightenment.

An Obstreperous Individual

On the first Saturday of August 1982, I once again participated in the folklore parade that preceded the Fifty-first Annual International Kayak Race
from Arriondas to the sea and the seaport town of Ribadesella.[1] I later observed the race from the special fluvial train that accompanies the racers
along the west side of the river. And later yet I participated in the seaside
afternoon and evening festivities in Ribadesella that follow the race. I
should say that this year, as opposed to previous years, I observed the
parade more than participated in it. Because of a friendship of some years
with the incumbent socialist mayor of Arriondas, I was invited onto the
reviewing stand along with the mayor and other friends, as well as some of
the assemblymen *(concejales)* and their friends. Not all of the *concejales*
were on the reviewing stand—some because of differences with the mayor
and his party and others because they were not so inclined. Those on the
stand were thus raised above the crowd which the parade always attracts
and which is often so numerous as to intermingle with the paraders and even
to interfere with the progress of the parade. It is often difficult to
distinguish the parade from the crowd that engulfs it.

We were not raised so far as to escape, early on before the parade
really got started, the loudly delivered and, for the most part, humorously

received observations of an obstreperous and slightly tipsy individual on the other side of the street. A young man in his late 20s, he began by calling out, "Mr. Mayor, Mr. Mayor. You of the opposition side there. [He meant both of the opposition party and the opposite side of the street.] What are you doing up in the stand placing yourself up above the people. Aren't you the party of horizontal democracy? What is this outmoded 'verticalism' [*verticalismo*] you practice there? Come down! Come down into the street with the rest of us!''

These and other similar observations continued to be shouted until the parade began in earnest, although the man's remarks were increasingly dampened by the rain, which is a frequent accompaniment of the fiestas and *romerias* of the Cantabrian slope of northern Spain. Disappointingly, the rain became more intense as the parade proceeded. And this obstreperous young man was, like practically all the young people and despite the justness of his remarks, without an umbrella—the indispensable accoutrement of Asturian life. Those of us in the reviewing stand were amply provided with umbrellas. The mayor, it ought to be said, stood the entire time without an umbrella and, furthermore, was bare-headed, a populist gesture that was perhaps not lost on the crowd.

Before an account of the parade itself is given, let us consider for a moment the humor involved in the remarks directed at the *tribuna* from the other side of the street. The humor played on several anomalies. First, there was the incongruity of having a reviewing stand at all for a folklore parade. The various floats and musical and dance groups had only the vaguest sense of passing in review. And the review process itself—a highly disciplined presentation to a select and judgmental group of authorities—which is integral and, indeed, the focus of the military parade, was largely absent. No prizes were to be awarded, at least not from the reviewing stand. More humorous, though, were the ideological issues. The previous authoritarian regime, in their "national socialism," argued for (and sought to impose) a "democracy" characterized by a syndicate organization of vertical communication between the ruling elite and its followers. This worked only by coercion, particularly in Asturias, a province with marked egalitarian values and a large working class of miners and metalworkers. During the Franco years, these workers maintained surreptitious "horizontal" unions and *verticalismo* was the subject of ironic commentary, if not derision, by such elements of Asturian society as were present in large numbers in this parade (e.g., smallholders, workers, small-town merchants and tradesmen, and members of the rural bureaucracy). That the socialist mayor and assemblymen of his party—a party whose politics were those of egalitarianism—should raise themselves about their countrymen on a reviewing stand, a structure on which, in any event, the former regime was much more at home—was clearly apt for humorous commentary.

Another issue ripe for irony, at least at the time of the parade, arose from the fact that the socialist party (meaning here the PSOE—Partido Socialista Obrero Español) seemed to be clinging to the opposition role despite its manifest strength in many provinces, and surely in Asturias. This continuing preference for "opposition" was a source of humor. Given the many economic difficulties with which Spain was confronted in the transitional years, coupled with the continuing presence of Francoist elements in the state bureaucracy and the army and other "forces of order," the party seemed to be strategically postponing its accession to power and settling into a more comfortable permanent opposition. This source of ironic commentary, however, was to be eliminated soon with the convincing electoral success and accession to power of the Socialists in the national elections of November 1982.

One has difficulty, in any event, imagining this kind of mocking commentary taking place in front of a municipal body during the Franco period, even though the use of Carneval and the carnival atmosphere to mock political authority has august ancestry in Spain and Europe.[2] Such commentary simply would be unimaginable as an intrusion into the military parades that were the favorite events of the former regime. Even folklore parades in that period were provided with large contingents of civil guards *(Guardia Civil)* and national police, not to mention local municipal police. And their presence was always quite evident. There were still many of these "forces of order" present on this Saturday in August 1982, but they kept much more in the background. The socialist mayor and his colleagues may have acquiesced to appear on a reviewing stand, yet they did not go so far as to surround themselves, as in the old days, with the "forces of order." They were willing to suffer the "indignities" of an "obstreperous individual" and an "unruly crowd"!

Ironic Incongruities of Situation

While one cannot easily imagine an "obstreperous individual" openly shouting out ironic and mocking observations to the authorities at public functions during the Franco period, irony was the main covert weapon against oppressive authoritarian situations of domination and subordination. As in contemporary Poland, ironic commentary in the form of jokes about the disparities between official pronouncements and pretentions and the actual state of affairs was extensive. One consequence of the democratic transition is, as we see, the opening up of public life to such heretofore more circumspect observations. But in any event, irony has the advantage, since it speaks by opposites and depends on a rather moot sense of incongruity, of not directly confronting authority. Authorities can tolerate ironies as relatively mild challenges to their hegemony and control of the means of violence. Ironies just work away in the rotten hulls of authoritarian repression—they do not attempt to seize the cannons on the deck.

By irony I mean any of a variety of standard rhetorical devices by which something is asserted in such a way that we understand just the opposite or at least something clearly different from what is asserted. Ironic awareness is essentially the awareness of incongruity. By dramatic irony I mean an incongruity between what is asserted in any form of discourse and the actual developing state of affairs. For example, the "obstreperous individual" was pointing out the incongruity between socialist rhetoric and the actual "verticalism" being acquiesced to by the mayor and his *concejales*. Such incongruities are inevitable and inescapable in human social and political life, and no laudable commitment to sincerity and authenticity in that life should allow us to forget their abundance. Incongruities are more present in some social and political situations than in others, however. Here it should be recognized that the years following the 40 years of the Franco regime are transitional in the evolution of Spanish political life and hence are full of ironies apt for humorous interpolation. That is, they are full of incongruities in which people are saying one thing or being told one thing but are aware that they are living another. Thus the irony of a situation of apparent new freedom and new hopes and new options while the "forces of order" of the former regime are still in place—the army, the civil guard, the national police, the state and provincial bureaucracy. Their continuing presence in the Spanish situation makes the rhetoric of democratic freedom and equality sound dramatically ironic and incongruous with the actual state of affairs.

Whatever ironies are a part of these transitional times in a much larger sense, there is an incongruity and a dramatic irony in Spanish history bound up in Spanish decline. The developing situation, beginning in the late 16th century, of loss of empire and increasing economic and political disorganization and impoverishment at home, the increasing falling out of contact with the science, technology, and industry of the rest of Western Europe, stands in ironic contrast with and reveals the inappropriateness of the continuing rhetoric of empire and Spanish universality. The bold posturing of successive military regimes—the *triunfalismo,* as the Spanish ironically call it—is simply belied by the empirical situation. This seems to have been sensed already by Cervantes in Quixote's ironic commentary on the adventurous promise of picaresque tradition. There is a deep irony in Spanish history itself, in the development of a state of affairs—drastic decline—the very opposite of what was to be expected of an empire. It is my experience that these historical ironies are not lost on the Spanish, at least not on the Asturians. Provincial literature is abundant in "humorous histories." In more austere parts of Spain, these ironies may give rise to the pessimistic and ultimately "eschatological dignity" of a "tragic sense of life." This is not the case in the province, except perhaps in the very highest echelons of the Asturian intelligentsia. Asturians readily see the irony in their situation, as this *desfile folklorico* shows. The ironies are not only those of an obstreperous individual.

A Joyful if Rainsoaked Procession

This particular kayak race has gained such renown in the province[3]—indeed, it is well known nationally and internationally, and points gained there qualify racers for the annual international championships—that this Saturday in August attracts people from all over the province and much of northern Spain. They begin arriving the day before the event. On Friday evening and well into the next morning Arriondas is alive with roaming groups of young people, with street dancing and street music. Often, the crowds that attend the parade and the subsequent race have had very little sleep the night before. This adds a readiness to participate as well as a certain indiscipline and intermingling that makes it difficult to bring the parade off with any precision. The "obstreperous individual" on the opposite sidewalk showed all the signs of all-night revelry.

Participation in the parade is invited from anyone who takes an interest in it. International kayak teams and their representatives are especially invited. Since the race begins just after the parade, very few foreign visitors participate as the crews and their support teams are busy preparing the start. Also, the foreign teams are puzzled as how to take the parade. Is it a serious review and authentic presentation of self? Or is there something essentially frivolous about it? In any event, only an English, an Australian, and a Dutch group paraded in 1982. Indeed, the sincere demeanor of these groups did seem out of place amidst the cavorting multitude. Perennial elements in the parade are folklore groups from various parts of the province, all similarly dressed in their black, red, and white traditional costumes. They are most often young people in their late teens and early 20s led by two elderly men playing the bagpipe and drum. Periodically, these groups stop to form a circle and dance. There were eight groups from various parts of the province in the 1982 parade. Since these folklore groups are ubiquitous at practically any celebration—*romerias,* patronal fiestas and holy days, fairs and *certamenes* (e.g., *ferias de muestra*)—they are not as interesting a challenge to explanation as the other less traditional and more calculatingly composed and presented elements in the parade. That is, these classic folkdance groups make their obviously important contribution to the definition of situation, and definition of provincial identity, but they are not subject to a very complex reading. Essentially, their presence signals the folklore situation and demarks the phases of its progress, but they are not part of the play of tropes.

Most interesting is the attempt on the part of the organizers of the parade[4] to present a kind of historical overview of the province. The word went out to various kayak groups and booster organizations *(peñas)* of the vicinity that such was the intention. But specific assignments were not made and it was left to these various groups to communicate among themselves. William Lloyd Warner's (1961) study of the parade of town and state history in the bicentennial celebration of Yankee City (Newburyport), Massachusetts, is relevant here. As Warner (1961:89–159) points out, "the town fathers of Yankee City decided that the successive floats of their parade should develop their history . . . the Aboriginal Indians and the Forest Primeval, The Coming of the White Man, the settling of the town, the Revolutionary War etc. . . ." In this way the leading citizens, and especially the Protestants, sought to legitimate their past and to state collectively what they thought themselves to be. Nothing so well organized and intentional was ever worked out in Arriondas. No deep study of local history accompanied by distinguished lectures was made. No attempt was made to assign the various historical events to specific groups. It was simply suggested to the various groups that historical motifs were in order. The result, naturally, was desultory. But the chief difference between the two events is the utter seriousness with which the town fathers and citizens of Yankee City sought to portray their history through the parade. The only irony, and that was inadvertent and existed largely in the eyes of Warner and his readers, was the initial assignment to the local Jewish community of the Benedict Arnold float. In Arriondas, by contrast, every historical presentation was designed to make ironic commentary, to make light of that history by interpreting it within a framework of comic portrayal of some of its main elements.

Thus, the only float—it came along after a bagpipe, drum, and dance group and the alternates for a number of provincial kayak teams—was a wagon drawn by a tractor. It held some 15 or 20 men, all dressed in cavemen skins and carrying the red and yellow plastic billy clubs common to Carneval, as well as some rough-hewn hand axes. A very large papier-mâché hand ax covered with tin foil towered over the wagon. Although this float was labeled España, to set it off from the foreign groups that were to precede it (but did not), it carried Asturian flags and was intended as the first entry in the historical series representing the Stone Age ancestors of the Asturians. It was an ancestry amply confirmed by the paleolithic sites and considerable cave art actually present in the province. The seaside town of Ribadesella, in fact, possesses one of the finest examples of paleolithic polychrome art of Franco-Cantabrian Europe.[5] Note the emphasis on mock weaponry in this float, in playful relation to the real instruments of violence of the military parade. The *porras* (plastic billy clubs) were not only in the possession of the men on this float but had been widely distributed among the young people marching in the parade. As the marchers danced along they beat tattoos on each other in time to the music and occasionally "menaced" bystanders in the crowd who had lined up on each side of the street. The cavemen with their mock weapons were so calculatedly brutish as to make obvious the ironic contrast with any serious image of paleolithic Asturian forebears.

Following the Stone Age float were members of the Ribadesella canoe club—*Unión las Piraguas*—dressed in roman togas and led by a monarchical figure in a tin crown. From time to time they knelt before and around him as he delivered a peroration praising Asturias, its people, and its climate while the "famous" Asturian rain poured down. This group was obviously a conflated representation of Roman and Visigothic history and the eventual conquest of Rome, as well as of the Romans in Asturias, by the Visigoths. They were accompanied by musicians playing instruments made of stovepipes, water hoses, and plastic toilet pipes and by a considerable number of young people flailing around with their *porras*. The Visigothic king and his Roman court were followed by a kayak team carrying paddles and dressed as pirates. One sensed that they were out of place because after them appeared a group dressed as Arabs and immediately after them was a group of capitalists in black suits with stovepipe hats scattering play money—in thousand-dollar denominations—to the crowd. The Arabs harassed the Romans and the Visigoths with large clubs and were themselves engulfed by the capitalists and the swirling green stuff they scattered around. Subsequently, the pirates fell back to mingle with a kazoo band whose instruments also were made of plastic, plumber's piping. This band, from the port city of Gijon, were inveterate participants in events of this kind. They traveled many weekends a year to participate in such events wherever they were held. Their worldliness gave them some sense of superiority over the other groups, and they did not hesitate to take center stage and monopolize the space in front of the reviewing stand until asked to move on by a sign from the mayor.

After this, the historical representations ceased. Various kayak teams then passed by, and finally, at the very end of the parade and preceded by a sports team from Avilles dressed as Neptune's minions with trident spears mounted on their paddles, came the Giants and Bigheads. The tiny Bigheads marched around under the feet of the Giants, presented in provincial costume as the traditional countryman and countrywoman, Pin and Tielva. The final units of the parade were composed of other sports groups, including the three foreign representatives mentioned earlier.

Because of the rain, the bagpipe drum and dance team assigned to bring up the rear had tired of waiting and had joined the procession much earlier on. So without any final marker the parade really faded off with a very large crowd of people tailing after it. No one, at least on the reviewing stand, was quite sure whether the parade was really over or whether there were several more groups to come. By the time the decision had been made that it was over, the street was so crowded that the mayor and his assembly, even with the aid of the municipal police, had difficulty making their way the several blocks to their reserved platform at the river's edge. When they arrived, the kayak race had already started—an ironic outcome of their supposed supervisory role, something the "obstreperous individual," had he been present, would have been sure to note. The irony also would not have been lost on sympathizers of the former authoritarian regime. Had the mayor made use of the civil guard, he would have arrived on time.

The Phases of a Festival of Two Towns and a River

Although the main focus is on the "folklore parade," something further must be said about the events of the day in order to understand the festivities in their entirety. After the start of the kayak race, the town empties and as many people as can by car and autocar, by the fluvial train, by biking or hitchiking, follow the kayaks the 25 km or so of their strenuous passage to the sea (see Figure 1, which puts this competitive phase into ironic perspective). For most of this distance the Sella River winds through the steep canyons of the coastal range and is flanked by the railroad and the highway. The race is usually over by 1:30 P.M.—all racers who are going to arrive (that is, who have not foundered) doing so in two and á half hours.[6] At that time the *romerias* begin. I use this term in the most general sense to mean a convivial gathering in an extramural, necessarily outdoor milieu, although all the stages of the classic Asturian *romeria* (see Fernandez and Fernandez 1976)—in particular, the religious functions—are not present. For families from the origin town of Arriondas, and for their relatives and friends, the race is followed by a *romeria*-type picnic on a riverside meadow on the outskirts of Ribadesella. Many clusters of extended family groups, each gathered around their food and drink, are spread around the meadow more or less oriented toward a platform next to the willows by the river where a string of performers of the Asturian bagpipe, the deepsong, and the dialect country-bumpkin monologues all appear. Their performances may be followed by general singing and dancing. This *romeria* is very much an Asturian affair and few of the multitude of strangers in attendance participate here. It is a time of provincial and local conviviality.

In the streets of Ribadesella it is another matter. Here, all the other visitors gather—those from distant parts of the province, from other provinces, and from other countries. All of the thousand or so kayakers, with their team associates, are gathered here. The various teams congregate and technique and technology are compared, perhaps a kayak is traded or sold, and T-shirts are exchanged. Shortly, multinational groupings of young people begin to make the rounds of the tents set up on the wharfs purveying *calamares, gambas a la planca,* fried *chorizo, churros,* and all the other *tapas* Spain is known for. Ever-present and a challenge that is laughingly engaged in by the foreigners is the drinking of Asturian hard cider. It must be poured from its bottle, while held high over the head, into a large glass held at the knee. There is always a great crowd at this urban *romeria* added to late in the afternoon by those who join it from the other *romerias*. And if

Figure 1. Festival poster by Alfonso commenting humorously on the kayak race itself.

things go well—if the rain stops, for example, as it did in 1982—it goes on until late into the evening or into the early morning hours. The various provincial and national groups lose some of their awkward sense of difference and carouse together, feeling themselves, perhaps, part of a greater human whole.

If we now consider the festivities in their entirety, we note that there are phases of participation and observation, intensification and dispersion, in the crowd's experience. These are the phases of foregathering, of the parade itself, of the kayak race, of the *romerias,* and of the aftergathering. The foregathering—of the evening and morning before the parade and race—and the aftergathering—after the *romerias*—are phases of relatively unorganized conviviality in which the different identifiable groups—familial, provincial, and national—are of slight importance. One promenades about, and full participation is possible simply on the basis of attendance and membership in the crowd. In the parade there is separation between the performers and the observing crowd, but this is not tightly controlled and some of the crowd is regularly inspired into full participation in the parade. In the race there is, necessarily, full separation, and the crowd become merely observers of the event. At the same time they are, each and every man and woman, each and every family, engaged in their own race to keep up with the kayaks and make their way through the crowd to the seaport city. Indeed, after the conviviality of the foregathering and the parade, there is a pell-mell, everyone-for-oneself atmosphere. The crowd undergoes a separation phase. Finally, it is gathered together again, first in the *romerias*—in which the separateness of family units and sports teams and groups is still featured—but more assuredly in the subsequent aftergathering.

This festival, more complex than the usual rite of passage, is also unusual, perhaps, because it is not the festival of one locality and one community. It moves from one town to another and thus escapes the sociocentrism, the community focus, of traditional Spanish festival. It is really the festival of two towns linked by a river. It is also, in its way, a provincial, an interprovincial, and, indeed, an international festival. It is equally a composite of several varieties of street life.

The Varieties of Street Life

It is useful to briefly review the three genres of street life in this northern .Spanish province so as to more adequately frame this "folklore parade" and grasp the contexts that, in part, give it its meaning. I make a simple distinction between orientation toward images of the self and orientation toward images of the significant other for the shift from self-interest to other-interest in the fundamental creation of moral order. We note that the festival shows a mix of all these genres.

Paseo (Promenade)

Every evening after 7:30, and on Sunday afternoons after 4:00, the streets of Asturian towns, except in the smallest hamlets, and except during rainy weather, fill with the *paseo*. The *paseo* is a social promenade, and primary to it is the presentation of self—along with a secondary interest, complementary to the first, in observing *(fisgando)* "significant others" of the town. One might say that one purpose of the *paseo* is to make the self over into a significant other. Many parts of the kayak festival have a *paseo* feeling.

The "Procession"

The images one sees presented in the *paseo* are largely the images of self that individuals and families want to make public, putting their best foot forward. The religious procession is also an occasion for self-presentation, but the attention is given over here to the religious images being transported—the image of the significant other that can define the self is of dominant importance. With the greatest sincerity there is the presentation of group belief and group identity. It is the religious icons—those images of saintly devotion, of human weakness and betrayal; of suffering and crucifixion; of sorrow, hope, and exaltation; of maternal love; of saintly martydom and saintly equanimity—from which the townspeople learn both about themselves—the potentialities of their most authentic humanity—and about the ultimate circumstances and values of life as embodied in these imaged others who are the ultimate referents of their identity. In the kayak festival parade there is a progression of images of significant historical others. But ironic rather than sincere presentation is the norm.

Parades *(desfiles)*

The events focused on here make us aware of two kinds of parade: the military parade, the normal unmarked category; and the folklore parade, the marked category to be understood within the frame of the military parade. Military parades have been a pronounced presence in Spanish national life not only because of the imperial past but because of the succession of military regimes that have appropriated and exercised power since the mid-19th century. These regimes have sought to consolidate and manifest their power by frequent displays of the instruments of violence. Military parades are largely the parades of provincial and national capitals—very large cities where large numbers of troops and weapons are quartered and can be martialed.

With present democratization, military parades are on the decline. But it is still necessary to read the *desfile folklorico* in the context of the military parade and as standing in meaningful contrast with it. In both cases of procession and parade the self is caught up in the greater whole attracted by the display of the significant other. The spectator is reimpressed, constrained, and loyally reconverted to expected allegiances by that display. Parades and processions are, I argue, moments of both constraint and conversion in the presence of the significant other, though there is much more constraint in the former and conversion in the latter; there is also more imposed sincerity in the latter and voluntary sincerity in the former.

There are other kinds of street activity that have characterized northern Spanish life. There have been many spontaneous and disgruntled crowds in the history of Asturias, such as those that have appeared regularly in the mining zones of Asturias since the turn of the century. These crowds—an example is the one that gave rise to the miners' revolution of October 1934—have a high potential for concerted and destructive action. Because of the potential volatility of such crowds in Spanish history, indeed in European history (Rude 1981), successive regimes have been uncomfortable about crowds of any kind, including festival crowds. They have always sought to send among these crowds the "forces of order" to make sure that the crowds do not suddenly change the framework of their being, shifting from playful representations to serious protestations, from desultory and self-interested milling about to concerted action. Bateson (1974) discusses with instructive subtlety the ever-presence of the possible shift from the "this is play" frame to the "is this play?" frame in the life of human groups. The "forces of order" are present in large numbers, paradoxically to guarantee continuing playfulness. In the festival before us—the summer crowd of 1982—there was, first of all, very little if any latent disgruntlement or resistance to the "willing suspension of disbelief" which might shift the festivities into something much more serious and challenging, so far as the authorities were concerned. Second, the ironies were too patent in this curious and playful mix of *paseo*, procession, and parade.

The Festival Crowd: Its Composition and Dynamic

One takes away from this festival day of the descent of the Sella a memorable impression of the crowd. Total participation in 1982 was estimated at well over a hundred thousand people. The town of Arriondas was crowded, as was the town of Ribadesella after it. The fluvial train was packed and the highway to the sea was congested with cars, buses, bikes, and hitchhikers. Even the river was crowded with kayaks (some 700 kayaks and 1050 kayakers participated in 1982). Indeed, as more and more competitors show up for this race over the years, the start of the race has become increasingly cumbersome and disadvantageous for those kayak teams who draw low numbers and must start hundreds of yards upstream. There has been, in recent years, a great melee of kayaks at the start of the race, and many founder. At the same time, in order to be successful in the minds of the organizers and participants, not to mention the dozens of itinerant vendors and tent merchants, the festival must attract a crowd. The fact of the crowd is an obviously important, and memorable, part of the experience.

Everyone loves the crowd on this occasion, just as they love the parade as a sign of the success of the proceedings.

We have only to remember Albert Einstein's profound mistrust of parades and the crowds they enchant to recognize how problematic the phenomenon is—and not only for authoritarian regimes who suspect its volatility. On the one hand, from the Durkheimian (1965) point of view, a crowd is a crucible that, working through the law of large numbers, guarantees that kind of intensification of social experience in which the moral order and community ideals often embodied in images of significant others can be revivified, in which egocentrism can be restrained in favor of altruism, and in which the obligatory can be made the desirable. Einstein, on the other hand, had good reason for his mistrust of the "altruism" inspired by the parade and motivated by the crowd. And, quite beside the bigotry parades and crowds inspire, the martial spirit and the particular kind of "mindlessness" characteristic of parades and enthusiastic crowds are very far removed from the cerebral and inner-sanctum atmosphere in which a theory of relativity could be worked out. Still, the crowd "mind" has long been postulated and its working has intrigued its students since Gustave Le Bon (1920[1895]), the pioneer in this study, as the general epigraph of this paper indicates.

Before addressing the question raised by Le Bon, one that is central to our interest here—the way in which the collective mind works—it is instructive to consider several other implications of his work having to do with the broader historical context in which the *desfile folklorico* appears, for profound questions of "attitudes toward history" are before us. Up to this point in the discussion, the *desfile folklorico* is framed mainly within the context of the Spanish military parade. If we take note of Le Bon's conservative preoccupations and realize the influence of his own thought on the "forces of order," we find even more reason for regarding the military parade as the relevant ground from which to consider the folklore parade. Also, while Le Bon tended to, with one exception, generalize about all crowds, subsequent work has sought to differentiate between the types of crowds. The exception to Le Bon's lumping of all kinds of crowds together sprang from his ideas on race. He distinguished crowds according to the "national soul" of the nationality composing them. Thus he distinguished sharply between a Latin and an Anglo-Saxon crowd: "Crowds are everywhere distinguished by feminine characteristics [he meant that they were volatile, willful, and changeably fickle] but Latin crowds are the most feminine of all. Whoever trusts in them may attain a lofty destiny with the certainty of being soon precipitated" (Le Bon 1920:96).

It should be remembered that the most avid readers of Le Bon's work and the quickest to exploit this new knowledge of crowd behavior were the military minds of his time. In particular, the French General Staff studied this new discipline of collective psychology in an effort to raise the level of commitment and the esprit de corps of French troops in the face of the highly disciplined and self-abnegating German armies (Nye 1975). Le Bon's "collective psychology of the crowd" promised knowledge of the phenomenon useful to those who would motivate and/or control large congregations of people. On the positive side, from the military perspective, such knowledge could be used more effectively to animate troops (and public spectators) to higher levels of commitment in nationalistic enterprises and foreign wars. Parades, with all their glamorous and romantic display, surely had that result. On the negative side, at a time in history when, as a consequence of the industrial revolution, class-conscious crowds were having an increasingly turbulent effect on orderly government, the military charged also with maintaining internal order could profit from this new knowledge of crowd psychology. In any event, the emerging totalitarian—mostly military—regimes of the 20th century have been quick to'appropriate this knowledge for their authoritarian purposes. Military parades with their somber, cold-spirited display of these "instruments of violence," which it is the state's legitimate right to employ, are effective means for the control of the crowds they attract.

To say that because these processions of folk images in the *desfile folklorico* are called parades brings them into meaningful contrast with military parades is to make, in its way, a historical statement about the interaction of varieties of contemporary experiences. It is to say that a part of the meaning of the *desfile folklorico* derives from its play on the resonance, in the minds of the participants, with the military parade.[7] Indeed, the use of the term *desfile* for this folklore procession is very much a 20th-century usage, one of the authoritarian era dating from the 1920s dictatorship of Primo de Rivera and confirmed in the unilateral encouragement of folklore by the Franco regime.[8]

But there is another term in the phrase which has historical dimension—and that is the term "folklore." This is, as is well known, a 19th-century term invented to conceptualize popular culture at a time when nation building and centralization of administration acted to peripheralize local popular culture. This centralization both threatened popular culture and, as well, created an awareness of it by contrast to emerging national culture. Involved, then, in the contrast between the *desfile folklorico* and the *desfile militar* is also the contrast between local provincial culture and national culture. This contrast in levels of cultural allegiance contained in the term *desfile folklorico* itself is actually seen in the rows of small paper flags hanging above the parade route. The blue and white provincial flag hangs side by side with the red and yellow national flag.

A folklore procession is, by definition, a show of local culture and a manifestation of local identity, just as a military parade is a parade of national culture and national identity (in Spain, for many decades it was a parade by a nationalist party dominated by the military). The military parade is a parade of the "instruments of violence" of which the nation-state enjoys sole possession and legitimate use (Weber 1958), just as a folk-lore parade is a parade of the instruments of conviviality. Weber asks in his discussion of the state, defined as a relation of men dominating men sup-ported by the means of legitimate violence, "If the state is to exist the dominated must obey the authority claimed by the powers that be. When and why do men obey? Upon what inner justification and upon what exter-nal means does this domination rest?" (1958:79).[9] The use of the military parade is one of these means. The question of inner justification, a propos, is a more subtle question and one more Durkheimian than Weberian in im-port. It is a question that mainly concerns us here.

The *desfile folklorico* appears very much, then, in the historical con-text of "nationalist centralization" and provincial peripheralization—in the context of the creation of national culture. It stands as a playful counter-statement to these historical developments. If we ask, rephrasing Weber, What inner justification does it have? Toward what end is it directed? the obvious answer is that its inner justification lies in its resistance to domina-tion by the center and in its reestablishment of the claims of local culture. But in this parade the answer is more complicated. For not only does it, on the one hand, stand as a counterstatement to the nationalization of culture in favor of provincial and local culture, but on the other hand, it stands as a counterstatement to both local and national culture in favor of internation-al culture.

Crowd Formation

If there is an international counterstatement in this kayak festival and race it is in part because the composition of the crowd is international. Although the actual number of foreigners present in the various phases is never above 3000 to 5000, or 5 percent of the total,[10] they give a flavor to the crowd, constrain the representations presented to it, and are thus inescapably a part of its thinking about itself. We might call this crowd "postindustrial," keeping in mind Rude's (1981:chapter 4) distinction between preindustrial and industrial crowds. It is certainly not simply a preindustrial crowd—a crowd such as the "menu people" who participated in the French Revolu-tion: tenant farmers, rural smallholders, landless laborers, rural and urban craftsmen and journeymen, small shopkeepers, peddlers, artisans, students, clerks, and servants. Nor is it a proletarian industrial crowd of factory or mine workers more or less of the locality where they gather. The Arriondas-Ribadesella crowd is international and postindustrial. It is a crowd that gathers very much as the consequence of mass transportation and relaxed provincial and national frontiers. It is a crowd made possible by trains, motorcars, automobiles, and even airplanes. Only because of such modernity could this diverse multitude congregate in these small provincial towns whose resources are greatly taxed by their presence. Even though many of the images out of which the *desfile folklorico* is composed are found in carnival processions of earlier centuries—the Giants and the Bigheads, for example, or the obstreperous young people armed with plastic billy clubs (formerly, inflated pig bladders), or the floats representing diverse topical tableaux—the sheer numbers who participate in and observe these proceedings and performances are very much a 20th-century phenomenon, and in Spain a late 20th-century one at that. A law of large numbers and a law of diversity in large numbers rule in this *desfile* that did not rule in the genres of street life antecedent to it.

If we look at the composition of the crowd in local, provincial, and extraprovincial terms, some distinctions are in order. There are, for example, elements of all three crowds present. There are rural smallholders, clerks, servants, craftsmen, small shopkeepers, and beggars. Because of the relatively high wages of Asturian miners and metalworkers and their relative prosperity of the late 1970s, many of these people are present with their cars and their families. Particularly in evidence are those individuals associated with the various kayak clubs from industrial cities such as Aviles or Sama de Langreo, which are working class in origin. We also see many of the middle classes: bureaucrats, owners of small businesses, businessmen, and professional people such as doctors and lawyers. In short, it is a crowd of great diversity. It is true, withal, that it is predominantly a "young peoples" crowd, the average age of the participants being not over 30. There are, above all, many students of *instituto* and university age, perhaps 50 percent.

Because of the history of class conflict in Asturias, something more should be said about the presence of the class dynamic in the crowd and at the parade. The early industrialization of Asturias, by Spanish standards, led to the formation of a working class of miners and metalworkers who periodically gathered in disgruntled crowds. This was a phenomenon of the late 19th century onward, and it is a constant preoccupation to authorities whether of the right or the left. Indeed, such preoccupation has a basis in fact, for the miners' revolution of October 1934—the first Socialist revolution in Spain—virtually rose out of the decision of a crowd of long-disgruntled miners gathered to protest working conditions and salaries, to march on the provincial capital of Oviedo, and to take over the government.[11] This uprising was suppressed bloodily by the military. Throughout the Franco years, particularly in the last two decades of the regime, miners gathered in large crowds, seemingly spontaneously, to protest work conditions and wages and to mark the deaths of fellow miners in mine accidents. These disgruntled gatherings of the working classes were a significant worry to the Franco regime, particularly because of the infiltration in the last decades of the regime of socialist and communist organizers from France.

As a consequence, there were as many constraints on public events and as heavy a presence of the "forces of order" in whatever gathering in Asturias as in any province.

In the democratic period, crowd events were no longer under authoritarian constraints and the "forces of order" kept a low profile. Their manifest presence, their silent bodying forth of the potential of state-legitimated violence, was a technique of control of the authoritarian government hardly compatible with democratic aspirations and rhetoric. Nevertheless, on the side streets in Arriondas, in national police and civil guard vans, they were waiting for any spontaneous disorder or unruliness in the crowd that might be a threat to property, to the orderliness of civic life, or to provincial or state institutions.

Gilmore (1975), in an article on the contribution to working-class unity made by pre-Lenten Carneval in a *campiña* agro-town of southern Spain (Andalusia), shows that the main participants are lower-class agricultural laborers *(jornaleros)* or smallholders. The ritualized intraclass aggressions that take place in Andalusia Carneval—present to a mild extent in the *desfile folklorico*—serve cathartically to bind these lower classes more tightly together against the upper classes *(señoritos),* who in any event absent themselves from Carneval lest they be the direct objects of aggression. Their absence confirms both the class system and Carneval as a lower-class festival. Similarly, the wealthy class in the Asturian towns of Arriondas and Ribadesella do not participate directly in the *desfile* or mingle with the crowd, although they do observe the race and attend the *romeria* picnic down at the sea. There are nonetheless some important differences between the class system of southern Spain, with its privileged elite of large landowners contrasting with a large class of landless laborers, and the class system of northern Spain and particularly of Asturias. In Asturias we find, as a context of a festival of this kind, a "minifundia" system whereby practically all countrymen are landholders. The very large landholders—the Asturian "aristocracy," based mostly on bought titles of the late 19th century—have their holdings in very dispersed parcels. These large landholders, perhaps several dozen in the province, live in the capital city or in Madrid and are hardly known locally except through their administrators *(mayordomos).* Class antagonism based on very marked differences in landholding is thus neither a significant provincial dynamic nor an Asturian town dynamic in the 20th century.

The predominant dynamic of class is that between the mining and metallurgy working classes, on the one hand, and the mine and factory owners and managers, and the administrators, managerial staff, and bureaucrats in their service, on the other. This dynamic, which was at the base of much crowd disgruntlement in the late 19th and early 20th centuries, was considerably transformed during the Franco years by the nationalization of most of the mines and factories. The antagonism was thus directed away from local or provincial personages—known representatives of their class—toward the national corporate state. In recent years, the "multi-national manipulators" of the Spanish middle class and its corporations have become one of the main objects of antagonism. In the 1982 parade this antagonism was jocularly represented in the personages of the black-suited, black-hatted capitalists *(los multinacionalistas)* who danced around scattering handfuls of thousand-dollar "bills." This was the only representation, frivolous to be sure, of class antagonism in the parade. There was, in short, little land-based local class antagonism to begin with, and the composition of the parade was otherwise too diverse to admit a generalized middle-class proletarian antagonism. The parade was understood as an Asturian parade—and more than that, as an international parade.

Given the diversity and size of the crowd, questions arise as to the dynamics of crowd formation, the way that, to use the vocabulary of the theory of collective behavior (Milgram and Toch 1969), an unformed aggregate of individuals and small family units is formed into a crowd defined as a collective phenomenon oriented around joint stimuli and whose members respond to each other in an interactive way.

As the theory of crowd dynamics well recognizes, the convergence of such numbers of diverse outsiders, many with different languages, creates a special turbulence and poses a special difficulty for crowd formation. In the "foregathering phase" there is much milling about in the streets, with small knots of people in multiple foci ringed about many different points of attraction. The parade provides the first joint stimulus for this entire collectivity, although there are still many people confined to the side streets who are unable to watch and to participate in the performance, and there are many others who prefer to assure their viewing position for the start of the race at the riverside. The parade is thus essential to the dynamic of crowd formation in that it provides a common stimulus that the crowd can observe and with which its members can interact. Even more fundamental to crowd formation, however, is the race itself, the central common stimulus of the day, even though the nature of the race over so many downriver miles puts the crowd through a strenuous pell-mell experience of accompaniment. When the crowd gathers again in the seaside port town of Ribadesella, they have all had not only their experience of trying to keep up with the race but their common interest and commentary about the conduct of the race and the winners. This "forms" the crowd in a way that carries over into the *romerias*. It persists in the "aftergathering" in which, once again, the former crowd begins to disperse into small groups milling about scattered points of attraction, finally returning to an aggregate of individuals and family and friendship groups beginning to think about their departure.

Commanding Images and the Elementary Play of Tropes

In one of the most systematic, and in that sense satisfying, theories of collective behavior, Smelser (1963) introduces what is in my view the unsatisfactory notion of "generalized belief"—the set of ideas or ideologies that emerge (and, indeed, must emerge for proper crowd "formation") to define the crowd's objectives. Assuming we know what belief means, Smelser's notion is unsatisfactory because it overestimates the consensual situation prevailing in the crowd at the cultural level of belief (see Fernandez 1965). It thus ignores the diversity of "faces in the crowd" that emerges even to historians working only with documents when they inquire into crowd composition and crowd belief (Rude 1981:chapter 5). Not only do the subtleties of consensus pose a challenge to the notion of "generalized belief," there is also the problem of the processes of collective mentation—the kind of information processing that goes on in the crowd. It is my view, and here I am in agreement with Le Bon, that the crowd's thinking mainly takes place through an "argument of images" (Fernandez in press). The set of images presented to all or most members of the crowd plays a powerful role in the coalescence of these members and in the transformation in feeling, tone, and attitude set which they experience and which have been widely observed in crowd activity.

Lang and Lang (1968:556) account for the rise of collective action on the basis of a failure of commanding and centralizing images.

> Problematic situations [those that give rise to collective behavior] are defined here as those in which participants lack adequate guides to conduct. Whenever imagery that is conventionally accepted or officially sanctioned fails to take account of or runs counter to deeply felt sentiments or common perceptions of reality people create currents of agitation by whose actions they are stirred from the planes along which they normally move and remain agitated until they settle back again into a pattern resistant to further change. What takes place during the interlude is *elementary* collective problem solving rather than structured social action.

It is just this elementary collective problem solving that is involved in the argument of images.

Although I think the kayak festival crowd can be understood as undergoing "formation" in terms of image loss and image gain, the more obvious case is the crowd of miners that forms in Asturian mining valleys the day after an accidental death in the mines of one or more of their comrades. Such a gathering is at the time of the funeral. The crowd mills about at first in an agitated state, but it is quiet and not turbulent. The miners seek to show their solidarity and fraternity with the lost miner(s). Usually, funeral services are going on in the church for the families involved, but the great majority of the miners gathered do not enter because they are anticlerical or irreligious and cannot satisfactorily coalesce around that set of images. When the coffin exits from the church to be carried to the grave on the shoulders of fellow miners, then one can *feel* the coalescence of the crowd around these images of ultimate circumstances. The entire crowd becomes oriented around these images and, as one, follows these coffins to their grave. The coalescence of the crowd is such that this is an apt time for directed agitation and crowd organization—the lesson of Antony at Caesar's grave. The coffins, the yawning grave, and the burial are powerful images with which to make an argument.

There are no images in the kayak festival parade before us that are as compelling—as coalescing and authentic—as a comrade's coffin being borne along to the grave. The racers in their kayaks, paddling furiously as they are carried along to the sea, and the images of the funeral procession are similarly authentic; so, too, are the victors, raised on the shoulders of their comrades or stepping onto the awards platform as very live heroes, and the dead heroes of Asturian mining accidents, in coffins carried on their comrade's shoulders. But the intensity is much different.

Still, the emphasis here should rather be on the authenticity of these images and not on the intensity. Like religious icons, all of these icons are authentic because, following the dictionary sense of the word, they are not open to challenge; they are worthy of acceptance because they are not contradicted by evidence; they conform to fact or reality. There is nothing playful or ironic in either the coffin or the kayak racer. No double vision is involved; no suspension of disbelief is required in observing or participating in these activities; no incongruity is being addressed. What the crowd sees is what it gets from life—what life is in the end all about: a matter of being dominated or subordinated, of winning or losing, of living or dying. Since what the crowd feels it is getting from life may be incongruous with its images of itself, these images of victory or defeat, life or death, can be used, if the crowd takes itself seriously, to animate it to excited collective behavior in favor of its perceived interests and desired images. Burial ceremonies are not the only occasions for motivating crowds. The results of athletic contests often lead to disgruntlement and destructive crowd action despite the supposedly playful character of the events. What started out as a statement, "This is play!" to recall Bateson again, is rapidly transformed because of the disagreeable consequences of the play into the statement, "This is not play!" because this is unfair and an affront to our dignity and images of ourself.

This disgruntled transformation of a playful crowd into an authentically destructive crowd has never happened in the Arriondas-Ribadesella kayak race. Playfulness is always maintained, and not just by the "forces of order." Among the most important reasons for this, I believe, is the ironic presentation of the Spanish and Asturian self that occurs in the parade. The parade takes mock arms against taking oneself and one's situation seriously. It makes a playful counterstatement to the "sincerities" of the military parade, though in no sense is it a direct mockery of those parades. It is a parade in which the citizens of Arriondas and all of Asturias, in contrast to the serious presentations of self by the citizens of Warner's Yankee City, tell themselves not what they are but, ironically, what they are supposed to be. The parade makes a playful counterstatement and takes an ironic attitude toward the serious pretentions of Asturian history.

With this point in mind, let us recall just how the parade does this. The historical tableaux and groups of historical personages, for example, all burlesque the ancestral Asturians: the grubby prehistoric aboriginals, the pretentious Visigoths, the subservient Romans, the shifty-eyed Moors. And bringing up the rear, after all of these playful images of self, come the Asturian giant couple, Pin and Tielva, with the frolicsome Bigheads at their knees. How should we interpret these most commanding images? If one thinks that these Giants, because of their towering size, are exalted and celebratory images of Asturian country identity, that they are icons to be taken as seriously, somehow, as the religious icons of patronal processions, then one overlooks the incongruities involved. Not only are their physiognomies virtually those of simpletons—representations writ very large of the well-known country bumpkin, the *tonto Asturiano*—but their swaying dance through the streets is more ungainly than stately (see Figure 2). They are awkward giants—*gigantes torpes*. Periodically, their occasional mock embracing of each other, their stateliness subverted by public display of visceral impulse, is another incongruity. Altogether these Giants are anomalous and have to be read in ironic terms.

Brandes (1980) has given us a notable study of the Giants' and Bigheads' parades in Andalusia, analyzing the psychological seriousness underlying the playfulness. In the Andalusian parade the regal, stately Giants represent at once both parental figures and the upper classes dominant over the Bigheads, who represent at once impulsive children and the impulsive lower classes. The parade plays out and confirms both class and generational relations. The Asturian Giants and Bigheads, I believe, must be otherwise understood, for they are commanding images that playfully mock the image of Asturian traditional rural identity. The seriousness that underlies their playfulness is the seriousness of the Asturian self-image, undercut at once by its impulses (the Bigheads) and magnified and burlesqued. These final figures in the parade are symbolic types[12] in the sense that they stand for that traditional rurality that undergirds Asturian identity. They are allegorical types[13] in the sense that they play out the bumptiousness (or bumpkinness), the "mistakenness," that is implicit in this type.

If one is persuaded, as I think we must be, to read these folklore parade images in playful counterstatement to the solemn icons loftily displayed and carried along in religious processions, one must also recognize that these images have simply replaced carnival images in this function. In previous centuries, of course, it was the carnival processions that stood in contrast to religious processions, for the pieties and projections of sacred commitment and secular order bound up in religious processions found their meaningful counterstatement in carnival processions, with their im-

Figure 2. The Giant countrymen bring up the rear of the parade, preceded by the Bigheads.

pieties and representations of misrule and disorder. The folklore parade is a kind of carnival, then, freed from confinement to a single time of year—the pre-Lenten period. It is a carnival that contextualizes and to some degree undercuts the seriousness and authenticity of the ensuing competition.

Commanding Images and a Theory of Transcendent Humanization

We cannot pretend that all members of the festival crowd understand in the same way the images paraded before them in the *desfile folklorico,* or even that all members of the crowd can be present at the parade to understand it. What can be argued is that though these images are particularly Asturian or Spanish, there are enough elements in them of broader, even universal, communicability to make them comprehensible to extraprovincials and foreigners alike.[14] It can also be argued that the ironic overtone of the parade presentation is widely understood and is part of the uncertainty foreigners have about participation. And it is certainly arguable that the parade is instrumental in setting for Asturians a convivial tone to their festivities and in facilitating an inclusive rather than an exclusive and discriminating—and invidious—interaction in the crowd. This was done in 1982 by playfully bringing into ironic perspective the commanding images of the Asturian past and present.

At the risk of considerable simplification, it can be argued that crowd formation really has two fundamental dynamics: the achievement and celebration of exclusiveness, which is to say the crowd's employ of the classificatory and specifying impulse in human mental activity, and the celebration of inclusiveness, which is to say the employ of the collection-oriented (collectivist) and genericizing impulse distinctive in human mental activity.[15] In the former, wholes are discriminated into parts by attention to features; and in the latter, relational matters become dominant and parts are amalgamated into wholes. The latter is the best strategy for a truly convivial and noninvidious festival. One of the ways that it is accomplished is to take the various specifics of a whole identity—the Spanish-Asturian one, in this case—and present them ironically, suggesting another possible whole than the one that has been specified and on which irony has given us a new perspective. In the particular dynamics of the Asturian parade, it might be said that this new whole is given to us in those towering and hence truly commanding images, the giant Asturian couple, who follow after all else and, in a way, sum up all the ironic particularities that have gone before. But this "commanding" couple is presented in such a way as to undercut and mock itself. Pretending to overwhelm the spectator, they come to be seen for what they are: giants with feet of clay . . . that is, very human feet! They suggest an even more transcendent perspective, an ever larger, more human whole from which these successively larger ironic perspectives are taken. What I suggest here is the humanity of irony, or at least the humanity that lies in ironic detachment from the self—in reflexive irony, as it were.

Of course, irony can be sharp, satirical, and disdainful. But the sense of incongruity in which irony reposes—the sense of human "mistakenness"—need not be invidious and painful.

There are many theories of Carneval and of the playful misrule and disorder that prevails in impious carnivallike processions—theories of catharsis, theories of class formation and political organization and protest, theories of psychic integration. But the theory I advance here is simply a theory of "transcendent humanization," an experience evoked by Carneval and surely present in the *desfile folklorico*. This theory rests on a theory of figurative predication of social identity, which argues simply that the inchoateness of the human condition requires that we recurrently escape literal mindedness and, making use of the various rhetorical devices, recurrently predicate figurative identities upon ourselves. We inescapably turn to *tropes*. In these predications we significantly transform ourselves and escape the stultifying routinizations of our structured existence—in the modern world, our existence in the "iron cage" of organizational and bureaucratic responsibility. The point is that we recurrently transcend these routines and commitments and we do that in a variety of ways. We can exalt ourselves by practicing a kind of verticalism (to recall the shouts of the obstreperous individual); that is, we can separate ourselves out by various processes of competition and struggle and establish our primacy and uniqueness. We can become heroes or, failing that, we can celebrate heroes and identify with them (the transcendence taking place in the kayak race itself). Or, we can turn to the leveling, the horizontal, trope of irony and point up—celebrate, as it were—the incongruities and the recurrent "mistakenness" in the human situation, and in ourselves. Rather than taking the images of one's self and society seriously and trying to make such sober images stick both to self and to other, we can suspend belief in ourselves (I am more inclined to twist the Coleridgian phrase and say that we can finally and voluntarily accede to the gnawing disbelief in ourselves) and celebrate incongruities. We can recognize our "mistakes" for what they are—recurrent in the human condition. This accession is what the folklore parade is about—an ironic leveling of the pretentious images of the Asturian historic identity. And it is a leveling that, at the same time, suggests the potentiality for a greater festival inclusiveness.

Thus, this "irony" has important humanizing consequences for the continuing playfulness of this international kayak festival. Of course, one could argue as a general principle that in the human equation it is easier for unknowns or casual acquaintances to relate to each other in a relaxed way when they show that they are not taking themselves too seriously, when they are not pretending to their virtues but recognizing their foibles and their vices, when they are displaying the contrarieties of their humanity. This recognition sets the tone for their carnival interaction and is certainly the consequence of the *desfile folklorico* of Arriondas.

I further argue that a theory of play necessarily involves a theory of transcendent humanization. Such an argument is lodged in a theory of tropes. It is not enough to identify simply the "this is play" frame and to say that it is recurrent in human and protohuman activity. It is important to recognize that play is a predication of nonliteral, or inauthentic, identities on the players, and in that sense play is always a play of tropes. (Of course, that play may suddenly be taken quite seriously and literally, and thus transform the play frame.) To really understand play we must understand the play of tropes and the transcendence involved in that play.

The trope that interests us here is irony—the ultimate trope, really—which emerges from the recognition of the dramatic incongruities in the human situation. To point out these incongruities by ironic commentary is to suggest their transcendence, to suggest the passing beyond the necessarily pretentious claims of our roles in particular social organizations and institutions.[16] A truly persistent playful and joyful festival, one must argue, will be based on a vision of our ultimate humanness in this sense. The *desfile folklorico* helps very much to achieve this for the kayak festival of the two towns and a river. In doing so, in creating reflexive images of incongruity in which the crowd can find some unpretentious bemusement, the *desfile folklorico* creates a relaxed atmosphere of celebration that will withstand the competitive pressures exerted on both racers and the hurrying spectators by the race itself and its necessarily hierarchical, zero-sum result. The ironic comments with which I began, then, set a certain playful tone for the festival as a horizontal celebration of common humanity. And it is a celebration of that humanity which makes a convivial collection of Le Bon's (1920) two great European classes of human (Anglo-Saxon and Latin) "races."

It is true that I use a very broad definition of irony here. I want to resist such narrow definitions as superciliousness, indiviousness, disdainfulness, with which we often associate ironic attitudes, because I want to see irony for what it essentially is: one of the tropes. That is, one of the devices we have for dealing with the perception of differences and of incongruity—one of the devices other than the ordinary logical devices of conceptualization. In truth, the kind of self-conscious reflexive irony before us is generally felt to be a modern attitude. Recall that Nietzsche, who blamed irony on Plato and the Platonic sense of the incongruity between the ephemera of everyday experience and the reality of the pure and enduring forms, felt irony to be, like romanticism, a pusillanimous attitude. He had in mind the idealism and informed irony of liberal humanism. He wished to eradicate such attitudes in favor of robust comedy and heroic tragedy.

Nietzsche's alternating "frolicking in the images of comedy and tragedy" may have been appealing in the late and sedate 19th century. But in this 20th century of total war, and particularly in the Spanish Civil War and the subsequent "heroic crusade" rhetoric of Francoism, it is hard to conceive of a comedy that could possibly alternate with such manifest tragedy. We are forced back, as I think these Asturian townsmen and countrymen are, to the ironic awareness, the quixotic awareness, of the differences between what men and women—at least Iberian men and women—are and what they pretend to be. I see nothing pusillanimous in such recognition. I see, and I think this is what the folklore parade shows us, the basis for transcendent humanization.

This parade is essentially to be situated in Asturian and Spanish history and suggests, to recall Kenneth Burke (1937), a humanizing set of attitudes toward that history. But in its implicit ironic comment on military parades, on the one hand, and on "international competition," on the other, it also situates itself in world history. Indeed, it situates itself in the most contemporary world history struggling to find terms of order for the mischievousness of competition and for the burdensome threat of self-willed tools of destruction. This parade suggests an appropriate framework for both the acceptance of that history in its long-term engagements and a rejection of that history in its short-term hysterias.

Notes

Acknowledgments. This paper is one of a series that expands on and seeks to clarify various aspects of a behavioral "theory of tropes" first put forth by me in 1974. Of particular relevance here are the two most recent papers in this series (Fernandez 1981, in press). The ethnography on which this paper is based was undertaken as part of the Princeton University-University of Madrid Anthropology Project supported by the Spanish-North American Joint Committee. I am indebted to the committee for their support. I thank my colleagues at the 1983 AES Symposium on "Text, Play, and Story," and particularly Alton Becker, Edward M. Bruner, Roberto DaMatta, Bruce Kapferer, Smadar Lavie, and Emiko Ohnuki-Tierney. David Kertzer has asked good questions about the context and content of the kayak festival, not all of which I have been able to answer here. Celina Canteli de Pando provided valuable supplementary ethnographic information, and Honorio Valesco Maillo commented on the *desfile folklorico* from the vantage point of his wide knowledge of Spanish folklore. I am grateful to the Center for Advanced Study in Behavioral Sciences for its facilities and support during my fellowship year, 1982–83.

1. I have attended this kayak festival for a number of years. It is one of the best known of the summer fiestas in Asturias. There is considerable variation in the content of the *desfile folklorico* from year to year, although the generally playful tone is constant. The phases of the festival remain the same also.

2. The literature on this topic is extensive, but see the pioneering piece by Natalie Z. Davis (1971).

3. The race was first organized in 1930 by Dionesio de la Huerta of the further upriver town of Infiesto. He still holds honorary leadership of the event. Before and after the Spanish Civil War, the race was a competition between towns in Asturias and did not become truly international until the late 1950s.

4. The parade is organized in only a very general way by a committee composed of the two mayors of Arriondas and Ribadesella and their assistants, and by representatives of the national and provincial kayak federations.

5. This is the recently discovered cave of Tito Bustillo.

6. On this Saturday in 1982 the two-man kayak team (K2) winners, a Basque team, paddled the course in 1 hour, 11 minutes, 30 seconds. The record (set in 1980) is held by the Spanish Olympic team of Misione (Galicia) and Menendez (Asturias) in 1 hour, 10 minutes, 47 seconds. In 1982 the first foreign team, from Portugal, placed seventh. Generally, over the years, the North Europeans have done much better, and particularly the English, Danes, and Dutch have been frequent winners. The American Olympic team did much better in 1982 women's and K1 events.

7. The resonant interaction of carnival and military parades as two kinds of national ritual that compose a total ritual statement in Latin cultures has been examined by Roberto DaMatta (1978).

8. It is well known that authoritarian regimes make use of "folklore" to celebrate national identities, on the one hand, and to allow for the relatively innocuous expression of regional identities, on the other. The term *desfile* in relation to folklore, besides being a 20th-century usage, has in other parts of Spain mainly been used for brotherhood and religious society *(cofradia)* parades, for parades made up of floats (a basic meaning in Asturias), for parades of masked personages representing various stereotyped groups, and for parades of ethnic celebration such as the Moros and Cristianos parades (Honorio Velasco, personal communication). In other words, the term seems to be used where nonreligious or quasi-religious solidarity groups are involved (sodalities).

9. Weber (1958:79) defines the state: "We have to say that a state is a human commodity that (successfully) claims the monopoly of the legitimate use of physical force within a given territory. The state is considered the sole source of the right to use violence."

10. Foreign participation in the canoe race itself was much higher: 20 percent of the total, or about 200 kayakers.

11. As Shubert (1982) points out, there were long-standing reasons for the deep mistrust of the Asturian miners by both the Republican government and their own mine unions. Still, the uprising was unpredictable and spontaneous and not desired by the union structure itself.

12. This is a term introduced into the literature by Handelman and Kapferer (1980) to focus our attention on the social tendency to concentrate norms in selected personae.

13. This is a term introduced by Smadar Lavie (1983) to capture those standardized melodramatic events in a culture, in which symbolic types may well participate to be sure, that communicate a "metamessage" about the general social structure and essential norms.

14. Needham (1978) has recently advanced an archetypal theory of images in

behavior in which he identifies the various elements that, for example, go into the making of the image of the witch. These elements, if not universal, are found in many cultures but are synthesized in particular cultures in particular ways. Not all the elements are synthesized in any one culture at any one time, but enough elements are present to enable cross-cultural understanding.

15. In previous work (e.g., Fernandez 1974) I analyze the play of tropes in terms of the interplay (transformative predication) of metaphor and metonym in relation to inchoate social subjects. Leach (1976) should be consulted for a statement—curiously ironic—of the logic of this interplay. Always involved in this interplay are the two logics of classification and collection. The trope of irony points us more to this underlying logic than do discussions of metaphors and metonyms, and that is why this logic is featured here. See Markman (1981) for a psychologist's summary of this classification-collection interplay in children's concept information.

16. It is Victor Turner's (1969) work on *communitas* that constitutes the basic statement in anthropology on the periodic—liminal—escape in human experience from the constraints, separations, and distantiations of normative social structure. The emphasis here is on seeing that process in terms of the logical transcendence of categories and not of the collapse of categories.

References Cited

Bateson, G.
    1974   A Theory of Play and Fantasy. *In* Steps to an Ecology of Mind. pp. 177–193. San Francisco: Chandler.
Brandes, S.
    1980   Giants and Big-Heads. *In* Metaphors of Masculinity. pp. 17–36. Philadelphia: University of Pennsylvania Press.
Burke, Kenneth
    1937   Attitudes towards History. New York: The New Republic.
DaMatta, R.
    1978   Constraint and License: A Preliminary Study of Two Brazilian National Rituals. *In* Secular Ritual. S. F. Moore and B. Myerhoff, eds. pp. 244–264. Ithaca: Cornell University Press.
Davis, Natalie Z.
    1971   The Reasons of Misrule: Youth Groups and Charivaris in Sixteenth Century France. Past and Present 50:41–75.
Durkheim, E.
    1965   The Elementary Forms of the Religious Life. New York: Collier.
Fernandez, J. W.
    1965   Symbolic Consensus in a Fang Reformative Cult. American Anthropologist 67:902–927.
    1974   The Mission of Metaphor in Expressive Culture. Current Anthropology 15:119–145.
    1981   "Moving Up in the World"—Transcendence as a Problem for Symbolic Anthropology. Paper read at the Center for Art and Symbolic Studies, November 1981. University of Pennsylvania.

in press The Argument of Images and the Experience of Returning to the
    Whole. *In* The Anthropology of Experience. E. M. Bruner and V. Turner, eds.
    Urbana: University of Illinois Press.
Fernandez, J. W., and R. L. Fernandez
    1976 El Escenario de la Romeria Asturiana. *In* Expresiones Actuales de la Cul-
    tura del Pueblo. C. Lison, ed. pp. 230–261. Madrid.
Gilmore, D. D.
    1975 "Carneval" in Fuenmayer: Class Conflict and Social Cohesion in an Anda-
    lusian Town. Journal of Anthropological Research 31:331–349.
Handelman, Don, and Bruce Kapferer
    1980 Symbolic Types, Mediation and the Transformation of Ritual Context:
    Sinhalese Demons and Tewa Clowns. Semiotica 30 (1/2):41–71.
Illich, Ivan
    1975 Tools of Conviviality. New York: Macmillan.
Lang, Kurt, and Gladys Engel Lang
    1968 Collective Behavior. *In* The Encyclopedia of the Social Sciences, Vol. 3.
    David Sills, ed. pp. 556–564.
Lavie, Smadar
    1983 "The Madwoman": Spontaneous Theater and Social Inconsistencies
    among the Mzeina Bedouin of the Sinai. Ms. Files of the author.
Leach, E.
    1976 Culture and Communication: The Logic by Which Symbols Are Con-
    nected. New York: Cambridge University Press.
Le Bon, Gustave
    1920[1895] The Crowd: A Study of the Popular Mind. New York.
Markman, E.
    1981 Two Different Principles of Conceptual Organization. *In* Advances in
    Developmental Psychology, Vol. 1. Michael E. Lamb and Ann L. Brown, eds.
    pp. 199–235. Hillsdale, NJ: L. Erlbaum.
Milgram, S., and H. Toch
    1969 Collective Behavior: Crowds and Social Movements. *In* The Handbook of
    Social Psychology, Vol. 4. Gardner Lindzey and Elliot Aronson, eds. pp.
    507–610. Reading, PA: Addison Wesley.
Needham, R.
    1978 Primordial Characters. Charlottesville: University of Virginia Press.
Nye, R.
    1975 The Origins of Crowd Psychology: Gustave Le Bon and the Crisis of Mass
    Democracy in the Third Republic. New York: Sage.
Rude, George
    1981 The Crowd in History: 1730–1848. London: Lawrence and Wishout.
Shubert, A.
    1982 Revolution in Self-Defense: The Radicalization of the Asturian Coal-
    Miners, 1921–34. Social History 7(3):265–282.
Smelser, Neil J.
    1963 Theory of Collective Behavior. New York: Free Press.

Turner, Victor
  1969   The Ritual Process. Chicago: Aldine.
Warner, W. L.
  1961   The Protestants Legitimate Their Past. *In* The Family of God. pp. 89–154.
  New Haven: Yale University Press.
Weber, Max
  1958   Politics as a Vocation. *In* From Max Weber: Essays in Sociology. H. Gerth
  and C. Wright Mills, eds. pp. 77–128. New York: Oxford University Press.

10

On Carnaval, Informality, and Magic: A Point of View from Brazil

Roberto DaMatta
Musei Nacional, Rio de Janeiro

Translated from the Portuguese by Barbara Geddes

Carnaval and Social Relations

For many years I have sought a sociological interpretation of the Brazilian Carnaval and its relationship to similar phenomena in other societies. I do not have sufficient space here to present all the dimensions of Carnaval, but any interpretation must take into account the complex set of relationships that are explicitly defined as *carnavalesco*—that which one wants to do or say, along with everything that one does not want to do, during Carnaval. The formula is quite obvious, and its implications for the study of formal situations are very important. Anthropologists are too often satisfied with defining the ritual under study, leaving aside everything that the ritual conceals or inhibits. The fact is, however, that each social event—magic or secular, formal or informal—always possesses two sides. There is an explicit dimension where we find rules relative to the orientation and direction of the event as a singular social episode: a funeral, a carnival, a birthday party, a healing ritual, and so on. And there is an implicit dimension that includes everything that one should not do so that the event one desires to construct will have the desired form and cultural content. Most important, these two sides are both fundamental to the study of an event.

It is not enough, then, to study the event as such. We must look to the relationships in which it is regularly obliged to manifest itself, or in those in which it is inhibited from manifesting itself. Carnival is thus an inversion of daily reality, banishing work and creating a utopia of pleasures and abundance. Most specifically in the Brazilian case, Carnaval provides a time and space where people can disconnect themselves from the web of obligatory social relationships—from family responsibilities and from other relationships of institutionalized loyalty, such as *compadrio* and kinship. Participants can then form new, voluntary social groups: Carnaval groups. Thus, if Brazilians in everyday life are defined by their relationships with their homes, jobs, skin color, way of speaking, academic degrees, family names, type of friends, prestige of their *compadres,* and so on, what is important at Carnaval is a kind of negative social determination; on this one occasion they gain the freedom to choose the group with which they wish to "play at Carnaval," as they say.

If a person's daily life is determined by established relationships, then Carnaval opens up the possibility of individual determination, entirely based on a choice from within, as is the case with everything that is defined as ludic and festive in Brazilian society. Although I cannot choose my family or even some of my friends, I can choose the saints to whom I pray, the soccer clubs that excite me and give me some experience of social justice (see DaMatta 1982a), and the Carnaval groups that allow me a much more individualized perspective on the social universe. At the same time, Carnaval permits me to wear special clothes, a disguise that in Brazil is called *fantasia.* In one sense, as I have pointed out elsewhere (DaMatta 1973), a *fantasia* is a type of Carnaval uniform. But while a uniform leads to uniformity, making people similar and accentuating their relationships with and immersion in a corporation or social group, a *fantasia* does the exact opposite: it permits the expression of individual desires that are socially negative or, at times, impossible. Thus, in contrast to vestments and robes which hide and protect the person performing a particular social role—as is the case with judges, ministers, priests, and soldiers, whose emotions are hidden beneath their uniforms—the *fantasia* relates what the person really is in daily life (what in Brazil is called the real world or "the hard reality of life") and what he or she would like to be or could have been. The *fantasia* of Carnaval permits men to relate to women (in the case of transvestites) and the anonymous, urban poor to relate to the aristocracy. It accentuates a specific social group (e.g., Samba School X) without ceasing to permit the full expression of individuality, since in the parade of the samba schools, people dressed in the same way alternate with people dressed in an individualistic way (called *destagues,* "persons with distinction," because they are in effect distinguished from the group, like superstars or superindividuals).

Carnaval, then, has a recipe or formula that orders and coordinates social life by means of certain relationships, values, and emotions, while necessarily inhibiting other sentiments and relationships. It would be impossible to have Carnaval in Brazil if Brazilians insisted on thinking about the secular and problematic aspects of their lives, such as the formidable external debt, the high rates of both infant mortality and illiteracy, the chronic absence of political liberties, and the shocking socioeconomic contrasts. But it is necessary to emphasize that these aspects are absent only explicitly from the celebration; they are absent formally, paradigmatically. But, in fact, their presence is remembered, not only by social critics of Carnaval (who condemn the orgy of Carnaval using precisely these facts to support their arguments) but also through their presence as part of the structure of the celebration itself. It is this overwhelming presence of contrasts and contradictions that explains the energy that Brazilians expend on the creation of Carnaval. If social misery did not exist, if there was not enormous familial repression, if society did not discriminate brutally against women in the public sphere, and if there was a fair distribution of income, then Brazilian Carnaval might exist but certainly it would have a different configuration and style. What explains the style of Brazilian Carnaval is the necessity of inventing a celebration where things that must be forgotten can be forgotten if the celebration is to be experienced as a social utopia. Just as the dream makes reality even more vehement, Carnaval can only be understood when we discover what it must hide in order to be a celebration of pleasure, sexuality, and laughter.

What I am saying, then, is very simple: all delimited social events involve a complex relationship between what they reveal and what they conceal; between what is said and what is left unsaid; between what they make possible and what they prohibit. Both aspects are essential for a correct sociological interpretation. Without the search for links between the explicit and the implicit, we run the risk of proposing a purely formal theory of social events. I know that Carnaval is a ritual of reversal. Hubert and Mauss, Van Gennep, Leach, Turner, Douglas, and Needham (to cite only the most well known) have already made this point. But it is necessary to go beyond this, to note the type of reversal that occurs in the Brazilian Carnaval in contrast to other carnivals. It is necessary to determine which objects, scenarios, social relationships, and persons are systematically reversed. My thesis is that we can only do this when we try to discover the relationships between what the event reveals and makes explicit and what it hides or simply makes irrelevant.

The comparison of the Carnaval of Rio de Janeiro with other carnivals is, in this sense, important. The "festival of liberty," the celebration of happiness and pleasure, the occasion on which everything is possible and which Brazilians call *loucura* (madness), is a moment when social categories separated by daily life are clearly and dramatically linked to each other.

The Categories of Social Life

Basically, Brazilian social life takes place in three social domains: the home *(casa),* the street *(rua),*[1] and the other world (DaMatta 1981, in press). The sphere of the home is a region where the physical being is created, maintained, and dispatched to the other world by people who are very close, people who share the same "nature" (i.e., the same flesh and blood, the same tendencies and aversions). There the *person* has direct, ongoing, and inalienable relationships, as well as a singular position, special and exclusive, one that is accentuated by the fundamental hierarchies of sex and age. The world of the street, however, is entirely different. There, universal values and an individualistic ideology, lived and conceived negatively, predominate. Thus, if in my home I am a supercitizen, in the street I am defined by what I am not able to do. If at home there are no laws, in the street I am subordinated to all the laws. I am subject to the impersonality of the laws of the market and run the risk of being equal to everyone before the law, a situation that is irksome for all Brazilians of whatever social strata and that seems to characterize semitraditional societies with double or multiple ethics (see DaMatta 1982b; on the question of double ethics see Weber 1967). The supernatural sphere of the other world permits the reconciliation of all the contradictions between life in the home and on the street.

In a society thus constituted there is a morality based on personal relationships and the fact that membership in the family group is perpetuated and derives from the substance that passes from one generation to another. On the other hand, there exists an ethic based on the individual as the moral center of the world and on universal laws that guarantee his liberty and public equality as a citizen. This, of course, is the legacy that came to Brazil by means of the French and American revolutions and that simultaneously operates in the country with the morality of personal relationships. In the street, therefore, all are equal before the law, and for this reason the street is seen as a dangerous space: there, the authorities can dehumanize the person, transforming him into an individual.

There is nothing worse in Brazil than being an individual and thus running the risk of having no relations, being "undivided" and alone. In a certain sense, the existence of the individual is very complicated. Although everyone is theoretically an individual before the laws of the state, those who have connections and prestige can slip under or over legal barriers, invoking a special relationship with those who control the legal resources of the state. Thus, the law tends to be applied in a rigorous way only to the masses who have neither powerful relatives nor important family names. From this perspective, it can be observed that in a society like Brazil's universal laws may be used for the exploitation of labor rather than for the liberation of society, as happened in Europe as a result of both the Protestant Reformation and the French Revolution.

The relationships between these two ethics are complex and fundamental for understanding societies where both individualism and hierarchy exist.[2] The point I want to emphasize, however, is this: in a system so structured, the social universe is perceived as divided, segmented, crosscut by social spaces and ethics that are distinct but complementary. Psychological space is similarly divided, like the God of Roman Catholicism, into three persons. In Brazil, I am one person at home, another on the street, and still another in church or in a cult. The result is a vision of the world based on alternation and complementarity. From the point of view of home and family, of friends and cronies, I see the world as a conservative by means of relations that I desire to remain immutable and from within a space based on hierarchy and substance. Here I am the mediator and provider, defending my family from the world with its modernities and, evidently, aggressions. But if I look at the system from the point of view of the street, and if I am in the street, then everything changes. Now I am a relentless individualist who believes more strongly than the English that time is money and business is business. Now I am a revolutionary and advanced in business, ideas, and morality. By the same logic, I become noble and advocate the renunciation of the world when I am in church or when I face death and suffering. Thus, I am convinced that social life goes on in this way in the majority of societies that have to some extent adopted an individualistic code of ethics without, however, modifying the system of personal and familial relationships.

For a Puritan observer trained in a world where home, street, and the other world operate by the same ethic, systems like the Brazilian one appear to be systems where cynicism, amorality, and the absence of "public spirit" are dominant. It might be suggested that the Brazilian Carnaval is the most developed instance of this socially irresponsible society that can tolerate without moral indignation such incredible contrasts between fine houses, inhabited by persons who have every privilege; streets full of the poor and the marginal, subject to the hard and cold letter of universal laws; and finally, baroque churches full of gold and silver, with their virgins and saints that look like us.

Totality and Inversion

From my perspective, however, Carnaval should be interpreted as an extraordinary moment, precisely because it permits the system to transcend its internal divisions. The Brazilian Carnaval turns society into a coherent totality by means of a single ethic and an exclusive pattern of behavior. It is not surprising that this ethic is based on a hedonism that abolishes all duties and distributes to all a type of supercitizenship. At Carnaval the ideal is that everyone can do everything. It is not uncommon that in a society with a hierarchical framework the symbolism of the body takes on exceptional salience during Carnaval. It may be because everyone has a body; it may be because it is through the body that it is possible to bring about the basic equality that joins all men as members of humanity. Also, it is not fortuitous that the Brazilian world of carnival gives enormous emphasis to women and makes the world feminine during Carnaval. Here, also, the reversal is perfect, since if men are responsible for mediating between the home and the street in the everyday world, at Carnaval it is women who are permitted to create a utopia of abundance and pleasure. Thus, the social world becomes feminine because it is through the woman that all the contradictions can be reconciled in the framework of values of this society. Woman is not only the mother of God—Virgin Mother, that is, as Leach notes, a contradiction in terms—but she is also the mother of Carnaval, as if her body were the center toward which everything gravitates and from which, naturally, everything comes.

Neither is it fortuitous that Carnaval permits all gestures and practices in the streets and in clubs, opening enormous space for the expression of individual sentiments of all types. Carnaval does not really create anything new, but it permits doing in the street or in public what is usually only done at home. One can, for example, eat, urinate, defecate, or go naked in the street. One can make love in the street, which becomes a secure and inviting space, even in the great cities like Rio de Janeiro, Sao Paulo, Belo Horizonte, and Salvador. The uninhibited universe of the home is abandoned and the individualistic impersonality of the street is decreased. Carnaval thus permits a merging of these two poles of Brazilian social life, making it possible to "forget" everyday morality that opposes sin and is concerned with the control of eroticism and sexuality. Putting morality aside, the moment of Carnaval opens up possibilities for pleasure as something positive, free, and naturally, individualized. Pleasure is no longer controlled by parents, brothers, and spouses, or by the institution of marriage and the family. Now pleasure is treated as magic, intransitive, pleasure for its own sake that permits the transformation of a highly repressive society into an open and highly democratic system. At Carnaval all are equal with regard to pleasure and the body. In this underlying sense, Carnaval permits a profound link between equality and hierarchy, between the individual and the person, family and voluntary associations, relatives and unknown persons, compatriots and foreigners, home and street, morality and pleasure, citizenship and individual desires, wives and casual and inconsequential lovers.

The basic question in all this is, Do other rituals of inversion and other carnivals have the same characteristics? Brazilian Carnaval is interesting because it seems to create a space in which connections between home, street, and the other world are possible. The presence of angels, devils, and death itself results from the creation of such a space. But what would a carnival be like in a society without such marked internal divisions? One example is the carnival of New Orleans—Mardi Gras—which is regional, partial, and borderline. Mardi Gras happens in one city inserted in a social environment whose ideology is egalitarian and whose impersonal laws operate everywhere. What is this carnival like that also inverts and creates, according to Victor Turner (1969), a *communitas* in a society where home, street, and the other world are merged and are much closer to each other than they are in Brazil?

Everything indicates that in New Orleans the carnival movement is one of separation instead of merging. While the Brazilian Carnaval invents a moment when all are equal before the laws of Carnaval—and the laws of Carnaval reconcile home, street, and the other world—in the universe of Mardi Gras the event seems to intend to create a hierarchy, with the consequent exclusion of persons and groups from the most precious moments. Thus, the carnival of Mardi Gras does not lead to individualization or even to the creation of an egalitarian ambience. In fact, to do this would be not to *carnavalizar*[3] in a society where individualism and equality are precisely the ideas that Mardi Gras inhibits or keeps in the background. In contrast with Brazil, where inequality is a fact of life, in New Orleans equality is a basic tenet of social and political faith and, as such, part of social reality. Therefore, "to carnival" in Brazil involves equalizing and creating relationships where none previously existed; "to carnival" in the United States, however, involves inventing hierarchies and exclusions.

It is therefore in seeking to understand the relationship between the implicit and the explicit that we can really discover the way inversion operates. We see in Brazil that inversion tends toward inclusion and connections. But in New Orleans the inversion seems to go in the opposite direction, creating temporary differentiation and inequality. In both cases it is necessary to understand what precedes and follows the moment of ritual. Here, I repeat an argument made by Leach (1966), but I hope also to deepen the study of certain problems. To make this more clear, let me speak of the carnival ball in Brazil.

The Embrace of Carnaval

The Carnaval Ball

As a carnival event, the Carnaval ball is everything of which I have spoken in capsule form. Really, this occasion marks not only a special time but also a space where the world appears clothed in extraordinary elements that everyday life insists on hiding. The magic of Carnaval consists of the possibility of relating all these worlds to each other.

What is a carnival ball in Brazil? Primarily, it is the creation of a space where people can "cavort" and "play," which means use the whole body, ceasing to control it as one would in everyday life. It is interesting, in this context, to observe that the word *brincar* (to play) comes from the Latin *vinculu,* which means to relate by means of an earring (in Portuguese, a *brinco).* Thus, the basic idea of the carnival ball, of playing, is to be open to relationships with all persons in that environment, independent of their position or social status. Together with the idea of playing, a special way of moving the body and gesticulating is implicit; or, as Marcel Mauss (1969 [1921]) has noted, the idea of playing at Carnaval implies a "body technique." Primarily, it is necessary that the body follow—discretely or outrageously—the rhythm of the music of Carnaval[4] that is played by a band on the stage. To do this, it is necessary to learn to differentiate the body into parts, divorcing the hips, shoulders, arms, and face from the body as a whole so that it is possible to do the following: while the hips (and consequently the legs, thighs, and feet) move rhythmically to the cadence of the music, the arms are open in a circle toward the multitude or toward the person with whom one is then "playing." The face is resolutely expressive, with the eyes focused on the person or groups of persons with whom one is playing, and the mouth is moving, singing the melody obligatorily sung by everyone. One can also throw kisses to persons (or person), or, even more erotically, show her (or them) the point of the tongue in a suggestion of a French kiss, or in gestures more daring.

At a Carnaval ball or at Carnaval, then, gestures always reveal what I interpret as a symbolic embrace that all give to everyone. This is significant because in Brazil, as in other countries, social relations are manifested in personal gestures that vary in intensity. Thus, in Brazil I shake hands with recent friends, stay distant from enemies, and embrace quickly or slowly people with whom I maintain a relationship of lesser or greater intensity. A long embrace indicates not only a prolonged, loving relationship but also the level of intensity of certain emotional states. Together with the embrace comes the touching of faces that can occur between men when the relationship is very intense. The embrace is thus a means of expressing social relations and only takes place between people who have a relationship at a certain level of intimacy.

Carnaval permits this kind of logic to be subverted because during Carnaval one can embrace anyone, both symbolically and in practice. At the beginning of the ball a man or a woman can face his or her partner with open arms, in the rhythmic movement already described, only suggesting an embrace, as if the person were being "encircled." But after some minutes, if some sympathy exists, the embrace can be concretized and then the two people, paired together, go through the ballroom, singing, hugging, in the same rhythm, and having necessarily to express happiness. Eventually, in going through the dance, they can embrace each other front to front and kiss on the mouth in a sexually open manner. A man can also embrace a woman from behind, suggesting an inverted and inhibited sexual act, sodomy. At Carnaval balls, this kind of "playing" is common, leading me to suggest that on this occasion a form of sexuality usually concealed in Brazil becomes publicly legitimate in the orgy of Carnaval.

I mentioned above that the Carnaval ball permits people to be "encircled." I want to explore this a little further because in sexual relationships in Brazil (whether hetero- or homosexual) the metaphor of the hunt is constant. Thus, the sexual object is "encircled," "hunted," *paguerado* (as when one is going to hunt the animal called the *paca*), and finally "seduced" and "eaten." Sexual excitement can be described in terms of heat, with people becoming "hot" or "catching fire," and the sex act is always described as a meal, where the dominant person (in general, the male) takes in (swallows) the female. At a Carnaval ball, what seems to happen is that everyone wants to "eat" everyone else. The possibility of having an erotic visual relationship with everyone is central, I believe, to the Carnaval situation. Above all, it suggests an equality that the situation of each person in everyday life obviously prevents.

If in the world of the home, the street, and the other world, Brazilians know that they will never be able to see "in the flesh," as they say, a television or film actor, at a Carnaval ball it becomes possible. Here, obviously, we have a critical difference between Carnaval in Brazil and Mardi Gras in New Orleans. In Brazil, one can buy an invitation to all the Carnaval balls in the large cities. Of course, some are expensive, but the fact is that Carnaval brings everyone together through money, making Brazilian society "democratic" in this sense. In other words, street and home, family and masses, are related by the logic of money. The purchased invitation confers the right to enter the balls of the most exclusive clubs of the city, such as the Yacht Club in Rio de Janeiro. But in New Orleans, exactly the opposite occurs. There the ball is controlled by a semisecret, exclusive group, a krewe, and only those with invitations can take part in the ball. The invitation then, in an egalitarian society has the function of excluding, while in a hierarchical society it has the function of permitting inclusion.

The enormous social opening that the ball permits in a closed physical space creates a situation of social and erotic intimacy that seems very important for understanding the direction and style of the Brazilian Carnaval. At the Carnaval ball three well-marked social spaces exist. First, there is an open space for dancing, where people circulate as described above. This area is the focus of all the watchers, and it is here that people dance. The dance floor, by being an open and free space with areas that need not be definitely occupied by anyone, is thus a perfect symbol of the street. The dance floor permits movement and, as they say in Brazil, "animation."

Second, there is a more closed space where tables are placed. In general, the tables are at the top of a little wooden stairway so that people there can see the whole dance floor, as the audience sees the stage in a theater. At the tables one can eat lightly (Carnaval is not a festival of eating), drink, or relax with relatives and/or friends. There is no better metaphor for home than this group of tables where one can refresh the body that comes in tired from the dance floor (the street). The third space complements the other two: private rooms like theater boxes are located above both the dance floor and the tables and appear to be the privileged locations for the ball. There, people are served in a more refined way and can also enjoy a more complete view of the entire scene. In the boxes, people can also do anything they desire because they have privacy.

The dynamic of the ball comes from constant movement back and forth among these three spaces, with people able to leave the boxes for the tables and the dance floor. This possibility of theoretically changing positions is joined to another that actually occurs and gives to the ball its definition as an orgiastic, carnival event. I refer to the fact that at the ball in Brazil, in contrast to a theater or the ball in New Orleans, there is no single zone that dominates the focus of all the watchers and centralizes the actions and even the way the celebration unfolds. In a theater, of course, the stage dominates everything, although flirtations and penetrating looks can pass freely between people in the boxes and seats, on the stage and in the boxes, in the orchestra pit and on the stage. These possibilities of visual relationship, frequently dramatic in traditional societies, occur in the theater and give rise to the question of whether it is not precisely this that makes (or made) the theater one of the most significant social experiences in the Western world. In other words, is not the magic of the theater precisely this enormous possibility of allowing the glance to circulate freely, without curb or censure, in a society in which each social segment had its own exclusive area, as was the case in Europe before the French Revolution?

A Carnaval ball does more than this, however. In New Orleans, as we know, the logic of the ball is much closer to that of a theater than is the case in Rio de Janeiro or in Brazil in general. In New Orleans the ball is ordered in circles. There is a group of central persons, made up of the king and queen of the krewe and their court; there is a controller or captain of the ball; there are honored guests, and spectators in general who do not dance but instead only watch the members of the krewe dance. The hierarchy is patent. For me, the Mardi Gras ball in New Orleans is a perfect metaphor for social differentiation.

In Rio de Janeiro, the ball has no defined center. There, the stage where a band plays carnival music is least important. What counts more is the possibility of everyone's eyes meeting everyone else's in a highly individualized world only marked by spatial divisions. An atmosphere of almost concrete eroticism penetrates all the spaces and brings about a series of social situations fascinating from the point of view of a theory of ritual and magic.

Magic and Time

At the Carnaval ball in Brazil, the rules of circumspection that divide and give meaning to social actions are definitely suspended. Hence, it is possible to do in public what is only permitted in private during everyday life. One can look freely at everyone—which cannot be done in daily life without fear of the "evil eye" or bad luck. But at the ball no one is afraid, no one hides his wealth or beauty, his body or soul. Open and uninhibited observation corresponds in an exemplary and complementary way to exhibitionism. Those on the dance floor put on a show for those at the tables and in the boxes. Later, those at the tables put on a show for those on the dance floor and in the boxes. The simultaneous occurrence of exhibitions and small events of a markedly erotic character, such as people making love, women taking off their clothes, men and women engaged in acts of complete grotesqueness, makes the situation highly explosive and magical.

Brazilians call this highly fragmented and exciting atmosphere, where something new happens every minute and at any moment anything can happen, *loucura* (madness). In fact, the French word *foliao* (from *folie*) is used to describe those who love to play at Carnaval in Brazil. But why is all this perceived as madness? I believe that the answer to this question brings us to some theoretically important issues. I approach these issues from the perspective that the Brazilian Carnaval situation suggests.

The first point is that Carnaval invents a powerful form of totality. In reality there can be no society without the idea of limits and frontiers, but the totality that is created when a social event is delimited is radically different from the secular or everyday idea of totality. In fact, in a ritual, spectacle, show, festival, and so on, it is possible to experience concretely something fundamental, that is, the beginning, the middle, and the end of an important event. It is precisely this that we cannot accomplish in any society. That is, I know that my life follows a trajectory with a beginning, middle, and end, but I am also sure of a paradox: my society, made up of men like me, existed before me and will survive after my death. Although I can see the end of many men, I cannot see the end of a society. It is clear, at least, that a society's physical extermination would be something extraordinary and, in addition, recent in the history of mankind. In general, societies are transformed, but they survive.

At issue, however, not only with respect to concrete societies but also to a much more complicated problem that seems to have preoccupied Durkheim his entire lifetime, is the relationship between individual existence and collective existence. What I am saying is that individual existence is always perceived as transient and finite, while social life is always seen as permanent and eternal. Durkheim taught us that these views correspond universally to the idea of the body (symbol of the individual and of individual desires) and the soul, which is typically social and collective, and, as a result, immortal. If the body and soul are in disparity and out of step during the routine of daily life, then rituals are a means of social harmonization where these disparities and contradictions can be reconciled. Why? Because the bounded event provides a possibility of experiencing totality as something concrete. Thus, after the festivity, everyone can go home thinking about another kind of social reality that is much more open and complex. But at a Carnaval ball or ritual of healing, at a civic festival or mass, we are faced with an event that has a limited duration, thus permitting the dialogue between the soul, which is social, and the body, which is individual.

I believe that one of the basic elements of magic is this syncretic totalization, solid and closed, where compromise and complicity are required of all in everything. I am, then, in full accord with Lévi-Strauss (1962a, 1962b) when he says that the savage mind desires to be ultradeterministic, going beyond science. And I am in full sympathy with Bergson (1932) and Evans-Pritchard (1937) when both, at the same moment, discover that magic is a machine for finding out the meaning of coincidences and accidents, all that reminds us that the social totality—the society with its rules, myths, limits, and frontiers—is something that leaves much to be desired from the point of view of the individual. That is, following moral rules is not sufficient to avoid misfortune. The only way of exorcising misfortune is by means of the discovery of its social significance, by using logical principles contrary to the logic of the accident, for they affirm that misfortune has a direction, a goal, and a will behind it. If the accident or misfortune leads us to doubt and eventually to discover that the world is indifferent to our moral norms, then belief in witchcraft guarantees us that everything is linked morally with everything else. And this again permits the merging of body and soul, will and indifference, open and closed totality.

Carnaval, like all "sacred," liminal, or extraordinary events, thus permits us to experience totality concretely. In Brazil this is done through the institution of an individualism and egalitarianism that daily life tends to deny or exclude. The world of Carnaval permits a vision of a coherent world. This seems to me to be a basic experience of formal or ritual events. In fact, if daily life oscillates between conflict and harmony, individual and group, personal desire and moral rules, ritual creates a possibility of harmonizing all this, setting everything on the same course. Thus, even when the ritual invents something opposed to the everyday world, as Carnaval does, this "chaos" is ordered according to rules that it inhibits or does not allow to surface. At base, in social life we always have a gestalt of pattern and form such that the oscillation between dimensions seen as opposed or contrary is a fundamental experience of human society.

This experience of harmonization of things of the world in a bounded event (or at least more bounded than the world) has something to do with the idea of time. Here we come to a fundamental dimension of the human condition. Leach (1961) was one of the first to note that ritual fabricated time and, beyond this, could make it concrete and even permit the manipulation of its rhythm. I could not agree more. I would only add that ritual—or better, the forms of delimited social events—create different kinds of time.

I am convinced (see DaMatta 1982b) that in the Brazilian case many kinds of time exist simultaneously. I do not believe, however, that Brazil is an abnormal society in this regard. In fact, I think that all societies experience different temporalities and that diverse rituals create and recreate different kinds of time. All ritual forms tend to invent eternal and equal temporalities since the ritual is a repetitive social act. But this does very little to discern and advance our understanding of the problem. It is necessary to discover, as Leach suggests, the configuration of the ritual as a whole: what comes before and what comes after. Thus, I suggest that in societies where history as a form of temporality tends to be dominant, the most important rituals may be rites that try to stop time and eternalize values. By contrast, in societies dominated by a cyclical conception of time, the ritual is more likely to be a moment when the introduction of change or the establishment of some rule or historical personage is desired or required. The repetition seems to me to be closely linked to a certain guarantee of perpetuity and finite alternation, as of day and night, while the idea of history and progress suggests to me an opening world with a course I can no longer experience. In a universe thus constituted, the experience of the spectacle with finite and well-marked duration can be a constant.

Finally, it is necessary to investigate why a society always has well-marked social spaces, all liable to specific forms of ritualization. In Brazil, for example, home, street, and the other world are expressed by means of specific rituals, and I suspect that each of these rituals works with a different idea of time. Thus, birthdays, funerals, weddings, baptisms, engagements, and individual rites of healing are rites of the home and tend to occur within a repetitive temporal framework. Here, the event and the experience are more important than the time at which they occur, their place on the calendar. But the rituals of the street, that is, the ceremonials supported by the state—are events always located in historical time. What they mark explicitly is a singular, Brazilian time, although its implicit and occult side may be oriented toward the eternity of the values of the country.

The case of Carnaval is interesting because in Carnaval time we have a clear sensation of very rapid passage, as happens with weekends, vacations, and holidays in general. But the duration of Carnaval is empty, by which I mean that it does not imply differentiations capable of separating the days or even some carnivals from others. It is only possible to know that a Carnaval of the past is being dealt with when a considerable period of time has passed. All Carnavals are seen as equal. Is that because they permit an explosion of happenings simultaneously? We know that time can only pass when we have some way of "measuring" its duration. It is alternation that permits the feeling and crystalization of time. Thus, a period very full of events would make impossible such an alternation, confounding everything.

This is precisely what does not occur in formal rituals, where actions are delimited and the unfolding of the ritual demarcates all the positions. Rites of order permit a more precise focus on the events. Perhaps they also imply a lesser mobilization of feelings. Thus, a lecture only requires that I remain quiet and listen. I can even close my eyes and not cause surprise or commit a gaffe. But I cannot do the same while eating at the home of a friend. At a dinner, I am obliged to be present, to listen, to speak . . . and also to drink and eat. A dinner is not possible if people do not like the food or are not hungry. The same thing seems to occur at Carnaval, in contrast to the inauguration of the president. At a presidential inauguration only the president appears central, and only he speaks. All the other people are part of the ritual, but they are backstage, as Goffman would say. It is impossible, however, to be in the shadows at Carnaval because the logic of the event involves eliminating precisely those zones. All are actors and spectators simultaneously. Thus, it appears that Bakhtin (1968) is correct when he says that "to carnival" *(carnavalizar)* is to be able to exchange positions, to be able to act and watch at the same time. I suggest that this is the most flagrant characteristic of informal occasions and that the opposite occurs during formal ones. Thus, the more centralized the event and the better defined by its objective, the more possibilities that exist for a divorce between what we do and what we feel. By the same token, there will be a lesser mobilization of the feelings, in contrast to informal situations.

A last point should be made with regard to magic. At the Carnaval ball in Brazil, what is magical is precisely its power to reconcile a divided social universe, creating an opportunity to link everyone with everyone else. But the magic of Carnaval is also related to the fact that at the ball we are singing what we do, so that words, actions, persons, and objects come to be a single thing. Tambiah (1968) has called attention to a very important aspect of magical acts: the power of words. It is clear that he is correct when he invokes the theories of Austin (1962) to suggest that the magical act has a "performative" aspect. Thus, in the magical act, the word does not speak of the world but is, in a certain sense, the world itself.

The same thing occurs in poetry, or better, in the "intransitivity of poetry." I recall, following Todorov (1979), that Novalis uses the classic distinction of Kant between practical and intransitive things. The language of poetry, the language of magic, and the language of Carnaval are languages of the "second order." They are expressions for their own sake as much as they are expressions that intend to be entirely practical. Thus, as Todorov (1979:182) tells us:

> The paradox of intransitive language is the fact that expressions that say nothing outside themselves can have, or better, are loaded with, the deepest meaning. It is precisely at the moment when we do not speak of anything that we say the most. When someone speaks only for the sake of speaking, he enunciates the most magnificent and original truths.

This also occurs in magic formulas that enunciate hermetic and/or disconnected realities, or in the orgiastic or carnavalesque rituals, where the secular and utilitarian practical side of life is totally abandoned for a much more dense, rich, and complex vision of the world. That vision is, in reality, unsustainable since it promises a utopia of eternal pleasure or a subversion of the social universe that goes against itself. Such seems to be the case of Mardi Gras in New Orleans, which imposes temporary hierarchy, exclusion, and inequality in a society whose creed is just the opposite.

Magic formulas, like oaths, declarations, and the music of Carnaval, are acts that accomplish two processes simultaneously: they speak of the world and they are the world. The act of symbolizing is, according to Todorov, also an act that calls something into existence. Thus, the symbolizing is part of the symbolized in the same way that the act of magic has to do with a definition or clarification of the world. Its basic question is, without doubt, that of attributing meaning, making the world cease to be indifferent to the moral norms that should govern it. But it is also important, as the study of Carnaval reveals, to understand those situations where words and things, persons and actions, form and meaning, emotions and social rules are confused and are merged in a closed and well-defined totality. What seems to be magic in these situations is that finally the world can cease being based on a division between utility and intransitivity, means and ends. At Carnaval we are far from the practical and the utilitarian: it is perhaps this divorce between means and ends that creates the magic of Carnaval and the symbolic forms.

While the everyday world goes on necessarily searching for a form of compromise between means and ends, form and meaning, command and obedience, the universe of rituals and symbols desires to establish a grammar of incoherence between means and ends. Its goal is not to find the means adequate to certain ends but to use the cannon to kill the sparrow, or the magic formula to make the plants grow or to prevent an earthquake. Thus, this separation can be magic. And to be magic is to discover that at times words are more important than the things to which they refer, and that gestures are more basic than the emotions that engender them. It is to discover, as have all Brazilians, that it was not Brazil that invented Carnaval; on the contrary, it was Carnaval that invented Brazil.

Notes

1. The Brazilian word *casa*, translated here as "home," and *rua*, translated here as "street," have somewhat different connotations from their English counterparts. *Casa* refers to both the home, in the sense of home and hearth, and also to the dwelling or shelter itself. It cannot be used to refer to other sorts of "homes," such as a home state or a prison cell. *Rua*, by contrast, has a less literal meaning in Portuguese than in English. It refers to the real world outside the home, to the place, in an urban setting, where life outside the family occurs.

2. With regard to this problematic, I must mention the work of Louis Dumont (1965, 1970a, 1970b), which opens up the possibility of recovering the German discussion that attempted to join universal social mechanisms with their concrete historical content and foundations.

3. There is no English equivalent for *carnavalizar*, which means, more or less, "to carnival."

4. A type of music composed specially for the occasion.

References Cited

Austin, J. L.
    1962   How to Do Things with Words. Cambridge: A Harvard Paperback.
Bakhtin, Mikhail
    1968   Rabelais and His World. Cambridge: M.I.T. Press.
Bergson, Henri
    1932   Les Deux Sources de la Morale et de la Religion. Paris: Presses Universitaires de France.
DaMatta, Roberto
    1973   O Carnaval como um Rito de Passagem. *In* Ensaios de Antropologia Estrutural. pp. 121–168. Rio de Janeiro: Vozes.
    1981   Universo do Carnaval: Imagens e Reflexões. Rio de Janeiro: Edições Pinakotheke.

1982a   Esporte na Sociedade: Um Ensaio sobre Futebol Brasileiro. *In* Universo do Futebol. pp. 19–42. Rio de Janeiro: Edições Pinakotheke.

1982b   Carnavais, Malandros e Herois. Rio de Janeiro: Zahar.

in press   Carnival in Multiple Planes. *In* Rite, Drama, Festival, Spectacle: Rehearsals toward a Theory of Cultural Performance. J. MacAloon, ed. Philadelphia: ISHI.

Dumont, Louis

1965   The Modern Conception of the Individual. Contributions to Indian Sociology 8:13–61.

1970a   Homo Hierarchicus. Mark Swainbury, transl. Chicago: University of Chicago Press.

1970b   Religion, Politics, and History in India. The Hague: Mouton and Co.

Evans-Pritchard, E. E.

1937   Witchcraft, Oracles and Magic among the Azande. Oxford: Clarendon Press.

Leach, Sir Edmund R.

1961   Rethinking Anthropology. London: Athlone Press.

1966   Ritualization in Man in Relation to Conceptual and Social Development. Philosophical Transactions of the Royal Society of London (Series B) 251:403–408.

Lévi-Strauss, Claude

1962a   Totemism. Rodney Needham, transl. Boston: Beacon Press.

1962b   La Pensée Sauvage. Paris: Plon.

Mauss, Marcel

1969[1921]   L'expression Obligatoire des Sentiments (Rituels Oraux Funéraires Australiens). Oeuvres 3:269–278 (Paris: Les Editions de Minuit).

Tambiah, Stanley

1968   The Magical Power of Words. Man (NS) 3:175–208.

Todorov, Tzvetan

1979   Teorias do Símbolo. Lisbon: Edições 70.

Turner, Victor

1969   The Ritual Process. Chicago: Aldine.

Weber, Max

1967   A Ética Protestante e o Espírito do Capitalismo. São Paulo: Pioneira.

11

Inside-Out, Outside-In: Concealment and Revelation in Newfoundland Christmas Mumming

Don Handelman
The Hebrew University of Jerusalem

In symbol there is concealment and yet revelation. . . .
—Carlyle quoted in N. O. Brown (1966:190)

To mum well is to conceal and then reveal.
—Sider (1976:103)

Concealment and revelation often alternate in the inversion of social personhood. Opposed yet complementary, their relationship encompasses a recurrent mechanism of the deconstruction and reconstruction of social order. Of the two, the concealment or alteration of one's familiar and public persona has been accorded pride of place in numerous analyses. Modes of symbolic inversion have been termed rituals of reversal (V. Turner 1969), dramas of conflict (Norbeck 1967:209), and rituals of rebellion (Gluckman 1954). Leach (1961:135) likens role reversal to the playing of everyday life "back to front," in its systematic inversion of signs. Such inversions often are associated with the periodicity of transition (Phythian-Adams 1972:67–68; Davis 1971) and are marked by mockery, mimicry, and the ridiculing of one category or conception of person by another (Handelman 1982).

Inherent in the logic of inversion is the cultural recognition that such states are unusual and temporary. These are conditions that mark the incorrectness of such transformations and the validity of a further reversion to normal personae. Thus, the concealment of personhood leads also to its revelation. As scholars have argued, an inversion of personhood and the revelation of its reversion to familiarity strongly underscore the moral correctness of everyday social order (Handelman 1977, 1979, 1981).

If much attention is paid to the aspect of concealment in inversion, then little is focused on its complement—that of revelation, when the mask is removed, when the masquerade is over, when the inversion proves to be a false representation of person, and when inverted personhood reverts to its everyday analog. To decipher the significance of inversion, however, in dramatizations of personhood and collectivity, one should recognize that its mechanics operate through two aspects of a single device: concealment and revelation. For the moment, let me state that with inversion to conceal is to reveal, while to ask what is concealed is also to pose the question of what is revealed.

This essay considers the logic of concealment and revelation that operated in "mumming," as this custom was practiced during the Twelve Days of Christmas, from Christmas Eve to Epiphany, in the small, rural fishing communities (outports) of Newfoundland. In outport Newfoundland, Christmas mumming flourished during the period of the family fishery, roughly from the mid-19th century until World War II.[1] Sider (1976) argues that this form of mumming was isomorphic with the outport community; and so attributes of this kind of community, and of personhood found within it, should offer the suitable context for an explanation of how mumming operated there.[2]

In order to mum, persons disguised in costume. As mummers they visited households in the community, and if householders guessed their identities, then the mummers removed their facial coverings and accepted food and drink before departing for the next house. I argue here that this deceptively simple device of concealment and revelation effaced a disjunctive duality in perceptions of the exterior person and the interior self, a duality that was echoed in perceptions of the social relationship within the community and in the absence of such bonds beyond its external boundary. Mumming not only harmonized person and self but also the community in relation to itself. I argue for a notion of personhood in outport Newfoundland that was predicated on a disjunction between perceptions of the self, perceived by others as hidden, and perceptions of the social person. In accordance with this notion, the presence of selfhood was masked in much of daily life, while that of personhood was revealed and open to inspection.[3]

My interpretation of mumming depends on the ethnographies of others. I first turn to a consideration of these materials, one that permits the emergence of the distinctions discussed above and their relatedness in a semiotic or ideal sense. Then I detail the outport mumming complex itself. The third section of this paper examines certain safeguards, of sign and structure, that protected the collectivity against the deconstructive force of mumming. Such safeguards included the taming of mumming through shifts in social space; through the sequential shift in control in the discourse between disorder and moral order; and through the guessing game, as a rule-governed medium. The fourth section addresses the mechanics of inversion and reversion in mumming to demonstrate how this mechanism erased disjunctions in the domains of personhood and community. In the conclusion I discuss certain general issues that emerge from this analysis: that the ongoing inversion of signs between domains of personhood and community maintained the relational separation of these domains, even while disjunctions within each domain were erased; and the relevance of inversion and reversion for a comparative semiotics of concealment and revelation.

Interior and Exterior Attributes of Person and Community

Scattered along the rugged 9600 km of Newfoundland shoreline, outport villages were physically isolated and numerically small in population. The basic unit of social organization was the household, and ties of kinship among households constituted, in the main, the lineaments of community. Beyond the household there were virtually no communal institutions that organized the village in terms of administration, adjudication, conflict regulation, or the management of work and production.

The household was akin to a solidary and enduring bastion in the village: a dense locus of sentiments of solidarity and of comparative openness and cooperation in interpersonal bonds. Only within the household was information shared freely among its members, including the children, while it was kept strategically from other familiars (Chiaramonte 1970; Faris 1966). The emotional bond between husband and wife likely was the most resilient tie within the household, as such ties were stronger than those between familiars from different households. Relationships between households were characterized by "separateness," with each household a highly privatized and self-contained locale that conserved information about itself (Chiaramonte 1970:13) and that was somewhat analogous to the relative insularity of the community of households. Social relationships between members of different households were largely dyadic, reciprocal, instrumental, and fragile, and were open to ongoing renegotiation.

Houses, often built close to one another, reproduced in their use of space the duality of, on the one hand, extreme privacy and containment, and, on the other, an openness and transparency before others—a dualism echoing that of interpersonal relationships between members of different households. Houses presented an overt or surface appearance of openness to familiars, while keeping the great bulk of household space hidden from view. The main entrance to a house was through the kitchen, and familiars freely entered this region without knocking or otherwise signaling their approach. Still, once within they were restricted solely to the kitchen, where householders commonly socialized with one another and where they kept their social personae on view. Moreover, in the kitchen familiars were constrained by the strict etiquette of the host-guest relationship that, like most interpersonal contacts, was permeated by high degrees of formality, reserve, respect, and outward cordiality (Faris 1969:142; Szwed 1969:108; Firestone 1967; Chiaramonte 1970).

Most outport households earned their livelihood through the inshore or family fishery. Fishing was based, in the main, on relationships of kinship and also was pervaded by the perceptual and behavioral attributes noted above. The ideal unit of fishing production consisted of a group of brothers who held property for fishing in common, who fished together, and who divided the returns into equal shares. As the sons of the brothers grew older, they fished with their fathers; later on, these sons would fish together as a group of brothers (Firestone 1967, 1969). In ideal terms, this suggests a phase in the domestic and productive cycles—when a father fished with his sons—that made the household quite autonomous of other households, and therefore a solidary bastion. This did not occur in practice, for a variety of demographic and social reasons, but such a contraction of a village into relatively self-sufficient households was perceived as hypothetically possible, at least on certain parts of the island.

The average crew of the family fishery was composed of two to four men, who were closely related. The skipper owned the boat, but he rarely told his crew where, when, or how to fish, or how hard to work (Sider 1976:109). Complementing the work of the crew was that of the "shore crowd": the wives, mothers, elder daughters, and other children of the crew, who together did the technically complex jobs of processing the fish on shore and preparing the catch for sale. As Sider (1976:109) argues, villagers not only controlled their means of production but also the social relationships of production. Still, given the attributes of these communities, the tasks of maintaining crew and shore crowd generated much tension. Even brothers who worked together intensively during the fishing season would drift apart afterward until the Christmas season, after which they would prepare the equipment for the coming season (Nemec 1972; in this context, McFeat's 1974:34–36 discussion of task groups and therapeutic groups is relevant).

The exigencies of living in a small face-to-face collectivity created conditions of what Firestone (1978) terms "role-transparency": familiars knew well the social personae of one another and they lived fully in one another's gaze. Within the home the same held for the kitchen, the interface between transparency and privacy that was protected rigidly by host-guest etiquette. Ethnographies of outports imply that the transparency and moral restraint of social personae were complemented by the deep interior privatization of the self. There, in accordance with the perceptions of familiars, hidden from view and rarely exposed, an individual was at home to himself and was not restrained by the moral strictures of the social person. Here, too, others perceived that one experienced the motivations, the desires and emotions, that were not to be shown to familiars; one's "face" reflected the moral and social cordiality of good neighbor and workmate that one also saw reflected in the visages of others.[4] This, at least, seems to be the manner in which familiars perceived one another. However, ethnographers of rural Newfoundland are much more forthcoming on how familiars perceived one another and are quite reticent on how persons perceived themselves.

These ethnographic accounts imply that familiars were perceived in terms of a dualism composed, on the one hand, of the overt moral aspect of personhood, bound in different ways by ties of kinship and social contract and corresponding to the social person; and, on the other hand, in terms of an inner and hidden self, freed of moral restraint and composed, in part, of feelings and sentiments that if given rein would destroy social ties. This is a crude separation that hardly serves to encompass the complexities of social personae and the convolutions of selfhood, yet it does highlight a distinction that had currency in the daily calculus of outport life.

Faris (1968, 1972:161) writes that adult behavior was marked by formality, reserve, caution, inhibition, and rigid role expectations (see also Faris 1969:142). Children were taught to avoid close personal ties with peers and, in general, to suppress emotional expression, for any exposure of self could lead to exploitation by others. Szwed (1966) echoes these observations, noting that children were taught to be aware of possible deceptions in their social relationships.

In daily life there was little social visiting among households, especially on the part of men (Chiaramonte 1969). To some extent this was due to the necessities of the fishing season. Still, outside the household men tended to congregate in small groups only in neutral locations (shops, the churchyard, the government wharf; see Faris 1966). There, conversation took the shape of sequential monologues rather than discussion (Chiaramonte 1970:15). The women who were present were quite silent (Faris 1966). And the men could avoid making any commitments to one another, even of proffering hospitality (Chiaramonte 1970).

Ethnographies of the outport emphasize the centrality of an ethos of egalitarianism and reciprocity among villagers. Szwed (1969:107) argues that this stressed equality was maintained, in part, by "the highly ritualized nature of interpersonal relations." Any striving for mobility, for status, was met by techniques of leveling, such as gossip, ridicule, satire, and the withdrawal of reciprocity (see also Firestone 1967, 1978:102).

The caution, the reserve and wariness, that marked interpersonal contacts outside the household (Szwed 1969:108; Firestone 1967; Faris 1968) were conjoined by the deep suspicion persons held of what they perceived as the amoral but hidden attitudes and motives of others. Feelings of suspicion and hostility were kept well concealed and "masked," and there were strong proscriptions against verbal confrontation and physical violence (Faris 1966, 1969:139; Szwed 1969:108). It is clear that the formality and distance of moral etiquette protected social persons from one another—on the surface, as it were—and buffered them against the unknown but socially dangerous desires with which their inner selves were suspected of being infused. Chiaramonte's (1970:12) informants could state, "A man doesn't have a friend here." As social persons, community members were familiars of one another while their inner selves, secluded and privatized, were mysterious and forbidding and, so to speak, "strangers" to one another. Szwed (1969:108) notes that social relationships were known only as "surface facts," while the motivations of social persons which underwrote such ties were perceived as unknown and as a "threatening mystery."

These observations support the interpretation of a duality of social person and private self. The social person was perceived as a "surface fact," well known in various personae, while social relationships themselves were characterized by role transparency. By contrast, there was the deep suspicion that if the social person were quite transparent, the self would be opaque to the perceptions of others. It was to the workings of the self that villagers appeared to ascribe the causality of motivation, a point that fits well with their emphasis on individualism and self-reliance. In turn, this suggests that villagers conceived of the inner person, of the self, as the location of "authentic" feelings and sentiments that animated personae yet that were not to be revealed to others.

The term "authentic" is used here with reservation. I do not suggest that the outport perception of the self and others was constituted wholly and simply in terms of attributes and accents of emotion that potentially threatened the idea of social contract and the persons thus connected. But I do argue that outport people conceived of the almost inaccessible self as composed, in part, of hidden qualities that were both authentic and dangerous to the social fabric. If the self were a wellspring of authentic motivation and causation of danger to others, then the social person and the social contract between persons did not accurately reflect such authenticity—and so they contained significant elements of artifice, of inauthenticity. Just as the social person masked the self, so the social relationship, that linchpin of community, masked the selves of persons thereby brought into conjunction. If, in terms of social contract, persons were familiars, then their concealed and dangerous selves were strangers.

Together, the households of an outport constituted a moral community of familiars (Faris 1968; Sider 1976:111). Within the household this was predicated on bonds of close kinship, trust, and ongoing interdependence. Among households, morality depended on a code of etiquette and social contract, mainly between individuals. Within the community, familiars "masked" their grievances, their suspicions and hostilities, through privacy and social distance, through formality and reserve, through egalitarianism, and through an avoidance of the expression of emotion.

Although categories of social differentiation within the moral community were ill defined and weak, its external boundary was well defined,

strong, and resilient. Nonfamiliars—that is, anonymous and morally unformed and uncontrolled strangers—were regarded openly in precisely the
ways in which familiars were perceived covertly by one another within the
community. The typical stranger was received with courtesy, formality, and
hospitality. But he was perceived as "unpredictable, unreliable, not to be
trusted, deviant, and . . . potentially dangerous and malevolent. . . . The
category 'stranger' is edged with suspicion" (Faris 1969:134). The devil, the
night, and things dark by nature, including the dangerous interior state of
anger (termed "getting black"), were associated with evil, and evil with
strangerhood (Faris 1969:138; see also Firestone 1969).

Two contrasts and two affinities, in the domains of collectivity and
personhood, emerge from the preceding discussion. These are restated here,
for they are used intensively in my analysis of concealment and revelation in
mumming. One must emphasize that in the daily life of the outport, these
contrasts and affinities were better regarded as tendencies. Nonetheless, in
mumming, as in so much of other ritualistic activity, these themes were con-
centrated and were honed to a greater clarity (Handelman in press).

The first contrast distinguishes between the inside of the community,
its social relationships, and the strangerhood that lies beyond it. This contrast is of a disjunctive dualism, since it opposes the morality of community
to the amorality of strangerhood. The second contrast distinguishes between the social person, the exterior of personhood, and the interior self.
This contrast also is of a disjunctive dualism, for it opposes the moral social
person to amoral aspects of self. The first affinity is between the interior of
the social person, the self, and the exterior of community, the realm of
strangerhood. The second affinity is between the exterior of the social person and the interior of community. These contrasts and affinities are summarized in Figure 1.

Aspects of the self, of the submerged desires and antagonisms that
were suspected to exist there, were negatively valued but were regarded as
"authentic," in the sense used previously. The covert self contained certain
negative attributes that charged motivation toward familiars, that were per-

CONTRAST

		exterior	interior	
	exterior	PERSON	COMMUNITY	interior
AFFINITY				
	interior	SELF	STRANGERHOOD	exterior
		interior	exterior	

Figure 1.

ceived as "true," but that were concealed from view by the exterior social person who, in no small measure, was a creation of the exigencies and instrumentalities of a moral code of conduct. The self was affective, charged with emotion; the social person was oriented instrumentally and showed little feeling. The exterior of the social person was positively valued but was perceived as inauthentic, since it was the product of the constraints of community and of interpersonal relationships, and not of a person's inner sentiments, as these were perceived by others.[5]

In this interpretation, mumming was a drama of deception and truth, of concealment and revelation, that the collectivity played on itself. It was a dramatic construction on the value and, as it were, the authenticity of person and community—one that manipulated the dualism of interior and exterior, of the covert and the overt, to invert their everyday contrasts and affinities. In so doing, mumming showed what the person, and the community of relationships, were "really" like. But then it reversed this apparent "truth" and demonstrated that it was indeed artifice, a deception and falsehood. The mechanics of inversion and reversion effaced the dualism of person and self, of familiar and stranger, and brought these into congruency with one another. There emerged an analogous structure of person and community that was harmonic in its moral valency. Later in this paper I suggest that the above was accomplished through the manipulation of three major sets of opposition: the covert and the overt, the positive and the negative, and the authentic and the inauthentic.

The Mumming Complex in Outport Newfoundland

The Christmas season was perhaps the only continuous period during the year when villagers refrained from work (Faris 1972:140). The men slept late; Sunday clothing was worn daily; the evenings were given over to drinking, dancing, and singing; and special foods were eaten (Chiaramonte 1969). Apart from celebrations within the home, the Christmas interlude also was a time of social intensification through which the isolation, alienation, and self-containment of households was broken down.

There was a sharp increase in social visiting between households during this season, whether by entire families or by groups of male social drinkers who stopped in succession at the houses of each of their number, who in turn became a host and reciprocated the hospitality received previously (Chiaramonte 1969). Unlike much of the more infrequent and sporadic visiting of daily life, visiting during the Christmas season appears not to have had any special instrumental purpose. Villagers participated together in many events—card parties, dances, Christmas Eve gift giving, variety shows—that were held in locations central to the community, such as the local hall of the Orangemen's Lodge and the church (Faris 1972:160; Chiaramonte 1969:83). These trends toward social solidarity were clear-cut and unproblematic. They involved, in additive fashion, increasingly inclusive levels of social integration: the household in relation to itself, links between households, the giving over of public space to sociable interaction, and the collective participation of villagers in communitywide events.

Transversing this movement of increasing solidarity was the countervailing flow of groups of mummers, commonly called "janneys" or, in places, the "Dark Ones" (Faris 1968). The basic features of the mumming complex here were quite simple (see Halpert 1969). Groups of adults—mainly men, but including women and, in more recent times, young persons—donned costumes. These were put together from oddments of clothing, often belonging to other persons. Special attention was given to the concealment of the well-known features of the social person. Thus, faces were covered with pieces of transparent cloth, commonly called "veils", and more infrequently by masks. In some villages such coverings were called "false faces" (Faris 1969:131). Hands, usually well known in the village, were also covered. Padding changed body shape and image, while voice was altered through ingressive speech. Although men often dressed as women, and women as men, the emphasis was not on the inversion of gender as such, nor on the impersonation of particular characters. Instead, in virtually all such costuming, preeminence was given to dis-guise, to concealing one's known and everyday personae and to becoming unknown and anonymous—in other words, to becoming strange, mysterious, and indeterminate, since one concealed social knowledge about oneself and so about one's relationships (Sider 1976:118).

Disguised, anonymous, and anomalous, the mummers intruded into the community after dark and made their way among houses along the pathways of the village. There is no doubt that, in general, they were perceived as malevolent, frightening, and threatening creatures (Widdowson 1977:233) who, in earlier times, may have had connotations of the supernatural: of amorphous ghosts, spirits, and other malign beings ordinarily kept at bay beyond the borders of community (Widdowson 1977:229). Mummers especially were fearsome and feared when encountered along the byways between houses: in the interstices, so to speak, among dense nodes of solidary intimacy within the community. Here their behavior was patently aggressive and threatening toward those they met. It was not playful. In extreme cases, persons were reported to run from them, to climb trees, or to jump into the harbor to escape them (Widdowson 1977:233–234; Firestone 1969:68). Groups of mummers sometimes fought one another with staves and clubs, physically attacking those they encountered (Halpert 1969:44). Faris (1969:132) notes that in earlier times, mummers could be especially rough with socially peripheral persons: "those most offensive to the general order, were often beaten if caught out by the janneys." Williams (1969) quotes an informant: "Outdoors you're more afraid of them than in the house—you never know what they're gonna do. You try to keep away from 'em as much as you can.'' Intruding into the community, the mummers brought disorder into its open public spaces and controlled these by their presence. One did not reason or negotiate with mummers out-of-doors; one submitted, resisted, or bolted. Out-of-doors, after dark, the definition of context and contact was quite that of the mummer: wild, emotional, aggressive, and menacing.

When the mummers reached a house they intended to visit, they knocked on the kitchen door and requested admittance. In this, they acted as would strangers to the community. Once within, their behavior continued to be the inverse of that expected of familiars, and people would say that "anything can happen" (Faris 1969:132). Unrestrained, the mummers acted oddly. They shouted, made sudden and violent movements, and engaged in horseplay, trickery, and mock intercourse with the women of the household (Faris 1969:132). They nudged and jostled householders and poked fun at them (Szwed 1969:110–111). Mummers intruded within the private and prohibited regions of the house (Faris 1969) and frightened the children, on occasion by threatening to abduct them (Widdowson 1977:234). Although much of this behavior was scary, like the out-of-doors, it also was perceived as playful and "fun."

In turn, the hosts would initiate a guessing game with the mummers, to unravel the "true" personae of the guisers. They, too, were not restrained by customary morality and formality: householders felt the bodies of the mummers, tickled and poked them, and in former times occasionally were known to forcibly rip off the facial coverings (Faris 1969:132). The mummers could respond by raising their staves at the householders. The latter commonly asked the mummers to perform—to sing and dance—in order to discern some familiarity in voice, gesture, and movement. The transitions from outright fear, out-of-doors, to an admixture of playful and scary interaction within the home, and then to the guessing game, are important. I return to these shifts later in the paper.

If the social persona of a mummer were guessed correctly, he removed his facial covering. The householder then became host and the mummer, the guest. Customary etiquette prevailed, and all chaotic behavior ceased. The host greeted his guest, placed him in a seat, controlled the conversation, and offered food and drink (Szwed 1969). If the persona of a mummer were not guessed correctly, he would depart, concealed and anonymous, without partaking of commensality.

This invasion by grotesque and malign beings was most discomfiting for the family. Yet the overall house visit usually was summarized as "fun." There was no fun, however, for either householder or mummer if the persona of the latter was not guessed correctly and the mummer left without revealing himself. There also was no fun if the mummer's persona were guessed too quickly. Crucial to an accomplished performance of mumming was, first, successful concealment, and second, successful revelation.

Why mumming in its outport form? Explanations have tended to focus on the social conditions that fostered mumming and on the functions of this activity. Little attention has been paid to the logic of mechanisms that permitted the controlled accomplishment of mumming (with the exception of Firestone 1978). Explications understand mumming to be a period of reversal, a time of sanctioned license (Faris 1966),[6] that offered cognitive variations from everyday arrangements. Faris and Firestone link the mummer to the idea of strangerhood: by taking on the anonymous and chaotic personae of strangers, mummers were freed from the daily strictures of role and relation. By behaving as surrogate strangers, suggests Firestone and, more implicitly, Faris, mummers were permitted to express suppressed hostilities. Szwed (1969), who does not use the metaphor of mummer as stranger, nonetheless echoes these comments. Sider (1976) understands mumming as commenting on egalitarian relationships that controlled means of production. Chiaramonte (1969) considers mumming, and associated social drinking, as shattering the isolation, alienation, and self-containment of households while it allowed dyadic ties to be formed or renewed. All of these interpreters, to varying degrees, agree that through such activities the outport celebrated and reaffirmed its sense of communal identity.

In a recent reanalysis of the materials on mumming, Firestone (1978) departs from the more functionalist arguments noted above and takes a position closer to that of this essay. He argues that in facing the anonymous mummers, the householder also faced the anonymous community on whom his perception of self depended. By unmasking them, and "the fantasmagora of what one might be in others' eyes" (1978:109), the householder revealed the familiar personae and the honorable intentions that lay beneath the mask. This legitimized his perception of himself through their eyes. For the mummer, too, disguise provided an occasion to celebrate not being himself, to escape from the knowledge that others had of him in the everyday.

My own understanding of mumming borrows from all of the above: the affinity of mummer to stranger; the expression of suppressed suspicion and hostility through licensed behavior; the revelation of self and other through unmasking; and the ways in which the above commented on and contributed to social relationships and a sense of community. Yet, I seek an interpretation at a more abstract level of understanding, one that is not dependent on a direct relationship of form and function and does not rely on the vagaries of persons in interaction for the logic of its structure. Moreover, the interpretation that is offered here operates at one and the same time on the domains of both personhood and collectivity. These domains are linked together through affinities of analogy and through a common mechanism of inversion and reversion that harmonizes the incipient duality in each domain, bringing each into congruence with itself, with implications for the other. This, I think, should be a primary aim of the study of public events as dramatizations of personhood through performance and as media for the replication and possible change of social order through operations on the self in performance.

Time, Space, and Control in Mumming

That mumming first came to be associated with the idea of Christmas and with this period of celebration and leisure in the outport may have been idiosyncratic and practical. That this association continued to exist in outports contributed profoundly to the circumscription of mumming with devices of protection that tempered the degree to which it was permitted to spread chaos within the collectivity. Examined closely, the contexualization of mumming emphasized its control, although its anomic voice was permitted extensive expression. Such safeguards became evident in the social intensification that surrounded mumming, in its timing, in the spatial locations of its practice, and in the taming of mummerhood through the medium of a game. These safeguards are discussed in turn in this section.

Two kinds of intensification were at work during the Christmas season. One was the great increase in social visiting among households, in the social drinking among groups of men, and in the holding of social events in which many of the community participated. Such socializing encompassed the major social configurations of the collectivity: dyads, groups of familiars, households, and the community as a whole. Given the paucity of information on religious beliefs and practices in the outport, I cannot discuss the significance of the embedment of mumming in the Christmas period.[7] Still, the intensification of collective solidarity likely gained import from a central theological tenet of Christmas: the birth of moral community among Christians. The time of Christmas, with its encompassing cosmogenic properties, provided a broad context able to withstand the license of mumming.

The second process of intensification flowed in the obverse direction, toward that of the deconstruction of relationships and of the idea of community. Its vehicle was that of mumming. Successful mumming was predicated on the turning of familiars into strangers. Alienation and unpredictability, I argue, were suspected to exist within the selves of others and beyond the community. These two loci of strangeness, beyond the social person but inward and beyond the community but outward, were the basic signs of the paradigm of mumming that linked personhood and collectivity. The appearance of the mummer—shapeless, formless, and anonymous—keyed the strangeness and potential for evil hidden within the self of everyman to the external boundary of the collectivity of persons, beyond which everyman openly was suspect.

In mumming, the insider became an outsider who was inside—that is, a stranger. The disguise of this outsider brought out the shadow side of person and community: the breakdown of moral communication, as the basis for interpersonal contact, through disorder, for the mummer fit no accepted category of familiar. The implication is that through mumming the person-as-mummer was turned inside-out, while the mummer-as-stranger, who intruded within the moral community, was turned outside-in.

These two processes of intensification pulled the community in opposing directions: mumming was centrifugal, vacuous, and anomic, and so reified the worst fears of the villagers; socializing was centripetal, warm, and friendly, and so confirmed their hopes. One sees here two contrary conceptions of collectivity, one of moral and social solidarity and the other of alienation and chaos; and the second, ordinarily hidden in the everyday, stared forth. If the first could be likened to a sort of renewal of the moral community, then the second was akin more to its demise. Still, this was temporary: the very cessation of morality contained within itself the embryo of moral rebirth, for the amoral mummer, unmasked and revealed, was again a basis for significant communication among persons. This suggests strongly that mumming mediated these two processes of centrifugality and centripetality. Mumming began with the premises of centrifugality and, by falsifying its own claim to authenticity, transformed these into the premises of centripetality.

In the daily life of the outport, contacts were mediated by the formality and morality of etiquette among familiars, on the one hand, and by that of trust and intimacy among householders, on the other. Through mumming, such links were mediated by anonymous and monstrous strangers. In more semiotic terms, relationships among signs, as media of communication, were blocked and displaced. Unable to relate to others who had become strangers, one also may have peered within oneself, to one's strangeness of self, to that which one suspected to be secreted within others, and to that which one thereby discovered to be present in oneself as others saw one. One's strangeness of self, in relation to others who were strangers, was amplified.

This sort of blockage of communication suggests that mummers, as strangers, infiltrated the interstices of contact between familiars; they inserted themselves into the social fabric and displaced and replaced everyday signs of connectivity. Such a semiotic displacement was a key to the deconstruction that mummers brought in their wake: disorder was not accomplished simply by the presence of these feared characters but by the displacement of the known sign, in the connective substance of relationships, that in turn made the mummer the fulcrum of interpersonal contact.

Any sense of relationship and community then passed through the matrix of the mummer figure who turned the network of the known—from its closure as the external boundary of the collectivity to its highest density in the intimacy of the home—into a frayed fabric of indeterminacies.

To use the conception that Bruce Kapferer and I have taken from Grathoff (1970), the mummer was a "symbolic type" (Handelman and Kapferer 1980; Handelman 1983). The symbolic type is an internally consistent form that is then wholly true to itself. In other words, its appearance, attributes, and logic of composition are not open to give-and-take, to negotiation. One either accepts a symbolic type for what it is, and for what it communicates, or one rejects its validity. Unlike interaction among social roles that modify one another through their mutual tending, a symbolic type presents itself as wholly valid and relatively unaffected by context. Therefore, to no small degree it is reified above context. Its appearance, and the logic of its composition, thus have the tendency to determine context, to mold context into congruence with the messages of its own internal composition and consistency. The presence of the mummer, given the composition of this form, deconstructed the unity of context into disparate signs that lacked connectivity. Still, this capacity for the dissolution of mundane contexts by the mummer depended on the extent to which others accepted this type as wholly consistent and invariant in relation to itself. And such acceptance varied in different locales within the community. Outside, in the dark, mummers were most accepted as authentic, as beings that were fully consistent with their form. Inside the home they became the least accepted as such, for there the authenticity of the mummer was made problematic.

An inspection of mumming in different loci indicates that the capacity of the mummer to mediate the chaotic into the known, and so to deconstruct the latter, was a graduated one in which the known began to be mediated back into the amorphic, as control shifted from mummer to familiar. Mummers were most true-to-type when outside, in spatial interstices between homes; and such locations, in an ideal sense, were closest to the moral boundary of the community. In daily life the use of such locations was quite dependent on the formality of etiquette and was least leavened by the intimacy and the open sharing of the home. The night, of course, heightened the vulnerability of these spaces and impartially blurred the seen and the unknown in its dark cloak. It was in such locations that persons ran from mummers. Here the latter were most violent toward others, and others toward them. Here mummers were without restraint or obligations of mutuality toward others, and others toward them. Here one could be uncertain whether a familiar, indeed anyone human, lay beneath the costume: in other words, whether appearance was guise or authenticity.

As mummers knocked for admittance, the internal consistency of their typification began to alter. On the one hand, they behaved as did strangers; yet on the other, they acknowledged the moral integrity of the home. Control began to shift toward the reconstitution of morality at the very interface of public and private space, of exterior and interior. However, with their entrance, the mummers penetrated this elementary unit of solidarity and intimacy. Moreover, they intruded into a domain that was highly protective of the most vulnerable core of the community—its children, who were the products of its past and the predictors of its future. A longer range view suggests that the contact between mummer and child was one of the more profound of the entire mumming complex. The capacity of children, and parents, to withstand and tame the onslaught of the mummers also was an implicit commentary on the likelihood of the community to reproduce itself through youngsters who would become properly socialized adults.

Within the home, control oscillated between householders and mummers. The latter inserted themselves between householders by behaving like intimates of the former. In a sense, they behaved as householders could toward one another, albeit in exaggerated ways, were they to share intimacy. Yet the mummers mocked such closeness and interdependence, and so questioned its significance. They teased and threatened householders; they entered the inner reaches of the dwelling, forbidden to nonmembers of the family; and, on occasion, they chased and threatened to chastise the children, thereby usurping parental functions. For their part, householders ridiculed the mummers and took liberties with them, touching and feeling their bodies and rough-housing with them.

Although mummers and householders dropped the relevance of rules of etiquette, the result was not intimacy, as it was understood within the home, but its converse: a condition of distance that bore certain icy resemblances to intimacy. As the mummers mimicked intimate behavior within the family, so the character of trust among householders also was mocked and mediated by strangeness. Metaphorically, the home, the moral core of community here, teetered on the edge of its own deconstruction. In the anonymous and forbidding mummer, the householders likely saw not simply a mirror image of themselves but perhaps their extinction as a family. This may be the deepest, if implicit, truth that mumming touched on—and so the importance of proving the artifice and pretense of the mummer. Such revelation then would mediate moral knowledge back into the chaotic unknown, and so extirpate the latter. Strangeness would be concealed once again within the self and beyond the collectivity.

The guessing game, enacted within the home, was crucial to the resurrection of familiarity. The behavior of mummers within the home has been described as frightening and yet playful. There is no contradiction between these if one comprehends the significance of play here. Elsewhere, in part following the works of others, I suggest that the power of the idea of play lies in its capacities for dissolution, although it does not offer viable alternatives to that which it deconstructs (see Handelman 1977). In other words, it is an amoral medium, and this is its particular terror. It can "play" with any foundation-for-form, rendering alien the known. Let loose in a playful medium, this is what symbolic types like mummers accomplish: they are true to their own internal composition and to its consistency, with little regard for external constraints; and so they deconstruct context by shaping it in accordance with their own amorphic agglomeration.

But the medium of "game" is a ruled domain. The freedom of symbolic types is keyed to rules that specify the conditions of their existence and therefore limit their action, as Grathoff (1970) discusses. In such a medium, types are controlled by context; that is, the medium of game is a moral domain in which symbolic types accept the rules of context, even though these may specify the destruction of the type under particular conditions. This was the case in the guessing game. The mummer no longer could continue to play out his own authenticity and destructive design, for these were made conditional by the rules of the game. The acceptance of the game placed the mummer in a moral domain within which the type no longer commanded its own fate. Therefore, degrees of control continued to pass to the householders, since they held a mandate to falsify the presumed authenticity of the mummers. With the transition to game, morality was ascendant, although its triumph was hardly assured until the mummer was shown up as sheer disguise.

If the identity of the mummer were guessed accurately, then control passed wholly to the householders. In this regard, one should pay special attention to the act of naming oneself: this revelation of biographical person was a moral act that committed the ex-mummer to the obligations of humanity and to the responsibilities of sociality. This is one reason why mummers whose personae were not guessed, and who departed still retaining their authenticity as types, left both themselves and householders anxious and dissatisfied. The revelation of personhood was a triumph of morality and civility, in a contest won by the household over those concealed forces, within person and community, that could erode and destroy it. Once the mummer was revealed as familiar, the determinate form of the host-guest relationship replaced the agonistic oscillation of the guessing game, the outcome of which was conditional and not predetermined, at least in accordance with the ideal form of mumming.[8]

The banishment of the strangeness and amorality of the mummer, through inversion and reversion, is now considered. I suggest that the mechanics of mumming linked perceptions of personhood to those of community, such that concealment and revelation operated at one and the same time in both domains.

Inside-Out, Outside-In: Inversion and Congruency in Mumming

The ethnographic evidence suggests that perception of outport personhood was dualistic. The exterior of personhood, the social person, was accorded positive value. Yet this exterior, molded by social strictures, also was perceived as inauthentic—to a degree as camouflage. Lurking within the interior of the person were aspects of a more authentic self that were not to be trusted, and these were accorded negative value. Not that the self as a whole was perceived as negative, but aspects of it that were significant for interpersonal contacts were comprehended in this way. One rarely saw these negative aspects of self, for the social person conducted his everyday life in accordance with the cordiality of formality. Yet one suspected that they were indeed present. People might have been overtly correct and courteously sociable to one another, but they also were deeply suspicious and distrustful of one another's so-called true but secret motives, intentions, and sentiments. I argue that the outport perception of personhood differentiated, if implicitly, between one's overt social person and one's covert self; that each of these was accorded a relatively positive or negative value (rendered in Figure 2 by + or −, respectively); and that each of these was perceived as relatively authentic or inauthentic. In numerous versions of daily life, then, outport personhood could be summarized, if simplistically, in accordance with the coordinates of Figure 2.

In daily life the overt social person was accorded positive value but was perceived as inauthentic, as a moral artifice of social relationships; by contrast, the covert self was perceived as authentic but was accorded negative value, since it was not constrained by morality.[9] In other words, the outport perception of personhood contained striking incongruencies between the exterior person and the interior self.

An analogous relational set can be posited for the outport perception of community and strangerhood, with one significant difference. The condition of strangerhood lay outside the community, covert and hidden from view and beyond moral compact. And, although strangerhood was accord-

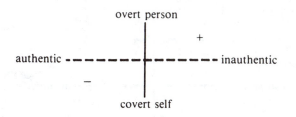

Figure 2. Daily life.

ed a negative value, it also was perceived as authentic and "true," if indeterminate, amoral, and dangerous. This suggests an affinity among signs that connoted aspects of the perceived covert self of a person within the community and those that connoted the covert but external state of strangerhood beyond the community; and an affinity of signs that connoted the perceived overt social person and those of membership within the community. Significant aspects of both the overt social person and the social relationships of community were accorded a positive value but were perceived as inauthentic. The overt appearance of the person masked the suspected and negatively valued authenticity hidden within the self, while the etiquette of relationships between persons masked the suspected and negatively valued authenticity that underlay sociality but was banished to hidden regions exterior to the community.

The mummer raised this submerged quality of personhood into view and made others anxious that it indeed could be authentic—that there was no different quality of being beneath the mummer's surface, nor any different implications for social relationships. Yet it was precisely this turnabout, in which what had been concealed was revealed and what had been revealed was concealed, that erased the disjunction between the authentic but negatively valued covert character of self and the community of familiars, and their inauthentic but positively valued overt character. In each of the separate domains of personhood and community, exterior and interior attributes were made congruent and harmonious with one another.

The donning of mummerhood was an exercise in concealment, the hiding of the overt and familiar person. Yet it also was a revelation, for it brought to the surface and reified a representation of the negatively valued but authentic aspects of self that persons were suspected of having. Inside-out, negative aspects of selfhood were revealed; and aspects of the social person, positive but inauthentic, were concealed. The signs of personhood were inverted in a manner in keeping with the deepest fears of villagers about others and perhaps about themselves. Authentic strangerhood, which lurked in everyman, was among them. This is summarized in Figure 3, as negative and positive signs move through the coordinates of personhood and authenticity.

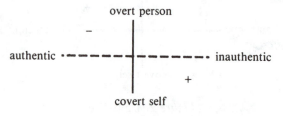

Figure 3. Mumming.

With the presence of mummers in the community, outside-in, strangerhood struck at the interior and burrowed into the collectivity. Mummers,
as strangers, inverted the relationship between interior and exterior, replacing familiars and reversing the signs of social relations. The concealed
character of the social relationship, suspect but authentic, was revealed. To
interact with the mummer was to experience the authentic fragility of the
mundane social relationship, a vulnerability ordinarily hidden in the everyday. Mumming inverted person in relation to self and in relation to others;
and so it also inverted the social relationship. The inversion of a number of
relationships exponentially subverted the very idea of community as a nexus
of connectivity among households.

If mumming revealed a suspected "truth" about personhood and
about the social relationship, then it did so as dis-guise. The deep structure
of disguise, as concealment, once again implied that surface appearance was
not authentic. Should it be penetrated, it would become mask and therefore
inauthentic. Thus, the rendition of personhood that would emerge from
within would be perceived as authentic. Since the personhood of mummer
was of negative value, its replacement likely would be perceived in a positive
vein. But this phase depended on the validation of mumming as mask; as an
artifice that concealed another version of personhood within itself. Yet the
demonstration of deception was conditional, not predetermined: this
penetration of artifice could be unsuccessful, in programmatic terms, and
then the mummer would exit as such, as an authentic representation of personhood. Until this issue was resolved, in the duration between concealment
and revelation (or its absence), the overt but negative mummer and the
covert but positive character it was suspected of concealing were likely to
oscillate between authentic and inauthentic versions of personhood.

The guessing game that located the mummer firmly within a moral
nexus of rules tested the falsity or validity of the mumming version of personhood. If the mumming version were falsified, it was peeled away to
reveal both a familiar *and* an authentic personhood, now proven to have
been concealed within the mummer. Once the validty of mummerhood was
nullified, the mummer removed his head covering, and the now authentic
person-as-self emerged from within. This was a reversion and a cancellation
of those negative qualities of self that were concealed within an everyday
version of personhood. In this moment of revelation there was no contradiction between social personhood and covert selfhood. The outcome of
the successful reversion of mumming is shown in Figure 4. Personhood,
authenticity, and valency are conjoined in a way that is precisely the reverse
of their everyday disjunction.

The revelation of the falsification of mummerhood likely was one of
the few occasions in the outport when, apart from relationships within the
home, there was no disjunction between the positively valued perception of

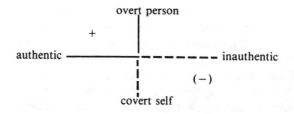

Figure 4. Revelation.

the person and its authenticity. Instead, these qualities of personhood were harmonized with one another, while the negatively valued perception of the covert self momentarily became inauthentic and so rendered itself irrelevant. I suggest that in such moments the harmonics of personhood and selfhood were experienced fully and holistically as "surface facts." Their congruency was open wholly to public inspection and validation.[10]

One understands once more why both mummers and householders were uneasy and distressed if the deception of the former was not falsified. Then the mummer's version of personhood remained authentic and negative, a confirmation of the worst suspicions of the villagers about familiars. The mummer departed as he had come, an anonymous stranger outside the morality of etiquette and beyond the incorporation of commensality. As villagers said, then there was no "fun," for mummerhood froze in its phase of authenticity and so continued to signify the deconstruction of sociality.

I argue that the intrusion of mummers into the community, the outside-in flow of strangeness, reified fears that amoral disorder was the authentic basis of relationships. However, the revelation of the familiar, hidden within the mummer-stranger, falsified the latter and authenticated the former, in accordance with the logic of the above interpretation. In programmatic terms, the mummer-as-stranger, who belonged outside the community, once again was banished beyond its borders. Then, within the community, relationships were governed by a morality of etiquette that no longer was merely formal but also was both positive and authentic. Therefore, in the domain of community, the falsity that was suspected to lurk within everyday relationships was banished, inside-out, beyond the collectivity of familiars. Here, too, the previous disjunctions between the overt and the covert, between the positive and the negative, and between the authentic and the inauthentic, were brought into harmony with one another.

In these small settlements a sizable number of individuals, especially adult men, participated in mumming and took turns being host and mummer. Programmatically, one can state that the idea of personhood, if not all persons, underwent the harmonic process that, to my mind, composes the deeper structure of mumming. In turn, relationships were composed, in the main, of persons who underwent the host-mummer interchange. Bonds also went through this process. The collection of bonds that connected households to one another and that constituted the sense of community consisted of persons who underwent this process . . . and so forth.

In circles of increasing breadth, the entire community annually underwent this comprehensive discourse of concealment and revelation, emerging within as a more solidary unit and protected from without by a strengthened redoubt no longer eroded by internal doubts. Still, as individuals returned to the strictures and strains of daily living, the pattern of duality would re-form: outside-in, suspect qualities of self would be perceived to take shape within others and would be perceived as authentic, if negative; inside-out, the community would regard with suspicion any incursion from without its circle of familiars. Overlaying all this would be the formalism and reserve of the code of etiquette, dimly perceived as necessary but as artifice—a mask that precariously hid from view the anarchy of the mummer's blank visage.

Convergence and Divergence, Concealment and Revelation

This interpretation of mumming links one series of harmonic operations in the domain of personhood to an analogous series in the domain of the collectivity. These linkages are presented as analogic affinities between these two domains. Yet it is crucial to stress that these affinities are not homologies and that this point addresses what I take to be a prime function of devices of inversion, one that has to do with convergence and divergence in connections among signs.

In mumming, the relationship between the two domains was of an inversion of signs, so that each domain remained a representation of what the other was not. If personhood turned itself on an axis of inside-out, then the collectivity was involuted, outside-in. Therefore, these domains were not related through a simple connection of signifier to signified, of idea to image, in which one could be understood as a derivation of the other, brought into being and formed by it. Such a reductionist position, still not that uncommon, would suggest either that personhood could be derived from collective representations or that community could be constructed as an additive collection of personae.

Instead, the ongoing inversion of signs, of each domain in the other, permits a continuing relationship of what might be called *intimate separation* among these respective domains. This kind of connectivity among signs maintains the autonomy, integrity, and internal consistency of their respective referential domains. It continues to produce the integrity of the distinction between personhood and collectivity while reproducing their intimate separation. Therefore, neither domain is concealed in the other nor subsumed by it, although the disjunctions within each momentarily are effaced.

These points highlight an elementary principle in the logic of devices of inversion: the divergence of signs, their opposition that is inherent in inversion, maintains their domains of signification as distinctly separate yet intimately related. A divergence of signs, in devices of inversion, is to be distinguished clearly from the condition of a convergence of signification. Such a convergence of signifiers erases boundaries that separate domains, permitting either their coalescence into a single domain or the subsumation of one by another. Perhaps the most radical example of a convergence of signs and a coalescence of domains is found in the condition that Victor Turner calls "communitas," in which distinctions of selfhood, personhood, and other categories are altered in terms of overriding and cross-cutting common denominators.[11]

In the case of mumming, both convergence and divergence appear to operate. Within each of the respective domains of personhood and community there is the signification of convergence, erasing disjunctions. Yet the continuing inversion of signs between domains, while convergence occurs in each, ensures their intimate separation.

Christmas mumming shows the importance of giving equal attention to both concealment and revelation in what commonly are called reversals or inversions, instead of glossing such operations. In mumming, inversion and reversion form an integral sequence of two phases that revolves around notions of concealment and revelation. More generally, recognition should be accorded the following proposition: if inversion and reversion operate in sequence, as a two-part set, then inversion maintains mode of discourse (see Handelman 1979). "Reversal" does not do this, since this term does not contain its own negation that is reversion. Instead, "reversal" potentially indexes a radical overturning of social order, however defined in terms of magnitude, for it is open-ended and developmental in its implications. Inversion is a highly conservative and conservationist mechanism that indexes "reversion" and therefore does not threaten social order. Those who look to "inversion" as a seedbed of radical change likely are in error. Clearly, the usage of inversion-reversion as a complementary set should be kept separate from that of "reversal."

Still in a general vein, I also suggest that when events (including those of ritual) are organized in accordance with a logic of inversion-reversion, then their dynamic is that of a "dialectic of encapsulation," as I have come to understand this. Classical Hegelian dialectics, predicated on a dynamic of thesis-antithesis-synthesis, are generative and developmental. By contrast, the dialectics of encapsulation are closed and regenerative. The encapsulated dialectic is predicated on a major thesis and its relationship to a minor antithesis, such that the latter is subsumed by, or encapsulated within, the former. Then the emergence of antithesis revalidates the thesis, instead of generating a new synthesis.

For example, numerous public events of a ritualistic order are constructed through the interplay of a major thesis of "solidarity" and a minor antithesis of "opposition" to the major thesis. Since members of the social unit (however defined) who enact the event accept the validity of the major thesis, their statements of opposition—the minor antitheses—remain in the mode of discourse of the major thesis. Therefore, expressions of opposition, of conflict and difference, of deconstructive tendencies, are contained and controlled by the assumptions of the major thesis. The emergence of opposition thus demonstrates the strength and viability of, in this instance, solidarity. In turn, this demonstration of its own resiliency encourages the social unit to continue to express opposition to itself through controlled and ritualistic media, thereby reasserting its own coherence time and again by the containment of minor antitheses. Such a dialectical process is predicated on an unbalanced relationship between major thesis and minor antithesis. The relationship is kept closed, or bounded, in the sense that other factors are held in abeyance, permitting the controlled generation of major thesis and minor antithesis. Since the outcome of such interplay is a resynthesis of the major thesis of solidarity, and not a new synthesis, it is likely that this dynamic is found in numerous events whose primary aims are concerned with the regeneration of moral, social, and natural orders. Where the relationship of inversion to reversion provides a structure to such events, in many instances the relationship of minor antithesis to major thesis provides a dynamic that explicates the replicative character and outcome of such a structure.

Max Gluckman (1954) came very close to enunciating the logic of an "encapsulated dialectic," one that I state in all but name in a previous work (Handelman 1976), in his formulation of "rituals of rebellion." This is of interest because Beidelman (1966) roundly criticizes Gluckman's sociological analysis of the Swazi Incwala rites for not accounting for the meanings that these rites had for the Swazi themselves. Beidelman argues that a cultural analysis of these rites, like the one he did, would demonstrate quite a different logic of organization—one not only closer to Swazi understandings of their cosmos and of themselves but also one that would explain why these rites were put together as they were. I suggest that a rereading of Gluckman's sociological analysis of the Incwala rites in terms of rituals of rebellion and of Beidelman's explication of the cultural logic of these rites would lead one to conclude that on a more abstract and therefore encompassing level there is no basic contradiction between these analyses. The dynamics on which both (and so, perhaps, the Incwala rites as well) are predicated are those of the dialectics of encapsulation.

The recognition of this basic dynamic has many implications, and here I list only a few. One is that the processual logics of ritualistic events should not be mistaken for or thought simply to mirror other societal processes whose logic of organization, and whose dynamics, may well be closer to that of classical dialectics. On a very abstract level, a social order is moved by a variety of processes that should not be confused with one another. A second implication, then, is that such events should not be confused for the social orders that produce them. As selective and particularistic microcosms, in the fuller sense of "model" as a more systemic simulation of macrocosm, such events are "fictive"; and they are all the more coherent and powerful for that, in comparison to the ongoing social orders from which they emerge. A third implication, and this restates the commonplace, is that a major thesis of, say, solidarity gains its very shape and significance by being posited against a minor antithesis whose thrust is deconstructive. Thesis gets its own coherence and thrust from its relationship to antithesis; and it then becomes able to contain and subsume the latter, thereby resynthesizing itself. Only by coming to know and to recognize and enunciate regularly the deconstructive forces that are glossed or taken for granted in everyday living can a social order take account of itself as an integral whole. Even if such an awareness of integrity is transitory and fleeting, its rythmic transmission is not.

An appreciation of inversion and reversion as a two-part set can open the way to a comparative semiotic of concealment and revelation and their relation to moral order through a consideration of some variants of this set. For example, there are numerous dramatic and ritual events that emphasize only the concealment of social personhood. In such instances concealment reveals an authentic replacement. Such authentic types often channel powerful forces, frequently paranatural, from the exterior of a collectivity into its interior. Where the stress is on the concealment of personhood, the authenticity of revealed paranatural types is not questioned, even when their force clearly is amoral. Examples close to this variant abound: the visits of the Japanese Namahage (Yamamoto 1978); Hopi "ogres" (Kealiinohomoku 1980); Austrian village Krampuses (Honigmann 1977); Inuit Naluyuks (Ben-Dor 1969); Eastern Cherokee Boogers (Speck and Broom 1951); and Nova Scotian Belsnickles (Bauman 1972), to name some.

Such amoral types do the work of morality because they authentically are out of place in a moral context. In the main, their task is the posing of a sharp contrast between morality and amorality and the testing of community members, especially children, for these qualities. They are authentic admonitions of the dangers of amorality, and they evoke correct reactions from community members. Such moral responses provide the social unit with a homogeneous valency in relation to the intruders, who depart still as authentic types.

A second variant may be termed *transparent concealment*. Here the concealed is not hidden completely from perception, nor is the revealed granted authenticity. Instead, concealment and revelation, authenticity and falsity, are perceived as a superimposed or double image in the composition of the figures. The disguise of costume often signifies that concealment and revelation will cancel out one another. Close to this variant are well-known varieties of impersonation, like those of the carnivalesque, where one perceives that what is revealed by the concealment of the social person is an undoubted deception. Given the transparency of concealment, one can state that deception is inherent in the authenticity of that which is revealed. Therefore, the revelation of concealment is understood as inauthentic, and the figure or type automatically falsifies its own validity and reverts to its everyday analog, the social person.

The inherent deception of transparent concealment commonly is said to underscore moral order and customary arrangements. This is indeed so, for the initial inversion of costuming never fully places such order in doubt: the reversion to normality is built into the initial inversion of disguise. Transparent concealment encourages the perception of an authentic reality within the costume or disguise, and so renders this surface appearance inauthentic from the outset.

A third variant is the one discussed in this essay. Here, concealment of the social person reveals and posits an authentic alternative to what was hidden. Hence the significance of the guessing game, within which the falsification of the validity of disguise is not inherent, in programmatic terms. Concealment of the social person, and its revelation of an alternative, must be falsified; otherwise it remains authentic. This variant uses the full set of inversion and reversion in distinct sequence. Of the three variants briefly discussed here, it is the closest to the systematic renewal of moral order through inversion and reversion. Yet this overall instrument of renewal, as yet unamed and still hardly revealed, deserves careful thought, lest it remain concealed within superficially similar phenomena.

Notes

Acknowledgments. My debts are to Jean Briggs, who first suggested that I think about mumming, and to Robert Paine and George Story, who read and criticized an earlier draft of this essay; all are at Memorial University of Newfoundland. That first draft was read in colloquia at the University of Chicago, Duke University, Harvard University, and the University of Illinois, Chicago. My thanks to the participants for their comments.

1. Notions of selfhood, personhood, and community emerged from my reading of outport ethnographies and were not part of a predetermined scheme of analysis intended to apply to such materials. These distinctions are said to be common in Western social orders, but my first concern here is to decipher outports in terms of their own implications. Therefore, it is not incumbent on this interpretation to discuss whether outports are distinct in this regard from other North American or European collectivities.

2. Sider (1976) distinguishes this form of mumming from that of urban New-

foundland. There, mumming flourished during the 19th century. Taking the shape of a public parade and the performance of hero-combat plays by lower-class men in upper-class homes, urban mumming was pervaded by a symbolism of hierarchy and by religious and ethnic distinctions. Urban mumming gave over the control of public space to both the orderly and the riotous behavior of lower-class participants, whose costuming pointedly reversed social-class distinctions and who intruded into upper-class homes to perform and to "collect" monies. As with similar carnivalesque vehicles for social protest in Europe (see Burke 1978; Handelman 1982), urban mumming virtually ended when such activities were banned throughout the island in 1861 (Story 1969:179), although its outport form continued to flourish.

3. Outport mumming must be understood in the context of this kind of community and its associated family fishery. There was no mumming during the period of the servant fishery, roughly from 1600 to 1840, when fishermen worked for a "master" who exercised great control over the lives of his workers. When this fishery system collapsed (Sider 1976:107), the family fishery emerged, based on families who organized fishing along lines of kin and community. By contrast to the servant fishery, these outport fishermen sold the product of their labor—salt-fish—and not the labor power itself; and so they controlled their social relationships of production. Mumming, according to Sider (1976:117), was especially about a collectivity in which such relationships were prevalent and which declined with the onset of the mechanized processing of fish and with an exodus to factory work, especially after World War II (Sider 1976:111–114).

4. Available data limn how outport men perceived one another. Yet there are hints that the perceptions of women were not necessarily different from those of men. Indirect evidence, for example, comes from the design and placement in the home of hooked rugs made by outport women. Pocius (1979) argues that rugs with a symmetrical and geometrically repetitive pattern were those with a community-wide provenance. Rugs of such standardized designs were used almost exclusively in the kitchen, the spatial interface between household selves and community personae. Such rugs, like persons, were perceived as equal in quality and worth to one another, and so were interchangeable, in a communitywide sense. Rugs with idiosyncratic or innovative designs were used solely in the inner recesses of the home, in the parlor or front room. Here, guests of high status, who were not substitutable for one another, were received. And here the household revealed aspects of its individualistic and creative selves that were not interchangeable with those of others. Like the self, "the innovative rug kept in the front room was rarely seen, although its existence was acknowledged" (Pocius 1979:284).

5. The relationship between person and self hardly was unitary in outport culture. Alternative versions of this relationship are found, for example, in the "cuffer" (Faris 1966) and in the craftsman-client "contract" (Chiaramonte 1970). The cuffer is a tale of licensed exaggeration based on a core of truth, told by men before an audience of men, usually in neutral and public settings. The cuffer temporarily permits the suspect self to emerge when moral constraints of etiquette are relaxed but are buffered by messages of play. The cuffer validates the relationship between person and self in the image of selfhood. That is, personhood is constructed here as a version of selfhood. However, this is perceived as pretense, thereby denying the serious implications of such revelation.

By comparison, the contract between craftsman and client is negotiated with a view to establishing trust and sincerity between these persons to accomplish a clearly defined, instrumental goal (i.e., the building of a boat). Such trust depends on the validation of the relationship between self and person in the image of personhood. Here, selfhood is constructed as a version of personhood. Only then can the parties rely fully on one another to fulfill their respective obligations over a lengthy duration, as specified by the contract.

In contrast to both of the above, the device of mumming operated not to construct selfhood and personhood as alternative versions of one another but to efface their incipient dualism. I am indebted to Robert Paine for bringing "cuffer" and "contract" to my attention in this context. Still, the above interpretations are my own.

6. Chiaramonte (1969) is least explicit on this point.

7. Still, one may point to the comparative paucity of communal ritual activity in outports to appreciate the power of mumming there.

8. To my mind there is a fascinating "cultural catch" in the programmatics of the guessing game. Through the guessing game the outcome of the program of mumming was left indeterminate, since revelation was not assured—although in practice, through their interaction the participants likely had ways to raise the probabilities of unmasking the mummers. Nonetheless, the dependency of successful mumming on this game suggests an implicit cultural recognition on the part of villagers of the contingent character of their community. A lengthy series of unsuccessful mummings, which the program of this activity allowed for, could produce for villagers a highly negative version of community, one that would reify their worst fears about one another. This possibility was built into the logic of the event of mumming. In seminars and discussions it was put to me that such a contingent reconstruction of community is not unusual. I think that it is, in terms of the cultural logics of such events. Other ritualistic events have correct outcomes built into their texts or programs, although errors in practice can circumvent or destroy such outcomes on particular ritual occasions. In mumming, the program is contingent while practice must overcome this. Other events of deconstruction and reconstruction are, in the main, rigged contests in which reconstruction is built into the premises of the event (see Handelman in press). The premises of mumming imply that households, and so too the community, could fail this test. In turn, this would imply that the community could be rendered invalid as such, for it would be reduced to a collection of solitary and autonomous households.

9. Although I summarize the everyday in the above manner, this is intended to highlight aspects of personhood and selfhood that are of special relevance to this interpretation of mumming. This summation is not intended to encompass all predispositions of perception and behavior among outport people (see, e.g., note 4).

10. The interplay of concealment and revelation in connecting selfhood and personhood, community and strangerhood, likely had wider ramifications that through inversion related the home to the community. In many of these small outports, households were related closely to one another, and women tended to marry into these communities. Therefore, women as wives often were strangers to the community. The interior of the home was perceived largely as a female domain (the male counterpart being the "stage," the wharf where men of the household stored and

repaired their equipment). Homes, too, were strangers to one another, for each contained a privatized interior that was hidden to familiars. The intimate and solidary tie between husband and wife implies that this elementary relationship, on which the home rested, also was embued with strangeness in the perceptions of others. From the perspective of familiar personhood and community, the collective self of the household was covert and authentic but strange and therefore negative.

The aggressive intrusion of mummers, their roaming through interior portions of the home and their rough-housing with women of the house, unmasked the strangeness of the household to others and made it more known and familiar. In a similar vein, wives-as-strangers who controlled the interiors of homes were made more known to familiars. In other words, homes also were turned inside-out. Of course, the agents of these revelations were the strange mummers, who flowed outside-in and who themselves would be revealed within the home in a meeting between familiars who ordinarily were perceived as strangers. One could say that the authentic collective self of the household was revealed in a positive light; and that this revelation, in turn, revealed those of the mummers, so that both the members of the household and the ex-mummers were on display and were open to inspection, in relation to one another.

I owe the above points to a discussion with Jane Guyer. Although I am not certain that the insights she had are clear to me, my gratitude to her is.

11. I began to understand the significance of signs of convergence and divergence in extending Bateson's interpretation of *naven* behavior among the Iatmul (see Handelman 1979). In *naven* activity, inversion enables particular roles to maintain their distinctive contours when situational conditions increasingly signify their convergence, coalescence, and the effacement of their attributes of differentiation.

References Cited

Bauman, Richard
   1972   Belsnickling in a Nova Scotia Island Community. Western Folklore 31: 229–243.
Beidelman, T. O.
   1966   Swazi Royal Ritual. Africa 36:373–405.
Ben-Dor, Shmuel
   1969   The "Naluyuks" of Northern Labrador: A Mechanism of Social Control. *In* Christmas Mumming in Newfoundland. H. Halpert and G. M. Story, eds. pp. 119–127. Toronto: University of Toronto Press.
Brown, Norman O.
   1960   Love's Body. New York.
Burke, Peter
   1978   Popular Culture in Early Modern Europe. London: Temple Smith.
Chiaramonte, Louis J.
   1969   Mumming in "Deep Harbor": Aspects of Social Organization in Mumming and Drinking. *In* Christmas Mumming in Newfoundland. H. Halpert and G. M. Story, eds. pp. 76–103. Toronto: University of Toronto Press.
   1970   Craftsman-Client Contracts: Interpersonal Relations in a Newfoundland

Fishing Community. St. John's: Institute of Social and Economic Research, Memorial University of Newfoundland.

Davis, Natalie Zemon

1971   The Reasons of Misrule: Youth Groups and Charivaris in Sixteenth-Century France. Past and Present 50:41-75.

Faris, James C.

1966   The Dynamics of Verbal Exchange: A Newfoundland Example. Anthropologica (NS) 8:236-248.

1968   Validation in Ethnographic Description: The Lexicon of "Occasions" in Cat Harbour. Man (NS) 3:112-124.

1969   Mumming in an Outport Fishing Settlement: A Description and Suggestions on the Cognitive Complex. *In* Christmas Mumming in Newfoundland. H. Halpert and G. M. Story, eds. pp. 129-144. Toronto: University of Toronto Press.

1972   Cat Harbor: A Newfoundland Fishing Settlement. St. John's: Institute of Social and Economic Research, Memorial University of Newfoundland.

Firestone, Melvin M.

1967   Brothers and Rivals: Patrilocality in Savage Cove. St. John's: Institute of Social and Economic Research, Memorial University of Newfoundland.

1969   Mummers and Strangers in Northern Newfoundland. *In* Christmas Mumming in Newfoundland. H. Halpert and G. M. Story, eds. pp. 63-75. Toronto: University of Toronto Press.

1978   Christmas Mumming and Symbolic Interactionism. Ethos 6:92-113.

Gluckman, Max

1954   Rituals of Rebellion in South East Africa. Manchester: Manchester University Press.

Grathoff, Richard

1970   The Structure of Social Inconsistencies. The Hague: Martinus Nijhoff.

Halpert, Herbert

1969   A Typology of Mumming. *In* Christmas Mumming in Newfoundland. H. Halpert and G. M. Story, eds. pp. 35-61. Toronto: University of Toronto Press.

Handelman, Don

1976   Re-thinking "Banana Time": Symbolic Integration in a Work Setting. Urban Life 4:433-448.

1977   Play and Ritual: Complementary Frames of Metacommunication. *In* It's a Funny Thing, Humour. A. J. Chapman and H. Foot, eds. pp. 185-192. London: Pergamon.

1979   Is Naven Ludic?: Paradox and the Communication of Identity. Social Analysis 1:177-191.

1981   The Ritual Clown: Attributes and Affinities. Anthropos 76:321-370.

1982   Reflexivity in Festival and Other Cultural Events. *In* Essays in the Sociology of Perception. Mary Douglas, ed. pp. 162-190. London: Routledge and Kegan Paul.

1983   Charisma, Liminality, and Symbolic Types. Ms. Files of the author.

in press   The Madonna and the Mare: Symbolic Organization in the Palio of

Siena. *In* The Anthropology of Spectacle and Entertainment. M. Yamaguchi, ed. Tokyo: Sanseido.

Handelman, Don, and Bruce Kapferer
1980 Symbolic Types, Mediation and the Transformation of Ritual Context: Sinhalese Demons and Tewa Clowns. Semiotica 30:41–71.

Honigmann, John J.
1977 The Masked Face. Ethos 5:262–280.

Kealiinohomoku, Joann W.
1980 The Drama of the Hopi Ogres. *In* Southwestern Indian Ritual Drama. C. J. Frisbie, ed. pp. 37–69. Albuquerque: University of New Mexico Press.

Leach, Edmund R.
1961 Two Essays Concerning the Symbolic Representation of Time. *In* Rethinking Anthropology. London: Athlone Press.

McFeat, Tom
1974 Small-Group Cultures. London: Pergamon.

Nemec, Thomas F.
1972 I Fish with My Brother: The Structure and Behavior of Agnatic-based Fishing Crews in a Newfoundland Irish Outport. *In* North Atlantic Fishermen. R. Anderson and C. Wadel, eds. pp. 9–34. St. John's: Institute of Social and Economic Research, Memorial University of Newfoundland.

Norbeck, Edward
1967 African Rituals of Conflict. *In* Gods and Rituals. John Middleton, ed. New York: Natural History Press.

Phythian-Adams, Charles
1972 Ceremony and the Citizen: The Communal Year at Coventry, 1450–1550. *In* Crisis and Order in English Towns. P. Clark and P. Slack, eds. London: Routledge and Kegan Paul.

Pocius, Gerald R.
1979 Hooked Rugs in Newfoundland: The Representation of Social Structure in Design. Journal of American Folklore 92:273–284.

Sider, Gerald
1976 Christmas Mumming and the New Year in Outport Newfoundland. Past and Present 71:102–125.

Speck, Frank G., and Leonard Broom, with the assistance of Will West Long
1951 Cherokee Dance and Drama. Berkeley: University of California Press.

Story, George M.
1969 Mummers in Newfoundland History: A Survey of the Printed Record. *In* Christmas Mumming in Newfoundland. H. Halpert and G. M. Story, eds. pp. 167–185. Toronto: University of Toronto Press.

Szwed, John F.
1966 Private Cultures and Public Imagery: Interpersonal Relations in a Newfoundland Peasant Society. St. John's: Institute of Social and Economic Research, Memorial University of Newfoundland.
1969 The Mask of Friendship: Mumming as a Ritual of Social Relations. *In* Christmas Mumming in Newfoundland. H. Halpert and G. M. Story, eds. Toronto: University of Toronto Press.

Turner, Victor W.
  1969   The Ritual Process: Structure and Antistructure. Chicago: Aldine.
Yamamoto, Yoshiko
  1978   The Namahage: A Festival in the Northeast of Japan. Philadelphia: Institute for the Study of Human Issues.
Widdowson, John
  1977   If You Don't Be Good: Verbal Social Control in Newfoundland. St. John's: Institute of Social and Economic Research, Memorial University of Newfoundland.
Williams, Clyde E.
  1969   Janneying in "Coughlin Cove." *In* Christmas Mumming in Newfoundland. H. Halpert and G. M. Story, eds. pp. 209–215. Toronto: University of Toronto Press.

12

Monkey Performances: A Multiple Structure of Meaning and Reflexivity in Japanese Culture

Emiko Ohnuki-Tierney
University of Wisconsin, Madison

My interest in monkey performances began to develop in 1980, when I was invited to visit a group of monkey trainers in Hikari City, Yamaguchi Prefecture. I had heard of these young *burakumin* (so-called former out-castes)[1] who had revived the art of monkey performances, once a "traditional" occupation of the outcastes, in an effort to assert their own identity. On the first day, I observed the training of monkeys and had extensive discussions with the young men and their families in the yard of one of the families. A recurrent theme in the discussion of their experiences in training the monkeys was the almost life-and-death struggle involved in the process. Thus, while referring to the monkeys as if they were their own children, they emphasized the ferocity of the "beast," which can instantly rip off a person's nose, ears, or fingers, as evidenced by the scars on the arms of the trainers. I was struck by their serious dedication in selecting monkey performances as a way of asserting their own identity.

On the second day, I accompanied the trainers to a festival in a fishing community for which they had been invited to give monkey performances. The performances were held at the shrine of Ebisu, a guardian deity of fishermen closely associated with the monkey. There was no overt, discernible difference between the *burakumin*'s perception of the event and that of the non-*burakumin* audience, just as there is no discernible physical difference between two groups of Japanese. In fact, the two groups visibly shared the conviviality, viewing the performing monkeys as "cute" *(kawaii)*. Yet, the seriousness which underscored the attitude of the trainers contrasted markedly with the simple lightheartedness of the spectators, who were children, women, and men, some of them quite intoxicated.

Although monkey performances was not my research topic at the time, the complexity and ambiguity I sensed at the festival were too intriguing to forget, and I subsequently undertook a two-pronged study: a historical study of monkey symbolism in Japanese culture and the cultural/symbolic meaning assigned to the *burakumin*. From a theoretical-methodological perspective, this study is an attempt to use history for an anthropological reading of the present. Since I began my study of Japanese culture, I have encountered specific incidences to illustrate how a strictly synchronic study leads to a definitely erroneous, not an alternative, interpretation of the meaning of a present event.

This paper first examines the meaning of the monkey in various aspects of Japanese culture—folk beliefs, oral tradition, and visual arts—from a historical perspective. The monkey, being one of the dominant symbols[2] in Japanese culture, has a wide range of meanings assigned to it. Yet there also are persistently common themes about the monkey that run through these aspects of Japanese culture. From a historical perspective, the polysemy contains at least two major meanings that are apparently contradictory to each other, with each dominating the other in a different historical context. Next, I examine the history of outcastes in general and of the monkey trainers in particular, with an emphasis on the cultural/symbolic meanings assigned to both in different historical periods by the non-*burakumin* Japanese. The study of the monkey and of outcastes presents the peculiarly parallel symbolic meanings assigned to each, as well as the parallel changes in those meanings through time. The remainder of the paper presents two major theoretical points. I examine the relationship among the positive power of mediation, the negative values of pollution and taboo, and the positive power assigned to tricksters/clowns. All of these roles, powers, and meanings are assigned to the monkey in Japanese culture. I also discuss the interplay and relationship between the context-free basic structure of meaning and the context-determined structure which I call "the processual-contextual structure."[3]

This paper is deliberately organized so that relevant historical and ethnographic information is presented before the analysis. The reader must go through the background information without knowing the reason for it. This somewhat unusual approach is a replication of my research process, during which I spent countless hours combing through historical and ethnographic data without predicting the ultimate answer to the puzzle, or to the patterns of meaning in the historical and ethnographic information. This contrasts to a presentation whereby information to substantiate the author's interpretations is neatly interwoven, giving the reader the impression that the author started with an a priori conception of the interpretations/analyses. By no means does this indicate that I consider there to be an objective reality of history and ethnography or "objective" data separate from the investigator's own perceptual framework (for a discussion of the inseparable nature of interpretation and data see Ohnuki-Tierney 1984).

The topic of this paper is indeed very complex and enormous in scope, ultimately involving both Japanese history and cosmology through time. Further research is now in progress, in the form of a book-length manuscript. This paper should be considered as a summary of preliminary analyses; a great deal of additional historical and ethnographic information and other theoretical points are omitted from this discussion.

Monkeys in Japanese Culture

Monkeys in Folk Religions

In Japanese folk religions, the most dominant role of monkeys is that of mediator or messenger. Although the monkey itself may be referred to as a deity *(sarugami),* it is characterized mainly as the messenger of various deities.[4] In particular, the monkey is the messenger of the powerful Mountain Deity (Origuchi 1965b:299, 324–325; Yanagita 1951:240), one of the most important deities in the pantheon of Japanese folk religions (Blacker 1975; Yanagita 1951:642–644). As messenger, the monkey mediates between the supernatural world and the human world.

The mediating role of the monkey is again evident in the monkey's association with several relatively minor deities whose roles are those of mediators. For example, in the *Kojiki,* the oldest document of Japan (dated A.D. 712), Saruta Biko is depicted as the deity who guided the offspring of the deities in their descent from Heaven to rule the land below (Philippi 1969:138, 140, 142; Shimonaka 1941:118). In the Japanese origin myth, then, Saruta Biko serves as the mediator between deities and humans, and Heaven and Earth.

The identification of Saruta Biko with the monkey is based on the inclusion of the term *saru* (monkey) in the name of this deity. In addition, its physical characteristics include a red rear end—a prominent characteristic of the Japanese macaque (Shimonaka 1941:118). Furthermore, in the *Kojiki,* Saruta Biko is said to have had his hand caught in a shell while fishing (Philippi 1969:142)—a behavioral characteristic of macaques, which gather shellfish at low tide. Minakata (quoted in Philippi 1969:142) uses this information to identify Saruta Biko as the monkey deity.[5] Later, Saruta Biko became fused with Saeno-kami, Deity of the Roadside (Dōso-shin), who dwells at the border of a community, the edge of a bridge, the foot of a hill, and other spatial boundaries. Dōso-shin is believed to have the power to prevent the assault of epidemics thought to come from outside the community (Hirose 1979:244, 265–268; Shimonaka 1941:93, 118; Yanagita 1951:400–401).

The fusion of belief in the monkey deity and belief in Kōshin-sama, a deity of Taoist origin, also demonstrates the role of the monkey as a mediator. The forms of belief in Kōshin-sama have undergone a series of transformations, often resulting in diverse syncretic beliefs because of influence from Shintoism, Buddhism, and folk religions. Most dominant and persistent, however, is the concept expressed in the term *kōshin* (i.e., *kō*-monkey or *kōshin* day). *Kōshin* is the 57th day or year of each 60-day or 60-year cycle in the Taoist calendar. On that day, the three worms (black, green, and white) believed to dwell in a person's body are said to ascend to Heaven. There they report to the Emperor of Heaven their host's transgressions during the previous cycle (Blacker 1975:329; Yanagita 1951:196–197). On the evening of that day, people gather to pray to Kōshin-sama for protection. Because of the association between Kōshin-sama and the temporal liminality (between the two cycles of 60 days or years), Kōshin-sama belief and the monkey-god belief were fused during the last phase of the Muromachi period (1392–1602) (Yanagita 1951:196). A concrete expression of the fusion appears in one of the amulets used by those believing in the sanctity of Mt. Fuji, which has been closely linked with Kōshin-sama belief. On this amulet, Saruta Biko and more than 60 monkeys worshiping Mt. Fuji at its foothills are depicted (Miyata 1975:148; a most detailed work on Kōshin-sama is in Kubo 1961).

Another fusion occurred during the Kinsei period (1603–1867). The fusion may have started with the merging of the aforementioned Saenokami and Jizō, a roadside Buddha and a guardian of children (Shimonaka 1941:93). This merging is vividly expressed, for example, in stone statues of a monkey wearing a bib (Hirose 1979:268–271); being a guardian Buddha of children, Jizō wears a bib, which has become almost a trademark.

The monkey, together with all of these supernaturals, is thought to have healing power (for details of these supernaturals and their medical roles see Ohnuki-Tierney 1984) and was used extensively in folk medicine in the past (and, to a much lesser degree, is so used at present). A charred monkey's head is pounded into powder and taken as medicine for illnesses of the head and brain, including mental illnesses, mental retardation, and headaches. The monkey's remaining body parts, as well as various representations of the monkey—such as *kukurizaru* (small stuffed monkeys)—are prescribed for illnesses of various types, as well as for childbirth (for a survey of the medicinal uses of the monkey see Hirose 1979:76–94, 199–202).

Not only is the monkey potent medicine for human ailments, but it is also the healer of horses. Among its other assigned meanings, the monkey as guardian of horses is perhaps next in importance to that of the monkey as messenger of the Mountain Deity. A monkey was often tied to a leash in a stable to keep a horse company, because of a belief that the monkey would keep the horse healthy and tamed in spirit. Although the practice must have started much earlier (Yanagita 1964:336), it reached its height during the Kamakura period (1185–1313). At that time horses were vital for warriors (Hirose 1979:151), who wrested the political power of the nation from the emperor. But the practice was not confined to warriors; farmers, too, kept monkeys in their stables for the work horses.

The transformation of the monkey tied to the stable into the monkey performing dances is not well understood. In *Ryōjin Hishō* (1169–79), a monkey is described leaving the stable to "play" *(asobu)*. Yanagita (1964:336–337) interprets the description as depicting a monkey performing a dance. Elsewhere, Yanagita (1951:241–242) explains the transformation as a process whereby diviners in charge of prayers for the horses gradually became entertainers. At any rate, the dance performances of the monkey became a part of the solemn ritual on the third or fifth day of the New Year at the Imperial Court in Kyoto, and later at the Shogunate in Edo (Tokyo). The purpose of the ritual was to ensure the welfare of the horses (Yanagita 1964:336). The ritual/religious privilege of having a trained monkey perform for the occasion was held exclusively by certain families, as we shall see in the next section.

As the monkey became "the performing monkey," it entered the field of street entertainment, breaking out of its confinement to religious rituals. *Yuzu Nenbutsu Engi Emaki,* an illustrated Buddhistic document dated 1391 (Umezu 1972), contains a picture of a monkey and its trainer with a few spectators. The monkey, tied to a leash, is not attired and is standing on its hind legs while holding a pole. The trainer wears no special attire and is barefooted (painting reproduced in Suō Sarumawashinokai Jimukyoku 1978). But the picture shows the monkey performance on its way to becoming an established street entertainment. On the basis of such drawings in *Nenjū Gyōji Emaki* (Illustrated Annual Events, early 12th century) and the *Yūzū Nenbutsu Engi Emaki,* Oda (1978) proposes that the monkey performance had been established as a performing art by the beginning of the Chūsei period (794–1603) (see also Miyamoto 1981:82).

Praying for the health and welfare of horses gave birth to a related practice, *ema* (literally, "picture-horse"). People drew pictures of horses on votive plaques and offered them at shrines to ensure the health of their horses. Yanagita (1951:70–71) refutes a popular interpretation that *ema,* as offerings to the deities, were substitutes for real horses. Through time, the original idea was broadened and people began to use *ema* for many other reasons. People did and still do use *ema* for the maintenance of health, recovery from illnesses, and even for passing the entrance examination of a university. At any rate, a large number of *ema* from differing regions of Japan and from differing historical periods depict a horse pulled by a monkey, providing rich evidence for the role of the monkey as guardian of horses.

For a further understanding of the meaning of the monkey as guardian of horses in Japanese culture, it must be noted that horses had a significant role in Japanese religion. As Yanagita (1964:342) explains, Japanese deities are believed to have come down from the mountains on horseback. Accordingly, horses had possessed religious significance for the Japanese even before they were used for work in paddy fields and by warriors.

The symbolic association between the two animals in Japanese cultural context is not altogether clear. Yanagita (quoted in Miyamoto 1981:82) speculates that since the horses used by the Japanese in early times were wild, the monkey was employed to tame the wild horses. Although Yanagita does not further explicate this idea, it does allow me to interpret the monkey's role as a mediator. The performing monkey may be viewed as a tamed wild animal assigned the role of taming a truly wild animal—the horse. On one level, then, the monkey mediates between humans and wild nature (horses); on another level, the monkey mediates between humans and the deities who ride horses.

Leaving further discussion of the monkey as mediator to a later section, I point out here that the folk beliefs described in this section are found primarily in western Japan, where hunting of the monkey is prohibited. It is not prohibited in northeastern Japan (Tōhoku), where the monkey is eagerly hunted for meat and medicinal purposes (Hirose 1979:47, 53; regional variation in Japanese culture and its relevance to the cultural meaning assigned to the monkey are discussed in note 2).

The Monkey in Oral Tradition

While the beliefs and practices just described are confined to western Japan, there is little geographic restriction of popular folktales in which the monkey is a major character. The themes in these ubiquitous folktales include the monkey as mediator, a cunning / evil character, and the monkey as an unsuccessful imitator of human beings.

The monkey as mediator appears in a well-known folktale called *Saru Jizō*. In this tale, an old man goes to a field in the mountains with his lunch. A group of monkeys appears and eats his lunch. The man simply sits in the field and watches them, whereupon the monkeys believe him to be Jizō Buddha and decide to place him in a temple across the river. They carry the old man on their arms and ensconce him in the temple. Although he finds the event amusing, he tries not to laugh; he sits still with his eyes closed. Several monkeys then pray to him, making money offerings. The old man gathers the money, leaves the temple to purchase kimonos and other things, and returns home. But a neighbor-woman becomes envious and sends her husband to the mountain field with the hope of repeating the event. Her husband, however, laughs when the monkeys try to carry him across the river to the temple. Surprised and angry, the monkeys drop him into the river and the man barely escapes drowning (Yanagita

1963:219–233). In this tale the monkey, together with Jizō, the aforementioned roadside Buddha of mediation, acts as mediator sent by Japanese deities, who can punish or reward humans depending on their conduct.

Saru Muko Iri (Monkey Groom), another widespread folktale, presents perhaps a most dominant characterization of the monkey in Japanese culture, that of an unsuccessful imitator of human beings. The tale is about a foiled attempt of a monkey to marry a human. It begins with an old man either tilling the soil or harvesting root crops, depending on the region in which the tale is told. When he becomes tired, a monkey appears and offers to do the task for him, provided he gives the monkey one of his daughters as a bride. The monkey finishes the job for the man and says that he will come to get the daughter the next morning. After returning home, the old man feels ill and goes to bed, unable to disclose to his daughters the deal he made with the monkey. The older daughters ask him what his trouble is, and on hearing the story they flatly refuse to marry the monkey. The youngest daughter agrees, however, but asks for a large mortar (in eastern Japan; a large water jar in western Japan) as her dowry. The next morning the monkey goes to the man's house to claim a daughter and then heads home with his human bride. Coming to a river, she spots some pretty blossoms on a tree hanging over the water and asks the monkey to pick them. She urges him to climb higher up and farther out over the river for prettier flowers, until he falls into the river with his mortar (or water jar) on his back. The story ends with the monkey drowning due to the weight of the mortar (or water jar) (for details of the story see Hirose 1979:38–41; Yanagita 1951:242; 1962:451–463).

While the monkey in this folktale is not an object of ridicule, a laughable monkey unsuccessfully imitating human beings is a repeated theme in folktales and sayings. For example, a tale from Yamagata Prefecture in northeastern Japan describes an uncontrollable monkey that likes to imitate humans. A hunter ties himself up with a rope, whereupon the monkey imitates him. The hunter, of course, captures the monkey alive (Hirose 1979:54). In songs recorded from all over Japan (Hirose 1979: 251–258), the monkey is ridiculed because of its red rear end. The songs urge throwing a chestnut, a *gobō* root, and so on, at it. In other words, monkeys are not left alone as animals; if they were, the color of the rear end should not be the concern of humans.

A negative picture of the monkey as a cheater is found in *Saru Kani Kassen* (Combat between a Monkey and a Crab), one of the best-known folktales of the past and present. The monkey is depicted as cunning and evil, the epitome of a bully, whereas the crab is powerless but hardworking. Eventually, though, the monkey is punished by the crab, with whom others (a chestnut, a needle, a wasp, a mortar, dung, etc., depending on the region) join forces out of sympathy (Yanagita 1951:240–241; 1963:391–414). Not to be a bully *(yowaimono ijime)* is one of the most important values in Japanese society, and this tale appears even in contemporary textbooks for elementary school children, who are taught the folly of shortsighted cleverness, the virtue of perseverance, and the collective punishment accorded a bully by society. The monkey in this tale portrays evil human beings.

The negative side of the monkey is not only portrayed in folktales but has drawn considerable attention among scholars of folklore who consider the "mythical" figure *kappa* (a water creature) as a metamorphosis of the monkey. Although the morphological and behavioral characteristics assigned to the *kappa* vary from region to region, the common characteristics include: its portrayal as a childlike figure; a dish full of water on the top of its head (when the water spills, it dies); flexible, stretchable, or otherwise abnormal arms; and mischievous/malevolent behavior. In some regions the *kappa* is said to be the chief enemy of the monkey. Nonetheless, as Ouwehand (1964:203–220) painstakingly demonstrates, the two may be seen as structural opposites, one being a transformation of the other. When they are paired, the monkey represents the positive side of the trickster, whose negative side is expressed in *kappa,* which is thought to threaten humans through various tricks, some benign but others quite dangerous (see Ouwehand 1979:309–314; 326–327; for the monkey-*kappa* relationship see Ishida 1966; Yanagita 1951:111, 240; 1964:49–110).

The "Monkey": Gibbons and Macaques in Visual Art[6]

An intriguing facet of the history of Japanese art is that two types of *saru* (a Japanese word for both apes and monkeys)—gibbons and macaques—are represented in visual arts, while macaques alone live in Japan. Furthermore, as far as I can now determine, gibbons of Southeast Asia are the main motif of paintings set against the background of nature, whereas macaques appear in human setting, either anthropomorphized or among people as a part of human activity. This preliminary finding tells us something significant about the Japanese perception of monkeys. Let me first briefly discuss gibbons and monkeys in Japanese visual art.

Gibbons, as opposed to native macaques, first became the objects of artistic creation under somewhat unusual circumstances. Mu-Ch'i, a Chinese Zen priest-artist, emigrated from Szechwan Province of China to Kyoto in Japan. Although Mu-Ch'i was not well recognized in his own country, he became very influential in Japan. Three of his paintings in particular, the Goddess of Mercy (Kannon), Monkeys, and a Crane, were considered masterpieces of art. The mother-infant monkeys dated circa 1291 in this set of paintings gave rise to the tradition known as *Bokkei-zaru* (Bokkei's [Mu-Ch'i, in Japanese] monkey). A number of well-known Japanese painters, including Hasegawa Tōhaku (1539–1610), used Mu-Ch'i's gibbon as their model and so perpetuated the tradition of "Mu-Ch'i's monkey." These Japanese artists, whom I assume never saw a live gibbon, drew gibbons in nature using the Chinese method of painting. I may even venture to say that to the Japanese of that time, Mu-Ch'i's gibbons represented *Kanga* (Chinese art), rather than gibbons as such (for details of Mu-Ch'i's life see Toda 1978; for information on Tōhaku see Doi 1973 and Nakajima 1979).

The history of Japanese macaques in art is quite different from that of gibbons. The macaques appeared first either in caricatures or in Buddhist paintings. For example, in a 12th-century text, *Chōjū Giga* (Scrolls of Animal Caricatures; Kaneko 1969) monkeys, together with hares and other animals, are drawn in animal form but are either wearing pieces of human attire or engaged in human activities. The *Hōnen Shōnin Gyōjō Ezu* (Illustrated Deeds of St. Hōnen; Kadokawa Shoten 1961) provides an example of monkeys in Buddhist paintings. This series of paintings in 48 volumes, also known as *Hōnen Shōnin E-den* (Illustrated Biography of St. Hōnen), illustrates the life of Hōnen, founder of the Jōdo (Pure Land of Paradise) sect of Buddhism. Reportedly, the volumes were edited by Shunshō between 1307 and 1317. Therefore, the paintings are illustrations of the life of Hōnen (1133–1212) during the 12th and 13th centuries as perceived or envisioned in the 14th century. Naturalistically drawn monkeys appear in these volumes, but they are always in a human setting—playing on the roof of a temple or on a temple gate (two of these pictures are in Kadokawa Shoten 1961: Plate 14). Similarly, in another illustrated biography of a Buddhist monk, *Ippen Shōnin Eden,* dated circa 1299, a scene shows a naturalistically drawn monkey tied to a stable (reproduced in Miyamoto 1981:81).

During the 17th century, around the time when the Tokugawa Shogunate became well established and the culture of the commoners *(shomin)* started to flourish, a series of interrelated changes took place in Japanese society and in Japanese art: for society, the end of the political power of the Imperial Court in Kyoto and the establishment of political control of Japan by the Shogunate in Edo (Tokyo); for art, the end of the *Yamato-e* tradition—the so-called Japanese style which embraced various art styles, including *Kanga* (Chinese-style art). The *Yamato-e* tradition was identified with the Imperial Court, and many distinguished artists of the *Yamato-e* school were *machishū* (wealthy merchants) in the Kyoto, Osaka, and Sakai regions who gained civil control over those cities (for a detailed study of *machishū* see Hayashiya 1978; for a good summary of social history and its impact on the art at the time see Mizuo 1965:55–75).

With the transfer of political power from the Imperial Court in Kyoto to the Shogunate in Tokyo, the center of culture also shifted to Tokyo. In terms of art, this meant not only the end of the *Yamato-e* tradition but the birth of the *ukiyo-e* tradition, developed by the newly established merchant class known as *chōnin* in Tokyo. Like *machishū* (the character for *machi* in *machishū* and that for *chō* in *chōnin* is the same, meaning "town"), *chōnin* also belonged to the merchant class. But during the feudal period under the Shogunate the merchant class was rigidly defined in the feudal caste system as the bottom of society—the outcaste being the only caste below them. The flexibility that had been available to the *machishū* during the previous period no longer existed. The 17th century was also the period when naturalistic painting began to flourish both as an indigenous movement (known as *shijōha*) and as a result of influence from the West.

These dramatic changes in Japanese society and art during the 17th century are reflected vividly in the paintings of gibbons and macaques. The end of *Yamato-e* meant the disappearance of Mu-Ch'i's gibbons from Japanese art. In their stead, with the rise of naturalistic paintings, Japanese macaques for the first time appeared in nature, just as the gibbons used to. The macaques become the major motif of paintings by such famous artists of the Edo period (1603–1867) as Maruyama Ōkyo, Nagasawa Rosetsu, Kawai Gyokudō, Watanabe Nangaku, and Mori Sosen (Hirose 1979:169–182). By contrast, macaques continued to appear in human settings in various forms of visual art. Thus we see performing monkeys in the *ukiyo-e* woodblock paintings of 18th- and 19th-century masters such as Suzuki Harunobu and Katsushika Hokusai. Above all, the famous three monkeys *(mizaru, kikazaru, yuwazaru*—"see no evil, hear no evil, say no evil") appeared in 1650 at Tōshōgū Shrine.

Relegating the interpretation of the performing monkeys and how they were perceived by the Japanese to a later section, I conclude this section by describing a piece of visual art that expresses a theme about monkeys as revealed in folktales. It is a lacquerware stationery container made by an anonymous artist during the 19th century and now housed in the Freer Gallery at the Smithsonian Institution. On the cover of the box are three macaques, all wearing glasses and opening a scroll while night falcons hover over them. The picture carries a moral message: "Do not attempt things beyond one's capacity." The monkeys, of course, do not have the ability to read, an ability which, to the Japanese, distinguishes humans from animals. While the monkeys are attempting the impossible, they are risking their lives by letting their chief enemies, night falcons, approach them; the night falcon *(yodaka)* is also a euphemism for a prostitute or a night stalker. The moral message, then, is based on the Japanese characterization of the monkeys—clever enough to imitate humans but not wise enough to be human, a theme evident in the motifs of folktales.

A cursory survey of the meanings of the monkey in various aspects of Japanese culture suggests two dominant themes: (1) as a sacred mediator, appearing most conspicuously in folk religions; and (2) as a quasi human, emphasized in folktales and arts. The monkey as a sacred mediator appears as early as the 8th century. This meaning has not disappeared entirely since these folk religions are still practiced. By contrast, the quasi-human characteristic is a dominant image given to the monkey not only in the past but also in the present. A hunting taboo, the profound meaning of which I did not understand at first, most succinctly illustrates this point. Hunters regard a lone monkey as something unusual and it is taboo to hunt and kill it (Hirose 1979:47–48). I do not think that the taboo is singularly based on the hunter's observation that monkeys are usually in a group and a lone monkey is unusual. Instead, I think the fact that the monkey is a social animal and almost always lives in a group is significant to the Japanese, who regard humans as beings in the company of other humans. This notion is clearly expressed by the Japanese characters for humans—*ningen; nin* means "humans" and *gen* means "among." An isolated individual is antithetical to the Japanese notion of humans (Ohnuki-Tierney 1984; Plath 1982:120), and the monkey mirrors human beings, who engage in collective reflexivity. Various characteristics assigned to the monkey, including that of being unsuccessful imitators of humans, are the very characteristics the Japanese see in themselves. Therefore, in the daily discourse of contemporary Japanese, such phrases as *saru jie* (monkey wisdom = shortsighted cunning) or *saru mane* (monkey imitation = superficial imitation) are frequently used. Today, newspaper editorials often urge the Japanese not to engage in "monkey imitation" of the West.

The Burakumin *(Outcaste)*

Risking a somewhat lengthy detour to explain my interpretation of the monkey trainer, I introduce a history of the outcaste in Japan.

The Outcaste in Japanese History

The history of the formation of the *burakumin* as a category of people is not clear. In differing historical periods the so-called outcastes consisted of different types of people. No clear-cut linear descent links outcaste groups from one historic period to another (Harada 1978a, 1978b; Noguchi 1978; Ueda 1978a, 1978b).[7] Since they have not been a monolithic group of people throughout history, the single label "outcaste" may not be entirely appropriate.

Contrary to a stereotypic image of outcastes, which includes only those engaged in menial tasks considered "polluting," I believe there had been at least two broad categories of occupation for various discriminated people throughout much of Japanese history.[8] During the Kodai period (circa 350 B.C.–A.D. 794), the first category included diviners, itinerant priests, artisans, and entertainers, all of whom visited from village to village at regular intervals. In an agrarian society formed of permanent settlements, these men were stranger-outsiders, at least from the perspective of the farming population, although they may have had permanent residences elsewhere. The stranger-outsiders fulfilled a vital function for the agrarian population, however, in that they served as culture brokers, providing entertainment and thereby breaking the monotonous cycle of farming life. Diviners, healers, and itinerant priests were in charge of the fate of the people; they cured illnesses and became mediators between humans and deities. While they had the power to act on behalf of the agrarian population, they could also turn off that power; by doing so, they could bring calamities upon the population.

Included in this first category of occupation are the Korean artisans and craftsmen who came to Japan during the Tomb period (A.D. 250–650), and their descendants. Although they may have settled in communities, they were likely stranger-outsiders who possessed special skills absent among the Japanese. Their skills may have given them special power, at least in a symbolic sense. Later in history, perhaps when artists, architect-gardeners, and theatrical performers became more established as specialists, they too were included in the category of outcastes.

The second category of occupation involves death and dirt, that is, pollutants as defined in Japanese culture. Such occupations deal with the death of both animals and humans—butchers, tanners, makers of leather goods, falconers, cormorant fishermen, undertakers, caretakers of tombs, and executioners. As early as the oldest written records—*Kojiki,* dated A.D. 712, and *Norito,* dated A.D. 927—death is defined not only as the utmost impurity but also as a sin (see Philippi 1969:62–70 for *Kojiki;* Philippi 1959:46–47 for *Norito*). Since both footgear and floors are considered dirty in Japanese culture, makers of footgear of all types and makers of *tatami* straw mats for the floor have been outcastes (for the Japanese concept of impurity, see Ohnuki-Tierney 1984). The outcastes in this category, then, are the specialists in impurity, as Dumont (1970:48) would put it, who spare others the inevitable problems of dealing with pollution and dirt.

The cultural valuation of these two occupational categories was much more flexible and less rigidly demeaning until the establishment of the feudal society. Thus, during the long period (A.D. 794–1603) known as Chūsei (Middle Age), there were multiple systems of stratification with much mobility throughout. Some individuals from the lower rungs of the society, including the outcaste group, became warlords, while others, such as Zenami, who designed the Fushimi Castle, became famous for landscape architecture. Still others were renowned artists, such as Kanami and Zeami, the father-son pair who developed *sarugaku,* the forerunner of the *nō* play. The outcastes in Japan have had a close relationship with art, both established and popular.[9] An excellent study of the outcastes within the context of Chūsei culture and society is found in Yokoi (1975); see also Noguchi

(1978) for a summary of the complex systems of stratification during this period and their implications for the outcastes; see Hayashiya (1981) for artists during this period.

Individuals in both categories of occupation were officially outcastes throughout the history of Japan. Before the formation of the feudal society, however, individuals who excelled in their professional ability had direct access to the center of power. As artists and architect-gardeners, they were close to the Imperial Court and the powerful warlords. Even those in the second category held a special position because their services were vital. Those engaged in the killing of animals were also close to power: falconers served aristocrats. Tanners and makers of leather goods were close to the center of military power, since they alone could supply hides for armor. Similarly, without monkey performers, aristocrats, warriors, and farmers could not guarantee the welfare of their horses.

Toward the end of the Chūsei period, after about the mid-13th century, Japanese society went through fundamental changes (Yokoi, in H. Inoue et al. 1978:167–170). The subsequent historic period, called Kinsei (A.D. 1603–1868), witnessed the full development into the feudal system[10] with four castes (warriors, farmers, manufacturers, and merchants), plus two social categories outside the system—the emperor at the top and the outcaste at the bottom. Many scholars (e.g., Harada 1978b; Price 1966:23; Yokoi 1975:336) believe that the extreme legal and social discrimination against the *burakumin* that has persisted until recently originated in this period.

The effort toward military control over the entire nation, partly accomplished through forced settlement of the population for census purposes, had been underway since the latter half of the 13th century (Yokoi, in H. Inoue et al. 1978:169–170). However, this tendency reached its peak at the end of the 16th century, under the rule of Hideyoshi. In 1582 he recognized land tenure among the outcastes and, at the same time, registered them as *kawata,* a designation chosen to label and legally define them (Ueda 1978c:100–101). *Kawata* included both *hinin* ("nonhumans": beggars, criminals, orphans, etc.) and *eta* (the term used for outcastes until recently). Legally, the *eta* alone were assigned a permanent, hereditary status. Later, numerous rules placed the outcastes under the strict political control of the military government, with well-defined rules regulating their occupations (Ueda 1978c).

When feudal society came to an end in 1868, the Meiji government made many legal reforms, including the emancipation of the *burakumin* in 1871. It abolished the law forcing them to wear special clothing and removed the restriction confining them to traditional occupations only. The *burakumin,* however, have remained victims of social discrimination. Today a minority group in Japan, the *burakumin* are estimated to number three million, localized in 6000 communities.[11] They have been called

"Japan's invisible race" (DeVos and Wagatsuma 1966) because there are no physical characteristics to distinguish them from other Japanese.

Monkey Trainers

The changes through time in the social position of the outcaste and in the cultural meaning assigned to them by the dominant group in Japanese society are reflected both in the changes in the cultural valuation of monkey trainers and in the cultural image of monkeys. Recall from the section on the monkey in folk religions that by the Chūsei period the monkey, originally tied to a stable as guardian of horses, had become the performing monkey, providing vital services to the Imperial Court as well as contributing to the formation of a performing art. The Imperial Court specifically designated the Ono family at Ōmi to perform the New Year's ritual for its horses; and when the Shogunate in Edo did not have anyone to perform the ritual, it summoned Chōdayū Takiguchi to carry out the task (Yanagita 1964:337–339; a slightly different version of the incident is given in Ishii 1963:39). Later on, however, many monkey performers took to street entertainment. The monkey performance saw its efflorescence at the beginning of the Edo period, when monkeys performed on the stage, as shown in *Kii-no-kuni Meisho Zuroku* (cited in Oda 1978). It became a regular feature of the New Year celebration and at other times among the common people, whom the monkey and its trainer visited from door to door.

The relative significance of the monkey performance was gradually transformed from one of religion to one of entertainment. The transformation was paralleled by the above-outlined changes in the cultural codification of the outcastes in general and the monkey trainers in particular. *Ukiyo-e* is one of the best sources of evidence for the transformation. In some paintings, both monkey and trainer are elaborately clothed, attesting to the popularity of the performing art, while in others they are depicted as the objects of fun and ridicule. For example, in a print by an anonymous artist of the Edo period, now housed in Freer Gallery, Washington, DC, a trainer wears a *samurai* outfit with a pair of swords, but unlike *samurai* he is barefooted, like people of lower status at that time. The print is meant to be a visualization of the mid-17th-century satirical maxim, "The long sword of a monkey trainer is something the world can do without" *(Yononaka ni iranu mono sarumawashi no chōtō)*. Note the similarity between the trainers in this print and the monkeys in the aforementioned lacquerware. Just as the monkeys cannot read and hence cannot be humans, neither can the trainers become *samurai;* they only attempt in vain to do so. Hirose (1979:140–168) provides massive evidence for the low status of monkey performers during the Edo period, using visual art, *senryu* (a special genre of poetry), and other evidence (see also Yanagita 1964:93–95, 336–340, 370–387).

We see, then, the changes in the cultural valuation of both the monkey and the monkey trainers. Until the establishment of feudal society, monkey trainers, despite their low social status, did have a special power because of the religious significance of their occupation. During the feudal period, however, the trainers, except for their leaders, became merely entertainers of low esteem. The cultural meaning of the monkey, too, seems to have changed in a similar manner: semideified animals until the early Kinsei period, and afterward, laughable "human beings minus three pieces of hair"—a Japanese "definition" of the monkey.

The popularity of the monkey performance nonetheless continued to grow during the subsequent period, the modern period (1868–present). Although we know little about where the trainers were located, during tthe Meiji (1868–1911), Taishō (1912–1925), and Shōwa (1926–present) periods, one of the centers was the Suō District in Yamaguchi Prefecture, from whence many trainers traveled all over Japan. At the height of the popularity of this art during the Meiji and Taishō periods, there were 150 trained monkeys and an equal number of performers (Murasaki 1980:13–30).

Despite the legal liberation of the *burakumin* in 1871, prejudice and stigma attached to them remained unchanged. To engage in monkey performances was to identify oneself as *burakumin,* inviting prejudice from non-*burakumin* Japanese who would otherwise have no way to identify the person as such. The negative attitude of non-*burakumin* Japanese, then, eventually caused the complete disappearance of this performing art at the beginning of the Shōwa period (1926–present) (Murasaki 1980:39). In 1977, a group of young *burakumin* revived the monkey performance as a way of asserting their own identity (Murasaki 1980; Suō Sarumawashinokai Jimukyoku 1978:2, 17).

In the midst of the 1979 festival, while *sumō* (Japanese wrestling) was taking place on the other side of the shrine compound, I observed one of the trainers announcing the beginning of the monkey performances by beating on a drum, which was also used as a part of the signaling system throughout the performance. A set of performances by a monkey was preceded by a narration by his trainer, the same story being told by all trainers:

> One day I [the monkey] was happily swinging from tree branch to tree branch in the mountains with my family. I then heard the sound of a gun and saw that my father had fallen to the ground [here the monkey falls to the ground on its back]. Without our father, we had no means of supporting ourselves. I left our mountain home and came to the city to earn money by performing so that I can support my family back home. Here I begin [the monkey bows to the audience].

Every time the monkey fell to the ground at the onomatopoeia of a gunshot uttered by a trainer or when the monkey bowed at the end of the trainer's narration, the audience broke into smiles, laughter, and some cheers.

Taking turns, each trainer demonstrated several performances by his own monkey. The performances included relatively simple tasks, such as bicycle riding, jumping through hoops, and walking on a pair of bamboo stilts; all required bipedal posture. Dancing monkeys, so often described in historical records and depicted in visual arts, however, have not emerged. With too many cars and other dangers on the street, on the one hand, and movies, television, and other types of media entertainment, on the other, there is little hope that the monkey performance will regain its former popularity. It likely will be confined to special occasions, such as the festivals I attended.

The Monkey, the Monkey Trainer and the Monkey Performance in Japanese World View

In this section I engage in speculative interpretation, as presented in Figure 1. I suggest that from antiquity until the formation of feudal society, macaques were sacred mediators, messengers from the deities, while the outcastes who were itinerant priests, artisans, and minstrels were human mediators. These human mediators mediate between agrarian communities and between humans and deities. The specialists in impurity, by contrast, were marginals in the symbolic structure of Japanese culture. During the feudal period and after, the monkeys become marginals—wild animals on the borderline between nature and human society, which had become increasingly urbanized without the "natural" presence of monkeys. Their trainers, together with the rest of the outcastes in the artistic/religious category, join the specialists in impurity, becoming the equivalents of the monkey on the human side. During the earlier periods the mediators mediated between humans and the benevolent side of Japanese deities, but later they all became marginals occupying a position between the violent side of the deities and the humans, as illustrated in Figure 1.

I proceed to suggest that during the monkey performance a multiple structure of both meaning and reflexivity is presented. Thus, from the perspective of the trainer, the monkey transforms nature into the highest form of culture (i.e., the performing art), while the non-*burakumin* audience sees the transformation in the reverse direction. The transformation of nature into culture is seen also as the reflexive process whereby the *burakumin* present their collective self to the audience, whose perception is the inversion of that of the *burakumin*. Therefore, both the structure of meaning and that of reflexivity consist of a pair, each being the precise inversion of the other. Furthermore, I suggest that nature and culture are two

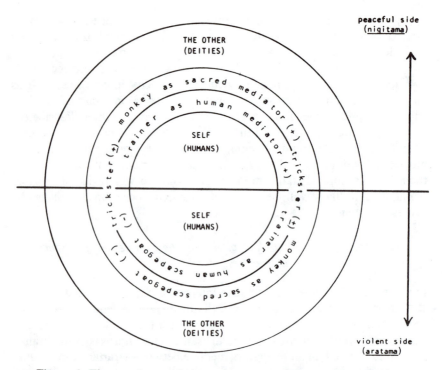

Figure 1. The monkey and the trainer as mediators and marginals.

sides of the monkey, the *burakumin,* the non-*burakumin,* and also the deities; that is, they are *nigitama* (peaceful side) and *aratama* (violent side) of the *marebito* deities. Thus, when the non-*burakumin* Japanese see the negative side of the *burakumin,* they are indeed projecting their own *aratama.* My explanation begins with a discussion of the dual nature of Japanese deities.

The Dual Nature of Japanese Deities

Among Japanese scholars today a predominant interpretation is that from the earliest times Japanese deities have been characterized by dual nature and/or power—both good and evil, creative and destructive (Higo 1942; Matsudaira 1977; Ouwehand 1958–59; Suzuki 1974, 1979; Yamaguchi 1977; Yoshida 1981). The concept of *marebito,* originally discussed in detail by Origuchi (1965a:79–82; 1965b:33–35; 1966:303–317), succinctly expresses this dualistic notion. According to Origuchi, the *marebito* was a god in ancient Japan from the world on the other side of the sea, where no aging and death were known. The god periodically visited the villagers in order to bring good luck, although he was also potentially dangerous.[12]

Higo (1942) and Matsudaira (1977) present incisive analyses of folk festivals in contemporary Japan and illustrate the persistence of the dual nature of Japanese deities. Introducing the argument presented by Higo (1942) and Matsudaira (1977:43-49), Ouwehand (1958-59:155) summarizes this view of Japanese gods:[13] "The attitude of the god towards man is ambiguous; it is either of a benevolent or of an evil character. Both possibilities are comprised in one and the same god. They can be abstracted as *nigimitama* (peaceful spirit) and *aramitama* (rough spirit)."

Yamaguchi (1977) sees a parallel in the traditional village between spatial classification and the classification of beings in the universe. According to his analysis, until about a hundred years ago each Japanese village had a clear line of demarcation separating the "inside" of the village from the "outside." The space beyond the boundary was associated with forces threatening the order of village society. These forces took the form of masked spirits, gods, epidemics, bandits, and itinerant merchants and priests (see also Embree 1958[1939]:246-248). Yamaguchi (1977:153-154) emphasizes that these forces had a dual quality; therefore, they could become either positive or negative, with ritual as the determinant—only a proper ritual can harness the benevolent power:

> The Japanese have always believed that the gods should visit each village community only at a certain seasonal time. If god's visit is at the proper season, then he can act in a benevolent way. However, if he visits the village at an unexpected period, he is thought to be out of place and a source of evil.

As is commonly known among Japanologists, these deities of dual nature in the Japanese pantheon are basically nature deities. They are exemplified by the Sun Goddess (Amaterasu O-o-mikami) and the Fox Deity, although they are usually anthropomorphized or personified. As explicitly stated in the *marebito* concept, Japanese deities are "strangers" or "outsiders."[14]

Japanese deities being characteristically outsiders, "the sacred" in Japanese symbolic structure includes not only beings of nature but also other outsiders, such as foreigners. Historically, the foreigners were Chinese, who brought "civilization" to then-illiterate and technologically "primitive" Japanese. Later in history and until very recently, the foreigners were Westerners who brought to the Japanese modern technology and science. However, foreigners have always been potentially threatening and must be kept clearly as "outsiders." Thus, when Christianity was seen to be threatening the political power of the Shogunate, with some exceptions all foreigners were excluded. Beyond these more dramatic incidents, the Japanese have been steadfastly reticent in admitting foreigners as bona fide members of their society (for details see Ohnuki-Tierney 1984).

At the most abstract level, "the outsiders" constitute the other, who provides a mirror against which the collective self of the Japanese becomes reflexive. Seen in this light, the explicit recognition of the dual nature of Japanese deities is an implicit recognition of the dual nature of the self, that is, humans or Japanese. I return to this point in a later section.

The Monkey and the Monkey Trainer as Mediators and Marginals

Within the framework of this Japanese world view, I now proceed to symbolic interpretations of the monkey and the monkey trainer, first during the Kodai period (circa 350 B.C.–A.D. 794) and the Chūsei period (A.D. 794–1603), then during the Kinsei period (A.D. 1185–1868). As seen in Figure 1, during the Kodai and Chūsei periods the monkey, a being from nature, is a sacred mediator which in the proper (i.e., ritual) context brings the beneficial power of the deities to humans; for example, the ability to tame horses.

The role of the monkey as a sacred mediator is amply substantiated in folk religions. There the monkey is associated with deities of mediation. The intriguing episode in art history of Mu-Ch'i's gibbons in nature and native macaques in human settings is also supportive of this interpretation. A striking consistency with which the gibbons were placed in natural settings in paintings whereas the native macaques were placed in human settings clearly indicates that the macaques were "the sacred" in human society and not "the sacred" in nature. That is, the macaques were the sacred messenger/mediators to the humans. By contrast, gibbons represented the "outsiders"—nature and foreigner, or in this case the Chinese. The gibbons, like the Chinese, were clearly "outsiders," ordinarily kept at a long distance. The Japanese brought them in only under culturally prescribed conditions—that is, in art forms—just as the *marebito* were brought into the villagers' lives through a culturally prescribed form—that is, ritual. Note that when Japanese society became a closed society under the Shogunate, shunning all "the other" out of contact, Mu-Ch'i's gibbons also disappeared. They shared the fate of human foreigners.

The monkey trainer during these periods was the human counterpart of the macaque; that is, the trainer was a member of society who mediated between humans and deities by facilitating the reception of the sacred mediator. The crucial role as mediator becomes even more impressive when the dual nature of the deities is taken into account. Mediators were relegated to the role of bringing the beneficial power/nature—not the harmful one—to humans.

By contrast to the monkey trainers and other outcastes associated with art and religion, the outcastes of the other "specialists in impurity" category were not mediators. Symbolically, they were marginals in human society. In a given symbolic structure, marginals are "deficient" members of a category, as it were, in that they are seen to lack those characteristics which would qualify them to be full-fledged members (for a detailed discussion of symbolic "anomaly" see Ohnuki-Tierney 1980, 1981).

The residential pattern of the outcastes at various historic times may be viewed as a symbolic expression of their marginal status. Historic records testify that these marginal outcastes often resided on the boundary of their community, such as on the river banks, under a bridge, or near a slope. Since rivers, hills, and mountains provided natural demarcation lines between settlements, these locations represented places away from the central or main part of the settlement. The term *kawaramono* ("people of the river banks") is indicative of this residential marginality. This designation was applied during the Chūsei period to those who resided at marginal places such as river banks and were not assessed a tax (Yokoi 1975:335–339). Another term, *sansho,* also is thought to apply to the outcastes or to the places they occupied. People in these *sansho* locations did not hold land, no land tax was levied on them, and they engaged in the occupations dealing with death and dirt (Noguchi 1978:89). The term *sansho* literally means "the scattered place"; it contrasts with the term *honsho,* which means either "central" or "real" place (Yokoi 1975:337–339). Hayashiya (1980:130–131) maintains that the term *san* means "nontaxable"; and "nontaxable" also can mean "marginal," other than normal in Japanese society in which tax was levied against land and earnings. Thus, the term *sansho* expresses spatial marginality, which in turn symbolizes the social marginality of the occupations.[15]

During the Kinsei period, when feudal society became solidified, the religious significance of the monkey and the monkey trainer declined. Both sacred and human mediators joined the ranks of marginals: the monkey became a marginal member of the Japanese pantheon and the trainer joined the marginals in human society (i.e., the specialists in impurity). Together, these human marginals formed the outcaste as codified in Tokugawa society. During the Kinsei period, then, the monkey and the trainer dealt with the negative side *(aratama)* of the deities (see Figure 1), and their proximity to the negative side of the deities rendered them objects of taboo and ridicule.

To emphasize the transformations in the cultural meaning of the monkey and the monkey trainer, I perhaps unduly emphasize contrasting features. Cautionary statements must be made here on two points. First, the term "mediator" denotes a role rather than a structurally defined status. As I elaborate elsewhere (Ohnuki-Tierney 1980, 1981), the role of mediator is often assigned to beings or people whose position within the ideological or social structure is marginal. In order to traverse categorical boundaries, either social-structural or ideological/symbolic, mediators often are not full-fledged members of a category and are too constrained by the existing structure to have the flexibility and freedom to deviate from and to traverse the boundary lines (see also Douglas 1966). My own terminological distinction in this study is that mediators, regardless of their structurally defined position, are assigned a positive and powerful role to mediate between categories. The term "marginal" refers to a structurally defined position. Due to their marginality with respect to a given category, marginals are often endowed with negative power, such as the power to defile, and are therefore subject to taboos. This negative power can threaten the structure, for example, with pollution; it nonetheless is not an active power like that of mediation. The distinction, then, between mediators and marginals is neither permanent nor basic. Marginals can become mediators and mediators can become marginals, as this study shows.

The second point is that the monkey, the monkey trainer (in particular), the outcastes (in general), and deities have always been polysemic in Japanese culture in that cultural meanings assigned to them have never been singular or simple. The historical transformations of these meanings are emphasized in the above discussion. It is a matter of relative importance of a particular meaning among others that receives prominence. Thus, the meaning of the monkey has always had two sides: the semideified side associated with the role of messenger from the deities, and the side associated with the "clever-but-not-wise-enough" animal. Other characteristics such as cunning or wildness are also among the bundle of meanings assigned to the monkey. When one meaning is emphasized in a given historical period or in an event, the other meanings lurk beneath the surface. In the case of Japanese deities, it is precisely because they have a negative, violent side that ritual is seen as important. The purpose of ritual is to bring forth the positive side of the deities, whose "slippery" nature may at any moment show its negative side and cause calamities for the humans. Ritual officiants, such as the monkey trainers, are held responsible in achieving that end.

The major difference between the two broadly demarcated periods in Figure 1 therefore lies not in basic changes in meaning of monkey, outcaste, or deities, but in the nature of cultural dynamics. During the periods before the consolidation of feudal society, Japanese culture and society were flexible; that is, the world view during these periods was dualistic. There was a tacit recognition, albeit unconscious, that good and evil were two sides of the same coin. And the coin was the collective self, as mirrored in the *marebito* deities, the other. The universe was in a constant flux in which meanings, even polar opposites in nature, were never in complete negation of each other; they changed sides, as it were, in giving meaning to symbols (i.e., objects, events, phenomena, people). The entire notion is best illustrated in the iconography of yin and yang, in which the presence of the two small eyes is of paramount importance. Yin always has an element of yang, as yang has an element of yin. When in yin the small eye of yang grows large enough, it then becomes yang with a small eye of yin in it. The curved dividing line between the two halves of the iconography consequently is not a permanent line; rather, it represents movement. The two principles, when conjoined, comprise a harmonious complementarity. Neither asserts hegemony over the other, since the two forces are constantly in gentle motion and are gradually changing sides (Freedman 1969; Granet 1977[1922]; Porkert 1974).

The dynamics of this type of dualistic cosmology mean also that the center and the periphery, whether those of social or of symbolic structure, were intimately linked. Therefore, the specialists in impurity were under the tutelage of the centers of religious power, that is, temples and shrines. The monkey and the monkey trainer were close to the center of political and military power, although neither ever held a high-ranking position in the formalized hierarchy of the pantheon and human society.

With the establishment of feudalism, Japanese society and culture seem to have become more rigid, reducing dynamics and flexibility. An increased intensity placed on the taboo against the impurity of the outcastes attests to the emphasis placed on the precise delineation of conceptual categories. It is beyond the scope of this paper to evaluate critically the neo-Durkheimian position which sees social structure as the causal agent in generating ideological/symbolic structure (for further discussion on this point see Ohnuki-Tierney 1981). I simply point out here that with hindsight what we see is parallelism between the changes in social structure and the changes in symbolic/ideological structure.

Monkey Performances—A Multiple Structure of Meaning and Reflexivity

My task in this final section is to illustrate how the polysemic monkey and monkey trainer, and the changes in their meaning through time, are related to my earlier claim that in monkey performances we see a multiple structure of both meaning and reflexivity. Let me explain my interpretation by referring to *Utsubozaru,* a well-known piece from *kyōgen* (comic interludes played between classical *nō* plays).

The story in *Utsubozaru* ("quiver-monkey"; Nonomura 1968: 158–166) begins with a *daimyō* (feudal lord) one morning pronouncing to his servant Tarō Kajo his intention to go hunting. As they set out they immediately encounter a monkey trainer with his monkey. The lord is impressed with the beautiful fur of the monkey and decides to ask for the monkey in order to use its hide to cover his quiver. The trainer begs the lord to spare the monkey since it is his only means of earning a living. The lord then asks to borrow the monkey, and the trainer again begs for it to be spared. The lord, becoming enraged, decides to shoot both the trainer and the monkey with one arrow. But the trainer points out that if the monkey is shot, the scar from the shot will ruin the hide. He then volunteers to clobber the monkey with a stick, saying that he knows how to kill a monkey with one stroke. When the trainer hits the monkey, the monkey, mistaking the blow for a signal to perform, begins its performance. The trainer, in tears, laments, "It is a sad fate for a creature when it cannot tell its life is in immediate danger." Observing this scene, the lord is moved; he tells the trainer not to hit the monkey any longer. Furthermore, the lord makes a gift of his fan, sword, and even his clothing. In gratitude the trainer has the monkey perform a dance. As the monkey dances, the lord joins in. *Utsubozaru* ends with the lord's servant begging the monkey to stop dancing so that his master also will stop dancing.

Utsubozaru is thought to be a product of the Muromachi period (1392–1603) (Yanagita 1964:339). Although it was created before the formation of feudal society, it succinctly illustrates the polysemy of the monkey and the monkey trainer, as well as the simultaneous presence of a multiple structure of meaning and reflexivity. The play begins with the lord viewing the monkey as an animal, but his request for its hide reveals his belief in the supernatural power of the monkey. Recall that the monkey was the guardian of horses, the animals most vital to warriors. The trainer, too, views the monkey as an animal which, unlike humans, cannot even tell when death is approaching.

While both the lord and the trainer see the monkey as a creature of nature, the lord's threat to kill the monkey and the trainer with one arrow reveals that the lord equates the monkey trainer with the monkey. Thus, in the ideological structure of the dominant Japanese, as represented by the lord, the outcaste and the monkey receive the same meaning—nonhuman creatures. As the story progresses, however, the monkey upstages both the trainer and the lord. Thus, during the performance, the monkey changes its identity from that of a beast to that of an artist who can transform its body (nature) into the rhythmically controlled movements of the performing art. Additionally, the monkey and the trainer transform the wild lord, a savage warrior ready to shoot them, into a peaceful lord who enjoys dancing, just as they have always transformed wild horses into tame horses both for warriors and farmers.

The monkey performance also involves music. In the past, the *shamisen* (three-stringed instrument) regularly accompanied the dancing (Ishii 1963:39), although drums were also used, as they are today. Like dancing, music creates patterned regularity, that is, the essence of culture (Lévi-Strauss 1969).

Utsubozaru expresses the essence of monkey performances in which the human mediator and the sacred mediator conjoin in their creation of culture (the performing art of dancing) from nature (the monkey). This process of transformation is identical with the process during which Japanese religions are created—beings of nature transformed into deified beings of culture. This capacity of transformation/creation characterizes not only monkey performances but other occupations held by outcastes. For example, architects and gardeners transform raw nature into culturally construed nature in the rock garden; the art of Japanese gardening is to reproduce nature without any trace of the human effort of re-creation. Similarly, *kabuki* actors, who also belonged to the outcaste class (Yamaguchi 1977), during their performances transcend the biological givens of age and sex, thereby transforming their own nature into the culturally construed personality in the play.

Rituals, as often pointed out in anthropological statements on reflexivity, are themselves reflexive processes during which performers achieve "the sense of distancing from self" (Fernandez 1980:28, 36). Ultimately, in the reflexive process the self becomes a sign (Babcock 1980:1). In an effort to present themselves to the audience during the monkey performance, the monkey and the trainer distance themselves from themselves. And this reflexive process enables them to transform their identity with nature into an identity with culture. The performance, then, represents the culturalization process in two ways: transformation of nature (monkey) into culture (performing art) and transformation of self into sign. The latter is a basic feature of the human ability to symbolize.

The above represents one set of structure of meaning and reflexivity, as schematized in the upper half of Figure 2. It is a set from the perspective of the *burakumin*. Paradoxically, there is, I think, another set of symbolic structure and reflexivity that presents the same structure in precise inversion, from the perspective of non-*burakumin* Japanese. While the monkey and trainer present the self as an agent to transform nature into culture, the audience of non-*burakumin* Japanese is amused at the animal attempting to be human and at the trainer, whom they see as being human and yet not quite fully human. The performing art of humans is reduced to an unsuccessful imitation by an animal. The monkey performance, then, reaffirms the monkey's identity as a "human minus three pieces of hair" and, by extension, the analogous identity of the trainer; the trainer, as in the *ukiyo-e* introduced earlier, might carry swords but must walk barefoot. The direction of the transformation is the reverse—from culture into nature, as shown in the bottom of half of Figure 2.

There are symbols in the performance which can be interpreted in opposite directions. I note earlier that music epitomizes culture. However, the *shamisen*, the particular musical instrument most frequently used in the

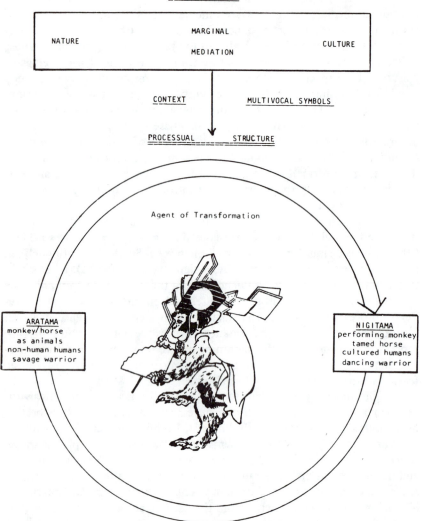

Figure 2. Transformations during monkey performances.

past by the monkey trainer, is associated with the merchant class, who occupied the lowest rung in the social strata during the feudal period. This contrasts to the *koto,* a "noble" instrument for the warrior class. Similarly, the type of drum used by the trainers both in the past and present is a folk instrument associated with folk festivals, rather than the one used in *no* plays and other forms of "great tradition." The trainer's attire, that of the

samurai but without the footgear, is not interpreted by the audience as the
trainer's ascendance and proximity to the symbolic and military power but
as a poor imitation of the warrior, in fact emphasizing his low status, as
symbolically expressed by barefootedness. (Footgear, a must in contemporary Japan when walking outside, was used by the upper class and
wealthy Japanese but not by others during earlier periods.) The audience
then perceives an analogy between the monkey and the trainer, both of
whom represent nature. This analogy is most explicitly revealed in the lord's
threat to kill both the monkey and the trainer with one arrow.

In other words, while the structure as described in the previous section corresponds, at least in the main, to the structure of perception of the
trainer during the performance, the structure of perception of the non-
burakumin audience is its precise inversion, as illustrated in Figure 1. This
finding calls for a distinction between the basic structure of meaning and
what I call the processual-contextual structure, which in this case consists of
two structures of meaning. Note that both structures in the processual-
contextual model—one being the precise inversion of the other—are derived
from the same basic structure of meaning which expresses itself in a number
of multivocal symbols, such as the monkey, outcastes, and musical instruments. It is the structure in the Lévi-Straussian sense that has remained
intact in Japanese culture, as far as my research demonstrates.

Although the basic structure corresponds to the upper half of the
processual-contextual structure, there is a real difference between the two.
While the basic structure is context-free, the processual-contextual structure
is not only contextualized but, in fact, the context determines the structure.
The context of the outcaste trainer and the nonoutcaste audience creates the
pair of structures. A context-free analysis of symbols of the monkey performance itself does not lead to the processual-contextual model, although it
suggests that possibility. The basic structure, as Lévi-Strauss
(1967:275–281) argues, has deductive power. Yet the particular processual
model induced from the contextually situated monkey performance is not
an automatic product of the basic structure, because it must presuppose a
particular kind of context.

The structure of reflexivity also is complex. As noted earlier, the
monkey performance may be seen as a ritual during which the outcastes
(burakumin) present themselves, using the monkey as their symbol.
However, when we examine the context of the performance, we see that the
presentation of the collective self of the *burakumin* is to the nonoutcaste audience. Therefore, by presenting themselves as the agent of the culturalization process, the outcastes force the nonoutcaste audience to be reflexive
about their own world, which should represent culture. From the perspective of the ritual process, the monkey performance begins with the lord, like
the audience, identifying the trainer with the monkey, both as beings of
nature. At the end of the performance, the lord/audience realizes that it was

they who were the untamed nature to be culturalized by the monkey. Put another way, the monkey and the outcaste are the small eyes in yin and yang. For this reason, I think, even amidst the laughter at the monkey performance the audience is reminded, albeit vaguely, of their darker side, as represented by the monkey and the outcaste trainer.

In this light, we see that the monkey is assigned an additional role of trickster/clown in Japanese culture. As a *kappa* (mythical water creature)-trickster, the monkey displays its negative side. But its dual nature makes it a Pierrot or Tonio Kröger who gently prods the Japanese to reflect on their basic assumptions.

The entire matter may be seen in terms of the dual nature of Japanese deities, which is the reflexive projection of the dual nature of human beings themselves. The peaceful and cultural side of human nature always has another side—the violent and natural side. The darker side lurks in the unconscious or at a deeper level of perception, even when on the surface the positive side has the upper hand. In the monkey performances the tension and pull between nature and culture, between the peaceful side *(nigitama)* and the violent side *(aratama),* are acted out.

Both the context and the process therefore make the structure of reflexivity expressed in the monkey peformance highly complex. The collective self of the outcaste as an agent for culturalization is one structure of reflexivity, whereas the other is the reflexive structure of the nonoutcaste Japanese whose universe topples upside-down. The dual structure of reflexivity, like the structure of meaning, is again symbolically facilitated by the multivocality of the monkey in Japanese culture. It is an explicit metaphor for the Japanese with their weaknesses of wickedness, shallow wisdom, and so on, whereas it also is an implicit metaphor for the outcaste.

The monkey peformance is similar in some ways to other rituals and performances. Leach (1965:266) points out that two versions of nearly the same Kachin myth, one structurally being the reverse of the other, have been recorded. In one version it is the elder brother who is jealous and drowned at the end of the story, whereas in the other version it is the younger brother who is drowned. Leach (1965:265) explains that the context determines the nature of storytelling, since for Kachins their tradition is to "validate the status of the individual who tells the story." He emphasizes that "there are bound to be different myths to validate the particular rights of different groups of people" (1965:277)—just as one structure of meaning and reflexivity of the monkey performance validates the status of the outcaste, while the other structure validates that of the nonoutcaste Japanese. The monkey performance is quite special, if not unique, in that both the structure and the inverted structure are simultaneously present during the same ritual, and their presence depends on the nature of the context of performance. The dual structure presupposes the presence of the two groups of Japanese.

My interpretation of the monkey performance is quite different from the Geertzian interpretation of the reading of text. The structure of a monkey performance is not a product of different individuals reading the text differently; nor is it due to intracultural variation as such. Two different groups of Japanese do not automatically produce the dual structure—it is the simultaneous presence of these two groups at the performance that is responsible for this. Furthermore, quite contrary to the Geertzian claim, it is the polysemants of each symbolic object and action that are *public,* in the sense that they are shared by the two groups (both groups being capable of drawing any of the several meanings of a symbolic object or an action). The processual-contextual structure, which lies closer to observable behavior—the only level which Geertz considers to be justifiable for his "interpretation"—is *not* public. In sum, the duality of the processual-contextual structure of the monkey performance is not due to individual differences, to intracultural differences, or even to the difference between the indigenous text as opposed to that of the anthropologist. It is due to a complex interplay between the basic structure of meaning in Japanese culture and the particular context of the performance.

Overtly, then, at the monkey performance the two groups of Japanese do *not* engage in "symbolic communication"—the basic definition of ritual (Tambiah 1981:119). Neither do the monkey performances "conjoin" initially separate groups and transform inequality and asymmetry into equality and symmetry, as rituals do, or accomplish the opposite, as games do (Lévi-Strauss 1966:32). Yet, a closer look reveals the difference in the reading of monkey performances and the apparent lack of communication that are indeed made known at a deeper level. The monkey performance is a ritual in the sense that it engages in symbolic communication. It communicates, during a temporarily egalitarian ritual time, the history of the hierarchically divided world within Japanese society and the inversion of the cosmology between the two groups. The monkey performance is equally an example of a ritual as a "language" of argument, not a "chorus of harmony" (Leach 1965:278). Ambiguity and indirectness, which are characteristic of ritual communication (Leach 1965:286; Tambiah 1981), prevent the monkey performance from becoming a ritual of rebellion—one of the topics explored further in my book in progress.

Summary

The main points of my preliminary study of the monkey symbolism and monkey performance in Japanese culture through time are two. First, there is massive historical/ethnographic evidence to support the approach that the structurally marginal member of a class, be it a person, a being, or an object, may be assigned the positive role/power of mediation, the negative meaning of pollution and taboo, or the role of a trickster/clown. Hitherto, ethnographic studies have pointed to the interrelatedness of marginality, taboo, pollution, mediation, trickster/clown, and the like. However, it has usually been a mediation here, a trickster there, and so on, either within a separate context within a culture or in different cultures. The historical/ethnographic evidence from Japanese culture tells us that all of these are indeed closely related and that one particular symbolic figure, the monkey, is assigned these interrelated roles and meanings in contexts which are different in time and space. Second, the contextual analysis of the monkey performance indicates that the complex interplay between the basic structure of meaning and the context of ritual performance specifies a context-specific structure which is multiplex as a structure of meaning and reflexivity.

Notes

Acknowledgments. I am grateful to the Institute for Research in the Humanities at the University of Wisconsin, Madison, which generously funded my full-time research on monkey symbolism in Japanese art and literature during Semester I, 1982–83. Without such a period of concentration and without warm encouragement from my colleagues at the Institute, this study would never have been completed in such a short time. The theoretical/interpretive part of the work was conducted during Semester II, 1982–83, during which my full-time research was funded by the Graduate School of the University of Wisconsin, Madison. I am indebted to the Research Committee for their generous support. I thank Professor Thomas A. Sebeok of Indiana University for inviting me to join him on his visit to the monkey performances in 1980 (Sebeok 1981). Professor Don Handelman of Hebrew University spent long hours discussing this research with me and later sent me a detailed and most helpful critique of the version of this paper that was read at the 1983 AES meetings in Baton Rouge. The written criticisms and suggestions by Professor Michael Herzfeld of Indiana University also have been most instructive. Numerous scholars offered their comments and suggestions at the Decennial Conference of the Association of Social Anthropologists at Cambridge University in July 1983, where I read a portion of my book which is in progress. I thank all of these scholars. I alone am responsible for any weaknesses in the interpretations presented in this paper.

1. The term *hisabetsu burakumin* (literally, "the people of settlements under discrimination") is the current official-legal term; however, the term *burakumin* is preferred by these people. In this paper I interchangeably use the term "outcaste," in part because it may be more meaningful to the English-speaking reader and in part to emphasize the outcaste status from the past. Needless to say, my use of the term "outcaste" is not intended to be derogatory in any way; and I hope it is not considered offensive to the *burakumin*.

2. I use the term "symbol" in its broadest sense, rather than only when metaphor is involved. A discussion of the use of this term in current symbolic anthropology is presented in Ohnuki-Tierney (1984).

3. In discussing Japanese culture on a very macro-level, as this paper does, we must remember the major intracultural variations: northeastern and southeastern

Japan have represented two distinct culture areas since prehistoric times. Another major intracultural variation is found along the line of rural/urban distinction. These two types of intracultural variations do not, however, constitute two distinct geographic areas with a sharp line demarcating the two. For example, the introduction of agriculture from the Asian continent via the Korean Peninsula to Kyushu in western Japan transformed southwestern Japan from a hunting-gathering society to an agrarian society. The same process of transformation gradually spread northeastward in successive waves, pushing the line dividing southwest and northeast Japan further to the north. Similar culture "traits" which profoundly affected Japanese culture and society include the introduction of writing, of Buddhism, and of other cultural complexes, all of which came first from China to western Japan. The process of urbanization, too, spread and transformed large sectors of rural Japan in different historic times (Smith 1974; Yazaki 1974).

Recognition of these intracultural variations is especially meaningful in discussing monkey symbolism, since there is a distinct lack of cultural elaboration of monkey symbolism in northeastern Japan. There, a hunting culture persisted more pervasively, and hunters hunted monkeys for practical uses. By contrast, in the southwestern agrarian areas a more elaborate symbolism of the monkey has developed, including a greater number of taboos. In these areas, farmers found the monkeys to be threatening to crops and yet did not simply eliminate them by killing. On close examination of the people's attitude toward the monkey and the cultural meaning assigned to it, Hirose (1979:47–48) finds the Shiroyama Mountain Range in Ishikawa Prefecture to be the dividing line: to the west of that mountain range monkey symbolism takes on a complex, often ambivalent, nature. Similarly, the attitude toward the monkey is different between rural and urban areas. Rural areas in Japan are often adjacent to mountains, and hence monkeys are familiar visitors to farmers; but they did (and do) not roam in Japanese cities as in India. Thus, although ecological conditions by no means act as determinants for symbolic meanings assigned to the monkey, a broad ecological basis nonetheless provides a certain basic framework within which rich symbolism is created.

4. The Japanese term *kami* (deity) may refer to a bona fide deity, such as Amaterasu O-omikami, the Sun Goddess, but it also refers to a spirit.

5. The interpretation of Saruta Biko is somewhat complex. In *Nihon Shoki,* an ancient document (dated A.D. 720), Saruta Biko is depicted as a hostile figure who opposed the descent of the heavenly deities (quoted in Philippi 1969:138; see also Hirose 1979:265–268).

6. Professor Sandy Kita of the University of Wisconsin, Madison, initiated me into the art history of Japan and generously has supplied information in answer to my questions. I am solely responsible, however, for the interpretation in this section.

7. During the Nara period (A.D. 650–794), common people were classified as *ryōmin* (good people) and *senmin* (base people), with the latter class subdivided into five ranked categories (Ueda 1978b). Some of the *senmin* may have been descendants of Koreans and Chinese who came to Japan during the preceding Tomb period (A.D. 250–650) with skills in various crafts unknown to the Japanese; others were not. Similarly, the *senmin* during the Nara period were not in toto ancestral to the outcastes of the subsequent periods.

8. Ninomiya (1933:74–76, 85–86) proposes four categories of outcaste occupations during the Kamakura (1185–1392) and Muromachi (1392–1603) periods;
although his categories are based on the data from these periods, they also apply to the
periods before and after. These categories are: (1) butchers, tanners, and makers of
leather goods; (2) dyers and manufacturers of bamboo articles; (3) entertainers, pros-
titutes, and diviners; and (4) undertakers and tomb caretakers. Itinerant priests and
minstrels are also included in the third category (Yamaguchi 1977). Noguchi
(1978:91), with a slightly different emphasis, describes the major occupations of
burakumin during the Chūsei period as: (1) cleaners of temples, shrines, and their
compounds, including the care of the dead; (2) landscape architects as well as general
construction workers; and (3) plasterers, carpenters, and arms manufacturers.

All of the occupations listed by Ninomiya and Noguchi have been held by
outcastes at one time or another. In addition, people of various other occupations
joined the outcastes at different times in history. For example, although falconry
had previously been a favorite sport of the elite, the Department of Falconry was
abolished under Buddhist pressure in A.D. 860 and the falconers are said to have
joined the outcastes as butchers (Price 1966; Noguchi 1978:88 cautions against
assuming a direct relationship between the falconers and the outcastes of later
periods). Cormorant fishing is another outcaste occupation (Kitahara 1974).

9. Literature on the outcastes-untouchables, of India or elsewhere, seldom
stresses the connection of the untouchables with art, architecture, and other
aesthetic genres. However, there is evidence of a strong connection between the two,
not only in Japan but also in India. As Kailasapathy (1968:95) documents, the
minstrels (the Pāṇar) were one of the four noble clans and were held in high esteem
until the medieval times when the caste system was formed and the word *pāṇar* came
to mean a lower caste.

10. Although I use the term "feudal" without qualifications, there has been
considerable scholarly debate about whether or not the Japanese system was truly
"feudal" (see, e.g., Dumont 1970).

11. More accurate figures are hard to come by. The government census is
probably inaccurate; its 1973 figure of 1,048,566 (Ueda 1978a:3–6), for example,
seems much too small. The *burakumin* communities are found primarily in western
Japan, with the highest concentration in the Kinki District. Many *burakumin* are
employed in small factories that deal with their traditional occupations, such as
leather and fur processing and butchering; however, most of them are farmers,
fishermen, and unskilled laborers. Although many individuals have become
economically or socially prominent, the average standard of living is far below that
of non-*burakumin*. In the main, *burakumin* have remained endogamous; marriage
with non-*burakumin* is rare because of acute prejudice. The most prominent feature
of prejudice against *burakumin* is the attribution of "dirtiness" (Donoghue
1966:138). For publications on the contemporary situation see Buraku Kaihō
Kenkyūjo (1978a, 1978b); see also several articles in DeVos and Wagatsuma (1966).

12. Several scholars (e.g., Higo 1942; Matsudaira 1977; Ouwehand 1958–59;
Yamaguchi 1977) see the prototype of the Japanese god with its dual nature in
Susano-o-no Mikoto, the brother of the Sun Goddess, Amaterasu, described in the
Kojiki.

13. Ouwehand's (1958:59:156–158) own interpretation moves further into an

elegant analysis of double ambivalence (both *nigitama* and *aramitama* consisting of the dual aspects) comprising the basically tripartite division (the opposition of the two aspects comprised in the totality of the god).

14. For the concept of "stranger" see Berger and Luckmann (1967:122, 156 ff.); Schutz (1971:91–105); Simmel (1950:402–408); Turner (1975:231–271); van Gennep (1961:26, 27ff.); Yamaguchi (1978). For use of the concept in ethnographic analysis see Frankenberg (1957); Myerhoff (1980).

15. There has been a controversy over the residential pattern of outcastes. Many scholars claim that the outcaste did not have permanent settlements but traveled from village to village. However, Ochiai (1972:66–67), citing Yanagita, emphatically states that many outcastes were not outsiders but members of a community. I suggest that the outcastes in the artistic/religious category were temporary visitors to farming communities, as noted in the text, but that the outcastes of the second type of occupation were permanent members of settled villages, occupying spatially marginal areas.

References Cited

Babcock, Barbara A.
   1980   Reflexivity: Definitions and Discriminations. Semiotica 30(1/2):14.
Berger, Peter L., and Thomas Luckmann
   1967   The Social Construction of Reality. New York: Doubleday.
Blacker, Carmen
   1975   The Catalpa Bow: A Study of Shamanistic Practices in Japan. London: George Allen & Unwin.
Buraku Kaihō Kenkyūjo, ed.
   1978a   Buraku Mondai Gaisetsu (Introduction to *Buraku* Problems). Osaka: Kaihō Shuppansha.
   1978b   Buraku Mondai Yōsetsu (Outline of *Buraku* Problems). Osaka: Kaihō Shuppansha.
DeVos, George, and H. Wagatsuma, eds.
   1966   Japan's Invisible Race: Caste in Culture and Personality. Berkeley: University of California Press.
Doi, Tsugiyoshi, ed.
   1973   Hasegawa Tōhaku. *In* Nihon no Bijutsu, Vol. 8, No. 87. Tokyo: Shibundō.
Donoghue, John
   1966   The Social Persistence of an Outcaste Group. *In* Japan's Invisible Race: Caste in Culture and Personality. George DeVos and Hiroshi Wagatsuma, eds. pp. 137–152. Berkeley: University of California Press.
Douglas, Mary
   1966   Purity and Danger. London: Routledge & Kegan Paul.
Dumont, Louis
   1970   Homo Hierarchicus. Mark Sainsbury, transl. Chicago: University of Chicago Press.
Embree, John F.
   1958[1939]   Suye Mura: A Japanese Village. Chicago: University of Chicago Press.

Fernandez, James W.
1980   Reflections on Looking into Mirrors. Semiotica 30(1/2):27–39.
Frankenberg, Ronald
1957   Village on the Border: A Social Study of Religion, Politics and Football in a North Wales Community. London: Cohen & West.
Freedman, Maurice
1969   Geomancy. *In* Proceedings of the Royal Anthropological Institute of Great Britain and Ireland for 1968. pp. 5–15. London.
Granet, Marcel
1977[1922]   The Religion of the Chinese People. Maurice Freedman, transl. New York: Harper & Row.
Harada, Tomohiko
1978a   Buraku no Zenshi (An Early History of *Buraku*). *In* Buraku Mondai Yōsetsu (Outline of *Buraku* Problems). Buraku Kaihō Kenkyūjo, ed. pp. 16–23. Osaka: Kaihō Shuppansha.
1978b   Kinsei Hōken Shakai to Buraku Keisei (The Feudal Society and the Formation of *Buraku*). *In* Buraku Mondai Yōsetsu (Outline of *Buraku* Problems). Buraku Kaihō Kenkyūjo, ed. pp. 24–33. Osaka: Kaihō Shuppansha.
Hayashiya, Tatsuburō
1978   Machishū ("Town Folks"). Tokyo: Chūō Kōronsha.
1980   Nihon Geino no Sekai (The World of Japanese Performing Arts). Tokyo: Nihon Hōsō Shuppan Kyōkai.
1981   Chūsei Geinō no Shakaiteki Kiban (The Social Foundation of Arts During Chūsei Period). *In* Yōkyoku Kyōgen *(Yōkyoku* and *Kyōgen).* Nihon Bungaku Kenkyū Shiryō Kankōkai, ed. pp. 201–209. Tokyo: Yūseidō Shuppan.
Higo, Kazuo
1942   Nihon Shinwa Kenkyū (Research in Japanese Mythology). Tokyo: Kawade Shobō.
Hirose, Shizumu
1979   Saru (The Monkey). Tokyo: Hōsei Daigaku Shuppankyoku.
Inoue, Hisashi, Kikuo Nomoto, Tamotsu Hirosue, Minoru Betsuyaku, Osamu Matsuda, Osamu Mihashi, Masao Yamaguchi, Kimiyoshi Yura, and Kiyoshi Yokoi
1978   Shinpojūmu Sabetsu no Seishinshi Josetsu (Introduction to a Spiritual History of Discrimination—A Symposium). Tokyo: Sanseidō.
Ishida, Eiichi
1966   Kappa Komahikikō (Kappa Komahiki Kō—-The *Kappa* Legend [*sic*]). Tokyo: University of Tokyo Press.
Ishii, Ryōsuke
1963   Zoku Edo Jidai Manpitsu (Essays on the Edo Period), Vol. 2. Tokyo: Inoue Shobō.
Kadokawa Shoten, ed.
1961   Nihon Emakimono Zenshū (Collection of Japanese Scroll Paintings). Vol. 13: Hōnen Shōnin E-den (Illustrated Deeds of St. Hōnen). Tokyo: Kadokawa Shoten.
Kailasapathy, K.
1968   Tamil Heroic Poetry. Oxford: Clarendon Press.

Kaneko, Shigetaka, ed.
   1969 Chūjū Giga (Scrolls of Animal Caricatures). Adapted from the Japanese text by Hideo Okudaira. Honolulu: East-West Center Press.
Kitahara, Taisaku
   1974 Senmin no Kōei (Descendants of the *Senmin* [humble people; outcaste]). Tokyo: Tsukuma Shobo.
Kubo, Tokutada
   1961 Kōshin Shinkō no Kenkyū (Research on the Belief in *Kōshin*). Tokyo: Maruzen.
Leach, Sir Edmund R.
   1965 Political Systems of Highland Burma. Boston: Beacon Press.
Lévi-Strauss, Claude
   1966 The Savage Mind. George Weidenfeld and Nicolson Ltd., transl. Chicago: University of Chicago Press.
   1967 Structural Anthropology. Claire Jacobson and Brooke Grundfest Schoepf, transls. New York: Doubleday.
   1969 The Raw and the Cooked: Introduction to a Science of Mythology, Vol. 1. John and Doreen Weightman, transl. New York: Harper Torchbooks.
Matsudaira, Narimitsu
   1977 Matsuri: Honshitsu to Shosō—Kodaijin no Uchū (Festivals: Their Essence and Dimensions—The Universe of Ancient Japanese). Tokyo: Asahi Shimbunsha.
Miyamoto, Tsuneichi
   1981 Emakimono ni Miru Nihon Shomin Seikatsushi (Life of Common People in Japan as Depicted in Picture Scrolls). Tokyo: Chūō Kōronsha.
Miyata, Noboru
   1975 Kinsei no Hayarigami (Gods of Epidemics in the Recent History of Japan). Tokyo: Hyōronsha.
Mizuo, Hiroshi
   1965 Sōtatsu to Kōrin (*Sōtatsu* and *Kōrin*). Tokyo: Heibonsha.
Murasaki, Yoshimasa
   1980 Sarumawashi Fukkatsu (The Revival of Monkey Performances). Kyōto: Buraku Mondai Kenkyūjo Shuppanbu.
Myerhoff, Barbara
   1980 Number Our Days. New York: Simon & Schuster.
Nakajima, Junji, ed.
   1979 Hasegawa Tōhaku. Tokyo: Shūeisha.
Ninomiya, Shigeaki
   1933 An Inquiry Concerning the Origin, Development, and Present Situation of the *Eta* in Relation to the History of Social Classes in Japan. Transactions of the Asiatic Society of Japan 10:47-154.
Noguchi, Michihiko
   1978 Chusei no Shomin Seikatsu to Hisabetsumin no Dōkō (The Life of Common People and Discrimination against *Burakumin* during the Middle Age). *In* Buraku Mondai Gaisetsu (Introduction to *Buraku* Problems). Buraku Kaihō Kenkyūjo, ed. pp. 86-99. Osaka: Kaihō Shuppansha.

Nonomura, Kaizō, ed.

1968 Kyōgenshū (Jō) (Collection of *Kyōgen*), Vol. 1. Tokyo: Asahi Shimbunsha.

Ochiai, Shigenobu

1972 Mikaihō Buraku no Kigen (Origin of Discrimination against *Buraku*). Kōbe: Kōbe Gakujutsu Shuppan.

Oda, Kōji

1978 Nihon Geinōshi eno Atarashii Hikari (New Light Toward the History of Japanese Performing Art). *In* Suō no Sarumawashi (Monkey Performances at Suō). Suō Sarumawashinokai Jimukyoku, ed. p. 15. Hikari City, Yamaguchi Prefecture: Suō Sarumawashinokai Jimukyoku.

Ohnuki-Tierney, Emiko

1980 Ainu Illness and Healing: A Symbolic Interpretation. American Ethnologist 7:132-151.

1981 Illness and Healing among the Sakhalin Ainu: A Symbolic Interpretation. Cambridge: Cambridge University Press.

1984 Illness and Culture in Japan: An Anthropological View. Cambridge: Cambridge University Press.

Origuchi, Shinobu

1965a Origuchi Shinobu Zenshū, Dai Ikkan (Collected Papers by Shinobu Origuchi), Vol. 1. Tokyo: Chūō Kōronsha.

1965b Origuchi Shinobu Zenshū, Dai Nikan (Collected Papers by Shinobu Origuchi), Vol. 2. Tokyo: Chūō Kōronsha.

1966 Origuchi Shinobu Zenshū, Dai Nanakan (Collected Papers by Shinobu Origuchi), Vol. 7. Tokyo: Chūō Kōronsha.

Ouwehand, Cornelius

1958-59 Some Notes on the God Susano-o. Monumenta Nipponica 14(3-4): 138-161, 384-407.

1964 *Namazu-e* and their Themes: An Interpretive Approach to Some Aspects of Japanese Folk Religion. Leiden: E. J. Brill.

Philippi, Donald L., transl.

1959 *Norito:* A New Translation of the Ancient Japanese Ritual Prayers. Tokyo: The Institute for Japanese Culture and Classics, Kokugakuin University.

1969 Kojiki. Princeton: Princeton University Press, and Tokyo: University of Tokyo Press.

Plath, David W.

1982 Resistance at Forty-eight: Old-Age Brinksmanship and Japanese Life Course Pathways. *In* Aging and Life Course Transitions. T. K. Hareven and K. J. Adams, eds. pp. 109-125. New York: The Guilford Press.

Porkert, Manfred

1974 The Theoretical Foundations of Chinese Medicine: Systems of Correspondence. Cambridge: Massachusetts Institute of Technology Press.

Price, John

1966 A History of Outcaste: Untouchablility in Japan. *In* Japan's Invisible Race. G. DeVos and H. Wagatsuma, eds. pp. 6-30. Berkeley: University of California Press.

Schutz, Alfred
    1971   Collected Papers. Vol. 2: Studies in Social Theory. Arvid Brodersen, ed.
        The Hague: Martinus Nijhoff.
Sebeok, Thomas A.
    1981   Japanese Monkey Performances—An Ancient Art Revived. Explorers
        Journal 59(1):34–37.
Shimonaka, Yasaburō, ed.
    1941   Shintō Daijiten (Encyclopedia of *Shintō*), Vol. 2. Tokyo: Heibonsha.
Simmel, Georg
    1950   The Sociology of Georg Simmel. Translated, edited, and with an introduc-
        tion by Kurt H. Wolff. Glencoe, IL: The Free Press.
Smith, Robert J.
    1974   Town and City in Pre-Modern Japan: Small Families, Small Households,
        and Residential Instability. *In* Urban Anthropology. A. Southall, ed. pp.
        163–210. Oxford: Oxford University Press.
Suō Sarumawashinokai Jimukyoku, ed.
    1978   Suō Sarumawashi (Monkey Performances of Suō). Hikari City, Yama-
        guchi Prefecture: Suō Sarumawashinokai Jimukyoku.
Suzuki, Mitsuo
    1974   Marebito no Kōzō—Higashi Ajiya Hikaku Minzokugaku Kenkyū (The
        Structure of *Marebito* [Stranger]—Comparative Folklore of East Asia). Tokyo:
        Sanichi Shobō.
    1979   Marebito (Visitors). *In* Kōza Nihon no Minzoku (Folk Cultures of Japan).
        Vol. 7: Shinkō (Belief Systems). T. Sakurai, ed. pp. 211–239. Tokyo: Yūseidō
        Shuppan.
Tambiah, S. J.
    1981   A Performative Approach to Ritual. Proceedings of the British Academy
        63:113–169.
Toda, Teiyū
    1978   Bokkei, Gyokkan. Tokyo: Kōdansha.
Turner, Victor
    1975   Dramas, Fields, and Metaphors: Symbolic Action in Human Society. Itha-
        ca: Cornell University Press.
Ueda, Kazuo
    1978a   Buraku no Bunpu to Jinkō (Distribution of *Buraku* Settlements and
        Population). *In* Buraku Mondai Gaisetsu (Introduction to *Buraku* Problems).
        Buraku Kaihō Kenkyūjo, ed. pp. 3–10. Osaka: Kaihō Shuppansha.
    1978b   Kodai Senminsei to Buraku Kigensetsu ("The Lowly People" in Ancient
        Japan and the Origin of *Buraku*). *In* Buraku Mondai Gaisetsu (Introduction to
        Buraku Problems). Buraku Kaihō Kenkyūjo, ed. pp. 73–85. Osaka: Kaihō
        Shuppansha.
    1978c   Kinsei Hōken Shakai to Mibunsei (The Caste System during the Feudal
        Period). *In* Buraku Mondai Gaisetsu (Introduction to *Buraku* Problems).
        Buraku Kaihō Kenkyūjo, ed. pp. 100–118. Osaka: Kaihō Shuppansha.
Umezu, Jirō
    1972   Emakimono Sōshi (A Collection of Picture Scrolls). Kyoto: Hōzōkan.

van Gennep, Arnold
   1961[1909]   The Rites of Passage. Chicago: University of Chicago Press.
Yamaguchi, Masao
   1977   Kinship, Theatricality, and Marginal Reality in Japan. *In* Text and Context:
      The Social Anthropology of Tradition. ASA Essays in Social Anthropology.
      Ranvindra K. Jain, ed. pp. 151–179. Philadelphia: Institute for the Study of
      Human Issues.
   1978   Bunka to Ryōgisei (Culture and Ambiguity). Tokyo: Iwanami Shoten.
Yanagita, Kunio
   1951   Minzokugaku Jiten (Dictionary of Ethnology). Tokyo: Tokyodō.
   1962   Teihon Yanagita Kunioshū (Collected Writings of Kunio Yanagita), Vol. 8.
      Tokyo: Chikuma Shobō.
   1963   Teihon Yanagita Kunioshū (Collected Writings of Kunio Yanagita), Vol. 6.
      Tokyo: Chikuma Shobō.
   1964   Teihon Yanagita Kunioshū (Collected Writings of Kunio Yanagita), Vol.
      27. Tokyo: Chikuma Shobō.
Yazaki, Takeo
   1974   The History of Urbanization in Japan. *In* Urban Anthropology. A. South-
      all, ed. pp. 139–161. Oxford: Oxford University Press.
Yokoi, Kiyoshi
   1975   Chūsei Minshū no Seikatsu Bunka (The Life of the Common People
      During the Middle Age). Tokyo: Tokyo Daigaku Shuppankai.
Yoshida, Teigo
   1981   The Stranger as God: The Place of the Outsider in Japanese Folk Religion.
      Ethnology 20(2):87–99.

13
La Pitada Olímpica: Puerto Rico, International Sport, and the Constitution of Politics

John J. MacAloon
University of Chicago

Two contrary directions in so-called symbolic anthropology have recently reemerged with particular clarity. Theorists seeking alliances with cognitive and linguistic researchers have outlined, on programmatic as well as methodological grounds, a "microanthropology" of symbolic forms and lexical or logical domains. Direct concern with dominant sociopolitical institutions and historical processes is considered to belong to other, "macroanthropological" branches of the discipline (Colby, Fernandez, and Kronenfeld 1981:423–425).[1] An opposing group of theorists, while equally committed to highly contextual and extended case studies or controlled comparisons as essentials of anthropological method, seeks to bring new knowledge of symbolic forms directly to bear on the analysis of large-scale historical transformations and the dominant institutions of political economy. Within this body of work one notes an increasing unease with endlessly repeated, jejune claims that symbolic forms and cultural performances "express," "depict," or "display" structural patterns and institutional interests. A growing number of studies have sought to demonstrate that ludic and ritual performances, for example, may play a primary role in *constituting* political formations and institutions in the first place, in actively *making* history rather than reactively expressing it (Appadurai 1981; DaMatta 1984; Geertz 1980; Gusfield 1981; Turner 1974; Sahlins 1981). This paper presents a case of this kind.

The Anthropological Study of Olympic Sport

The modern Olympic Games incorporate a 90-year-old tradition of cultural performances, an ideology, a set of formal organizations, and a network of sociopolitical interests that are each international in character. Indeed, the

Olympics are the closest approximation to a truly global ritual symbol system that humankind has yet generated. Over 150 national cultures are represented, to a greater or lesser degree, in the Olympic Movement and may participate in the Olympic festival or its ancillary celebrations. The number of subnational cultural entities involved is impossible to count. According to the most reasonable estimates, the broadcast and print audience for an Olympics now exceeds half the world's population and is steadily growing.

The vast social energies and representational powers commanded by the Olympics are almost entirely the result of the symbolic appropriation of a set of relatively simple performance forms: athletic games; ritual processions, pageants, and prize givings; and the civic festivals in which these are embedded. Thus, the study of the Olympic Games and, more broadly, the international sports system is an especially obvious and appropriate opportunity for cultural anthropologists and other social scientists preoccupied with symbolic processes on a macrosocial scale. At the same time, the bewildering multiplicity of sociocultural groups that actually generate, interpret, and appropriate to other ends the meanings of Olympic performances introduces methodological and theoretical problems of the most extreme sort. How does one empirically study even a minimal approximation of the world? The clear answer seems to be that one does not, that one must content oneself with case studies focused on manageable research problems in restricted cultural contexts, in which ethnographic and historical methods can be fully brought to bear on rich though narrowly circumscribed data sets.

Yet the world-order and world-historical character of the Olympic Games is an essential empirical fact about them, in one way or another very much on the minds of Olympic officials, participants, ideologists, and popular and professional commentators (MacAloon 1981:268–269). I know of no Olympic text or particular episode in which this international dimension, this question about the existence and nature of "the world," is not present, joined with the more local preoccupations of the authors or actors. Hence, even the most restricted case studies must take account of it.

At the same time, this macrosocial set of interests and ideas is not built up de novo for each event, at each Olympics, in each nation, in each of its communities, by each actor or observer. On the contrary, the Olympics by now present a concrete history of marked and paradigmatic events, a familiar ideology, and a set of stable symbolic vehicles and ritual practices. Although necessarily general and inevitably abstract, the working out of the content and structure of this transnational system of institutions and representations is essential to understanding its transformations in and living contributions to the lives of very particular persons and peoples. Thus, the study of Olympic sport must proceed in both directions simultaneously, from the macro- to the micro-, and vice versa, for it is where they meet that the fullest human significance of the Olympics lies. It is also here that the mass phenomenon of Olympic sport intersects with the project of professional symbolic anthropology. Olympic sport is, for better or worse, a capital instance of the peoples' ethnology and diplomacy, of symbolic anthropology as a popular concern (MacAloon 1981:134–136, 217–218, 236–241, 262–269).[2]

A social history of the origins of the modern Olympics is presented in an earlier volume (MacAloon 1981). There, I show the indivisibility of structure and history by demonstrating the interpenetration of the founder's individual struggle for identity; the social dramas of his class, nation, and era; and the creation of a new cultural institution in Athens in 1896. Elsewhere, I analyze the developed Olympics as a formal structure of cultural performances, a "ramified performance system" in which the genres of game, rite, festival, and spectacle—each with its own semantic and behavioral properties and Olympic history—are joined in relations of opposition and congruence (MacAloon 1984). This paper belongs to a series of studies of the encounter between the Olympic sport system and discrete national societies. I have written two shorter accounts of international sport and United States culture (MacAloon 1982a, 1982b), and a more detailed work is in progress. This paper considers Olympic sport and Puerto Rico, in particular what I argue is the mutual structuring of sport and politics on the island.

With Respect to the National Identity

The tortured political history of Puerto Rico has generated a large analytical literature (see Vivó 1973:52–71; Bravo 1975:11–19; United States–Puerto Rico Commission on the Status of Puerto Rico 1966a, 1966b; U.S. General Accounting Office 1981). Publications on Puerto Rican sport, however, have been largely limited to technical reports, journalistic biographies, and historical chronicles (Huyke 1969). To my knowledge there are no extended scholarly studies of the interrelation of these two cultural domains on the island, though such an analysis for neighboring Bermuda has appeared (Manning 1981). In the aftermath of events discussed in this paper, a few legal analyses and policy documents have incorporated brief considerations of international sport in their discussions of the constitutional future of Puerto Rico (Serrano Geyls and Gorrin Peralta 1980; U.S. General Accounting Office 1981:97). Puerto Ricans themselves, however, are acutely aware of the systematic interconnection of sport and politics in island life.

Comparative study of Olympic sport brings with it a strong awareness of the culture-bound character of popular discourse in the United

States and portions of Western Europe on sport and politics, a discourse marked by a generic opposition between the two domains and "interference" and "exploitation" as the dominant motifs of their interaction. Other national cultures conceive the relations between sport and politics quite differently. Still, I was not prepared to hear asserted, early in my field study, that international sport had played an important role in the decline of the New Progressive Party (NPP) and its leader, Governor Carlos Romero Barceló, from a 60,000-vote plurality in the 1976 elections to one of a mere 3000 votes in the 1980 elections (still disputed despite a recount of the ballots). I was even less prepared to accept the judgment of a well-placed and respected informant that international sport has become "the most important single issue at the level of the masses with respect to the national identity, more important than language."

The speaker is not only a distinguished jurist, professor of law, and author of important scholarly works on Puerto Rican constitutional and political history, including the cultural politics of language (García Passalacqua 1962, 1969, 1970, 1974), but he also was a close aide to former governors Luis Muñoz Marin and Roberto Sánchez Vilella and is excellently connected in Washington. His columns of political commentary are known for their Realpolitik and no-nonsense prose. Moreover, he has no personal interest in sport and hence no reason to romantically exaggerate its effects. Although survey data, such as voter polls, are lacking to confirm it, the consensus of all those with whom I spoke on the island, regardless of party affiliation, is that international sport *had* played a capital role in the 1980 electoral fate of the NPP or statehood party. Moreover, other informants, including NPP officials, concur with Juan García Passalacqua in asserting that if the masses are convinced that becoming the 51st state of the United States would put an end to the separate representation of Puerto Rico in international Olympic-style sport (as indeed it would), this alone would be sufficient to finish the statehood cause, regardless of any other practical or ideological considerations. When I first heard this asserted, I skeptically questioned whether this might be a case of the tail wagging the dog, whether it might be a little absurd to think that the matter of political status—the most momentous issue in Puerto Rican life—might be decided in such a large part by a "symbolic" cultural institution like sport. García Passalacqua simply shrugged his shoulders and replied, "You do not understand us yet."

Endeavoring to understand how such unlikely claims could be made by otherwise reasonable persons, I immediately suspected the lingering effects of some recent highly emotional, but transient public scandal. Indeed, one was ready at hand to explain what seemed to the naïve outsider to be distortions of political judgment. It is known on the island as *la pitada olímpica*.

The expression is difficult to translate. *Pitada* is literally a "whistle," in this context a public expression of disdain and disapproval, equivalent to "booing" or a "Bronx cheer." In Puerto Rico and other Latin countries, however, it contains additional semantic components of insult and a shaming attack on the honesty and effectiveness of the man or men against whom it is directed. In its main referential meaning, the Olympic *pitada* refers to a specific event in which Governor Romero Barceló was whistled down during the opening ceremonies of the 1979 Pan American Games in San Juan.

As is well known, the rituals of the Olympic Games and those of the regional games modeled on them prominently feature national flags and anthems as master symbols of the participating societies. The rigid protocol of these rites with respect to national symbols is controlled by international organizations, with ultimate authority residing with the International Olympic Committee (IOC). As a consequence of her political history and ambiguous political status, Puerto Rico has not one flag and one anthem but two: her own and those of the United States (Todd 1967). As governor of the island, NPP leader, and a man of legendary stubbornness in his devotion to the cause of full union with the United States, Romero waged war over which flags and anthems were to be used in the rituals of the Pan American Games. His immediate combatants were local and regional Olympic authorities, led by Germán Rieckehoff Sampayo, president of the Puerto Rican National Olympic Committee (PRNOC) and a public figure of equal obstinacy in devotion to his cause.[3] For their own reasons, all leading social and political formations and sectors of public opinion in Puerto Rico took sides in the dispute; and it divided the entire island. A face-saving compromise notwithstanding, Governor Romero lost the battle and was attacked with a *pitada* during his ritual appearance as chief of state in the opening ceremonies.

The *pitada olímpica* is no transient event, no passing controversy or unique failure of negotiation. It is a social drama in the full sense of the concept (Turner 1957, 1984). If the usual procedure for establishing this claim were to be followed here, I would pass immediately to a detailed narrative of the 1979 events, punctuated by accounts of the ritual symbolism of the games, the particular constellations of party and private interests brought to bear on them, and the connections of immediate circumstances with abiding issues in Puerto Rican history. But this analysis must be postponed for substantive and theoretical reasons. While the customary ritual drama analysis would certainly render more comprehensible the effects of international sport on the 1980 elections and the statehood cause claimed by Puerto Ricans, it would fail to reveal the true dimensions and character of the situation. Inadvertently, it would suggest that sports events and the rituals generated by them merely "express" or "display" independent and self-contained sociopolitical formations and historical movements on the island. Instead, what I show is the mutual constitution of sport and politics in contemporary Puerto Rico. This requires an account of how both politics and sport systematically reach in very particular ways throughout Puerto Rican life, an explanation of that which occasions their mutual structuring of one another, and the location of the events of 1979 in a continuous series of prior and later episodes shown to be historically variant but truly structural and, so to speak, inevitable.

Political Formations in Puerto Rico

An extended survey of Puerto Rican political formations is well beyond the scope of this paper (for recent historical overviews see Cruz Monclava 1966; Hunter 1966; Anderson 1965; U.S. General Accounting Office 1981), nor is one required to confirm what is obvious to all Puerto Ricans and to outside observers. For decades in Puerto Rico, not only political affairs but also much of daily social, cultural, and psychological life have been dominated by "the status question." Of late, the *autonomistas*—those who favor continuation, though "perfected," of the present commonwealth (Estado Libre Asociado) arrangement with the United States—have had their electoral fortunes rallied chiefly by the Popular Democratic Party (PDP). The PDP still bears the imprint of the late Luis Muñoz Marin, the party's main architect and Puerto Rico's leading statesman since World War II. The *estadistas*—those who favor incorporation as the 51st state of the United States—are politically organized by the NPP, led by Carlos Romero Barceló. Those who wish to bring about full independence and constitutional separation from the United States—the *independentistas*—have lately been represented in electoral and legislative affairs by the Puerto Rican Independence Party (PIP) of Rubén Berríos Martínez, a social democratic party, and by the Marxist-Leninist Puerto Rican Socialist Party (PSP) of Juan Mari Brás. The cause of independence is also expressed by extraparliamentary splinter parties and by extralegal groups, the terrorist Armed Forces of National Liberation being the most visible from the mainland.

This skeletal portrait of contemporary Puerto Rican political formations is, of course, oversimplified in numerous respects. The great majority of Puerto Ricans, regardless of party affiliation, share a measure of nationalist sentiment as a reaction to the colonial history of the island, invaded and ruled first by Spain and then by the United States, and of nativist sentiment, a sense of identity with the Puerto Rican people as forming a distinct culture and society (see Steward 1956; Mintz 1966). All parties, including the NPP, pronounce themselves committed to the preservation of Spanish language and Puerto Rican culture.

Puerto Ricans do not limit their perceptions of what a political party really represents to its explicit platform. For example, statehooders have traditionally regarded PDP leaders as *independentistas* in disguise, in part because Puerto Rican politics are highly personalistic, memories are long, and many PDP leaders including Muñoz Marin himself were partisans of independence in their youths. Moreover, *estadistas* (and conservative *autonomistas* who sometimes vote with them) profess not to see how striking from the 1950 Federal Relations Act all language referring to Puerto Rico as "belonging to the United States" (one favored PDP means of "perfecting" the commonwealth) would be anything but de jure independence, whatever other constitutional ties remained. *Independentistas,* by contrast, tend to scoff at the notion of the PDP leadership as closet partisans of independence, arguing that reform of the Federal Relations Act would do nothing to alter Puerto Rico's colonial status. To its enemies, the PSP is understood to favor not independence but a state satellite to Cuba and other socialist powers.

Party platforms and the programs of individual politicians are not concerned exclusively with the status question but with the whole range of domestic economic, social, and political questions facing Puerto Rico. Given the conditions of poverty and deprivation traditional on the island—conditions so steadily exacerbated over the last decade that Puerto Rico is now on the brink of insolvency—the economic and social programs of the parties are of the greatest importance to the voters. Indeed, Muñoz Marin and his PDP successors have tried to present an image of the party as one which puts pragmatic issues before the status question.[4] The number and variety of Puerto Ricans who take the status question as a kind of Trojan horse distracting islanders from the real socioeconomic challenges ought not to be underestimated. (These include political independents who nonetheless take Muñoz Marin as their own and the society's tutor, among them, by his own account, Germán Rieckehoff Sampayo.) While certain NPP candidates have also taken the pragmatic line in recent campaigns, most other statehooders join the *independentistas* in regarding this analysis as faulty, arguing that since the socioeconomic conditions on the island are consequences of its political status, only a change in that status will ameliorate them. The pragmatic line is further understood to be self-serving of PDP interests: turning attention away from the status question merely ensures continuation of the present commonwealth arrangement to which the PDP is committed.

The complexities of Puerto Rican political opinion, merely suggested here, are multiplied if class, occupational, and educational factors are taken into account (Mintz 1966). However, when all the nuances are considered, it remains the case that the status question directly or indirectly dominates Puerto Rican political formations and political process; that political parties are understood chiefly by their positions on status; and that the categories of *autonomista, estadista,* and *independentista* organize the rest of Puerto Rican political symbolism and discourse. One may not believe that one's own views on political and social history and policy derive from a priori commitments on the status question, but one tends to believe it of most of one's neighbors and all of one's opponents. Nor is such reckoning limited to explicitly electoral occasions. The putative political orientation of individuals, families, and associational groups is a constant exercise and counter in social interaction of all sorts.[5] Moreover, attempts to portray Puerto Rican "national character" or "modal personality" by outsiders (Dexter 1949; Reuter 1946; Brameld 1959; Lauria 1964) and by native *puertorriqueños* (Figueroa Mercado 1963; Maldonado Denis 1963; Vientos Gastón 1964)—including the two most controversial, the *insularismo* thesis of Antonio Pedreira (1946) and its successor, the portrait of "the docile Puerto Rican" drawn by the eminent writer René Marqués (1976)—all find a role being played, in one way or another, by Puerto Rico's political status and history as a colonial dependency (see Mintz 1966 for a general critique of this literature).

Prior to 1976, the statehooders had come to power once before. In 1968, Luis Ferré led the NPP into office with a plurality of 23,000 votes.[6] Barely a year before, a plebiscite on the status question had returned 60 percent of the vote for commonwealth, 39 percent for statehood, and only 0.6 percent for independence. Although NPP leaders tried to claim that Ferré's election was a repudiation of the plebiscite (the results of which were difficult to interpret in any case), it was more clearly a consequence of a split in the PDP ranks. During the campaign, Ferré had tried to downplay the status issue; but once in office, his full commitment showed itself plain, particularly in his avid courting of the Nixon administration in the vain hope of securing real support for Puerto Rico's incorporation into the Union. To many of his opponents this seemed demeaning, particularly in the context of the Vietnam War, which daily kept in the public eye, in the most poignant ways, the fact that Puerto Ricans were required to serve in the U.S. Armed Forces while being unable to vote for the U.S. president or to have their own voting representatives in the U.S. Congress. Although the issue had been present for decades, "assimilation," the fear of cultural and linguistic absorption by the United States, grew to an eminent position in the Puerto Rican political vocabulary in the 1960s (Ocampo 1964; Epstein 1967; Granda 1969; Rosario 1971; Marqués 1976).[7] The presence of the NPP in La Fortaleza increased these fears and brought attacks on the statehooders by Muñoz Marin and *independentistas* alike for wittingly or unwittingly promoting assimilation. It has remained a central political challenge for statehooders to convince voters that political union with the United States would not mean the end of Puerto Rican cultural identity. As we shall see, it was during this period that international Puerto Rican sport made its first noticeable public appearance as an assimilation issue, setting the stage for the major problem it would present for statehooders in the 1970s and 1980s.

A deadlocked legislature, the radicalization of the University of Puerto Rico, violent clashes between police and *independentistas,* growing crime, and, above all, continuing economic decline during the Ferré administration were among the factors that brought the PDP back to power in 1972. The party received 95,000 more votes than the NPP and 550,000 more than the PIP, which had nonetheless doubled its totals over the previous election. The governorship of Rafael Hernández Colon began with a poor augury suggestive of the main theme of this paper: most of his inaugural events were cancelled because the tragic death of baseball star Roberto Clemente, while delivering relief supplies to Nicaragua, had plunged all of Puerto Rico into mourning.

Worsening economic and social conditions helped bring the NPP back into power in 1976, led this time by Carlos Romero Barceló, who had shown his political skills by being returned to the office of mayor of San Juan despite the PDP blitz four years earlier. In the early years of his first term he missed no opportunity to demonstrate his commitment to the realization of statehood. Some Puerto Rican commentators believe that in spite of, or perhaps because of, increasing domestic turmoil, Romero was making progress in convincing larger numbers of Puerto Ricans that statehood was not only desirable but really possible. In this effort he was assisted by what appeared at the time to be new attitudes in the Carter administration. But among other pitfalls awaiting Romero were Puerto Rican sport, the 1979 Pan American Games, and *la pitada olímpica.*

A Nation Mad for Sport

Puerto Ricans are little distinguishable from many other peoples in their passion for sport, considered as an abstract cultural institution with certain functional features: popular entertainment and public theater; a rich source of metaphors, legends, and folklore; an arena for agonistic relations among schools, clubs, and towns; a cause of and outlet for manifold emotions, from aggression to aesthetic delight; entrepreneurial business or status group consolidation; a means of socioeconomic mobility for the few and the dream of such for the many; and so on. Instead, the unique significance in the expressions, "We Puerto Ricans are crazy for sport," "We are a nation mad for sport"—expressions sometimes uttered in fierce pride, sometimes in ironic self-amusement—lies in the relation between the subjects and objects of these sentences. "We Puerto Ricans" and "We, a nation": these assertions of sociocultural identity are entailed by and entwined in sport and effect sport's special "madness" on the island. Through a fortuitous combination of historical circumstances, some external and some internal, the sociopolitical categories and conditions most salient to Puerto Ricans have been mapped onto the social organization of sport, and vice versa, creating a unique situation of mutual structuring[8] (see Figure 1).

Puerto Ricans distinguish between "professional" and "Olympic" or "Olympic-style" sport. Certain distinctive features involved in the construction of these opposing categories are familiar in other Euro-American cultures; other, less obvious ones are distinctively Puerto Rican and render the native categorization of sport of far greater importance.

Professional sports—baseball and boxing being the two most passionately followed and culturally marked—involve playing for pay; private sector dealings between individual players (or their agents) and corporations or commercial entrepreneurs; and the world of contracts, bidding wars, bonuses, commercial endorsements, and purported (if not real) high living. In both baseball and boxing the highest level of skill and competition is clearly understood to be the professional level. Although baseball and boxing are pursued at the amateur level all over the island (and the latter is an

Categories of sport	Teams or individual contracts organized by	Major competitions	Competitions owned and governed by	Social identities constituted: *Puertorriqueño as*
Professional	Corporations, promoters, agents	Title fights, AL and NL championships, World Series, PR Winter League championships, and so on	Major League Baseball, World Boxing Council, and so on	*Norteamericano*
Olympic-style	PRNOC	Olympics	IOC	*Mundial*
		Pan American Games	PASO	*Americano*
		Central American & Carribean Games	CACSO	*Hispanoamericano • Caribeño*
	PR national federations	National championships	PR national federations	*Puertorriqueño*
	Schools, clubs, civic groups, and so on	Local championships	Local leagues	

Figure 1. The Puerto Rican sports system.

Olympic sport and the former will be soon, in part through the efforts of Puerto Ricans), it is clear to all that the professional versions of these sports are the central points of athletic and social reference.

In both sports, over the years, Puerto Ricans have attained significant representation and no small success in "the big leagues" (Huyke 1969: 79–98, 107–124). In both cases, the big leagues are centered in the United States. Players who have "made it" go to the mainland for their major performances, are certified as true "stars" in the United States by mainlanders as well as by Puerto Ricans, and, in the case of baseball, are teammates of U.S. players in what might be termed the "organic solidarity" of the baseball world. These athletes appear as individuals who happen to be Puerto Rican, rather than as formally marked representatives of Puerto Rico. Moreover, they incite a reverse flow of mainlanders to the island, of U.S. boxing promoters staging fights in San Juan, of North American ballplayers competing in the Puerto Rican winter leagues, and of major league scouts combing the island for another Roberto Clemente or Dickie Thon. Finally, ballplayers and boxers are summoned to the "big time" on the basis of individual talent and achievement, and on this basis earn money and status from rationally interested and impersonal commercial entities and from a "faceless" mass public. While individualism, in certain of its meanings, is taken by many Puerto Ricans and several social scientists of the "culture and personality" school to be a general Puerto Rican value, so are *personalismo, respeto,* and *relajo* based in part on a direct responsibility to or sense of representing one's community (Mintz 1966:388–423). The absence of these qualities, particularly with the admixture of nakedly utilitarian motives and the cash nexus, is taken in large quarters of public opinion as quintessentially *norteamericano* (Marqués 1976:111–112). Thus, as cultural constructions, professional athletes are often associated with U.S. values. In professional sports, in a variety of ways, the United States is thus the context of reference for Puerto Ricans. For all of the discrimination and exploitation that persists in these sports (indeed, in part because of them), Puerto Ricans see themselves, or experiment with seeing themselves, in these sports as U.S. citizens and North Americans.

Matters are quite different with respect to Olympic-style sport. Some sports in this category—track and field, swimming, gymnastics, shooting, weightlifting—have no corporate professional versions; and amateur values and organizational criteria in principle, and in large measure in fact, prevail. In other sports that do have professional versions—basketball, soccer, tennis—Puerto Ricans have rarely made it to the "big time," and the amateur games remain the primary points of reference. Olympic-style sport is socially organized on different lines than professional sport. At the basic level, athletes generally find opportunities to train and compete by joining sports clubs. These clubs are typically sponsored by and understood to represent one or another determined social entity, whether scholastic (schools, universities), associational (occupational, church, union, or status groups, including country clubs), or civic (neighborhoods, villages, towns, cities). Where commercial businesses do participate, it is through sponsorship of or donations to teams, not through the setting up of teams as separate business ventures. Thus, in contrast to professional sports, a group orientation or ethos, a sense of representing a determined social entity, tends to be the dominant motif in Olympic-style sport, just as it is taken to be, or desired to be, the dominant value in Puerto Rican sociopolitical life by many islanders.

This motif of the thorough conditioning of individual achievement by group identity and solidarity not only continues but intensifies as one moves up the competitive ladder and up the hierarchy of governing and sponsoring bodies in Olympic-style sport. Each amateur sport is governed by a national federation committed in principle and by charter to developing its sport throughout Puerto Rico, and each organizes national championships. Victors in national championships are understood to be *national* champions, not only in the sense of being certified the best in Puerto Rico but also in winning the right to *formally* represent Puerto Rico in international competitions, that is, *as a nation among and against other nations.* There are no real equivalents in professional sport.

Here we reach the crux of the whole matter, the peculiar historical circumstance that has led most instrumentally to the mutual structuring, in relations of opposition and congruence, of sport and politics in Puerto Rico: *in politics, the status of Puerto Rico as a nation is ambiguous, conflicted, disputed; in international Olympic sport, it is not.* Only athletes from countries with separate National Olympic Committees to certify them—NOCs recognized by the International Olympic Committee—can be entered for the Olympics, for such IOC-approved regional competitions as the Pan American Games and the Central American and Caribbean Games, and for world championships (though in the last case the actual certifying bodies are the national federations). Since 1948, in London, Puerto Rico has competed in the Olympics as a national team separate from the United States, and in 1952 the recognition of its NOC was changed from provisional to regular by the IOC. Puerto Rico has competed as a separate nation in the Central American and Caribbean Games since 1930, in every Pan American Games since the second in 1955, and in several world championships. In international sport, but nowhere else in international institutional life, Puerto Rico formally appears as a nation among nations.[9]

In the Central American and Caribbean, Pan American, and Olympic games, Puerto Ricans see themselves, or experiment with seeing themselves, as an independent nation, so seen by others. At the same time there are important and ordered differences among these athletic festivals for Puerto Ricans. These differences lie especially in the practical requirements of mounting teams, in athletic competitiveness, and in sociopolitical symbolism: What sort of nation is Puerto Rico represented to be and with respect to whom?

Per capita outfitting, preparation, travel, and lodging costs tend to be greatest for an Olympic team and least for a Central American and Caribbean Games team. Puerto Rico is a poor country, and such fiscal considerations are important, particularly in the context of disputes over private and public financing of teams. Because of the number and nature of the nations involved in each competition, competitive ranking and visibility (the number of athletes who meet qualifying standards, reach the finals, and win medals) flow in a direction opposite to that of financial commitment. In contrast to certain professional sports, Puerto Rican athletes are least competitive at the highest level of amateur sports, the Olympics; they are more competitive at the Pan American Games, and more competitive still at the Central American and Caribbean Games.

As we have seen, professional sports differentially conjoin with Puerto Rican identities as U.S. citizens and *norteamericanos*. In the Central American and Caribbean Games, the "structure of the conjuncture," to borrow a useful term from Sahlins (1981:35), is with Puerto Rico's identity as a Latin American nation, a richly conflicted identity for many Puerto Ricans. On the one hand, there are shared and generally esteemed traditions of language and culture; on the other, there are associations with "underdeveloped" Latin countries, "jungle societies" full of class and racial hatreds, with chaotic, authoritarian, "banana republic" political traditions. Puerto Ricans may find a measure of realism in the economic associations, but the rest is regarded as utterly distasteful and untrue to Puerto Rican lifestyle, internal social relations, and democratic political traditions. The fact that many persons in the United States, including those political and corporate elites who have the most to say about the fate of the island, are known or feared to be ignorant of the real Puerto Rico and to incorporate it into the generic stereotype of the Latin nation deepens the ambivalence.

In addition, the incorporation of Central American *and* Caribbean nations into these games embodies the further dilemma of whether Puerto Rico's historical and contemporary situation is most like that of her island neighbors (Institute of Caribbean Studies, University of Puerto Rico 1966; Mintz 1966:361–366), many of whom are quite different from her linguistically and culturally; or like continental Latin American nations, closer in language and culture but larger, more populous, and quite different in geographic and geoeconomic circumstances. The question of whether Puerto Rico is a Latin American nation, a Caribbean nation, neither, or both is a question of external as well as internal perceptions.

Puerto Ricans have often been made aware in recent years of the fact that many Latin American nations do not typically think of Puerto Rico as one of their own, either because she is taken to belong to the insular Caribbean or because of her special relationship with the United States, seen as privileged by some, demeaning by others (Urrutia Aparicio 1954). This latter set of ambivalences is known to color the perceptions of island neighbors as well.[10]

In international games, nations compete *with* each other, in the double sense of *against* and *alongside*. In regional international games, some nations are in, some nations are out. In the Central American and Caribbean Games, the United States is out; Puerto Rico is in, with all "other" Central American and Caribbean nations, and is highly visible athletically and organizationally; and Cuba is in and, for over a decade, not only athletically visible but dominant. In these games, Puerto Rico is a Central American and a Caribbean nation, alongside, with, and against the others, facts with which all Puerto Rican political formations, constituted as they are around the status question, must contend.

In the Pan American Games, Canada, the United States, and the nations of South America are in as well. Within the overarching identity of hemispheric America constituted by these games, a third permutation of national arrangements is arrayed for intersection with Puerto Rican political formations and historical conditions. As in professional sports, Puerto Rican and U.S. athletes take to the same playing fields together, but they do so as opposing nations. In the Pan American Games, the appearance of Puerto Rico as a separate nation is marked differently than in the Central American and Caribbean Games, in which the United States is simply absent. The U.S. presence here is an explicit assent to the athletic independence of Puerto Rico, which can be read as an emblem and proof of the successfulness of the Estado Libre Asociado arrangement in political life or, by contrast, as evidence for the need for full political sovereignty to match the cultural independence present here.

In these contests, as in all sports events, the fortuitous outcomes of competitions are appropriated by audiences and re-presented as texts, oral and written, in which popular interpretations of particular relations of opposition and solidarity are expressed. Such texts are often centered around the progress of Puerto Rican athletes in elimination events at the expense of North Americans and to the advantage of Latin Americans; at the expense of Latin Americans to the advantage of North Americans; or at the expense of both to the advantage of Puerto Ricans. Moreover, such "metasocial commentaries" (Geertz 1972) are not limited to events in which Puerto Rican athletes play major roles. Lately, the Pan American Games as a whole have centered on the rivalry between the "athletic superpower" (the United States) and the "little giant" (Cuba), with Puerto Rico among the less-competitive supporting cast. The United States-Cuba rivalry keys directly into the whole north/south, capitalist/socialist, Anglo/Hispanic, imperialist/revolutionary, democratic/autocratic system of oppositions that organizes discourse about much of cultural politics in the region in general and Puerto Rico in particular. Intentions and incidents among persons who are not athletes, but are organizers, sponsors, officials, and coaches, provide further opportunities for the generation of texts condensing in narrative form the mutuality of sport and politics.[11]

Though it was the dream of Germán Rieckehoff before the controversies of recent years, Puerto Rico can never realistically hope to host an Olympic Games in this century. The expense typically involved in the outfitting and travel of an Olympic team has meant that only in Montreal in 1976 has a Puerto Rican delegation approached the size of that generally sent to the Pan American Games, much less to the Central American and Caribbean Games. The higher athletic standards and fiercer competition in an Olympics, in which scores more nations take part, has meant only a tiny handful of medals for Puerto Rico and mostly has left Puerto Ricans to watch other nations' champions in the broadcast coverage. But if, in these respects, the Olympics are less salient than the regional games—a situation common in much of the so-called Third World—in other respects the Olympics occupy a valued and privileged place in Puerto Rican sport and its political concomitants.

It was and continues to be IOC recognition of the sporting independence of Puerto Rico that chiefly generated and presently ensures the legitimacy of this status. This is true not only with respect to the Olympics but to regional games as well, for any attempt to disfranchise Puerto Rico in the latter, on the grounds of her constitutional dependency on the United States, would likely be met by the loss of IOC patronage and by sanctions against the countries involved. Germán Rieckehoff is not only president of the PRNOC and of the Central American and Caribbean Sport Organization (CACSO), the body ruling over the Central American and Caribbean Games, but is also Puerto Rico's first member of the IOC. This is a matter of personal prestige, native pride to the masses, empowerment to his allies, and grudging admiration to at least some of his enemies.[12] Still another factor is the genuine devotion of many Puerto Ricans to the ideals of the Olympic Movement.[13]

The principal cause of the Puerto Rican valuation of the Olympics, however, is their place at the top of a hierarchy of appearances as a nation. In the regional games, Puerto Rico appears as a nation of Central America and then as a nation of hemispheric pan-America; in the Olympics, she appears as a nation of the world. Her independence from the United States is constituted before the maximum world audience and, as is the case with many smaller nations that do not fare well in the athletic contests, this is particularly marked and attended to in the Olympic opening ceremonies. I was told by several Puerto Ricans what a college professor expressed in the following words: "It does not matter that we don't win anything, it's that procession [of nations in the Olympic opening ceremonies] that we have to have."[14]

This is not to say that the games of the Olympics are unimportant to Puerto Ricans. On the contrary, like all Olympic audiences, Puerto Ricans become engrossed in the performances of other nations' athletes. Moreover, Olympic eligibility rules are such that Puerto Rican athletes who have lived or trained in the United States make a decision, irreversible and binding for life, whether to compete for the United States or for Puerto Rico. Needless to say, these decisions cause a great stir in Puerto Rico, not only for what they mean athletically—in certain sports, making the U.S. team means a real chance at an Olympic medal—but for what they are read to mean sociopolitically. In addition, "deep matches" (Geertz 1972), say between the United States and Puerto Rico, do on occasion occur. In 1976, Butch Lee, born in Puerto Rico, raised in New York, and a basketball star at Marquette University, elected to play for the Puerto Rican team. To the horror of U.S. managers and fans, and to the ecstatic delight of their Puerto Rican counterparts, Lee and his teammates nearly upset the U.S. team, which would have kept it from its longed-for rematch with the Soviets.

While Olympic contests may have great interest for the Puerto Rican public, the ritual appearance of Puerto Rico as a nation is the most continuous and predictable source of Puerto Rican preoccupation with the Olympics. It is essential to reiterate that Puerto Rico is a full and independent member of no other international organization of any significance, a matter of deep ideological feeling and practical consequence for Puerto Ricans (U.S. General Accounting Office 1981:94–97). When the capital issue of Puerto Rico's political status is debated in the United Nations, it is Cuba and her allies who put the issue before the Decolonization Committee and endeavor to bring it to the General Assembly, while the United States and her allies endeavor to prevent this. Although their fate is being debated, Puerto Ricans participate only as invited "expert witnesses" or as members of the U.S. delegation.

If Puerto Rico were to lose its Olympic team, and thereby lose its Pan American and Central American and Caribbean teams, it would lose its only international appearances as a self-constituted and sovereign nation. These losses are directly and necessarily entailed in Puerto Rico's becoming the 51st state of the United States, further making the sociocultural organization and tradition of Olympic-style sport political affairs in the fullest sense. Beginning in 1966, what had been largely a latent tension in the Puerto Rican system emerged into the public eye; and in 1979 it burst forth in *la pitada olímpica,* an episode in the historical collision between the statehood government, Olympism, and the mass and party political formations that find it crucial to stand with the Olympic Games.

Power, Money, and the Ownership of Symbols

Although the error is frequent in contemporary social science, analysis cannot move directly from general patterns of order to actual historical events and behaviors. Structures themselves have histories, and the role of structure *in* history is always conditioned and mediated instrumentally by particular agencies, material resources, individual intentions, and accidents of circumstance. In this section, I discuss the major factors among these and further sketch the antecedent and subsequent events that show *la pitada olímpica* to be neither a unique historical transient nor an unconditioned reflex of the Puerto Rican politico-athletic order.

As a condition of recognition, the IOC insists on the formal independence of NOCs from governments. In the Olympic Games and in regional games governed by IOC rules, athletes are accepted for inscription from NOCs, not from governments. NOC members must not be appointed en bloc by governments, and the NOC must not function as a mere appendage or department of a state bureaucracy. Although this doctrine is not adhered to in dozens of countries, nor can it be in those where there is no private sector, at least a front of independence is everywhere maintained. IOC investigations and sanctions for violations of these rules have tended to be selectively aimed at "developing" countries, and in the mid-1950s Puerto Rico was threatened with the loss of its NOC recognition in part on these grounds. But since its reorganization in 1958, under the tutelage of Miguel Angel Moenck, the IOC member in Cuba, the PRNOC has been compositionally and executively independent of the Puerto Rican government. At the same time, important practical ties cross-linking the PRNOC and the government necessarily remain, creating potentials for conflicting as well as common interests.

All international sports festivals under Olympic tutelage are awarded by regional governing bodies to cities, conceived broadly as civic constellations not narrowly as local or central governments. The organizers are expected, in theory, to retain a large measure of independence from governments on practical as well as ideological grounds. Those groups seeking a games and the organizing committee assembled after a successful bid are asked to demonstrate both this independence and broad civic support. In certain instances, NOCs may dominate the organizing committees; in others, they may not compose the leadership but are nevertheless expected to stand as guarantors that Olympic principles will be respected by that leadership, including any political figures who may be part of it. In both cases, however, the direct participation of government officials in the process is not only helpful but required. No city will be awarded a games without letters from local and central government officials legitimating and supporting the bid, and it is generally the case that such officials lead the delegation making the presentation to the governing sports body. No city can host such an undertaking without government commitment to provide those rights and services that for legal, technical, or financial reasons only it can provide: expediting or suspension of normal visa requirements for foreigners, security, work permits, major capital improvements or new construction, transportation, communications, and so on. Thus, a situation is created in which the government is expected to supply legitimation and large investments of monetary and political capital, while at the same time it is expected to conceive of itself and to act as a valued service agency, bowing to the wishes of the international governing body, the organizing committee of the games, and the NOC in any matter of principled dispute.

It is rarely the case that government officials of a host city and country settle for this conception of their role, and the 1979 Pan American Games was a fortiori not one of these occasions. In making San Juan's appeal to the Pan American Sports Organization (PASO) in 1973, PRNOC president José Arrarás was joined by Carlos Romero, then mayor of the city, and by Rafael Hernández, then governor of Puerto Rico, both of whom supplied vigorous testimonies of government support and guarantees of organizing committee independence. The bid was successful, most Puerto Ricans rejoiced, and Germán Rieckehoff was made president of the Pan American Games Organizing Committee (PAGOC). But in November 1976, Romero led the statehood NPP to power, and, at a chance meeting at the inauguration of President Lopez Portillo in Mexico the following month, Rieckehoff informed the new governor of his intention to resign from his PAGOC post. Certain of the conflicts to come with Romero, Rieckehoff also anticipated election as PRNOC president and IOC member. When he assumed these positions in the spring of 1977, his PAGOC resignation was publicly announced. While ostensibly "to ensure more effectively the operation of the PRNOC" and to host an IOC executive board meeting (International Olympic Committee 1981:3), the resignation caused worried speculation in San Juan, despite the fact that Rieckehoff personally presented the new PAGOC to Romero at La Fortaleza and saw to it that the NPP was well represented in their number. The storm clouds were gathering, seeded by the symbols of the Pan American Games rituals, as both structure and history dictated they would be.

The protocol of Olympic-style rites orders several appearances of the master symbols of the modern nation-state, its flag and anthem.[15] In the procession of the national teams in the opening ceremonies, each delegation is led by its flag and its anthem is played as it passes the reviewing stand. In the victory ceremonies, the flags of the three place-winners are raised and the champion's anthem is played. In the closing ceremonies, the flags of the nations make a final ritual appearance, though there is some variation among regional and Olympic games in their proximity to the athletes. Only the anthem and flag of the host country are presented in the closing ceremony (and sometimes of the subsequent host nation), reduplicating this additional ritual honor to the hosts in the opening ceremonies. Other ritual appearances of the national symbols are less central and more variable.[16]

The preeminence of national symbols and ritual identities in a festival ideologically devoted to internationalism and humankindness, and built around the exploits of individual athletes, generates the problem of identities that has made the Olympics and Olympic-style sports events so evocative in the modern world (MacAloon 1981:258–269; 1984). Flags and anthems, in but one aspect of this general problem, are richly multivocal symbols and may constitute national identities and sentiments of solidarity on the basis of shared sociocultural traditions, political allegiance to governments, or both. So, too, the marked presence and ritual role of the host country's head of state in the opening ceremonies tend to generate the same conflict of interpretations.

The head of state declares the opening of the games, after having been formally invited to do so by the president of the international sports body owning and governing the festival. This ritual role is understood as a reward for the investment of the host government and people, whom the chief of state is taken for ritual purposes to doubly represent. His performance of that role at the behest of the sporting authorities symbolically replicates the service conception of its contribution that the government is expected to maintain. The ritual moment is an especially dangerous one, as conflicts among the host government, the host people, and the sports authorities can easily break out in public form. As a consequence, in the Olympics the chief of state is permitted to utter only a one-sentence formula that is set in advance and is invariable. But in regional games the chief of state may be a bit more long-winded, multiplying the danger even when his words are, on the surface, in the spirit of the occasion.

In the 1948 Olympics, the Puerto Rican team marched under both a U.S. flag and a special flag bearing the seal of Puerto Rico on a white background; the same occurred in the opening ceremonies of the 1952 Olympics at Helsinki. Earlier at the 1952 games, only the U.S. flag had been raised in the village welcoming ceremonies, though in a second ceremony, conducted after news was received of congressional approval of the Federal Relations Act, the Puerto Rican flag was raised. Thereafter, the Puerto Rican flag and *La Borinqueña,* the Puerto Rican anthem, were used exclusively in the 16 Olympic, Pan American, and Central American and Caribbean games between 1954 and 1979. Although surely there was some public notice and commentary on the flag and anthem symbolism on these occasions, to my knowledge they aroused no noticeable public controversy in Puerto Rico until 1966, when San Juan hosted its first major international athletic meeting, the Central American and Caribbean Games. With the region coming to and training its attention on Puerto Rico, the governmental and civic resources committed to these games, the additional symbolic demonstrations afforded the host country, the increased importance of assimilation as a political issue, and the growing instability in the ruling PDP sensed by the statehooders, the issue of the flags and anthems was broached as an explicit question of government policy. Bursts of public light were sent reflecting and refracting through the conjoined structures of international sport and status politics.

By all accounts, as preparation for the 1966 Central American and Caribbean Games progressed, the 12-year-old tradition of exclusive use of the Puerto Rican symbols was simply being taken for granted by the authorities.[17] Neither the government nor the organizing committee had found it necessary to consult one another on the matter. But on 8 June, less than a week before the opening ceremonies, a letter of vigorous protest was received by Secretary of State Carlos Lastra, and copies were simultaneously made available to the newspapers. The letter came from the president of "Citizens for State 51," a pro-statehood lobbying group. It accused the PRNOC, the organizing committee, and the government of "authorizing a public belittlement of our national [U.S.] flag and anthem" and of "a campaign . . . to deprecate our American citizenship." The secretary of state was further accused of violating sections 7, 8, and 10 of his own department's regulations on the use of flags and anthems, which order the use of the anthems and flags of both the United States and the Commonwealth "in all official ceremonies or in events which are invested with public solemnity" or when "the Governor so orders it." The regulations further include detailed instructions for their presentation (the Commonwealth flag always to the left, the Commonwealth anthem always prior). The letter also cited Title 36, Section 175 of the U.S. Code of Laws, claiming a willful violation: "No person will display any flag in prominence of, or with more honor than, or in place of, the American flag in any place within the United States or in a territory or possession thereof." The president of Citizens for State 51 and the author of the letter was none other than Carlos Romero Barceló, still a private citizen in 1966.

Although taken by surprise and faced with a coordinated demonstration at the athletes' village by members of the Associated Students for Statehood, the organizing committee and the government responded quickly and with a common voice. The director of protocol for the games replied that permission on the use of the flags had not been sought from the secretary of state because it "was not necessary, since these are not official government ceremonies." At a press conference at La Fortaleza, Secretary Lastra and Parks and Recreation Administrator Octavio Wys reiterated the view that the games were "run by the Olympic Committee, a nongovernmental organization, and, being sporting events, are unofficial." Lastra called Romero's charge "unfortunate" and described it as "lamentable that this situation has been made public with political overtones which it does not have." In his letter of reply, Lastra reviewed the tradition of using only the Puerto Rican emblems, arguing that the use of both flags "would lead to confusion because it would look as if the United States team is participating in events, which is not the case." He strongly reaffirmed the decision in favor of the Puerto Rican symbols alone but announced that both flags and anthems would be used in the preliminary ceremony welcoming the head of state into the stadium for the opening ceremonies. This arrangement was deemed fitting since the governor arrives at the stadium, a public building, as *jefe de estado* but plays his role in the ritual, an internationally owned performance, as *patrono de los juegos*. In closing his letter to Romero, Lastra wrote: "I exhort your group and all Puerto Ricans to join fraternally in celebrating the games with a spirit of cordiality, avoiding problems which are in the province of the [United States-Puerto Rico] Status Commission but not of the Olympic Committee."

Romero was not prepared to be fraternal or cordial on the matter. In an ensuing letter to Governor Sánchez, he wrote:

> We cannot accept the explanations . . . that the games are not official acts since the Legislature has appropriated funds for their celebration, the government has obtained an insurance policy protecting both athletes and spectators of the games, and since there will be official ceremonies at the opening and closing of the games.

The partitioning of the opening ceremonies into official and unofficial components was unacceptable, since at the close of the former, *"Puerto Rico will be converted into a sovereign nation among other nations"* (emphasis added). Lastra had spoken of "political overtones"; Romero knew the games to *be* politics in a sporting idiom.

In the following days, press editorialists and cafe debaters were split over the issue of the flags and anthems. Some observers at the opening itself reported that in the preliminary ceremony *The Star-Spangled Banner* drew more applause than *La Borinqueña;* but what that meant was difficult to interpret. In the opening ceremonies themselves, Governor Sánchez was warmly applauded by the majority, and as the Puerto Rican flag became visible at the head of the team, "a thunderous, steady ovation" rose from the spectators. "The crowd chanted 'Esa es, Esa es' (That's the one) . . . [and] several hundred tiny Puerto Rican flags made their appearance in the stands.'' The only concerted whistling to be heard was at the first appearance of the Cuban delegation, though it was drowned out by applause as the Cubans passed the reviewing stand. The rest of the ceremony passed without incident, save when a Colombian athlete rescued a dove unable to join its fellows in flight because of a broken wing, the athlete later vowing in the press to nurse it back to health. In the general public satisfaction over the games, the press quickly lost interest in the flag controversy and no obvious mark was left on the Olympic or political authorities involved. But it had left its mark on Carlos Romero Barceló.

In his 1966 letters to the government, Romero had vowed not to forget ''the contempt shown the U.S. flag and anthem'' and to take revenge if the decision were not reversed.

> As soon as the games end, we will distribute copies of the articles and editorials that have appeared in the press to members of the Status Commission and to all senators and representatives in Congress as evidence of the truth of our charges that the Puerto Rican government . . . takes advantage of any opportunity to hide the flag and hymn of the United States, representing Puerto Rico as an independent and sovereign nation.

How thoroughly he followed through on these threats is not clear; and what influence his role in the protest played in his subsequent rise in the NPP is a matter of disagreement among observers, though some insiders believe it to have been significant. But ten years later, he was *jefe de estado,* situated to exorcise his memory and exercise his will. Except for the added presence of the U.S. team and a larger hemispheric audience, the 1979 Pan American Games brought forward exactly the same structural arrangements and conflicts as in 1966. In the intervening years, however, the actual circumstances of Puerto Rican politics and social life had changed. The result this time would not be a passing tiff, but *la pitada olímpica,* proving that while sociocultural structures do reproduce themselves over time, what is produced in time is chiefly governed by history.

Whistling in the Dark

As soon as he was inaugurated governor, Romero let it be known that he would insist that both Puerto Rican and U.S. symbols be used in all 1979 Pan American Games ceremonies. Later, realizing the special practical problems presented by the victory ceremonies and the absence of a single precedent in Olympic history for double flags and anthems in them, and perhaps wishing to appear to compromise at the outset, he amended his position to include only the opening and closing ceremonies. With his position known and the games still two years away, the attention of both the governor and the public focused on more pressing matters, notably the precipitously declining economy and the building of relations with the new administration in Washington. But through these two years, Romero did everything he could behind the scenes to prepare for working his will over the 1979 games. In this effort, his chief stalking horse was José Barbosa Muñiz, his newly appointed director of the Parks and Recreation Administration, a man loyal to the governor and to the statehood cause, and Puerto Rico's first athlete to attain any degree of success in Olympic competition. Together, Romero and Barbosa sought to tighten the financial link between the PRNOC and the government.

Unlike commercially organized professional sport, which is regulated by the government but not directly supported, Olympic-style sport is recognized as a public good and entitled to a measure of direct government assistance, particularly since it was believed (until 1982) that such sums could not be raised by solicitation of private individuals in a country as small and as poor as Puerto Rico. Occasional grants (such as one of $50,000 in 1966, to prepare the Central American and Caribbean Games team) were superseded in the 1970s by legislative actions providing for yearly operating support for the PRNOC and the national federations. In 1976, during the last year of Hernández Colón's PDP governorship, legislative Joint Resolution 59 called for substantial sums to be passed on to the PRNOC by the Parks and Recreation Administration from its regular yearly appropriation. In June 1978, after months of debate and with the support of Governor Romero, J.R. 37 increased the authorization for the PRNOC to $500,000 per year, the monies coming from a special yearly drawing of the National Lottery. At the same time, however, the Parks and Recreation Administration was renamed the Sport and Recreation Department and elevated to cabinet status. The bill strengthened its discretionary powers, in effect making Rieckehoff more administratively dependent on Barbosa and his government agency for funds.

From the proceeds of the special lotteries,[18] J.R. 37 further committed far more substantial sums, totaling $7.75 million, to two additional purposes. While the NOC alone selects and certifies the athletes and officials for regional and Olympic games, the bill committed the government to paying the expenses of these delegations to the 1978 Central American and Caribbean Games in Medellin, the 1979 Pan American Games in San Juan, the 1980 Olympic Games in Moscow, and the 1982 Central American and Caribbean Games in San Juan. The awarding of the 1979 Pan American and the 1982 Central American and Caribbean Games to San Juan necessitated the second set of appropriations to meet the considerable expenses of the organizing committees for these events.

Through the same period the other side was gathering its forces as well, and Rieckehoff's qualities as a master strategist began to reveal themselves. His decision to resign the presidency of the PAGOC, mentioned earlier, was a shrewd one. He avoided being placed in the compromising position of being at once the man most responsible for the success of the games and the person who, as an IOC member and NOC president, would have to threaten to cancel them should the governor persist in his resolve with respect to the ceremonies. Rieckehoff also set about quietly lobbying for the support of international sports officials should such an eventuality come to pass.

Meanwhile, those opposed to the government with respect to sport, statehood, or both, discovered they had a trump card, and they did not wait long to play it. The fear of "assimilation" had been used as a club against the NPP in the Ferré governorship, principally with respect to the fate of Hispanic language and culture should Puerto Rico become the 51st state. Now a new threat came to the fore within this general political issue: if Puerto Rico became a state, it would lose its right to compete as a national team in international sport. As early as March 1977, Barbosa was forced to respond to this challenge in the press. His not very coherent, scattergun response prefigured what would become the statehood government's position when the issue became the central one in the aftermath of *la pitada olímpica*. He argued that there was no necessity whatever that statehood would mean the loss of independent international teams; that neither the recent treatment of Taiwan nor any other Olympic precedent was really relevant to Puerto Rico; that U.S. sports history was full of disputes that had led to representation by teams certified by different bodies; that U.S. Olympic authorities would surely support continued Puerto Rican teams; that the IOC itself was against mixing sport and politics and in any case was an autocratic body free to do whatever it pleased. In sum, Barbosa averred, as he and his governor were to do many times in the ensuing years, the issue had no merit in fact and had been trumped up for exclusively political reasons.

Of course, the issue has absolute merit in fact. Its public appearance set Rieckehoff to seeking letters of judgment from high IOC officials and colleagues, the Romero government to requesting through its resident commissioner in Washington a Library of Congress study of the matter (never released and protected from discovery by executive privilege), and various independent commissions concerned with the status question to studying it as well (Serrano Geyls and Gorrin Peralta 1980). The unanimous conclusion of all of these documents, subsequently made public, was that Puerto Rico would necessarily lose her international teams should she become a state of the United States, that she would no more be entitled to separate teams than would Indiana, California, or Texas.

In the period prior to the 1979 Pan American Games, the longer-term risk to the very existence of Puerto Rican teams exacerbated the more immediate problems of the flags and anthems that dominated public attention. The arguments on the symbols that appeared in the perfect fury of public statements, newspaper columns, lobbying, rumors, and street debates as the games drew closer need not be reproduced here. They were, for the most part, the same ones that had been rehearsed in 1966, or else transformations of these. (In 1966, for example, it was argued that the use of the U.S. flag would be confusing because a U.S. team was not present; in 1979, the opposite was asserted by those who wanted only the Puerto Rican flag.) But in this instance, the arguments were made in new circumstances: both Romero and his backers and Rieckehoff and his had the power to cancel or to wreck the games. It was a more even match than in 1966, and it was a match fought to the brink: the governor insisting on both flags and anthems for Puerto Rico in the ceremonies, the Olympic authorities vowing cancellation if the Puerto Rican symbols were not the only ones used. In the end, Romero conceded. He had the most to lose, given the investment in facilities and the anticipated foreign exchange; the mass public expectations of Puerto Ricans at home; the absence of support from the Carter administration which, embroiled in its own difficulties, had turned away from what had earlier seemed to be a real concern for the island; and the certainty of public criticism in the United States where, despite the principles on which the governor's position was based, the general public would see only another Latin imbroglio leaving its team (preparing for the "big match" in Moscow in 1980) nowhere to compete. Frustrated and angry, Romero was forced to accept a variation on the 1966 solution he had then abhorred. Both flags and anthems were used in a beefed-up ceremonial "welcome" for the chief of state at the Bithorn Stadium on opening day and at a number of other ceremonies inaugurating facilities and welcoming delegations at airports and in drawing rooms. But in the ceremonies of the games proper, the U.S. flag and anthem were reserved for the U.S. team.

When the governor's limousine pulled up at the stadium, and again at the conclusion of *The Star-Spangled Banner* in the preliminary ceremony, a chorus of both cheers and whistles broke out among the tens of thousands of Puerto Ricans assembled for the opening ceremonies. Eyewitnesses differ on which was the loudest reaction from the greatest number. But when Romero rose during the formal ceremony to declare the games open, the chorus of whistles began and crescendoed as he continued his noticeably overlong speech, though it was filled with words of welcome, solidarity, and friendship. As noted earlier, such public whistling in Puerto Rico expresses not only disapproval but also insult and imputations of ineffectiveness and hypocrisy. The governor's supporters, with which (according to some accounts) he had tried to pack the stadium, responded either with applause or, as did some members of the police force, by attacking their whistling fellow citizens. Both actions only resulted in augmenting the uproar, further interrupting the governor and in the end nearly drowning him out. He contained himself with visible difficulty and finished his speech. Order was eventually restored and the ceremony continued, highlighted by the overwhelming tumult of cheering (necessarily by Romero's supporters and detractors alike) when the Puerto Rican team appeared, marching, of course, to *La Borinqueña* and under the Puerto Rican flag alone.

The governor left the ceremony absolutely enraged, personally insulted, and politically worried about the interpretations the large broadcast audience throughout Puerto Rico, Latin America, and the United States would place on what they had seen and heard. According to informants who watched the coverage and to one who subsequently reviewed the tapes, the cameras had focused away from the audience and on the governor during his speech, but the whistling and commotion were readily audible and Romero's agitation was apparent. Within no time Romero's aides were spreading the word to the press that La Fortaleza had clear evidence that the "small number" of demonstrators were communist led and inspired. The number of demonstrators was clearly not small, and though the government maintains to this day its claims of their communist allegiances, no evidence to that effect has ever been produced.[19] Indeed, the charge served to further alienate many Puerto Ricans who had been among the whistlers, had known persons who were, or who saw in the government's claim only a further, demeaning attempt to curry favor with Washington. Through the rest of the games the governor attempted in various ways to eliminate the memory of what was already being called *la pitada olímpica,* but he met with little success.

Rieckehoff and the other Olympic officials had won the skirmish, to their own satisfaction and to that of *autonomista* and *independentista* forces who took the victory to be their own. But unlike 1966, the conflict did not fade away with the conclusion of the games. For Romero and Barbosa, the battle with Rieckehoff and Olympic sport was just beginning.

For years afterward, the governor was subjected to the same vilifying gesture that assaulted him at the 1979 Pan American Games. A low whistle would greet him whenever he set foot on a sports field, a major inconvenience for a Puerto Rican politician. For his part, Romero set about using the PRNOC's financial dependence on the government, created by the 1978 law, to his own purposes. Aside from minor harrassments over rent and utilities for the PRNOC offices, Romero and Barbosa attempted to influence the selection and allegiance of national federation and PRNOC officials by selectively wielding the purse strings. The NPP government argued that the public trust represented by public funding required a more representative and "democratic" composition of these bodies. What they sought, of course, were PRNOC members less deferential to Rieckehoff and his established colleagues, who were continuously accused of *autonomista* or *independentista* motives. The budget transfers to the PRNOC, authorized by J.R. 37, were executively suspended, creating large PRNOC deficits for the 1979 and 1980 fiscal years. Rieckehoff, though seriously embattled, was uncompromising in what he regarded as the defense of Olympic Committee independence against the government, while simultaneously seeking to avoid any action that could be interpreted as indicating party allegiance. Against the backdrop of the ultimate issue of losing international teams under statehood, these continuous conflicts and the almost daily publicity given them in the press were already thought likely to influence the 1980 elections when the campaign broke out to boycott the Moscow Olympics.

The Carter administration suddenly rediscovered Puerto Rico and naturally counted her in their boycott camp. Governor Romero quickly announced allegiance and was sincerely convinced of the appropriateness of this American response to the Soviet invasion of Afghanistan. His enemies, however, attributed his position to revenge against Olympic sport and accused him of demeaning Puerto Rico by his ready acquiescence to the orders of Washington. Rieckehoff opposed the boycott and was summoned to the White House, where he delighted in fending off pressure from its officials. For this he was further lionized in some political quarters, while in others he was accused of feathering his own IOC nest or of being another "Olympic idealist" blind to Soviet aggression. Like his mainland counterparts, Romero was chagrined to discover that there was no legal means, short of declaring a national emergency, by which athletes could be prevented from going to Moscow. All depended on the votes of the NOC, and Romero and Barbosa fell to lobbying the individual federations, some of which voted not to send a delegation to Moscow. They pulled the financial plug on the PRNOC and those federations that did vote to attend by effecting, in May 1980, the passage of J.R. 55, which removed not only government support for the Moscow team but also the regular subsidy to the PRNOC. With private funding, Rieckehoff succeeded in defying the government by arranging transit to Moscow through other Latin American countries—most of which sent full delegations—for a small contingent of boxers, one of whom added to the fierce domestic debate by making statements in Moscow that attributed the poor Puerto Rican representation to U.S. hegemony over the island.

The results of the 1980 gubernatorial elections and the widely claimed effects of Olympic-style sport on them have already been cited. Romero was not put off, and barely was the recount completed when he announced that owing to the desperate economic conditions on the island, Puerto Rico would have to abandon hosting the 1982 Central American and Caribbean Games (thus avoiding a certain repetition of 1979). Economic conditions notwithstanding, the outcry of anger and disappointment was great; but unable to proceed without government support, Rieckehoff had no choice but to effect the transfer of the games elsewhere. Cuba readily presented herself, and for organizational and financial reasons her choice was an obvious one. But this decision further embarrassed Romero, and he responded by announcing that the government would contribute nothing toward the mounting of a Puerto Rican team.

Here a line was crossed and *la pitada olímpica* became *la Gran Cruzada Olímpica* (the Great Olympic Crusade), Rieckehoff's brilliantly suggestive name for his populist campaign to raise the tens of thousands of dollars necessary from the people of Puerto Rico. He pursued the crusade with a vengeance: from printing bumper stickers showing a forlorn soul with empty pockets saying "I am an Olympic beggar," to the provocative act of threatening to set up a booth in sight of the governor's office window on the grounds of La Fortaleza, to nightly crisscrossing the island to solicit scores of working-class sports clubs in impoverished rural districts. Several times I observed a common scene: anonymous peasants or small tradesmen would approach him in restaurants or on the streets of hamlets, address him as "Don Germán," inquire about the campaign, and push dollar bills into his hand. In one year, and against all apparent odds, the Olympic Crusade grossed an astounding $447,954. Cash collections amounted to $343,138, half of which came in such small donations and purchases of promotional items.[20] Governor Romero had been spectacularly outflanked by popular commitment to international sport as, almost overnight, the PRNOC was enabled to pay its debts, to fund fully its teams, and to maintain a cash balance ensuring its financial independence for the immediate future. The campaign affected party politics as well. Clearly reading the political signs, a number of politicians from the governor's own NPP abandoned him to join PDP, PIP, and PSP counterparts in endorsing *la Gran Cruzada Olímpica*. Hernán Padilla, NPP mayor of San Juan, was portentiously among them, raising $50,000 for the Olympic coffers himself.

The success of the Olympic Crusade ensured that Puerto Rico would be represented in Havana by its largest and best-outfitted team ever to compete on foreign soil. The conditions of its genesis led many to conceive of the team—and many team members to conceive of themselves—as even more the creatures and instruments of the Puerto Rican people than is customarily the case with a national athletic delegation. This helped to account for the special emotion of the July ceremony in Roberto Clemente Stadium during which a national television audience saw—and perhaps in part joined—athletes, Rieckehoff, and other PRNOC officials in openly weeping as the Puerto Rican flag was handed over to the team to the nativist strains of *La Borinqueña*. Ever since the days of Luis Ferré, this ritual act had been performed by the governor. On this occasion it was done by

Rafael Pagan del Toro, president of *la Gran Cruzada Olímpica,* in the name of the Puerto Rican people.

The official delegation was hardly to travel to Havana alone. Some 400 Puerto Ricans—whether friends and relatives going to support the team, citizens making a gesture against the governor, or persons desiring to visit Cuba—had signed up for a PRNOC tour of the Games. But some weeks before departure, the U.S. Treasury Department invoked an old law against U.S. citizens contributing to the economic well-being of a hostile nation and threatened prosecution of any such persons who made the trip. This action was consistent with Reagan administration policies toward Cuba, but Sr. Corrado del Rio, Puerto Rican resident commissioner in Washington, was known to be involved, and few Puerto Ricans believed Governor Romero's public posture of innocence in the matter. This new episode not only polarized Puerto Ricans on the question of Cuba but also raised the whole array of legal issues surrounding the status question. A U.S. District Court in Boston refused to issue an injunction against the Treasury Department order, but some 137 Puerto Rican U.S. citizens defied the ban and entered Cuba through Mexico. Some, like PIP leader Rubén Berríos Martínez, publicly dared the authorities to prosecute them, which was never done. As many as 170 Cuban émigrés, resident in Puerto Rico but not U.S. citizens, secured visas and traveled to Cuba as tourists with the PRNOC tour. As CACSO president and premier of the host nation respectively, Rieckehoff and Fidel Castro were often together. Photographs of these occasions were used to different effect in newspapers of various political orientations. President Castro's well-known devotion to international sport and his properly laconic remarks upon opening the Games suggested contrasts with Governor Romero that the latter's press supporters tried to counter. The pro-statehood *El Día* sent a Cuban-born reporter who had not secured the necessary visa. When he was turned back in Havana, the paper used this as an excuse to vilify Rieckehoff as a "dupe of Fidel Castro," a "communist" and "fascist" sports "czar." This campaign would have backfired at any rate, but the paper was even more roundly sanctioned and embarrassed as the accomplishments of the Puerto Rican athletes in Havana made Rieckehoff a national hero.

The 400 Puerto Rican competitors won an astonishing 105 medals. Brilliant performance followed brilliant performance in Puerto Rico's finest international showing ever. Whether the athletes would have done as well without their special feeling and status as "the people's team" cannot, of course, be known. Few, however, thought so. This became an episode in which athletic results were taken to be triumphant ritual divinations of sublime social meaning (MacAloon 1981:228). Angelita Lind, a modest girl from a poor religious family, overnight became "El Angel de Puerto Rico" after her track victories, "converted into a symbol of the unity of our entire people," as *Claridad* put it. The coach of the victorious softballers proclaimed, "The glorious unity of this team is the glory of the Puerto Rican flag." Such themes dominated the perfect wave of civic ecstasy surrounding these athletes who, in turn, proclaimed their gratitude to and affection for Germán Rieckehoff, the PRNOC, and the Puerto Rican people.

The position of Romero and Barbosa in the midst of all this was one of discomfort, to say the least. No number of statements lauding the athletes and rejoicing in their victories could overcome the broad public perception of the government as the enemy of Rieckehoff and the PRNOC. Mass celebrations were planned to welcome the delegation home, and the government failed in its efforts to win a major presence at these or to substitute its own. The celebrations were marred when the team planes were mysteriously delayed; the government was widely suspected, though no proof ever surfaced. When the athletes finally did land in the wee hours of the morning, thousands remained at the San Juan Airport and the Plaza de Americas to greet them. Prominent in the crowd were such opposition politicians as Juan Mari Brás of the PSP and Hernández Colon of the PDP, anxious once again to associate themselves with Puerto Rican sport and the anti-NPP sentiment generated in its favor over the past several years. The politicians were altogether too prominent to suit Rieckehoff. Exhausted and perturbed, he was publicly rude to Hernández Colon, refusing to go on television in his company, a conflict that was patched up the following day.

Rieckehoff could suddenly afford to be as magnanimous or combative as he pleased. Romero had no such luxury. The gubernatorial elections were but two years away, and the sports issue that had continuously bedeviled his governorship now left him as isolated from the voters as he had ever been. No compensating successes in other political arenas were present or on the horizon.

On the basis of the preceding analysis, completed in the autumn of 1982, it was possible to predict that Governor Romero would move to defuse the issue by seeking accommodation with Rieckehoff and the PRNOC before the 1984 election campaign began in earnest. Not only was Rafael Hernández Colon, his PDP gubernatorial opponent, a staunch partisan of government support for an independent PRNOC, but so was Hernán Padilla within the governor's own party. It was becoming increasingly evident that Padilla would create a new party or a splinter movement of the NPP, announce for the governorship, and seek to capitalize on the Olympic issue. Thus, Romero would be forced to move first. This prediction has been amply confirmed by subsequent events, unknown to me until a return field visit in July 1983.[21]

Politics by Another Name

In the previous section of this paper, I show that the mutual entailing of sport and politics in Puerto Rico occurs at the level of social action as well as that of structure. Although relative peace currently reigns in this aspect of public life, new conflicts and alliances will continue to break out as long as Puerto Rico's political status remains unresolved and Olympic-style sport continues to be organized and valued as it now is. The games and rites of international sport do not merely "symbolically express" or "functionally reinforce" or "reflexively comment on" preexisting and "real" political structures and formations in Puerto Rico, they have helped to constitute these—they *are* these. Moreover, through the preponderant issue of the loss of independent international teams in the event of statehood, Olympic sport has moved from contributing to the constitution of the most important sociopolitical question facing Puerto Rico to playing potentially a significant role in its outcome.

Pragmatists will hasten to point out that even if the issue is as important to the Puerto Rican masses as the events analyzed in this paper indicate, the question of Puerto Rico's status will ultimately be decided in the U.S. Congress and not by Puerto Ricans. Quite aside from the ideological and cultural barriers to a congressional vote in favor of or authorizing statehood, there are material barriers that will doubtless carry more weight. Should Puerto Rico become a state, the U.S. House of Representatives would be faced with a choice of either a significant growth in size or else reapportionment. If the latter were chosen, Puerto Rico would instantly have a congressional delegation larger than those of almost half of the present states. Either choice would immediately dilute the power of a large number of present congressmen, making a vote for statehood for Puerto Rico unlikely. Moreover, statehood would mean an immediate increase in U.S. federal financial responsibilities to Puerto Rico, calculated in 1981 to be $720 million (U.S. General Accounting Office 1981:54–56, 120–125), further making unlikely such an authorizing vote for statehood, particularly in the present political and economic climate on the mainland.

These arguments are correct ones. But the fact remains that successive administrations in Washington, including the two most recent ones, have committed themselves to "self-determination" for the Puerto Rican people, by which is meant choice by plebiscite of one or another final option, either ratifying that which is offered by the U.S. Congress or answering its request for a binding expression of popular will on the island, thereafter to be ratified by Congress. Some believe that current international and domestic conditions on the island are indeed rapidly bringing the status question to a head; others believe that no end is really in sight, that in the face of its complexities the matter will continue to drag on as it has for decades. It is impossible to foresee which will be the case. The point here is that should matters come to a decision, a plebiscite will be held and the statehood option—whether one of those offered or one desired against those on the ballot—will be foreclosed in the minds of many Puerto Ricans in large part because of the effects on international sport.

The anthropological and political sociological literatures are increasingly marked by claims that symbolic forms and processes have active and constitutive, and not merely reactive and expressive, effects on dominant sociopolitical institutions conceived as agencies of the most material praxis. But concrete demonstrations of these theoretical claims are not yet as common. The scenario for a final resolution of the status question outlined above need not come about for the case to be made with respect to international sport and the dominant political formations and institutions in Puerto Rico, a case which illustrates why symbolic anthropologists ought never to turn away from "macro-" concerns.

Notes

Acknowledgments. Jeffrey Colón brought Puerto Rican sport to my attention and provided invaluable assistance in the field. Research was chiefly conducted in San Juan and rural southeastern Puerto Rico in autumn 1981 and in San Juan in July 1983. It was supported by the Puerto Rican National Olympic Committee, whose president, Germán Rieckehoff Sampayo, afforded me full independence in my inquiries and never attempted to influence my conclusions, with some of which he will doubtless disagree. I am also grateful to numerous consultants and to Dr. and Mrs. Ernesto Colón Yordán and Mrs. Irma Rieckehoff for their kind hospitality. Professor Nikos Nissiotis provided me with the opportunity to conduct supplementary interviews with IOC and Latin American NOC officials at the International Olympic Academy in Greece in 1982. Chandra Mukerji, Bennett Berger, J. David Greenstone, James Fernandez, Keith Basso, and Edward M. Bruner made helpful comments on an earlier version of this paper.

1. Partisans of this approach might well be sobered by recalling the parallel experience of symbolic interactionism in sociology. The labeling of that perspective as "microsociology" was concomitant with its isolation and encystment as an orphan tradition within general sociology. Only recently have practitioners of symbolic interactionism begun to fight their way back into the mainstream by seeking to join the study of small groups and transient situations with analyses of the principal institutions of public order (Gusfield 1981). The lesson for symbolic anthropology here ought to be clear: to the extent that it merits the rubric "microanthropology," it will risk ghettoization within general anthropology. To be sure, one may wish for a "high-level convergence toward the analysis of meaningful content by valid methods revealing logical structures" (Colby et al. 1981:440). But if this is accomplished by turning away from macroanthropological concern with dominant institutions, historical events, and cultural structures at the societal scale, symbolic anthropology will earn Roy Campbell's reproach (used by Gouldner 1973:19 against another target): "They use the snaffle and the curb, all right, but where's the bloody horse?"

2. The fundamental questions underlying the project of cultural anthropology—relativism versus universalism; the impact of culture on human nature; relations between material and logico-meaningful interests and necessities; the existence of "national characters"; the effects of increased knowledge of "the others" in a

plural world armed to the teeth—are the same questions millions of human beings pose for themselves, often in other terms and ways, to be sure, through Olympic sport (MacAloon 1981:261-269).

3. As numerous commentators on Puerto Rican cultural life have pointed out, even the most institutionally based public conflicts tend to be understood in personalistic terms by islanders. Puerto Ricans notably discuss *la pitada olímpica* and its post-1979 repetitions as a *mano a mano* combat between Romero and Rieckehoff. The fact that they are evenly matched helps to make the conflict so culturally marked and publicly fascinating. Both are lawyers and issue from the middle ranks of the professional class and from well-known political families. Romero's grandfather was Don Antonio Barceló, long the leader of the Union Party and later the Liberal Party, which Josefina Barceló, Romero's mother, led in her turn. Rieckehoff's father was a famous legislator from Vieques. The personal connections between the two men are deep. Antonio Barceló was Rieckehoff's godfather, and Rieckehoff represented Romero in the latter's divorce from his first wife.

Successful Puerto Rican politicians are rarely known for quiet subtlety, but Romero is perceived as even more forceful than most. His two most popular nicknames are "the Bull" and "the Horse." Yale-educated and presently married to an Anglo woman from the mainland, his commitment to wielding the power of his office for his cause is thoroughgoing. Rieckehoff was also educated on the mainland. His successful career as a lawyer brought him into contact with international sports arbitration and, together with his own athletic passion, led him into full-time organization and leadership of Puerto Rican amateur sports governing bodies. "Leadership" is too weak a word, however, in the Puerto Rican cultural understanding of things. Although Rieckehoff is at pains to put down such talk, many informants suggested what one San Juan worker asserted to me: "Don Germán *is* Puerto Rican Olympism." Indefatigable despite advanced years—he is older than Romero and that counts for additional *respeto* in traditionally patriarchal Puerto Rico—Rieckehoff has no popular animal nickname, though several informants referred to him spontaneously as "the Fox." His obvious skill at political infighting and the dignity and prestige accorded him on account of his age and international reputation do not generally detract from his success at being taken for a "man of the people," an obstinant servant of the Puerto Rican masses' desire for Olympic sport, with no source or apparatus of power beyond their allegiance and support. Not only does the Romero-Rieckehoff combat fit with the preferred Puerto Rican understanding of institutional and structural conflict, the "cultural text" created by their battles features a motif familiar in Hispanoamerican literature and social life: the aging and popular *don* against the powerful and robust *caudillo*. With the possible exception of a few sports heroes and media celebrities, Romero and Rieckehoff are said to be the most recognized faces in Puerto Rico.

4. "Before the Popular Party, political status was conceived as an *a priori* condition in order to bring about change. If you were for independence, you were for independence because in the abstract it was a good thing. The same for statehood. Then you made your economic and social arguments as a rationalization to tally with your *a priori* conception on political status. But our approach was different. The people of Puerto Rico have no shoes for their feet, and they haven't enough food, or schools; wages are miserable, working hours aren't long. *This* we

must solve first. We made the political status the servant of what kind of civilization the people of Puerto Rico wanted for themselves, instead of making the civilization subservient to the political status conceived *a priori*'' (Luis Muñoz Marin, cited in Wagenheim 1975:100).

5. In San Juan, for example, even the color of one's clothing or of the paint on one's auto or business may be read as evidence of one's political orientation— blue for statehood, red for autonomy, green for independence.

6. Election turnouts in Puerto Rico are among the highest in the world, almost always over 80 percent. The 1967 plebiscite was one of the few exceptions, a boycott having been declared by several parties.

7. Mintz (1966) has suggested that such nativistic concerns are largely the preoccupation of the urban middle classes, not the rural working classes. I am not competent to judge, but there are many indications of a change in the 18 years since Mintz wrote, brought on in part by the penetration of radio and television in the hinterlands. In any case, if his claim remains true it is fully consistent with Juan García Passalacqua's assertion that the preservation of international sports teams is more important than language as an assimilation issue among the working classes.

8. I say "unique" because of the particular *combination* of features and terms in Puerto Rico, not because of the absence of those features elsewhere. In much of Africa, Southeast Asia, and Latin America, international sport likewise is an idiom for building a sense of national identity, though these countries have for the most part gained their political sovereignty and the decolonization process is further advanced. In Eastern Europe, Olympic sport is a means of preserving ethnic nationalism in the face of Soviet military and political domination, though here it is a case—particularly in East Germany—of peoples with strong senses of developed national cultures who once had political sovereignty and subsequently lost it. For the "superpowers," not sovereignty but hegemony is the issue with respect to the external world, and minority group relations is the issue with respect to the internal domestic world. The variations in the intersection of the Olympic sports system with national and geopolitical systems are numerous, but they are also highly ordered.

9. No social historian has attended to the matter of how Puerto Rico gained her Olympic independence. The bare chronicle of events that is known begins with an act of extraordinary personal initiative and audacity. Julio Monagas, government administrator of parks and recreation and president of the national athletic federation, simply turned up uninvited in London with a band of nine athletes and somehow convinced the 1948 Olympic authorities to accept their inscription. There is a Puerto Rican folk history, told with bittersweet humor, that attributes this to the fact that the London officials did not know where or what Puerto Rico was, but finding that her representatives spoke Spanish, *just knew* that they could not be Americans.

The later decision to recognize an NOC in Puerto Rico despite its constitutional dependency on the United States—a decision in which Avery Brundage played a capital role—was not entirely without precedent in Olympic annals. The Bermuda Olympic Committee was recognized in 1936 and the Olympic Committee of Hong Kong in 1951, while both were still British dependencies. Yet the practice has been rare and runs counter to many other decisions made by the IOC in recent decades. Doubtless, the IOC's eagerness at the time to expand Latin American representation was a factor in Monagas's success, as was Puerto Rico's longstanding independent participation in the Central American and Caribbean Games, the oldest of the regional games patronized by the IOC.

Among the nine athletes in London in 1948 was a pole vaulter who would make the Olympic finals, José Barbosa Muñiz. Years later, he would become Monagas's successor as parks and recreation administrator in the Romero government. Until his resignation in 1982, Barbosa served Romero faithfully in battling Germán Rieckehoff, Monagas's successor as PRNOC president.

10. The attitude of official Washington is but one more of the complicated reflections and refractions here. President Reagan's recent "economic initiative" toward the region—from which Puerto Rico was excluded, appropriately so given her constitutional status and inappropriately so given her regional ties and domestic economic condition—is called the "Caribbean Basin initiative" and not the "Central American initiative." The eyes of the Reagan administration are drawn not to the great semicircular splash of blue on the map but to the island in its center, namely, Cuba. Cuba is very much on the minds of Puerto Ricans as well: for some as a fearsome threat, for others as a model to be emulated, and for still others as a more complicated and ambivalent object of contemplation and relations (Arana Soto 1963). Moreover, Puerto Ricans know that they are very much on the minds of Cuba (Bayo 1966; Estéfano Pisani 1967). Cuba takes the lead in pushing the status question of Puerto Rico before the Decolonization Commission of the United Nations and before the Conference of Nonaligned Nations.

11. The grand example at the 1979 Pan American Games was the divisive *pitada olímpica,* but another cause célèbre united·all Puerto Ricans against a U.S. coach and what he represented in mainland values and culture. Basketball coach Bobby Knight, dissatisfied with practice arrangements for his team, attempted to make unscheduled use of a gymnasium, interferring in a most obnoxious way with the practice of another team. This led to an altercation with a policeman and Knight's arrest for assault. Fleeing Puerto Rico after the competition, Knight took refuge behind the absence of clear extradition arrangements between Puerto Rico and the United States. After being convicted in absentia and declared persona non grata on the island, Knight made chauvinistic and racist statements about Puerto Rico and Puerto Ricans. In 1982, to the absolute shock and revulsion of Puerto Ricans and many Olympic leaders around the world, Knight was named national coach for the U.S. men's basketball team for the 1984 Olympics in Los Angeles. In the name of the Puerto Rican people, Governor Romero and all island sports leaders have sent numerous letters to the U.S. Olympic Committee vigorously protesting the appointment of this "ugly American." It appears, however, that American desire for victory—Knight is a highly successful college coach—will take precedence, and this acute insult to the Olympic spirit will indeed be delivered.

12. Nor is Rieckehoff merely a member of what the founder of the modern Olympics characterized as the IOC's "third circle . . . a facade of more or less useful men whose presence satisfied national pretensions" (Coubertin, in MacAloon 1981:180). Rieckehoff is exceedingly active, influential with his colleagues and a member of important working commissions of the IOC and the association of NOCs. His struggles with his government during and after *la pitada olímpica* redound to his credit in the IOC, illustrated by its award of the Olympic Cup to the

PRNOC, and he has gained equal respect among U.S. and Latin American officials. All this is known to contribute to the practical benefit of Puerto Rican sport and, in turn, to the Puerto Rican valuation of the Olympics.

13. Pareto (1968:67–68, 82) argues for the association of declining or disfranchised elites with ideals of generic humankindness. With certain important corrections, this theory is born out in the early history of the Olympic Movement (MacAloon 1981:129, 314). There may be an equivalent tendency among disfranchised and recently decolonized peoples, a feature less widely appreciated than other aspects of the colonial *mentalité* anatomized by Frantz Fanon and others. One is repeatedly struck by the refusal of many Puerto Ricans to regard official Olympic ideology (MacAloon 1981:256–275; 1984) as elitist or hegemonic cant, and many Olympic researchers share among themselves the suspicion that it is in the Third World generally that orthodox Olympism is most widely accepted at face value.

14. This is one illustration of why it is essential to distinguish carefully among the various genres in the Olympic performance system (MacAloon 1984).

15. It is a fundamental principle of processual symbolic analysis (Turner 1974) that individual symbols and symbol sets cannot be analyzed in isolation from their relations with other symbols in the action sequences of ritual wholes. Elsewhere I so analyze the Olympic opening, victory, and closing rites from which the rituals of the Pan American and other regional games are copied and show their semantic relations with the games of these Games (MacAloon 1982a, 1984). In any case, save for general and vague claims about "tradition" and "disruptions of the whole ceremony," the actual disputes over the 1979 Pan American opening rites explicitly concerned themselves with the symbols of flag, anthem, and head of state's role taken in isolation from the rest of the ritual process.

16. In recent Pan American Games, for example, the raising of national flags on masts to fly over the main stadium for the duration of the games may be ritualized, whereas this is not done in the Olympics. In the Olympics, a ceremonial flag raising and anthem playing accompanies the entry of each team into the Olympic Village prior to the opening of the games. Not all regional games have separate athletes' villages, and these ceremonies may or may not be duplicated.

17. The accounts here of the disputes of the 1966 Central American and Caribbean Games and the 1979 Pan American Games are reconstructed from interviews with key participants and eyewitnesses and from the San Juan newspapers, notably *El Mundo* and the *San Juan Star*.

18. Lotteries, which are one very common means of supporting amateur sport throughout the world, are mechanisms at once private and voluntary—the monies are raised from the optional purchase of tickets by private citizens—and public and governmental—the state owning the lottery and the legislature controlling the dispersal of funds through government agencies. In Puerto Rico, as elsewhere, this mixed character of the financial means replicates the mixed character of the sociopolitical means exercised in favor of national and international sport, and it paves the way for disputes over the appropriate governance and application of such funds.

19. To be sure, many of the demonstrators were provisioned with identical plastic whistles and small Puerto Rican flags, but this in itself proves nothing. NPP partisans are not alone in claiming a PSP role in organizing *la pitada,* but no clear evidence has ever appeared and, in any case, the number of demonstrators was far larger than any one organized group.

20. An additional $90,000 came from corporations, notably Schaefer Beer, the first significant business support for Olympic-style sport in Puerto Rico. Such support grows today and is an important factor in assuring the PRNOC that it can declare full financial independence from the government at any time it needs to do so.

21. On 2 September 1982, the newspapers carried a photograph of Romero and Rieckehoff shaking hands at a "peace party" arranged by Junior Cruz, NPP mayor of Guaynabo and manager of the women's softball team that had won the gold medal in Havana. As taken aback as Puerto Ricans were by the photograph, it was a bare hint of things to come.

In late October, Rieckehoff was privately approached by emissaries from La Fortaleza, wishing to know how he would react to the dismissal of José Barbosa as secretary of sport and recreation and his replacement by Pedro Barez Rosario, then secretary of labor and human resources and one of Romero's most respected ministers. While demurring that the governor's cabinet appointments were no business of his, Rieckehoff approved both developments and promised to let it be known that he would be happy to see Barez's unanimous confirmation by the legislature. As negotiations continued behind the scenes, the press campaign against the government's sports policies continued—Barbosa was called "public enemy no. 1 of sport" in *El Reportero* and several newspapers called for an investigation of alleged improprieties in the disposition of funds appropriated but not used for the Central American and Caribbean Games. Hernán Padilla came out strongly for renewed government funding for the 1983 Pan American and 1984 Olympic teams just as the Schaefer corporation delivered a $103,000 check for that purpose to the PRNOC, derived from a special profit-sharing campaign that sold 25 million bottles and cans of beer.

On 9 November, word of Barbosa's impending resignation was leaked to the newspapers. On 23 November, a carefully arranged meeting that the newspapers would hail in banner headlines as "an historic peace pact" was held at La Fortaleza. After breakfasting with 42 PRNOC members and officials, the governor stood side by side with Rieckehoff as he announced his cabinet changes to a jammed press conference. During his statement, Romero remarked that it was time "to start with a clean slate" and that "the Olympic Committee would not change, so we had to change," extraordinary comments from a man who had waged a 16-year campaign against PRNOC policies and powerful testimony to the influence of international sport on electoral politics.

On 11 December, Barez was unanimously confirmed, and some days later he indicated his independence by announcing that he favored the exclusive use of the Puerto Rican flag and anthem in international games. On the day of Barez's swearing in, a new compromise proposal for state assistance to Olympic sport was revealed. Government appropriations earmarked for the PRNOC and the national federations would be administered by a commission of six members, three chosen by La Fortaleza and three by the PRNOC. Thus, Romero could protect his principle that public funds should not pass directly to a private body and Rieckehoff could maintain that the PRNOC was not accepting monies with any political strings attached. On 28 January 1983, the bill was presented by PDP senator Antonio Fas Alzamora, and it passed easily on 16 February.

In early March, however, Romero backed out of the compromise. Perhaps feeling that the sacrifice of Barbosa, the popular respect for Barez, and the almost euphoric public attitude toward the new relationship between the government and the PRNOC had sufficiently strengthened his political standing on the issue of international sport, Romero returned to his previous position that public funds could be channeled solely through the Sport and Recreation Department and only to the federations, not to Rieckehoff and the PRNOC. A last-ditch attempt at compromise through amending the language of the bill failed, and the governor vetoed it.

Word reached Rieckehoff on 27 March, while he was attending an IOC meeting in New Delhi. He raced home to find public opinion perfectly enflamed against the governor, Barez brooding in private, and PRNOC colleagues ready to do battle. To Rieckehoff, "the honeymoon was over"; but, having come to regret his acceptance of the idea of a commission, he was not entirely displeased with events. Once again Romero had seriously miscalculated and simply undone himself. The pressure on the governor grew overwhelmingly in the following week. Rumors of Barez's resignation swept the capital, the PRNOC publicly expressed its support for its president, and Rieckehoff announced that he was willing to launch *la Gran Cruzada Olímpica* all over again. On 6 April, the governor's representatives called on Rieckehoff once again, and the following day an accord on a new bill was reached and initialed by Barez, Rieckehoff, and Romero's aide Virgilio Ramos. The new J.R. 2203 provided $500,000 each for the 1983 Pan American and 1984 Olympic teams, $650,000 for the 1986 Central American and Caribbean team, and $900,000 per year for four years for the general sports development programs. The commission was abolished and, while the secretary of sport and recreation would "generally oversee" their use, the monies would be delivered directly to the PRNOC for their administration. The bill was announced in the press on 8 April, passed within ten days, and signed by the governor on 28 April. Public opinion and political circumstances, rooted in the importance of international sport as a cultural system in Puerto Rico, had delivered a final victory to the PRNOC. "We have gone from the ridiculous to the sublime," says Rieckehoff of the entire period from 1976 to 1983.

The continuing effects of these events on the 1984 electoral campaign remain to be seen. Romero's final acquiescence did not fully restore the new mood at the beginning of 1983, broken by his sudden *volte face* in March. On 13 June, Pedro Barez announced his resignation and the post of secretary of sport and recreation remains unfilled at this writing (September 1983). This nagging embarrassment and reminder to the voters may be compromising subsequent efforts by the governor to present himself to them as an ally of Olympic sport, such as his support of plans for a national training center, pushed by Rieckehoff in the new atmosphere of political and fiscal plenty. Hernán Padilla, through such efforts as personally gaining for San Juan the World Masters Games, continues to present himself, in contrast to Romero, as the true political friend of international Puerto Rican sport. In July 1983, Padilla announced his defection from the NPP to form a new party to contest for the governorship. This split in the NPP cannot but assist the electoral fortunes of Hernández Colon and the PDP in the 1984 elections and will be of long-term importance in Puerto Rican political history.

References Cited

Anderson, Robert W.
  1965   Party Politics in Puerto Rico. Stanford: Stanford University Press.

Appadurai, Arjun
  1981 Worship and Conflict under Colonial Rule. Cambridge: Cambridge University Press.
Arana Soto, Salvador
  1963 Cuba y Puerto Rico. San Juan: Luis D. Paret.
Bayo, Arundo
  1966 Puerto Rico. Havana: Casa de las Americas.
Brameld, Theodore
  1959 The Remaking of a Culture. New York: Harper Brothers.
Bravo, Enrique
  1975 Biliografía Puertorriqueña Selecta Anotada. New York: Columbia University Urban Center.
Colby, Benjamin N., James W. Fernandez, and David B. Kronenfeld
  1981 Toward a Convergence of Cognitive and Symbolic Anthropology. American Ethnologist 8:422–449.
Cruz, Monclava, Lidio
  1966 The Puerto Rican Political Movement in the Nineteenth Century. *In* Selected Background Studies. United States–Puerto Rico Status Commission, pp. 1–49. Washington, DC: U.S. Government Printing Office.
DaMatta, Roberto
  1984 Carnival in Multiple Planes. *In* Rite, Drama, Festival, Spectacle: Rehearsals toward a Theory of Cultural Performance. J. MacAloon, ed. pp. 208–240. Philadelphia: Institute for the Study of Human Issues Press.
Dexter, Lewis A.
  1949 A Dialogue on the Social Psychology of Colonialism and on Certain Puerto Rican Professional Personality Patterns. Human Relations 2:49–64.
Epstein, Erwin H.
  1967 National Identity and the Language Issue in Puerto Rico. Comparative Education Review 11:133–143.
Estéfano Pisani, Miguel A. d'
  1967 Puerto Rico: Análisis de un Plebiscito. Havana: Tricontinental.
Figueroa Mercado, Loida
  1963 Puerto Rico—Cultura y Personalidad. Revista de Ciencias Sociales 7: 93–103.
García Passalacqua, Juan M.
  1962 The Legality of Associated Statehood of Puerto Rico. Inter-American Law Review 4:287–315.
  1969 My Self! They Take Away My Self! Boletín de la Academia de Artes y Ciencias de Puerto Rico 5:337–345.
  1970 La Crisis Política en Puerto Rico. Río Piedras: Editorial Edil.
  1974 La Alternativa Liberal: Una Visión Histórica de Puerto Rico. San Juan: Editorial Universitaria.
Geertz, Clifford
  1972 Deep Play: Notes on the Balinese Cockfight. Daedalus 101:1–38.
  1980 Negara: The Theater State in Nineteenth Century Bali. Princeton: Princeton University Press.
Gouldner, Alvin
  1973 For Sociology: Renewal and Criticism in Sociology Today. New York: Basic Books.

Granda, Germán de
  1969 Transculturación e Interferencia Lingüística en el Puerto Rico Contem-
      poráneo. San Juan: Ateneo Puertorriqueño.
Gusfield, Joseph
  1981 The Culture of Public Problems: Drunk Driving and the Symbolic Order.
      Chicago: University of Chicago Press.
Hunter, Robert J.
  1966 Historical Survey of the Puerto Rico Status Question, 1898–1965. *In*
      Selected Background Studies. United States–Puerto Rico Status Commission,
      pp. 50–146. Washington, DC: U.S. Government Printing Office.
Huyke, Emilio
  1969 Los Deportes en Puerto Rico. Sharon, CT: Troutman Press.
Institute of Caribbean Studies, University of Puerto Rico
  1966 The Netherlands, French, and British Areas of the Caribbean. *In* Selected
      Background Studies. United States–Puerto Rico Status Commission, pp.
      554–688. Washington, DC: U.S. Government Printing Office.
International Olympic Committee
  1981 Encyclopedia of NOCs, Vol. 3. Lausanne.
Lauria, Anthony
  1964 *Respeto, Relajo,* and Interpersonal Relations in Puerto Rico. Anthropo-
      logical Quarterly 37:53–68.
MacAloon, John J.
  1981 This Great Symbol: Pierre de Coubertin and the Origins of the Modern
      Olympic Games. Chicago: University of Chicago Press.
  1982a Double Visions: Olympic Games and American Culture. Kenyon Review
      (NS) 4:99–112.
  1982b Sociation and Sociability in Political Celebrations. *In* Celebration:
      Studies in Ritual and Festivity. V. Turner, ed. pp. 255–271. Washington, DC:
      Smithsonian Institution Press.
  1984 Olympic Games and the Theory of Spectacle in Complex Societies. *In*
      Rite, Drama, Festival, Spectacle: Rehearsals toward a Theory of Cultural Per-
      formance. J. MacAloon, ed. pp. 241–280. Philadelphia: Institute for the Study
      of Human Issues Press.
Maldonado Denis, Manuel
  1963 Política y Cultura Puertorriqueña. Revista de Ciencias Sociales 7:141–148.
Manning, Frank E.
  1981 Celebrating Cricket: The Symbolic Construction of Caribbean Politics.
      American Ethnologist 8:616–632.
Marqués, René
  1976 The Docile Puerto Rican. Barbara Bockus Aponte, transl. Philadelphia:
      Temple University Press.
Mintz, Sidney W.
  1966 Puerto Rico: An Essay in the Definition of a National Culture. *In* Selected
      Background Studies. United States–Puerto Rico Status Commission, pp.
      339–434. Washington, DC: U.S. Government Printing Office.
Ocampo, Tarsicio, ed.
  1964 Puerto Rico: Idioma Escolar 1962–65, Reacciones de Prensa. Cuernavaca:
      Centro Intercultural de Documentación.

Pareto, Vilfredo
1968   The Rise and Fall of Elites. Totowa, NJ: Bedminster Press.
Pedreira, Antonio S.
1946   Insularismo. San Juan: Biblioteca de Autores Puertorriqueños.
Reuter, Edward B.
1946   Culture Contacts in Puerto Rico. American Journal of Sociology 52:91–101.
Rosario, Rubén del
1971   La Lingua de Puerto Rico. Río Piedras: Editorial Cultura.
Sahlins, Marshall
1981   Historical Metaphors and Mythic Realities. Ann Arbor: University of Michigan Press.
Serrano Geyls, Raul, and Carlos I. Gorrin Peralta
1980   Puerto Rico y la Estadidad. Revista del Colegio de Abogados de Puerto Rico 522:1–28.
Steward, Julian H., ed.
1956   The People of Puerto Rico. Urbana: University of Illinois Press.
Todd, Robert H.
1967   Genesis de la Bandera Puertorriqueña. Madrid: Ediciones Iberoamericanas.
Turner, Victor W.
1957   Schism and Continuity in an African Society. Manchester: Manchester University Press.
1974   Dramas, Fields, and Metaphors. Ithaca: Cornell University Press.
1984   Liminality and the Performative Genres. *In* Rite, Drama, Festival, Spectacle: Rehearsals toward a Theory of Cultural Performance. J. MacAloon, ed. pp. 19–41. Philadelphia: Institute for the Study of Human Issues Press.
U.S. General Accounting Office
1981   Puerto Rico's Political Future. Washington, DC: U.S. Government Printing Office.
United States-Puerto Rico Status Commission
1966a   Status of Puerto Rico: Hearings. 3 vols. Washington, DC: U.S. Government Printing Office.
1966b   Status of Puerto Rico: Selected Background Studies. Washington, DC: U.S. Government Printing Office.
Urrutia Aparicio, Carlos
1954   Puerto Rico, América, y las Naciones Unidas. Mexico City.
Vientos Gastón, Nilita
1964   The Identity Problem. San Juan Review 1:26–42.
Vivó, Paquita
1973   The Puerto Ricans: An Annotated Bibliography. New York: Bowker.
Wagenheim, Kal
1975   Puerto Rico. New York: Holt, Rinehart and Winston.

Conclusion:
Further Thoughts on
the Realm of Folly

Edmund Leach
Cambridge University

If the fireworks in James Boon's contribution had been capable of melting the snow in Ithaca and New York City so that he could have been present, perhaps our discussions would have followed rather different lines.[1] We had assembled in Baton Rouge to talk about Folly and we mistakenly tried to be serious. To appreciate the fireworks, we should have had to attend Mardi Gras in New Orleans at the beginning of our conference rather than at the end, for only then could we have seen that the freewheeling jumble of verbal metaphors, in which there is no unity of time or space or rational linearity, which characterizes Boon's paper provides a very accurate transformation into words of what, in Mardi Gras, is a chaos of visual images, noise, and movement.

Even without Boon's presence, we ought to have been more responsive to the basic paradoxes that were built into our original endeavor. Although the leitmotif of Carnival provided at least one of the original foci for our whole enterprise, the eventual collective title of the symposium does not make this apparent; only about half of the final papers could be said to have even a remote connection with this theme. Indeed, as I said at the time, the papers which, on first delivery, I myself found most immediately stimulating (Becker, Basso, Ohnuki-Tierney) were not, on the face of it, carnivalesque at all. But that, too, was perhaps an error of appreciation, for Folly is all-embracing.

The comprehensiveness of Folly is tied in with the fact that the behaviors we thus demean come very close to those we might otherwise be inclined to categorize as religious. And as every anthropologist must know, whenever we attempt to delve into the semantics of "religious" action, it almost always turns out that whatever is the case is also just the opposite: Durga, the preserver of all things, often equates with Kali, the goddess of death; Mahisasura, the Lord of the Demons, against whom the goddess wages eternal war, is only another form of her husband Siva; in myth, Ganesha loses one of his tusks in valiant defense of the door of his parents' room, but in vernacular Hindu thinking he is a Janus figure, the remover of obstacles rather than the guardian of thresholds.

And so it is with Carnival. "Mardi Gras" (fat Tuesday) is a feast to end all feasts; but just change a vowel and move the clock past midnight and we enter a fast to end all fasts. Folk etymology which is doubtless quite false reverses the emphasis: Carnival is glossed as *carne vale* ("farewell to meat"). By contrast, although the English Shrove Tuesday should be a day to be shriven and confess your sins, including those of gluttony, it still remains, even after four centuries of Protestant sobriety, "pancake day" among Folly-inspired schoolchildren.

Although several participants borrowed their jargon from Derrida and "poststructuralism," rather than from Lévi-Strauss, all this is a very classical type of structuralist argument. Any structure of thought is made up of elements (distinctive features), each of which consists of a relationship between a category "+A" and its binary opposite "−A." Reverse all the signs and the total structure remains the same as before, even though it may now appear upside-down or back-to-front. But at the margin, where structure S overlaps with its mirror image, structure ∼S, all values are arbitrarily assigned. Although this very abstract schema fits very nicely with much that was said, I do not think that we were just repeating this old-hat set of ideas all over again.

For the moment, then, let us forget about Carnival and role inversions and consider our formal and very odd collective title: "Text, Play, and Story: The Construction and Reconstruction of Self and Society." I presume that it started out as a kind of omnibus that might be made to include under a single rubric papers about narrative, about theater, and even about Carnival, if any happened to be available. It seems odd, however, in light of the actual contributions, that not only does this title make no mention of either Carnival or processions, but it also does not mention *landscape,* a prominent feature. What I myself learned from our symposium above all was that the long-recognized relational link between *stories (myths)* and *rituals,* which anthropologists have talked about ever since the days of Robertson Smith, contains a middle term we can call *place.* I will not try to reproduce here what others said about it; instead, let me formulate a general thesis in my own terms.

Spoken language is ephemeral. The details of an utterance have vanished, even as an impression on the memory, almost as soon as it is uttered. Stories and plays are devices for postponing this rapid evanescence of the spoken word. The text of a repeated story is seldom close to any possible conversational spoken utterance, but it can survive over time. If a story text is then linked with a regularly repeated dramatic performance, story and performance are mutually supportive. Likewise, if a story becomes "embedded" in features of the landscape, story and place are mutually supportive.

What Keith Basso and Edward M. Bruner and Phyllis Gorfain, in particular, have to say on these themes seems to me very thought-provoking. It is not just that "places" serve to remind us of the stories that are associated with them; in certain respects, the places only exist (in the sense that they can be identified by name) *because* they have stories associated with them. But when once they have acquired this story-based existence, the landscape itself acquires the power of "telling the story." This is not just a peculiarity of rock faces among the Apache or skillfully misinterpreted archaeological evidence in Israel. It is a very general, perhaps universal, phenomenon and one that deserves our attention.

An example from my own country illustrates my point. It is recorded in contemporary documents that the Magna Carta was signed at a locality on the banks of the river Thames near Windsor called Runnymede, but the tourists' Runnymede that now bears a memorial of this event is certainly a recently invented fiction. Even so, to all who now gather there, the place tells a story about the origins of parliamentary institutions, a story which, in historical reality, is just as fictitious as the place.

It might even be argued that a story can only acquire value of a mythical kind (in Malinowski's sense of the term—that is to say, a story can only serve as a charter for social action or moral injunction) if it is firmly located in a place on the map. Without this kind of anchoring into concrete details of the landscape, the fictional nature of stories becomes obvious. They may still have value but of quite a different kind. More generally, it is only when stories have a material reference that we ourselves can see and touch that we are prepared to suspend our faculty for disbelief. The important role played by material relics in religious systems of all kinds serves to reinforce my point.

I am reminded here of a theme from Vico. Vico is all things to all men, and no one in his senses would want to claim that he knew what any particular passage in *The New Science* "really means." But there are places where Vico appears to argue that human beings must have expressed their feelings as "poets" before they conducted arguments as rational men, and further that this primeval poetic expression entailed the use of material nature as a system of signs which was prior to the use of spoken language. Hence, "writing" was historically antecedent to "speaking." Of course, in detail, such fantasies, despite their "de-constructionist" flavor, are absurd, but they do contain an important truth: Language of the ordinary kind, whether spoken or written, does not exist in a field by itself. The relations *within* language, which linguists are only able to discuss after they have devised an appropriate set of linguistic categories, such as phonology, lexicon, or grammar and syntax, do not form a closed system. They are, as A. L. Becker was trying to tell us, only a special kind of "translation" of other sets of relationships existing out there in the world of material things. Human beings can manipulate these relationships in many other ways besides treating them as metaphors for verbal text.

References to tourists at Runnymede, and religious relics, provide me with a signpost for the next stage of my journey. Twentieth-century tourists are the equivalent of medieval pilgrims. They assemble at special places and on set occasions to hear the stories that these places, with their relics from the past, their staged processions, and other kinds of dramatic performance, have to tell. But if the tourists do not know the details of the landscape, as most of them do not, how much are they able to hear and to understand?

My own reaction to Mardi Gras is that the "parades" and the floats with their costumed "krewes" are of rather minor relevance; an excuse, as it were, to bring the crowds together to gawk and cheer and dress up and play the role-inverted games that Folly dictates on such occasions. The core of the matter is the behavior of the crowds, the tourist-pilgrims themselves. This is an aspect of Carnival that the papers contributed to our symposium hardly broach, yet it is a general feature of Carnival and not just something special to Mardi Gras in New Orleans. In a festival context, whether primarily religious or primarily secular, there are always two kinds of event going on simultaneously and in parallel. One example from the other side of the world is the annual Kataragama festival in southern Sri Lanka, where the assembled pilgrims number hundreds of thousands. The formal religious processions (*perahera,* "perambulation"), with bands of costumed drummers and troupes of dancers and sacred relics borne on the backs of elephants, are entirely in the "Carnival parade" tradition. A complex, permanent bureaucracy, one that is part lay and part priestly, must be maintained to ensure that everything takes place at the appropriate time, in the appropriate place, and in the appropriate manner. But, besides all this, there is the behavior of the crowds, a mixture of the secular-commercial and the religious-ecstatic and one that in detail is quite unpredictable.

Those who have tried to describe the Kataragama festival (or any of the other processional festivals occurring in Sri Lanka) nearly always concentrate on the formal, orderly, predictable part of the total event. Yet, after all, it is the pilgrims who matter. Without them, the processions would constitute a nonevent. It is because the pilgrims gain satisfaction from what they see and hear, and from what they themselves perform, that such affairs are perpetuated. For me, this is a surprising but very pleasing feature of Mardi Gras in New Orleans: the tourist-pilgrims (ourselves included) very quickly become participants rather than spectators. The distinction is important and we might well have given it more attention.

Perhaps we should draw the same kind of inference from Renato Rosaldo's intensely personal contribution. The standard convention, both in social and cultural anthropology, has been that the anthropologist's task is to study social institutions and the roles that individuals (considered as *social persons,* in Radcliffe-Brown's sense of the term) play in relation to such institutions, rather than the feelings that individuals experience in the course of such role playing. This certainly has been my own attitude. Indeed, I have gone further to argue with vigor that the individual's feelings are inaccessible to the anthropological investigator (or to any other kind of investigator). I reject altogether Radcliffe-Brown's view that participation in a ritual in "the prescribed manner" serves to generate in the participant the "proper sentiment."

I am not, of course, arguing that the participant in a ritual performance, such as a funeral, has no personal feelings with regard to what is going on. But it seems to me quite impossible to generalize about what these feelings are. Indeed, I would have thought it very clear that the institutionalized procedures that follow a death—corpse disposal, mourning, second funeral, "headhunt," or whatever—are not constructed or maintained in such a way as to benefit either materially or emotionally those most concerned (i.e., the close relatives or affines of the deceased). On the contrary, as often as not, society, through these cultural arrangements, seems to persecute the mourners as an act of vengeance on behalf of the deceased.

Rosaldo, however, seems to be arguing in quite a contrary sense. In the circumstances of traditional Ilongot culture, headhunting provided an emotional catharsis, first for frustrated bachelors in their youth and then for mourning adults in their seniority. The implication seems to be that it was *because* Ilongot headhunting provided in this way a legitimate vehicle for the expression of rage and pent-up emotion that it survived as it did. When anthropologists of the era of J. H. Hutton sought to explain the phenomenon of headhunting in terms of metaphysical ideology (e.g., Naga headhunters were supposed to be seeking crop fertilizing "soul stuff"!), they were, among other things, asserting that the headhunters in question were endowed with a primitive mentality completely unlike that of modern Western man. Rosaldo, through his moving account of his own personal experience, is saying just the opposite. His personal grief in the face of bereavement brought him to a better understanding of the sense of rage without which Ilongot headhunting could never have persisted at all. Ilongot emotions are like "our" emotions—they are triggered by similar circumstances, and it is only the form of manifestation that is peculiar to Ilongot culture.

This is a tightrope that anthropologists must negotiate with care. We can surely agree, however, that in any "ritual" situation there are different categories of "performers" and that, overall, it is those whom we are liable to categorize as only marginally participant—namely, "the spectators"—who are the most significant. Unless there is some general sense in which these spectators derive individual satisfaction from what they see and hear, then the ritual in question will rather quickly cease to be a viable, ongoing cultural institution.

It is time that I return to the elaborations of our symposium's global title. We are anthropologists, not literary critics. Neither are we child psychologists. Brian Sutton-Smith's contribution to this proceedings volume is quite different from the paper he delivered in Baton Rouge, but from a professional point of view I can make no contact with either. The stories that interest me are repetitive and in some degree "traditional"; I am not concerned with the one-off inventions of children struggling to gain control of syntax or learning to imitate models that meet with the approval of their elders. But I must emphasize that for the purposes of our symposium, the linear, verbal mode of telling a story was not privileged.

What I mean by this is that when "text" carries its ordinary meaning of a sequence of written words, we tend to assume first that the whole "story" of the text is embedded in those words, and further that the "events" in the story, however delimited, all happen sequentially. Until very recently, we would also have assumed that the "meaning" of such a text was something that had been put there "intentionally" by the "author" and that our task as "readers of the text" was to discover what that author's meaning might have been.

Our usage at the symposium was very different from this. We were inclined to adopt from Derrida et al. the notion that text is text and that the author's intentions are irrelevant. The reader's "self" can (and does) operate on the text in such a way that it yields a meaning that is personal to himself/herself.

I do not think we had too much difficulty in dispensing with the author in this way. After all, most cultural materials, whether they have a verbal or dramatic or architectural form, reach us from an anonymous past. If myth is capable of conveying a message to the listener, it is not a message that derives from any individual author. We were much less certain, however, of the degree to which each individual can "legitimately" interpret a body of cultural materials in his/her own private fashion. Is there really no limit to the variety of interpretations that may be placed on a single body of text? Alternatively, if there is such a limit, how can it be specified?

We must all be well aware of the difficulties here. There are thousands of different Christian sects, and most of them accept the sacred authenticity of exactly the same body of biblical text. But they differ from each other in their interpretation of particular details of these texts. Yet the adherents of each particular sect find their common identity in the certain fact that they, and they alone, know the "correct" interpretation of the text. What, then, is the status of any particular anthropologist's interpretation of any particular text, especially in cases where the text has plainly been designed to glorify Folly?

A more telling peculiarity of our global title is that we were concerned at least as much with texts expressed (or expressable) in dramatic performance as in sequences of words. For some of the participants, the key question was not a matter of how free is the individual to interpret such dramatic texts in any way he/she chooses, but how does the drama, as a cultural phenomenon, impose its own "interpretation" on the psyche of the participating individual.

This is tricky country and seems to border on the mystical, though the problem seems to be "real." If, as I suggest here, we feel from first-hand experience that in such performances a distinction must be drawn between being a spectator and being a participant, then we are surely assuming that the drama can, in appropriate circumstances, "reconstruct the self." Whether it also "reconstructs society" is a different question which, personally, I hardly understand.

More important than any of this is the fact that in dramatic (as distinct from verbal) text, there is no automatic constraint of linearity. Many things are going on simultaneously. The "message," if there is one, is somehow embedded in the collective jumble rather than in any particular linear sequence. The fact that the participating self is able to pick up some kind of message despite the disorder of space and time must tie in with the fact that, whereas in reading an ordinary written text we employ one sense only, that of sight, when we participate in a festival we are employing all our senses to apprehend the many things that are going on at once: we see, hear, touch, taste, and smell. Although we can experience the result, we cannot describe it in words. Perhaps this is why we find that in all parts of the world, manifestations of Folly and religious participation regularly include processions. Maybe we are alarmed when we must use all our senses simultaneously. Linearity suggests the rationality of ordered speech. We feel we can "understand" a procession even if the chaos of the total experience escapes conscious rationalization.

Even anthropologists are not immune from such optimism. James Fernandez's paper about a Carnival-like festival in Asturias is quite honest about the confusing mass of performances that all go on at the same time. Yet, he makes his analysis of the imagery of a particular linear procession, "the folklore parade," serve as model for his interpretation of the whole. By contrast, DaMatta's paper on Carnaval in Brazil carefully avoids direct reference to the linear processions which are, for the casual outside spectator, the most obvious characteristic of the performances. Instead, he writes as a participant-observer, describing what goes on in the private-public Carnaval balls. Here again, when it comes to the point, he endeavors to make sense of the timeless chaotic confusion of the dance floor by declaring that it is symbolic of *street* behavior. And the street, whatever way you look at it, is necessarily linear in both space and time.

My comments here are not intended as criticism; quite the contrary.

As academics engaged in discourse, we are constrained by the limitations of ordered speech; like drowning men, we are bound to cling to linearity as the only available life raft. All I am saying is that we must remember that the order thus revealed is man-made, not a true construction of the goddess Folly. It is an outsider's comment, not an insider's experience.

This clearly applies to a number of other papers in this proceedings volume. Handelman's highly sophisticated analysis of Newfoundland mumming is likely to be accepted by some and rejected by others, but what is quite clear is that it is an analysis of a culturally "other" institution by an outsider anthropologist. No Newfoundlander participant could possibly understand what Handelman is talking about. Whether that is a serious objection is a matter of personal viewpoint. One thing that is evident, however, is that the process of analysis has served to destroy the Festival of Folly which, from the local point of view, was quite certainly the occasion for the whole enterprise.

There is yet another point that I should like to make about our global title. It seems odd that no one, as I recall, made any explicit reference to the ambiguities of the word "play," though we were in fact using the concept in a variety of different senses, such as: (1) spontaneous fantasy generated either by children or by adults; (2) formal fantasy such as occurs in drama or traditional mythology; and (3) play as competitive contests, such as in football matches or the Olympic Games. Mind you, such categories overlap. For example, although most of the scenes depicted in DaMatta's picture book *Universo do Carnival: Imagens e Reflexoes* (1981) are wildly chaotic and seemingly spontaneous (as well as obscene), the Carnaval proceedings in Rio de Janeiro also include formalized parades with hand-drawn floats and elaborately costumed teams of dancers. To an outsider, these parades all look very much alike; and since each is given a named theme, they must rate as "plays" in the dramatic, formal sense. Unlike the equivalents in New Orleans, the performances of the dancers give an impression of spontaneity. To that extent they are "play" in the children's fantasy sense. Yet, in fact, the gaiety here is contrived. The "spontaneity" of the dance crews is carefully rehearsed and the different Samba Schools that organize the parades are in almost lethal competition.

Much the same applies to Fernandez's Asturias paper. The background of the buffoonery of the "folklore parade," which mixes children's play with adult drama, is deadly serious—an international kayak race, "play" in the competitive games sense. All this ties in with John MacAloon's stress on the paradox that institutions such as the modern Olympic Games, which formally symbolize the peaceful unity of all mankind through the medium of "play," have become occasions for exhibiting the most primitive forms of competitive nationalism. In Folly, as in Religion, whatever is the case is also just the opposite, which is what I say right at the beginning of this essay.

So, having gone around the moon, I had better stop. I have not taken our central theme too seriously, but that is my basic point. My plea is that as academic anthropologists we must be alert to the constraints imposed on us by the culture of Academia, but we do not have to conform. Indeed, if we are too serious about what is palpably foolish, we shall only make fools of ourselves. Helen Schwartzman concludes her paper with the remark, "Perhaps the most important aspect of the stories (and meetings) . . . is that they provide individuals with something to do in a system where everyone is unclear about what it is they should be doing. . . ." That account of the goings-on in a mental hospital—where Folly is likely to be in charge in any case—seems to be quite a good description of some of the contributions to this proceedings volume, including my own. But we need not feel ashamed. Nor should we hesitate to recognize the most preposterous cross-cultural analogies in situations where Folly reveals precisely that which Reason conceals.

In medieval Spain, Santiago (St. James) was the patron saint of warrior knights. In a paper by Ginger Farrer that was circulated to symposium participants in advance but was not presented, we are told of how in present-day New Mexico a Spanish Catholic priest, Fr. Roca, has made a shrine to Santiago the locale for a much-revised version of a "traditional" annual festival. It seems clear that even though Santiago has no part to play in the tourist-oriented entertainment that goes on outside on the occasion of his feast day, it is, in the eyes of Fr. Roca, the power of Santiago that brings success to his evangelical mission and renewed prosperity and social solidarity to the local community of Chimayo.

In medieval Japan, as Emiko Ohnuki-Tierney tells us, monkeys were the patron angels of warrior knights, but in the contemporary world they are reduced to performing circus tricks for the amusement of country-bumpkin villagers. Even so, in the eyes of their *burakumin* trainers, the monkeys are sacred animals who, through their performances, may perhaps bring a new sense of self-conscious dignity to what was formerly a pseudo-ethnic community of outcastes.

Such parallels are far-fetched, trivial, and haphazard, but they run through all the papers considered here as a set. There is no rhyme or reason to them, but they tell me more about Folly's constructions of the human mind than a whole shelf full of treatises on formal sociology.

Note

1. I now understand that it was a virus rather than an exceptional blizzard that kept Jim Boon away from Baton Rouge.